MCA

T0188632

Microsoft 365~
Certified Associate

Teams Administrator

Study Guide

Exam MS-700

Ben Lee

SYBEX®
A Wiley Brand

This book is dedicated to my family with thanks for their love and support: Jen, Jessica, and Daniel.
And to my parents: Arthur and Sue.

Acknowledgments

In my career I have been very fortunate to work with some great individuals who have shaped me into the person and IT Professional I am today (so if I ever get to write another book, I promise this will be a smaller list!):

Thank you first to my brother, **Jon Lee**, for helping me get my first work experience in a technical role, then to **David Drylie**, **Chris McKenna**, and **Alistair Wilson** for giving me such a great start to my professional career when I got my first full-time proper IT job. I learned a lot in those early days, and not just how to deal with dot matrix and Phaser solid ink printers! A huge thank you to **Michael Dawson** for showing me how important it is to care for the end-user experience when deploying any systems. Thank you to everyone at Waterstons, where I learned how to become a consultant and to treat customers the right way, as well as making some great friends, including **Shahid Ali**, **James Alderson**, **Nat Hazlett**, and **Kate Thomson**. Thank you to those at Modality Systems for creating and cultivating an amazing environment back then, where I was always surrounded by very clever people—especially to **Rick Eveleigh**, **Graham Cropley**, and **Iain Smith**. Special thanks to **Jo Sims** and **Adrian Chatto** for being the best project managers I have ever worked with and for teaching me that good PMs are worth their weight in gold! Then at my current role, thank you to all my consultant colleagues at LoopUp who have put up with me bouncing exam questions and ideas off them, I appreciate your feedback: **Karl Smith**, **Jason Sloan**, **Tino Nguyen**, **Octavian Spuderca**, and **Leigh Henderson**. Special thanks to **Zach Bennett** (you know what you did!).

Of course, the process of writing a book is not a simple one (as I've so recently learned!), so a big thank you to everyone at Wiley and beyond who have made this happen:

To **Kenyon Brown** for letting me loose with a keyboard, to **Patrick Walsh** for your guidance and assistance in shaping what this book has become (and I'm so sorry for all the deadline issues; this last year really didn't go to anyone's plan!), and to **Jon Buhagiar** for your technical reviews. There are a great many people behind the scenes at Wiley who have had input into this project and whom I do not know; to them I am also very grateful. Obviously, any issues and mistakes that remain are entirely mine!

Life is not all about work, so I must also thank my friends and family who have, over what has been a crazy 2020–21, helped keep the wheels on in day-to-day life:

So, thank you **Team North** (Nat, Tom, Kate, Fi, Mark, Scott, Ian, and Jen) and especially to **Kate** for being our pandemic-bubble-buddy friend!

Lastly, thank you to my family for being my family. Life hasn't been easy, but you have been with me through this whole thing and I hope we will get to have many more amazing (but less fraught) adventures together. I love you, Jen, Jessica, and Daniel.

About the Author

 **Ben Lee** has spent most of his professional career working with Microsoft technologies and has passed more than 30 MCP exams (some as a charter member), and for the last 10+ years he has specialized in its Unified Communications and Collaboration stack. Since Teams entered the market, he has been helping organizations to understand how to deploy and adopt it successfully.

Ben has organized and helped many IT User Groups over the years and enjoys sharing knowledge and lessons learned through online platforms and speaking engagements, including with these UC-related groups:

- UC Day/Evolve: Evolveconf.co.uk
- Commsverse: Commsverse.com
- MSUC.Chat: MSUC.Chat

He currently works as the Microsoft Technology Lead for a global premium communications company, helping them build a best-in-class Direct Routing as a Service offering, and works with companies of all shapes and sizes to help them smoothly migrate their telephony workloads to Teams.

You can contact Ben via his website (bibble-it.com or LearnTeams.Info), LinkedIn (https://linkedin.com/in/benleeuk), or on Twitter as @Bibbleq (https://twitter.com/bibbleq).

About the Technical Editor

Jon Buhagiar, BS/ITM, MCSE, CCNA, is an information technology professional with two decades of experience in higher education and the private sector.

Jon currently serves as supervisor of network operations at Pittsburgh Technical College. In this role, he manages datacenter and network infrastructure operations and IT operations and is involved in managing projects supporting the quality of education at the College. He also serves as an adjunct instructor in PTC's Information Technology department, where he has taught courses for Microsoft and Cisco certification. He has been an instructor for more than 22 years at several colleges in the Pittsburgh area, since the introduction of the Windows NT MCSE in 1998.

Jon earned a bachelor of science degree in information technology management from Western Governors University. He also achieved an associate degree in business management from Pittsburgh Technical College. He has recently become a Windows Server 2016 Microsoft Certified Solutions Expert (MCSE) and earned the Cisco Certified Network Associate (CCNA) certification. Other certifications include CompTIA Network+, CompTIA A+, and CompTIA Project+.

In addition to his professional and teaching roles, Jon has authored *CCNA Routing and Switching Practice Tests: Exam 100-105, Exam 200-105, and Exam 200-125*; *CompTIA Network+ Review Guide: Exam N10-007, 4th Edition*; *CompTIA A+ Deluxe Study Guide: Exam 220-1002* (all Sybex, 2016); and *CCNA Certification Practice Tests: Exam 200-301, 1st Edition*. He has also served as the technical editor for the second edition of the *CompTIA Cloud+ Study Guide* (Sybex, 2016), *CCNA Security Study Guide: Exam 210-260* (Sybex, 2018); *CCNA Cloud Complete Study Guide: Exam 210-451 and Exam 210-455* (Sybex, 2018); *CCNP Enterprise Certification Study Guide: Implementing* (Sybex, 2018); and *Operating Cisco Enterprise Network Core Technologies: Exam 300-401* (Sybex, 2020). He has spoken at several conferences about spam and email systems. He is an active radio electronics hobbyist and has held a ham radio license for the past 18 years, KB3KGS. He experiments with electronics and has a strong focus on the Internet of Things (IoT).

Contents at a Glance

Contents

Table of Exercises

Introduction

There could be many reasons why you are looking to learn more about Teams and are considering taking the MS-700 exam: to prove to a potential employer that you have the skills to use Teams, to get on-the-job training in a position you already have, or perhaps just because you are interested in it.

The Microsoft certification program is broken into three types of qualifications:

Fundamentals: Usually for people at the early part of their career or starting out, these certifications provide a good grounding in their subject areas.

Associate: These are role-based certificates aimed at people who are already doing or want to learn about the tasks needed in a particular job role.

Expert/Specialist: These are deep qualifications in their areas, and each provides a way to showcase specialist knowledge in a particular area.

This book covers the content required so that you can study for and, we hope, pass the Microsoft MS-700 exam. If you pass this exam, you will earn one of Microsoft's Associate-level certificates and become a Microsoft 365 Certified: Teams Administrator Associate.

This in turn can act as a prerequisite for the more advanced Expert-level certification (Microsoft 365 Certified: Enterprise Administrator Expert) should you want to continue your learning by digging deeper into the M365 services.

The MS-700 Exam

It is anticipated that to be ready to take this exam you have been working with Teams in the real world for approximately six months. While this is certainly not a requirement and it is possible to take and pass the exam with no hands-on experience (not that I recommend this approach!), it does give you an idea of what to expect when tackling the exam. There is a lot of ground to cover, and if you have been living and breathing Teams to some degree before taking it, you will certainly find things easier.

For this exam you are expected to have a good understanding of how to manage all the different workloads in Teams and especially how to migrate away from Skype for Business Online. You should have a good idea of how you manage features, either via the Teams Admin Console (or O365 Security and Compliance Center, Azure AD, or SharePoint Admin) or via the command line with PowerShell, but as this is an Associate-level exam, you are not expected to be an expert in advanced workloads, such as detailed call routing and so on.

However, do not underestimate the importance of the calling and media workloads. This can account for 30 percent of the exam and is something easily overlooked if you are used to dealing only with the collaboration aspects of Teams. This is something that is given a lot of attention by Microsoft because it is something visible to end users if it does not work right.

You need to take the time to understand how media works and how the network should be configured to accommodate it.

Remember that the exam is also targeting enterprise-level knowledge, so it will be discussing features that need an E5 license, particularly in the security and compliance space. If you work for a Microsoft Partner, the Demos (https://demos.microsoft.com/) site will let you create fully featured test or demo tenants that are prepopulated with sample users to practice with. If you are not able to access the Demos site, you may be eligible for a Teams Exploratory License (https://docs.microsoft.com/en-us/microsoftteams/teams-exploratory), which gives you functionality equivalent to an E3 license for a trial. There is a requirement here to already have a domain and Azure AD configured in O365. If all else fails, you can sign up for Teams free (https://www.microsoft.com/en-us/microsoft-teams/free) and at least get access to the core application and configuration options. Chapter 1 has some more ideas and information about how you can get access to your own Teams tenant for testing.

Exam Format

The exam will have between 45 and 60 questions. Some questions may be worth more than one point, and some may be worth nothing (as Microsoft may be testing new questions to enter the rotation), so the important thing is to try not to get ruffled by anything you are not sure about.

There is definitely a certain mindset that can help you take the MS certification exams; for example, as you go through the exam, later questions may jog your memory or give you a clue to something that you were stuck on earlier, so flag anything you are not sure about to come back to later. That said, some questions will not let you skip forward, as they could be part of a multiple-question scenario. The MS-700 exam will normally have at least one of these scenario sections that will be approximately 10 questions long.

Questions are traditionally multiple choice; however, there are several different formats that you might come across, including the following:

- Build list
- Active screen
- Drag and drop
- Case study

 You can see the full list of possible question types at https://docs.microsoft.com/en-us/learn/certifications/certification-exams.

Case study questions aim to give you some real-world information that is then used across multiple questions. The information usually takes the form of paragraphs of information and then some supplementary data, such as tables, and so on. You can refer to this data as you need to during the subsequent questions. When answering case study questions, the text of the question will usually give you a specific clue about which part of the case study you should pay close attention to. For example, it might ask about what policy will meet the HR security requirements, in which case make sure you read the security requirement section closely.

You may also find some simulation or lab-based questions where you are given access to a sample environment and are expected to configure particular things. This is where having some real-world experience with Teams is helpful, as the chances are that it may look slightly different in real life than it does in books or training materials (because of the ever-evolving nature of the product). Simulation questions come in and out of favor, so you may not have any.

To pass the exam, you need to score at least 700 out of a possible 1,000 points available on the test; however, this does not directly correlate with a percentage-based score, as some questions can be weighted up or down. There is no distinction between passing with 700 points or full marks; a pass is a pass.

 Don't just study the questions and answers! The questions on the actual exam will be different from the practice questions included in this book. The exam is designed to test your knowledge of a concept or objective, so use this book to learn the objectives behind the questions.

Tips for Taking the Exam

Here are some tips for taking the exam:

- Give yourself plenty of time to take the exam. The official run time is 2.5 hours, so there is no need to rush things.

- Read everything carefully; it can be easy to jump to conclusions about the right answer to a question and throw away points.

- If you are not sure about a question, do not get stuck staring at the screen. Flag it for review and move on. You should be able to come back to it later. The exam will notify you if you cannot return.

- PowerShell cmdlets used in questions can get you in a muddle, as often the cmdlets will vary by a single word or so. Look carefully at the other combinations in the other options, as this can help you rule out cmdlets that are definitely not valid. If in doubt, use the trick from the previous point and flag the question to come back to; another question or screenshot may clue you into what the right wording will be.

- Unless told otherwise, assume settings are left at the default, and for any simulation questions, try not to change any settings that are not directly related to the task you have been asked to perform.

- No points are deducted for getting a question wrong, so if in doubt make an educated guess. You should be able to narrow down your options by at least eliminating one or two incorrect answers.

- Put your day job to one side for the exam, and do not get caught up in the real world versus the material. Sometimes you just need to give the answer that Microsoft wants even if that does not match your experience of best practices. Remember that for the exam purposes you are a fully fledged enterprise administrator juggling many workloads for a large multinational company.

Building Knowledge Chapter by Chapter

The chapters in this book are not directly lined up with the MS-700 objectives but are instead laid out in what I would argue is a more logical manner that fits better with how you would actually deploy Teams.

Each chapter starts with an introduction that includes which sections are going to be covered in the chapter, but you can also refer to the table in the "MS-700 Objectives" section later in this introduction.

The following is a breakdown of what we will be covering together in each chapter:

Chapter 1, "Introducing Teams": This chapter covers an overview of what Teams is and the core concepts behind it and how that fits with the wider Office 365 and Microsoft 365 offerings. It will also introduce some of the core concepts you will need to understand about how Teams is configured and managed.

Chapter 2, "Getting Teams Up and Running": This chapter covers three main areas: Skype for Business migrations, network preparation, and client deployments. This chapter helps lay the foundations of understanding how Teams interacts with Skype for Business if you have it deployed and need to migrate away from it. It covers how to best prepare your network for dealing with Teams (mostly) media traffic and how to get the Teams client out to your end users and on your devices.

Chapter 3, "Teams Core Functionality": This chapter covers Teams bread-and-butter tasks such as different types of teams, how to manage basic policies, how to control access to your Teams, and how to manage meetings.

Chapter 4, "Advanced Teams Functionality and Management": This chapter covers how to apply security and governance against your Teams deployment and how to make sure your data is safe, secure, and available only to the people who need it. We will also look at things such as templates and app policies.

Chapter 5, "Adding Telephony": This chapter covers how to incorporate PSTN calling into Teams, the different ways this can be delivered, and how this functionality works.

Chapter 6, "Review Usage and Maintain Quality": It is all very well having Teams deployed and all your users enabled and configured, but you should also be proactively looking at how they are performing. This chapter will cover some of the tools you need to monitor usage and track down issues.

Who Should Buy This Book

While this book is targeted at those who want to study for and pass the MS-700 exam, really it was written for anyone who needs to manage (or aspires to manage) Teams at any type of scale for their organization.

That could mean you are the IT administrator for your company and want to understand how to get the most out of Teams, or it could be that you work in support but want to learn more about how Teams operates. Really, I would hope it can be picked up and used by anyone who wants to go beyond living on the "user" side of Teams. Come lift the curtain and see what is happening behind the scenes.

As with any study guide, there is a certain level of assumed knowledge that will be helpful, although the book is structured to start with the basics and work through to the more difficult concepts (see the section earlier called "Building Knowledge Chapter by Chapter"). You should have a good understanding of how Teams behaves from an end-user point of view, and the more knowledge about how Teams works you bring with you, the more you will get out of it.

The management behaviors we will cover also build on basic concepts of how Microsoft services operate and can be managed, so some familiarity with PowerShell and Office 365's core concepts will be helpful.

Study Guide Features

This study guide uses a number of common elements to help you prepare. These include the following:

Summary   The summary of each chapter briefly explains the chapter, allowing you to easily understand what it covers.

Exam Essentials   The exam essentials focus on major exam topics and critical knowledge that you should take into the test. The exam essentials focus on the exam objectives provided by Microsoft.

Chapter Review Questions   A set of questions at the end of each chapter will help you assess your knowledge and whether you are ready to take the exam, based on your knowledge of that chapter's topics.

The review questions, assessment test, and other testing elements included in this book are *not* derived from the actual exam questions, so don't memorize the answers to these questions and assume that doing so will enable you to pass the exam. You should learn the underlying topic, as described in the text of the book. This will let you answer the questions provided with this book *and* pass the exam. Learning the underlying topic is also the approach that will serve you best in the workplace—the ultimate goal of a certification.

Additional Study Tools

This book comes with additional study tools to help you prepare for the exam. They include the following.

> Go to https://www.wiley.com/go/sybextestprep, register your book to receive your unique PIN, and then once you have the PIN, return to https://www.wiley.com/go/sybextestprep and register a new account or add this book to an existing account.

Sybex Online Learning Environment

Sybex's online learning environment lets you prepare with electronic test versions of the review questions from each chapter and the practice exams that are included in this book. You can build and take tests on specific domains, by chapter, or cover the entire set of MS-700 exam objectives using randomized tests.

Electronic Flashcards

Our electronic flashcards are designed to help you prepare for the exam. More than 100 flashcards will ensure that you know critical terms and concepts.

Glossary

Sybex provides a full glossary of terms in PDF format, allowing quick searches and easy reference to the materials in this book.

Practice Exams

In addition to the practice questions for each chapter, this book includes access to two full 75-question online practice exams. We recommend that you use them both to test your preparedness for the certification exam.

Conventions Used in This Book

This book uses certain typographic styles to help you quickly identify important information and to avoid confusion over the meaning of words such as on-screen prompts. In particular, look for the following styles:

- *Italicized text* indicates key terms that are described at length for the first time in a chapter. (Italics are also used for emphasis.)

- A monospaced font indicates fragments of code such as PowerShell cmdlets.

- Underlined text indicates links to useful resources and content. As Teams functionality evolves over time, use these links to read more deeply about a subject or check on what the current behavior is.

In addition to these text conventions, which can apply to individual words or entire paragraphs, a few conventions highlight segments of text.

 A note indicates information that's useful or interesting but that's somewhat peripheral to the main text. A note might be a little bit of real-world knowledge that differs from what you may see in the exam, or some information that helps put things into context from the main body of text.

 References are used to give links to the relevant sections in Microsoft's documentation. Here you can dive deeper into a subject if you are interested, or you can check on what the current behavior is as the Teams service is updated and improves.

Exercises

An exercise is something that you can carry out from your own computer with your own Office 365 tenant. The steps in an exercise are there to act as a guide for how to perform a specific task, but the goal is to encourage you to go off and explore on your own, so don't be afraid to go off script and explore for yourself how things work or what happens when you change something. Being curious and exploring is one of the best ways to really learn the material. (Just don't change too much if you only have access to a live environment!)

MS-700 Objectives

The following table shows the high-level breakdown of the skills that Microsoft aims to measure with the MS-700 exam. This includes the approximate weightings toward each section. As you can see, there is a lot of emphasis placed on the core planning and configuration activities, which can account for up to half of the exam. The table also tells you which chapter will primarily cover this objective area, but some will, of course, also be covered to some degree in the other chapters. The MS-700 exam, like all Microsoft exams, evolves over time. For a more detailed list of the current objectives covered, refer to the MS-700 exam page and look for the section titled "Skills Measured," where you can download a PDF of the current Microsoft objectives: `https://docs.microsoft.com/en-us/learn/certifications/exams/ms-700`.

Objective	Percentage of Exam	Primary Chapter
Plan and configure a Microsoft Teams environment	40%–50%	
Upgrade from Skype for Business to Microsoft Teams		Chapter 2
Plan and configure network settings for Microsoft Teams		Chapter 2
Implement governance and lifecycle management for Microsoft Teams		Chapter 4
Configure and manage guest access		Chapter 3
Manage security and compliance		Chapter 4
Deploy and manage Microsoft Teams endpoints		Chapter 2
Monitor and analyze service usage		Chapter 6
Manage Chat, Calling, and Meetings	30%–35%	
Manage chat and collaboration experiences		Chapter 3
Manage meeting experiences		Chapter 3
Manage phone numbers		Chapter 5
Manage Phone System		Chapter 5
Manage Teams and app policies	20%–25%	
Manage a team		Chapter 3
Manage membership in a team		Chapter 4
Implement policies for Microsoft Teams apps		Chapter 4

Assessment Test

1. You want to configure a number of custom tags that can be used in chat messages for your product names. Where in TAC can you configure the tag settings for your teams?

   A.   Meeting policies

   B.   Under Teams settings

   C.   Messaging policies

   D.   Guest access

2. Your CTO has identified a risk where owners might lose track of who is a member of their teams. What feature can you configure to help mitigate this risk?

   A.   Group expiration

   B.   Sensitivity labels

   C.   Dynamic membership

   D.   Access reviews

3. You want to configure dynamic membership for one of your M365 groups. Where can you configure this?

   A.   In TAC

   B.   In the M365 Admin portal

   C.   In the Azure AD portal

   D.   On the Teams membership screen

4. You need to create a voice workflow that accepts incoming calls for your building reception. These calls must be sent to voicemail when the office is closed, but when it's open, the inbound call should ring between a group of users. What do you need to create to support this?

   A.   Two resource accounts

   B.   Two resource accounts, both with virtual user licenses

   C.   One resource account

   D.   Two resource accounts, one with a virtual user license

5. You have deployed some Microsoft Teams Rooms devices and need to make sure that the Azure AD account password does not expire. Which cmdlet could you run? (Select all that apply.)

   A.   `Set-MsolUserPassword`

   B.   `Set-MsolUser`

   C.   `Set-AzureADUser`

   D.   `Set-PasswordExpiration`

6. How long after deleting a team can you still recover it?

    A. 20 days

    B. 30 days

    C. 45 days

    D. 60 days

7. You need to be able to prevent forwarding of calls to external numbers. What type of policy would you use for this?

    A. Calling policy

    B. Permission policy

    C. Teams policy

    D. Messaging policy

8. You need to prevent two groups of users from communicating with each other. What would you need to create?

    A. One segment and two information barrier policies

    B. One segment and one information barrier policy

    C. Two segments and two information barrier policies

    D. Two segments and one information barrier policy

9. Which of the following compliance technologies would prevent users from sharing credit card information over chat?

    A. Data loss prevention (DLP)

    B. Information barriers

    C. Sensitivity labels

    D. eDiscovery

10. You are migrating to Teams from your current phone-based conferencing provider. You want to make sure you keep the same dial-in number that your users are used to. The number currently terminates on your PBX. What can you do?

    A. Port the number to Microsoft as a user number.

    B. Configure Direct Routing.

    C. Port the number to Microsoft as a service number.

    D. Request that Microsoft acquire the number from the current provider.

11. You have identified a requirement to make sure that QoS is deployed for your Teams environment. You have configured Group Policy and made sure that your Windows clients are picking it up. What else should you configure in TAC?

    A. Network topology in Locations

    B. Networks in Locations

    C. Network in Meeting settings

    D. Network planner in Planning

12. When planning to migrate from the previous meeting provider, a use case was identified where meetings should have an audible announcement played when dial-in users join or leave the call. What would you configure to meet this requirement?

A. Conference bridge settings

B. Meeting settings

C. Meeting policies

D. Live events policies

13. What PowerShell cmdlet would you run to change a user into Teams Only mode?

A. `Grant-CsTeamsUpgradePolicy`

B. `Set-CsTeamsUpgradePolicy`

C. `Apply-CsTeamsUpgradePolicy`

D. `Update-CsTeamsUpgradePolicy`

14. You get reports of poor calls from one of your sites; you look in the firewall and apply a filter to traffic coming from the user's computer. You see only the following destination port active: TCP 443. What should you open on the firewall to help improve the call quality?

A. UDP 3478

B. UDP 3748

C. TCP 3478

D. TCP 3748

15. You want to make sure that certain business keywords cannot be used when making new Teams. How would you handle this automatically?

A. Configure an M365 group naming policy.

B. Restrict the users who can create teams.

C. Add tags to the Teams settings.

D. Configure a team template.

16. You are creating a retention policy for your Teams users and need to make sure that files a user uploads during chats (not conversations) are included. What should you include in the retention scope?

A. M365 Groups

B. OneDrive for Business

C. SharePoint

D. Skype for Business

17. To easily configure a group for dynamic membership using PowerShell, which modules would you use? (Select all that apply.)

A. Exchange Online

B. Skype for Business Online

C. Azure AD

D. Teams

18. Which of the following location lookups can use the Wi-Fi access point that a user is connected to?

    A. Location Information Services (LIS)

    B. Trusted IP Lookup

    C. Network Planner

    D. Network Settings

19. You are planning to migrate users from Skype for Business on-premises to Teams but want to manage it in a controlled way, so you have configured everyone into SkypeOnly mode. A group of users has a requirement to start using Teams for meetings immediately. What mode should you put them in that does not affect your other planning timelines?

    A. Teams Only

    B. Skype for Business with Teams Collaboration and Meetings

    C. Skype for Business with Teams Collaboration

    D. Islands Mode

20. You need to block all custom apps from being used inside Teams. What type of policy should you create?

    A. Calling policy

    B. Permission policy

    C. Teams policy

    D. Messaging policy

21. You need to allow users to generate meetings that external users can join using a toll-free number. What licensing would you need?

    A. Users with E3 and communications credits in the tenant

    B. Users with E5 and communications credits in the tenant

    C. Users with E5 licenses and calling plans

    D. Users with F1 licenses

22. You are planning your migration to Teams and need to create some new teams based on current resources. Which of the following can you upgrade or convert directly into Teams? (Select all that apply.)

    A. An M365 group

    B. Distribution list

    C. SharePoint team site

    D. On-premises AD group

23. You are deploying some phones for use in a break room. What license type is most appropriate to assign to the phones?

    A. E3

    B. E5

    C. Meeting Room

    D. Common Area Phone

24. To mark a team as not discoverable, what cmdlets would you run?

    A. `Get-Team` and `Set-Team`

    B. `Get-Team` and `Update-Team`

    C. `Find-Team` and `Set-Team`

    D. `Find-Team` and `Update-Team`

25. If you have 250 domestic calling plan licenses and 250 domestic and international calling plan licenses in your tenant, how many user numbers would you have access to?

    A. 500

    B. 250

    C. 560

    D. 510

26. You have a requirement to host an external-facing meeting for 500+ participants. What should you consider doing to support the meeting?

    A. Make sure you have QoS deployed to optimize the network.

    B. Configure Teams Live Events.

    C. Deploy an eCDN solution to optimize the network traffic.

    D. Ensure that External Access is configured in the tenant.

27. You want to use Teams Advisor to help plan the deployment of your meeting workload. What licenses should you have assigned to your account to get the most out of Teams Advisor? (Select all that apply.)

    A. Teams

    B. Forms

    C. Planner

    D. Azure P1

28. Your company has decided to disable the use of all Giphys in conversations. What type of policy would you configure?

    A. Calling policy

    B. Permission policy

    C. Teams policy

    D. Messaging policy

29. What is the name of the service that will update users' Skype for Business meetings when they migrate fully to Teams?

    A. Automatic Calendar Update

    B. Teams Administrative Calendar Update

    C. Meeting Migration Service

    D. Meeting Update Service

30. You need to create a team for a department that is hidden and whose membership is controlled. What should you do?

    A. Create an org-wide team.

    B. Create a private team.

    C. Create a private team and make it not discoverable.

    D. Create a public team and make it not discoverable.

31. When planning your Teams deployment, you identify a requirement to allow a group of users to work on documents together. A subset of these users needs to work on part of the project that contains sensitive data. What would you create to meet this requirement?

    A. One team and a private channel

    B. Two teams

    C. One team and a separate SharePoint site

    D. One team and a OneDrive for Business shared folder

32. You need to be able to allow only HR users to send messages that alert the recipient for 20 minutes. What would you configure in TAC? Your solution should minimize the number of policies required.

    A. Create two new messaging policies.

    B. Update the org-wide Teams settings and create a messaging policy.

    C. Update org-wide Teams settings and create a meeting policy.

    D. Update the global messaging policy and create a dedicated messaging policy for HR users.

33. You deploy Direct Routing for your organization and need to purchase the right license for your users. Currently they all have E3 licenses. You want to ensure that you do not buy any additional services that you do not intend to use at this time. Which of the following licenses would you purchase?

    A. E5

    B. Phone System

    C. Communications credits

    D. M365 E3

34. You want to make sure that you can invite guests to work on documents with your users. Which of the following M365 services should you check initially to make sure that guests are allowed access?

    A. Teams

    B. Azure AD

    C. M365 Groups

    D. SharePoint Online

35. You are six months into your Teams migration and have noticed that some teams no long seem to be used. What can you do to manage removing these teams with the least administrative effort?

   A. Use the M365 activity reports to identify what teams are not used.

   B. Use CQD to monitor Teams usage and then remove the unused teams.

   C. Use Teams Usage reports to identify unused teams and then archive them.

   D. Configure an M365 Groups expiration policy.

36. When migrating from your PBX, you want to maintain the ability for users to dial 666 and reach your support desk. What voice feature could you use to meet this requirement?

   A. Create a caller ID policy.

   B. Create a call park policy.

   C. Create a calling policy.

   D. Create a dial plan.

37. Where would you go to see the status of your Direct Routing SBCs?

   A. Direct Routing Health Dashboard

   B. Call Quality Dashboard (CQD)

   C. Advanced Call Diagnostics (ACD)

   D. M365 Admin Portal

38. You need to purchase new desk phones for use with your Teams deployment and want to make sure you get the best possible user experience. What type of devices should you purchase?

   A. Microsoft Teams Rooms

   B. Skype for Business 3PIP phones

   C. Native Teams phones

   D. Teams Displays

39. You want to make sure that certain teams, when they are created, cannot allow guests as members. Your solution should not affect the use of guests in other teams. What would you do?

   A. Configure Access reviews.

   B. Create a Teams template.

   C. Modify guest access settings.

   D. Configure sensitivity labels for Teams that prevent guest access.

40. What RBAC permissions are required to create an org-wide team?

   A. Teams Administrator

   B. Global Administrator

   C. User Administrator

   D. Teams Communications Administrator

41. During a discovery session with the business you have identified that the Marketing department wants to have a way to publicize good-news stories about the company to employees. Only Marketing should be able to post updates. What should you do? (Select all that apply.)

    A. Create an org-wide team.

    B. Create a team with dynamic membership.

    C. Configure channel moderation.

    D. Configure access reviews.

42. You have created some Teams templates and sensitivity labels and want to make sure they are being used correctly. What would you do to receive a notification when a new team is created?

    A. Change the team template settings.

    B. Create an Office 365 alert policy in the Microsoft 365 Compliance portal.

    C. Update the org-wide settings.

    D. In Azure AD, create a notification policy.

43. You need to allow some users to create private channels but disable the setting for everyone else. What type of policies would you configure?

    A. Calling policy

    B. Permission policy

    C. Teams policy

    D. Messaging policy

44. You have helped schedule a live event for the Sales team members to promote a new product release. They have sent out the invitation containing the join information. A few days before the event is scheduled, they want to double-check that everything will work as expected. How would you make it possible for them to do this?

    A. Generate a new live event with the same settings that can be used to test the meeting behavior.

    B. Schedule a Teams meeting using the same users and presenters as the scheduled event.

    C. Join the live event early, but make sure to reset it afterward so the links still work.

    D. Start an ad hoc Teams meeting to test the features.

45. You are using Skype for Business across your estate, which contains a mixture of Windows 10 computers and mobile phones (iOS and Android). You want to upgrade from Skype for Business to Teams quickly and need to make sure that all devices install the client ready for your migration. What can you do to speed up the deployment?

    A. Place all users into Teams Only mode straightaway, forcing Teams to be installed.

    B. Create a Teams App Policy to deploy the Teams client.

    C. In TAC enable the Download Teams In The Background option.

    D. Use your mobile device management platform (such as InTune) to deploy the Teams client for you.

46. You need to be able to identify which of your sites have poor call quality. When you look in CQD, no sites are identifiable. What should you do? (Select all that apply.)

A. From TAC run the Network Planner.

B. Run the Network Testing Companion from each site to collect its data.

C. Upload building data via CQD.

D. In TAC configure reporting labels.

47. What eDiscovery role would you give an HR user who needs to process data from an eDiscovery request? They must not be able to perform other eDiscovery activities.

A. Compliance Admin

B. eDiscovery Administrator

C. Organization Management

D. Reviewer

48. You are about to enable your first set of users for Direct Routing and plan to do it via PowerShell so you can repeat the process easily. What cmdlets would you be likely to need to use?

A. `Set-CsUser`, `Set-AzureADUserLicense`, and `Grant-CsOnlineVoiceRouting Policy`

B. `Set-AzureADUserLicense` and `Set-CsOnlineVoiceUser`

C. `Set-AzureADUser` and `Grant-CsOnlineVoiceRoutingPolicy`

D. `Set-CSUser` and `Set-CsOnlineVoiceUser`

49. What is the name for the international number format used by Teams?

A. E.164

B. e911

C. H.264

D. G711

50. Which of the following (by default) can a guest *not* do when invited into your tenant? (Select all that apply.)

A. View the org chart for a user

B. Share files in a channel

C. Add an app into a channel

D. Have a private chat with another user

Answers to Assessment Test

1. B. Tagging settings can be controlled at a global level via Teams settings. Meeting policies (option A), messaging policies (option C), and guest access (option D) do not cover the use of tags.

2. D. Access reviews can be configured to require a team owner to confirm who is a member of their teams on a periodic basis. Group expiration (option A) would only help to remove unused groups, and sensitivity labels (option B) would apply categories and behaviors to a group but not help with controlling membership. Dynamic membership (option C) would help control who is in the team automatically but would not let the owner be explicitly aware of who is a member without them manually checking.

3. C. Dynamic membership rules are configured at a group level inside the Azure AD management portal. You cannot view or edit the rules through the other portals (options A, B, and D).

4. D. You would need two resource accounts, one for an Auto Attendant that would support the in-hours versus out-of-hours requirement and then one for a call queue that would answer the incoming calls passed from the Auto Attendant. You need only one virtual user license because only the Auto Attendant needs an external phone number.

5. B, C. `Set-MsolUser` is the older PowerShell cmdlet, and `Set-AzureADUser` is the newer version; both will let you configure a user's password to not expire. Option A lets you reset a password but not change the expiration, and option D is not valid.

6. B. You can recover a soft-deleted team for up to 30 days.

7. A. Telephony features are controlled via calling policies. Permission policies (option B) are used to control third-party app integrations, Teams policies (option C) are used to control who can create private channels, and messaging policies (option D) control chat type functionality.

8. C. You need to create two segments, one for each group of users, and then two policies as the block must be done in both directions, so the other options (A, B, and D) would not function correctly.

9. A. Data loss prevention (DLP) policies can be configured to look for sensitive information and prevent it from being shared (or just generate warning notifications). Information barriers (option B) segment users from each other; sensitivity labels (option C) can be used to tag teams themselves, not the chat inside; and lastly eDiscovery (option D) can be used to search for that kind of information but only retrospectively.

10. C. You should try to port the number to Microsoft from your current provider. Service numbers are what can be allocated to a conference bridge or voice app, so option A would not work. Currently Direct Routing does not let you add external-facing numbers as a conference bridge (option B), and port requests need to come from the customer of the current number, so in option D Microsoft cannot do anything.

11. C. QoS settings for the tenant are configured under Meeting settings. Option A is used for dynamic call routing, option B is used for location awareness, and option D is used to help plan and model the impact on the network.

12. A. Conference bridge settings let you configure audio announcements for dial-in users. Meeting settings (option B), meeting policies (option C), and live event policies (option D) do not control dial-in announcements.

13. A. To apply an upgrade policy, you need to use `Grant-CsTeamsUpgradePolicy`; when applying a policy to users, it is common for the verb to be `Grant-`. The other cmdlet varieties such as `Set-` (option B) are used to modify the policies themselves and in this case are not valid for upgrade policies as you cannot create or modify the included ones. Options C and D are not valid cmdlets.

14. A. Teams will fall back to using TCP 443 for media, but UDP 3478 is preferred (UDP 3478–3481 is the full preferred range). The ports in options B, C, and D are not used by Teams.

15. A. A group naming policy allows you to add blocked words or create prefix and suffix lists to the creation of groups. Restricting users (option B) could work so that only authorized users who know the rules can make teams, but it is not automatic. Tags (option C) are not used for blocked words, and templates (option D) control what a team structure looks like, not the naming.

16. B. Chats are outside of a team, so any files shared are linked to the sender's OneDrive for Business account. There is no M365 group involved in chat (option A), SharePoint would be for files shared in a team conversation (option C), and Skype for Business (option D) would cover messages for users who have not migrated yet.

17. A, C. You need the Azure AD PowerShell module to configure the dynamic membership for a group, but by also using the Exchange Online module, you can search for the groups by friendly names. Skype for Business Online (option B) and Teams (option D) modules do not allow the modification of membership rules.

18. A. Wi-Fi lookups can be included in LIS but are not part of the Trusted IP (option B) or Network Settings (option D) lookups. You do not need to include Wi-Fi information in Network Planner (option C).

19. B. By placing the users in Skype for Business with Teams Collaboration and Meetings mode, they can schedule Teams meetings but leave the other core workloads in Skype for Business until you are ready to migrate them. Options A and D would let them use Teams for meetings but confuses the rest of your migration plan, and option C does not allow the creation of Teams meetings.

20. B. The use of apps is controlled via permission policies (for Microsoft, third-party, and custom apps). Calling policies (option A) are used to control voice features, Teams policies (option C) are used to control who can create private channels, and messaging policies (option D) control chat type functionality.

21. B. To allow dial-in for meetings, users need an Audio Conferencing license; this can be added onto an E3 or is usually included in an E5. To allow toll-free numbers to be added to the tenant, you must have communications credits added to the tenant.

22. A, C. M365 Groups and SharePoint team sites can be easily converted into teams. Distribution lists need to be first converted into an M365 group (option B), and on-premises AD groups cannot directly synchronize with M365 groups (option D).

23. D. The Common Area Phone license contains the basic Teams license and Phone System that would be required. Options B and C also contain additional licenses that would not be required, and option A does not contain the Phone System license.

24. A. You can use `Set-Team -ShowInTeamsSearchandSuggestions $False` to hide a team, and you can use `Get-Team` to find the team you want to apply the setting against. `Find-Team` and `Update-Team` are not valid cmdlets (options B, C, and D).

25. C. The formula used is 1.1 times the calling plans plus 10, which gives you 560 numbers that can be requested in TAC. The type of calling plan is not relevant, just the total number.

26. B. While Microsoft is adding support for larger meetings into Teams, a meeting with this number of external users would be best served through Teams Live Events. Deploying QoS (option A) is something that would help with the quality of calls; it isn't important for this scenario, and an eCDN (option C) would be helpful when running lots of live events for an internal audience, but it would not help with external users. Lastly, External Access (option D) would help make sure external users can join meetings, but it would not help with this volume of users.

27. A, B, C. Teams Advisor creates a team with some sample content for you to track and plan your deployment. This content includes pre-created project plans (in Planner) and suggested surveys (in Forms) to gather information. Therefore, you should have a Teams license (usually as part of your E3 or E5), a Planner license, and a Forms license. You do not need an Azure P1 (option D) license.

28. D. Giphys are controlled at a tenant level in the messaging policy. Calling policies (option A) are used to control voice features, permission policies (option B) are used to control third-party app integrations, and Teams policies (option C) are used to control who can create private channels.

29. C. The Meeting Migration Service can update users' calendar appointments with new Teams details. The other tools do not exist for Teams (options A, B, and D).

30. C. To control membership, the team should be private, and then to hide it from view, it should be marked as not discoverable using PowerShell. An org-wide team (option A) would include all users in the company. By default private teams are still discoverable (option B), and public teams (option D) are always discoverable.

31. A. The neatest way to meet this requirement based on the information presented is to create one team and a private channel for the subset of users who need access to the sensitive data. This way there is only one team that needs to be managed. While two teams (option B) would meet the main goal, it would create multiple teams. Options C and D would place the sensitive data requirement outside of Teams so would be a different place for the users to remember to use.

32. D. Urgent messages can alert for up to 20 minutes; allowing this functionality is controlled via messaging policies, so to meet the requirement, they should be disabled at a global level, and then a custom policy should be created for the HR users who need to send them. While creating two messaging policies (option A) would solve the problem, this would not meet the requirement to minimize the number of policies needed. Teams settings and meeting policies do not control urgent messages (options B and C).

33. B. A Phone System license unlocks public switched telephone network (PSTN) calling in Teams. An E5 (option A) would include Phone System but comes with a lot of other licenses you might not need yet. Communications credits (option C) are not used for calling with Direct Routing, and an M365 E3 license (option D) still contains the same O365 subset, so it would not change your Teams entitlement.

34. A, B, C, D. For guest access to work, it must be enabled and configured across all of these services. Teams controls specific functionality available to guests inside Teams, Azure AD allows guests to be authenticated, M365 Groups needs to allow external users to be members, and SharePoint Online needs to allow sharing with guests.

35. D. Group expiration policies will allow the automatic detection and deletion of unused teams. M365 activity (option A) and Teams Usage reports (option C) would help you manually identify teams that are not being used. CQD (option B) does not provide usage about teams themselves; it is for the voice workload.

36. D. A dial plan lets you convert the numbers a user enters into another number. With a dial plan, you could convert 666 into the number of your service desk. A caller ID policy (option A) is used to alter outbound number presentation, a call park policy (option B) is used for holding calls, and a calling policy (option C) controls calling feature availability.

37. A. The SBCs show up in the Direct Routing health dashboard inside TAC. CQD (option B) is used for call-quality trending, ACD (option C) is used for troubleshooting specific calls or users, and the M365 Admin portal (option D) would not show this information.

38. C. Native Teams phones are designed to run the Teams client provided by Microsoft; they will offer the best calling experience and longevity. 3PIP phones (option B) should work with Teams through the interop gateway, but if you are buying new, they should not be considered as they have both limited functionality and a limited lifespan (the gateway will be decommissioned in future). Teams Rooms (option A) are designed for meeting rooms so are not suitable as every day phones, and Teams Displays (option D) are also used in more specialized circumstances.

39. D. You can create sensitivity labels that will not allow guests in a team when applied. Create a label and make sure it is used/applied to the correct teams. Access reviews (option A) will let you check membership but would not block guests, templates (option B) cannot control features like that, and changing guest access settings (option C) would apply to the whole tenant.

40. B. Only a Global Administrator can create new org-wide teams. The other roles will not have sufficient permissions (options A, C, and D).

41. A, C. To meet this requirement, you want an org-wide team to make sure that all staff members are always included, and you want moderation configured to ensure that only Marketing can post into the channel. Dynamic membership (option B) could work but is more complex, and access reviews (option D) don't really help for this scenario.

42. B. You can use O365 alert policies to trigger when a new M365 group is created. Team template settings do not include notification options (option A), and neither do org-wide settings (option C). Azure AD does not have notification policies out of the box (option D).

43. C. The creation of private channels is controlled through Teams policies. Calling policies (option A) are used to control voice features, and permission policies (option B) and messaging policies (option D) control chat-type functionality.

44. A. Once a live event has been started, it cannot be reused. To test any functionality, you should create a duplicate meeting with the same settings for testing. Do not start the scheduled meeting early, as the join details will not work (option C). Options B and D would not help as they are normal Teams meetings so have different behaviors.

45. D. An MDM solution such as InTune is the only way of deploying across desktop and mobile clients automatically. Using the setting in TAC (option C) will apply only to Windows clients. An App policy (option B) is used to deploy apps only inside the Teams client, and configuring Teams Only mode (option A) affects only the features and functionality available; it cannot control the client behavior.

46. C, D. To allow CQD to identify locations, you need to upload a building data file. You can do this either via CQD (in its settings page) or from TAC via reporting labels. The Network Planner (option A) doesn't apply data into CQD, and neither does the Network Testing Companion (option B).

47. D. The Reviewer role lets a user view data returned by an eDiscovery request. The other roles (options A, B, and C) would allow access to perform other tasks as well.

48. A. To configure a user for Direct Routing, you need to make sure they have a license (`Set-AzureADUserLicense`) that can do this, give them an online voice routing policy (`Grant-CsOnlineVoiceRoutingPolicy`), and enable them for Enterprise Voice (`Set-CsUser`). The other options (options B, C, and D) contain `Set-CsOnlineVoiceUser`, which you would use for calling plans to assign a number.

49. A. The international number format is called E.164. e911 (option B) is enhanced emergency dialing used in the United States, H.264 (option C) is a video format, and G711 (option D) is a voice codec used in calls.

50. A, C. By default a guest can share files in a channel and have private chats (options B and D). They are not allowed to view org information or change what is configured in a team.

Chapter

1

Introducing Teams

MICROSOFT EXAM OBJECTIVES COVERED IN THIS CHAPTER

While this chapter does not cover specific content areas of the exam, it does act as a grounding point to make sure you are aware of the basic principles behind Teams, including how it fits with other Office 365 services, how it is licensed, and where you can manage it from. This is the fundamental knowledge that you will need to develop your skills as a Teams administrator.

Teams is the latest (and greatest) productivity offering from Microsoft, released as part of its Office 365 suite (O365).

Because it builds on Microsoft's extensive history in this space, Teams is perhaps the most comprehensive communications and collaboration suite available on the market today.

Why is Teams so great? Teams is (almost) the one tool that you need for all things work related. It is built around the concept of, well, teams. It lets you share ideas and information with the people you work closely with. It is flexible in terms of both the daily usage and the configuration/expansion options available for it. You can mold it to fit your requirements in many different scenarios, which is great from an end-user perspective. As an information technology (IT) administrator, you need to be aware of its capabilities, how they can be controlled and managed, and how to help your end users get the most from it.

What can you do in Teams? Broadly speaking, you can split Teams into two types of workloads: collaboration and communications.

- **Collaboration:** Defined as "the action of working with someone to produce something," in the Teams world *collaboration* means that Teams acts as a platform where you can work closely with people from both inside and outside your organization (if you choose) in a shared space. Teammates access a shared set of resources and documents to work on them together—in real time if required. This can replace the more "traditional" ways of working such as using network file shares or emailing documents back and forth, creating versioning headaches! With Teams you open the app, open the team you need, and get to work.

- **Communications:** Defined as "the imparting or exchanging of information," *communications* is where Teams really shines. Along with all the collaboration goodness it offers, Teams is your go-to place for communicating with colleagues. If you need something quick and easy, start with a chat message. What if that chat gets complicated and it'd be better to speak to the person? Just hit a button and you are joined into an audio call with the option to include video and share your screen. Need to add more people or invite external parties? Teams has you covered, even if those people do not have access to their own Teams tenant; you can let people join via a standard phone call.

It is the combination of these two types of workloads into a single client that makes Teams so powerful. Email used to be the "killer app" for companies. In the past, if email was unavailable, then work would start to grind to a halt. While email certainly still has its place, tools and technologies like Teams are moving in quickly to take its crown away. If you talk to any forward-thinking organization, you will find they are probably looking into how to deploy and leverage Teams.

The main drivers for companies looking to deploy Teams are usually a mixture of the following factors:

- **Improve collaboration:** Let people work better together by putting all the things they need in one place. Chat messages will be seen in the same context as the documents they relate to so they can be found by anyone who needs them.

- **Improve flexible working:** Give people better tools that let them work flexibly by providing access to information from multiple devices across device types (mobile, laptop, desktop, etc.) at home, on the move, or in the office.

- **Reduce information sprawl:** Cut down on "information silos" where documents and information are locked away in inboxes or personal data stores and version tracking is nearly impossible. (Habits can be hard to break. We've all been guilty of emailing attachments called `My_Stuff_v1_final_BLedit_draft.docx`.)

- **Consolidate tools/reduce expenditure:** Where you might already have different "point solutions" in use across an organization—such as one for chat, perhaps two or three for meetings depending on if they are internal or external, and another tool for one-to-many broadcasts—you can consolidate them to a single platform. This can not only help reduce costs but also make things less confusing for end users, as they have only one product to learn and do not need to understand or choose what to use when.

- **Simplify management:** For an organization that has deployed O365, a lot of the traditional management headaches are removed (arguably replaced with a new set!) regarding keeping products current and patched with the latest security fixes. In theory, Microsoft handles this behind the scenes for you, and you are always on a current version of the product. This does not, however, mean that you can sit back and relax. As a proactive administrator, you should be keeping an eye on what features and product changes are coming and working out how to best make use of them for your company.

Using Teams: The Basics

If you are planning to take the MS-700 exam, you probably have at least a little bit of experience with Teams. However, it is always helpful to get a quick refresher on how Teams looks and the core functionality it provides (see Figure 1.1). Microsoft provides a nice demo of the Teams client at `teamsdemo.office.com`.

FIGURE 1.1 Teams client

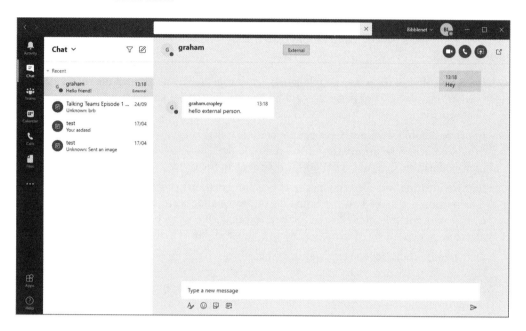

When you log into Teams on the desktop (either by using a modern browser or by downloading the app), you will see a menu bar on the left side. You can add or remove apps here as you require, but by default you will see the following areas:

- **Activity:** This is a feed of recent events relating to you in Teams. This includes where someone has @-mentioned you in a feed, reacted to one of your messages, or attempted to call you. This is the place to go to find out what you have missed.

- **Chat:** This is where you can see all the one-to-one or one-to-many conversations that you have been involved in (see Figure 1.2). You can pin frequently contacted people or groups to the top of the list so that they are always at hand. You will also see chat content from any meetings that you joined so you can find them again afterward.

- **Teams:** This is where you can see all the teams that you are a member or owner of (see Figure 1.3). A team (small *t*) is the core paradigm at the heart of Teams (big *T* for the product name). A team is the collection of people, content, and tools all related to something in one place. Underneath a team you can have more than one section called a *channel* to help keep things neatly arranged.

    As you become involved in more and more teams, you might find some will automatically "hide" if you have not participated in them for a long time, but don't worry—everything is still there when you need it.

    The same applies for channels in a team—you can choose to pin the ones you care about so they are easier to find.

FIGURE 1.2 Chat history

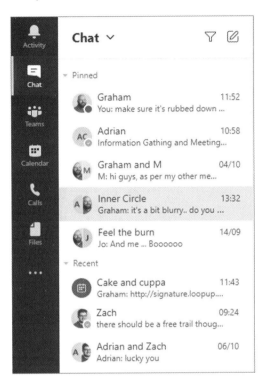

FIGURE 1.3 Teams list

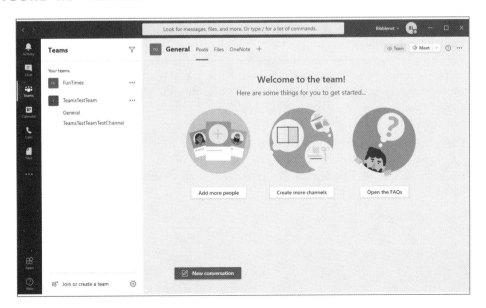

- **Calendar:** This gives you a view of your Exchange Online calendar (see Figure 1.4). You can create/schedule meetings here, join Teams meetings that you have been invited to, or click Meet Now to create a meeting there and then. While this view isn't as flexible as your full Outlook calendar, it is handy when you need to set something up quickly or jump into a meeting.

FIGURE 1.4 Calendar

- **Calls:** This lets you see contacts and create lists of speed-dial users/numbers (see Figure 1.5). You will also see a dial pad letting you dial phone numbers (assuming you are configured with the correct licensing, etc.). You used to only get the dial pad when your account was configured to use Microsoft Phone System, but now everyone should be able to see it as you can still "call" other users without going over the Public Switched Telephone Network (PSTN).

- **Files:** This shows you the most recent documents that you have been working on inside Teams along with any cloud storage providers that you have integrated (OneDrive will be the default here). This tab can act as a quick and easy way to continue working on whatever you were doing last (see Figure 1.6).

FIGURE 1.5   Calls list

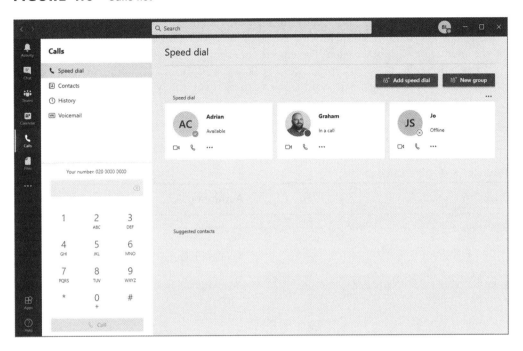

FIGURE 1.6   Files list

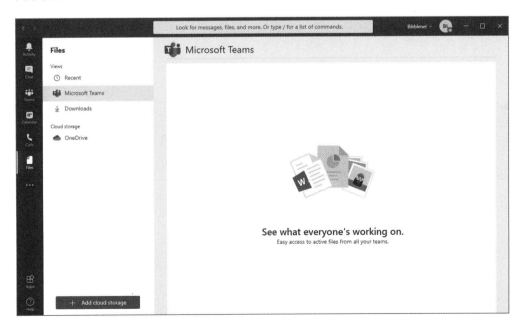

▪   **Presence, settings, and tenants:** At the top-right corner next to the minimize/maximize/close buttons you will see an icon for your user account with a colored dot. This dot is your presence indicator and usually automatically adjusts based on your activity and calendar information. You will see these colored dots in most places where you could be interacting with other users. Presence is core to what makes Teams a unified communications client and lets you (ideally) make smart decisions about how to contact someone. For example, there is little point calling them if they are already in a call or set to Do Not Disturb.

Your presence updates in near real time nowadays (this was not the case when Teams was first released) and can have the settings shown in Table 1.1.

TABLE 1.1   Presence Settings

User Configured	Automatic
Available	Available
	Available, Out of Office
Busy	Busy
	On a Call
	In a Meeting
	On a Call, Out of Office
Do Not Disturb	
	Presenting
	Focusing
Away	Away
	Away Last Seen <time>
Be Right Back	
	Off Work
	Offline
	Status unknown
	Blocked
	Out of Office

docs.microsoft.com/en-us/microsoftteams/presence-admins

If you click your icon, you can manually override your automatic presence or access various application settings.

Next to your icon you might see the name of the tenant you are signed into. Each user has a "home tenant," which is the O365 instance in which their account exists and is licensed for use with Teams. It is possible to be a member of more than one Teams tenant where you have been invited as a guest to work with other people. If you click here, you can swap in/out of these other tenants (but be careful because currently you will then miss any "activity" such as incoming calls, @-mentions, or messages happening in any tenant you are not active in until you switch back). See Figure 1.7.

FIGURE 1.7   Settings

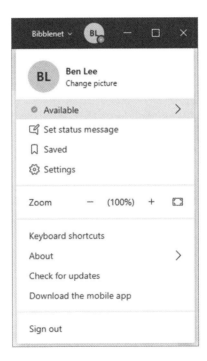

While there is much more to explore in Teams, this section gave you enough of an idea of the basics to start using your own Teams tenant later in the book.

Accessing Teams

To familiarize yourself with how Teams works behind the scenes, and for the exercises that we are going to cover in this book, it is important you have access to a real Teams deployment where you can experiment. While you may have access to an O365 tenant through your company, it is probably not a good idea to be testing things in an environment that has live users on it.

Ideally, you will have access to an environment with a few test users and E3 licensing to make sure the majority of features are available. Depending on your circumstances you might have the following options available to you:

- O365 E3 or E5 trial environment
- Customer Immersion Experience (CIE)—Microsoft Partner demo environment
- Fully paid E3 or E5 environment (but these usually have a minimum term!)

O365 E3 Trial

Microsoft does offer trial subscriptions for E3 (and E5, which is harder to find) from the E3 product overview page at `microsoft.com/en-us/microsoft-365/enterprise/office-365-e3`. You will be asked to enter some signup information but shouldn't need to enter any payment details unless you want to convert the trial into a full subscription. This trial should last for 30 days and let you have access to 25 licenses.

Customer Immersion Experience

If you work for a Microsoft Partner, you may have access to the Microsoft Partner demo site available at `demos.microsoft.com`. Here you can access temporary environments with full E5 licensing. These are intended for use by a partner organization to help run proof of concepts with their customers; however, you may also be able to use one for your own testing. After the trial period has expired, the tenant is deleted and reset. These environments can last for 90+ days.

Fully Paid E3

If you have the funds, or perhaps your company will support the expense as part of its training budget, you can sign up for a full-blown E3 tenant of your own. Be aware that this requires a full payment of a year up front.

Using Teams as Part of O365

O365 is a subscription service provided by Microsoft and includes elements of installable software (i.e., Word, Excel, etc.) mixed with cloud-hosted versions of its software solutions (Exchange, SharePoint, etc.). It is a way for Microsoft to bring together many of its enterprise offerings into a convenient wrapper that businesses can subscribe to. In O365, there are many different tiers of core subscription licenses that usually build on top of each other, and there are a plethora of add-on licenses to let a business pick and choose what additional features they want. Subscriptions come in three broad categories: Home, Business, and Enterprise.

You might see Office 365 and Microsoft 365 referenced together; it can get confusing, as Microsoft is rebranding some of the non-Enterprise plans from "Office" to "Microsoft." The difference used to be that the "Office" or "O" plans contained Office software or Office services (Exchange, SharePoint, Skype for Business, Teams, etc.), and the "Microsoft" or "M" plans took the included offerings further, incorporating Windows 10 Enterprise licenses as well as the Enterprise Mobility + Security (EMS) tools. For our purposes, when looking at the Enterprise plans, consider O365 plans as a subset of M365.

Teams is provided only as a cloud service, meaning that there is no edition that you can install on your own servers. It is generally provided as part of O365 subscriptions because it relies heavily on the rest of the Microsoft cloud offerings for its core functionality. (That said, Microsoft has released a cut-down version of Teams for free, but that is not something to consider for this exam. See `www.microsoft.com/en-us/microsoft-365/microsoft-teams/free` for more information.)

These integration points are as follows:

- Azure AD
    - Handles authentication and identity verification
    - Provides O365 Security Groups for Teams
    - Also controls guest access
- OneDrive for Business
    - Stores files a user uploads in chat
- SharePoint Online
    - Stores files/content uploaded into a channel
- Exchange Online
    - Stores channel messages (hidden in Group mailboxes)
    - Stores user chats (hidden in User mailboxes)
    - Calendar for scheduling Teams meetings
- Microsoft Stream
    - Stores recordings of meetings (at the time of writing, an upcoming update moves this into SharePoint Online)

You can find more information about the various Microsoft Teams architecture at docs.microsoft.com/en-us/MicrosoftTeams/teams-architecture-solutions-posters.

If you want to purchase O365, you have the following choices. (Note that all the information in the following tables, including prices, is correct at the time of writing but is subject to change as Microsoft does like to tinker with its licensing plans.)

Home User Plans

Home subscriptions are targeted at consumers and include Office applications as well as some cloud storage (OneDrive consumer: 1TB) and 60 minutes of Skype calling. See Table 1.2.

TABLE 1.2   Microsoft 365 for Home Subscriptions

Subscription	RRP (per Month)	Office Desktop	Cloud Services	Includes Teams?	Notes
Microsoft 365 Family	$9.99	Yes	OneDrive consumer (1TB storage) Skype consumer PSTN minutes	No	6 users
Microsoft 365 Personal	$6.99	Yes	OneDrive consumer (1TB storage) Skype consumer PSTN minutes	No	1 user

www.microsoft.com/en-us/microsoft-365/buy/compare-all-microsoft-365-products

These home user plans do not currently contain Teams; however, Microsoft is working on an edition of Teams for Home where you can share information with your family and close friends, but that isn't something you have to worry about for this exam or study guide. You can see more about that at www.microsoft.com/en-us/microsoft-365/microsoft-teams/teams-for-home.

Small/Medium Business Plans

Business subscriptions are for small to medium-sized companies up to 300 users. Where Teams is included in these packages, there are some restrictions about the use of advanced features such as calling plans and live events, but this will be covered when we get to the relevant chapters. See Table 1.3.

TABLE 1.3   Microsoft 365 for Business Subscriptions

Subscription	RRP (per Month)	Office Desktop	Cloud Services	Includes Teams?	Notes
Microsoft 365 Business Basic	$5	No	Teams Exchange OneDrive for Business SharePoint	Yes (No live events)	
Microsoft 365 Business Standard	$12.50	Yes	Teams Exchange OneDrive for Business SharePoint	Yes (No live events)	
Microsoft 365 Business Premium	$20	Yes	Teams Exchange OneDrive for Business SharePoint InTune Azure Information Protection	Yes (No live events)	Includes device management and additional security features
Microsoft 365 Apps	$8.25	Yes	OneDrive for Business	No	

www.microsoft.com/en-us/microsoft-365/business/compare-all-microsoft-365-business-products

Enterprise Plans

Finally, at the top end are the O365 enterprise plans. You will have probably seen these referred to as "E" plans, i.e., E3 or E5. There are variations of these plans for education, government, and nonprofit organizations. See Table 1.4. There are also add-on licenses specifically used for Teams telephony elements, but they are not covered here, as we will go into much more detail in the chapter on telephony.

TABLE 1.4 Office 365 for Enterprise Subscriptions

Subscription	RRP (per Month)	Office Desktop	Cloud Services	Includes Teams?	Notes
Microsoft 365 Apps for Enterprise	$12	Yes	OneDrive for Business (1TB)	No	
O365 E1	$8	No	Teams Exchange OneDrive for Business SharePoint	Yes	
O365 E3	$20	Yes	Teams Exchange OneDrive for Business SharePoint	Yes	
O365 E5	$35	Yes	Teams + Phone system and conferencing Exchange OneDrive for Business SharePoint	Yes	Also includes Phone System and Audio Conferencing Teams add-on licenses

www.microsoft.com/en-us/microsoft-365/enterprise/compare-office-365-plans

As you can see, Teams is considered by Microsoft as a core part of O365. Wherever you get any cloud software solution, Teams is included as part of that.

Teams is also due to take the baton from Skype for Business Online (SfBO) as the communications platform for O365. Microsoft has announced a date (currently July 31, 2021) when SfBO will be shuttered and no longer available for use, so you will see many organizations looking at how they can migrate their communications workloads to Teams. This is actually such an important part of the planning to deploy Teams that there is a whole part of the exam dedicated to it.

Teams is one of the most rapidly evolving products that Microsoft has ever produced and has come on in leaps and bounds since it was first launched in March 2017. This makes it exciting to work with but can also present challenges. What was not possible yesterday could be available tomorrow, buttons could move around the UI, or new sections could appear in the Teams Admin Center (TAC).

This section has set the scene for why Teams is a fun product to work with. It covers a lot of different areas, which may seem daunting a first, especially if you have not dealt with some of them before, such as PSTN telephony, but this is what makes Teams really rewarding to deploy. It is so powerful and can truly transform how companies operate, and you get to help them do that!

Managing Teams

It is important that we look at the different tools that are available to help you carry out management tasks in Teams and understand how different configuration settings take precedence when applied to your environment. For example, what happens when users have individual or group settings applied that are different from your company defaults?

Management Tools

Essentially, you will need to use two types of tools to accomplish the management tasks covered in the rest of this book: web portals and *PowerShell* (and if you advance, you can do some automations with the Microsoft Graph API, but that is beyond our scope for now).

Web Portals

Web-based portals are the bread and butter of modern management platforms; they can be accessed via pretty much any modern browser and are sophisticated in terms of the visibility and level of access they provide. For Teams, there are four main administration portals that you will be using:

- Microsoft 365 admin center
- Azure Active Directory admin center
- Microsoft Teams admin center (TAC)
- Call Quality Dashboard (CQD)

These portals will let you perform the most common configuration tasks and give you insights into what is happening in your tenant. Be aware that they are evolving rapidly, especially the Teams administration center, so you may find that items get moved or reorganized as new functionality is added.

Microsoft 365 Admin Center

This is the primary portal for managing your O365 tenant and is accessed via `portal.office.com/adminportal/home` (see Figure 1.8).

FIGURE 1.8   M365 admin center

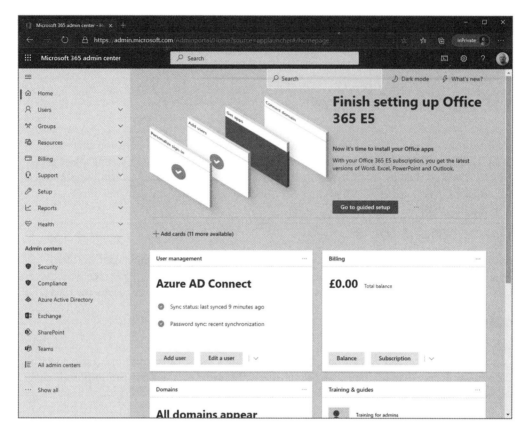

The landing page for the portal can be customized with "cards" to give you an overview of things relating to your tenant such as service health, domain issues, billing information, and service tips. You are likely to see some Teams adoption advice posted here.

USER MANAGEMENT

You can view all the users who are part of your tenant and perform basic configuration tasks for them such as changing names, setting primary email addresses, and choosing what user level licenses to assign. There is also section that shows guest users who have been given access to resources in your tenant without requiring you to provide a dedicated account or provide licenses.

BILLING

Here you can see what licensing subscriptions you are signed up to and can modify payment methods and view past and present invoices. Be aware that for most enterprise tenants, the majority of license billing will be handled through a third-party large account reseller (LAR), which will deal with the subscription plans, terms, and discounts.

SETTINGS

From here you can configure some settings to apply across your entire tenant, especially for applications/services that do not have their own dedicated management consoles (for example, you can disable sharing lists with external users for To-Do here). You can also control and manage the different domains that are associated with your tenant. When you first create a tenant, you will have to specify a unique subdomain of <something>.onmicrosoft. com, but chances are for any normal tenant, you will want to use your own custom domain with the service (these are called *vanity domains*). From here you can view the status of each domain you have added and modify DNS records if you have given O365 control of them. Many O365 services, such as Teams, rely on special DNS records for their correct operation, so this part of the console can check for any anomalies that may affect your service.

REPORTS

This gives you access to some reports that provide an overview of user activity for your tenant; here you can see the number of active users for each core service. This can be helpful when you are doing your Teams deployment to make sure that usage is tracking along with your deployment schedule, and if not, it lets you re-evaluate your user adoption planning.

HEALTH

This section gives an overview of each O365 service and any issues or service degradations that might be affecting your environment. The Message Center is used to provide notifications of upcoming changes in the O365 service that may impact your users.

Azure Active Directory Admin Center

This is available at aad.portal.azure.com (see Figure 1.9). You might wonder why you need to be aware of the Azure admin center to manage Teams, because Azure is not strictly part of the O365 suites. Behind each O365 tenant is an *Azure Active Directory* (AAD). This acts as the identity management platform storing user accounts, groups, and other security/ identity information needed to support the other Microsoft cloud-based products. Think of it in much the same way that the "traditional" Microsoft on-premises server products required *Active Directory* (AD) to operate.

The user data stored in Azure AD can be synchronized from an on-premises AD environment or it can operate in a stand-alone mode. It can have the following types of identities:

Cloud identity: Accounts that only exist in AAD.

Synchronized identity: Accounts that are synchronized from an on-premises AD along with their password information.

Federated identity: Synchronized from an on-premises AD but without a password. When an account needs to be authenticated this is done through some form of a federation gateway that checks the provided password against the one stored in the on-premises AD, for example using Active Directory Federation Services (ADFS).

FIGURE 1.9   AAD admin center

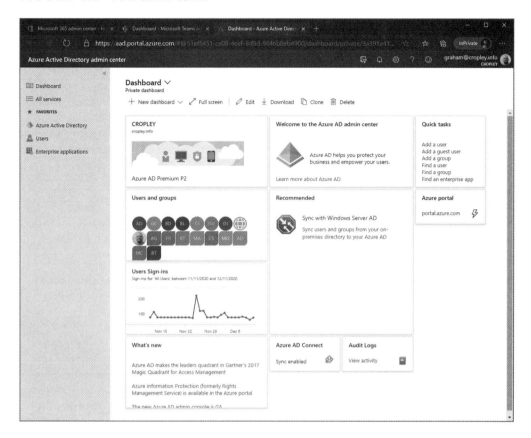

While the Microsoft 365 admin center lets you perform some basic user management tasks such as updating user information, the Azure Active Directory admin center lets you view and control any settings relating to your user accounts, security groups, permissions, and, most importantly for Teams, control over guest user accounts.

We will cover guest access and what controls are required via AAD in Chapter 3, "Teams Core Functionality," but for now just be aware that this portal exists and that it plays an important role in managing access to your Teams environment.

Microsoft Teams Admin Center

Found at admin.teams.microsoft.com (see Figure 1.10), this is the management interface you will be most familiar with for all things Teams. When Teams was first launched, a lot of its configuration settings were shared with Skype for Business Online, but over time Microsoft has been working on this portal to bring most of its Teams tooling together into one place. Similar to the Microsoft 365 admin center, the dashboard gives you some high-level stats about your organization's usage as well as links to hints/tips and training material that might be useful. If you have access to the Teams admin center (TAC), you can spend some time clicking through it to get familiar with the types of controls and settings you can control.

FIGURE 1.10   Microsoft Teams admin center

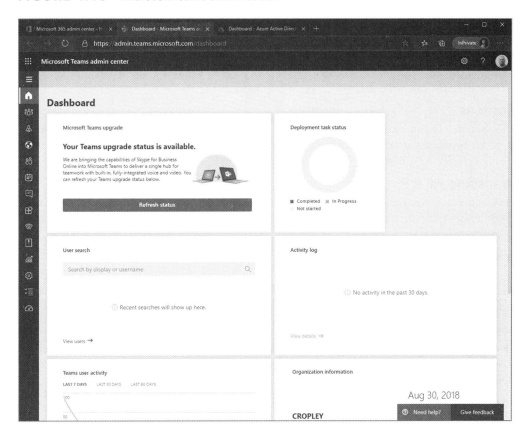

TEAMS

You can view, modify, and create teams for your organization as well as control settings relating to team creation, such as templates and policy settings (such as restricting the use of private channels).

DEVICES

This section gives visibility of (most) hardware devices connected to your Teams deployment. They are grouped by device type as they can have different management requirements, so meeting room hardware is separate from desk phones, etc.

LOCATIONS

This section contains settings related to your physical environment, such as networking topology details and office addresses. These are used mainly for either helping correctly handle calls to emergency services (via telephony) or helping to identify sites/subnets in call reports.

USERS

This section gives information about all Teams-enabled users in the environment. If you search for and click a user, you get a nice dashboard showing the user's call history for the past seven days, and you can dig into the call analytics to help identify any issues on specific calls. You can also view/modify the user-level policy settings that are applied or revert the user to using the org-wide default.

MEETINGS

This section lets you configure settings related to either Teams Meetings or Live Meetings (used for broadcast-style larger events). Here you can control some elements of branding (for example, including a company logo) or settings relating to guest behavior.

MESSAGING POLICY

This section lets you control chat functionality (either one to one or inside channels) such as the ability to delete messages or the use of images, stickers, and Giphys (animated images from a third-party service).

TEAMS APPS

Teams allows expansion through integrations with additional applications (both first and third party). Here you can control and manage what apps are available to your users for use inside Teams, as well as upload and distribute your own.

VOICE

This section controls the settings used to manage telephony functionality in Teams. You can view/manage numbers associated with your tenant, create and manage dialing rules, and view any gateways used for calling.

POLICY PACKAGES

This is a relatively new piece of functionality that Microsoft is introducing because it has recognized that many organizations need to apply the same policies across groups of their users in one go. In the future, you will be able to create bundles of policies to apply to the different types of users in your organization in one go. For now, Microsoft provides a number of pre-created packages that you cannot edit but may still be helpful in applying settings in bulk.

ANALYTICS AND REPORTS

This lets you view and track different usage information of Teams in your environment. You can also download the data to save and manipulate as you need. Don't underestimate how helpful this can be if you are embarking on a company-wide Teams deployment, as this can help show you where uptake is slow.

ORG-WIDE SETTINGS

This section lets you control some settings that apply across all users in your organization, such as coexistence settings with Skype for Business and controlling guest behavior in Teams.

PLANNING

This section offers tailored advice for help in deploying workloads in Teams such as completing a Skype for Business upgrade. This section also contains a network planning tool that you can use to model your network and perform network capacity planning.

Call Quality Dashboard

Found at `cqd.teams.microsoft.com` (see Figure 1.11), the *Call Quality Dashboard* (CQD) is used to detect trends in the quality of real-time media for your users in Teams. When users are making/receiving calls or participating in meetings, data is being collected about the calls that is then combined and displayed for analysis in CQD. If you are doing any real-time media stuff with Teams, you want to make sure that you are carrying out regular reviews of CQD so that you can be ahead of any issues that might be causing quality problems for your users. We will be covering how to use CQD in Chapter 6, "Review Usage and Maintain Quality."

FIGURE 1.11   CQD

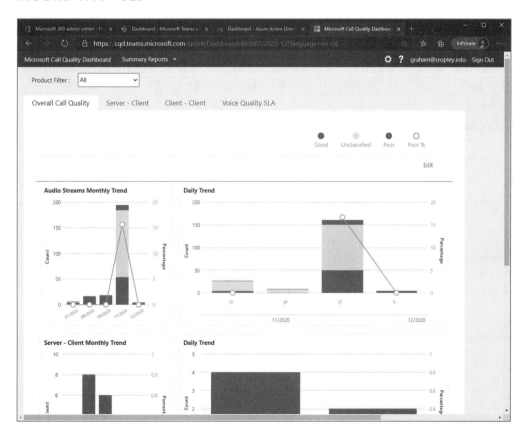

PowerShell

PowerShell is a command line–based management shell that is usually used for bulk management and automation tasks. One of the great advantages of PowerShell is that it is object oriented. This means that unlike in the traditional Windows shell (`cmd.exe`) that uses only text-based inputs, everything in PowerShell is an object complete with a list of properties. For example, if you retrieve a user in PowerShell, what you will actually get is an object representing that user complete with a list of properties that you can then read or update. Once you have the object you want to work with, you can then pass it between commands quickly (called *cmdlets*) and easily, allowing you to reliably and repeatedly perform operations against it.

PowerShell is also an extendable language, meaning you can import modules that give you access to new sets of cmdlets depending on what product you want to work with. Until recently you had to use the Skype for Business Online PowerShell module to work with the communications elements of Teams. The Teams PowerShell module (from version 1.1.6) has merged the required components of the Skype for Business Online modules with other Teams cmdlets, meaning that if you do not need to perform any Skype for Business Online–specific tasks, you only need to install the latest version of the Teams PowerShell module now. Be aware for the exam that some questions might have been written before this changed, so you may still see references to the Skype for Business Online Connector.

While the new Teams PowerShell Connector contains the relevant Skype for Business Online elements, you do still need to connect to them independently, depending on what tasks you are looking to carry out.

It is assumed for this guide that you have worked with PowerShell previously and are familiar with the standard formatting of PowerShell cmdlets (such as `Get-`, `Set-`, `Remove-`). If you haven't used PowerShell before, take a look in the reference list at the Microsoft PowerShell overview materials and get familiar with how PowerShell operates.

Install and Connect to Teams PowerShell

From a computer running PowerShell 5.1, first install the Teams module from the PowerShell Gallery at `powershellgallery.com`. If the machine has Internet access and administrative rights, you should be able do this directly from inside PowerShell itself by running the following command (see Figure 1.12):

```
Install-Module -Name MicrosoftTeams
```

You will need to accept the confirmation prompt, and if you have the Skype for Business Connector already installed, you will need to also use the `-AllowClobber` switch to overwrite some of the existing cmdlets with the ones from the Teams module (as Teams now includes the required Skype for Business components).

If you are unable to automatically download the module from the PowerShell Gallery repository, refer to the site where it provides instructions about how to manually download and copy files to the correct locations for PowerShell to find them.

FIGURE 1.12   Installing the Teams PowerShell module

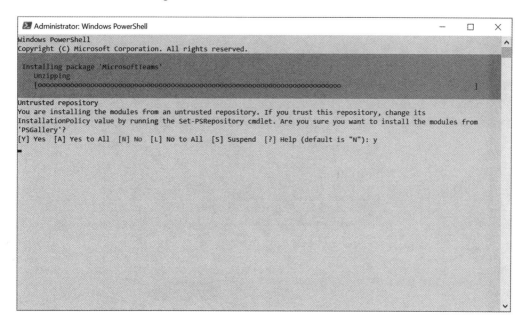

Next, we need to load up the Teams module and start a connection to our tenant. Depending on what you want to work with, you may have to connect twice: once to Teams and once to Skype for Business Online (remember that Teams shares a lot of its voice components with Skype for Business Online). When establishing the connection, there are several ways you can pass through credentials, depending on if you are using modern authentication with *multifactor authentication* (MFA) enabled. It is generally recommended that if you are going to perform automated scripting you have an account that does not require MFA (or at least does not require MFA from wherever you are running the script, for example, inside the company network) as this can be a challenge to automate.

```
#Import the Teams / SfBO module
Import-Module -Name MicrosoftTeams

#Connect to Teams
Connect-MicrosoftTeams

#Create an SfBO session and connect to it
$SfBOnlineSession = New-CsOnlineSession
Import-PSSession $SfBOnlineSession
```

As you are connecting to each service, you will see two modern authentication prompts (see Figure 1.13) where you can enter your credentials. (It should be an account with some Teams administrator permissions; otherwise, you won't be able to get very far, but more on that in later chapters!)

FIGURE 1.13   PowerShell modern authentication prompt

Now you have a connection to O365 and can start viewing and updating settings. Just be careful because while PowerShell is an amazing management tool, you can easily modify settings for large numbers of users in one go, so make sure you thoroughly test any scripts or commands you are going to run. Usually PowerShell cmdlets that modify settings have both a -WhatIf and -Confirm switch that you can use as a bit of a safety net.

To get an overview of PowerShell, visit docs.microsoft.com/en-us/ powershell/.

To find out more about the Microsoft Teams PowerShell module, visit power-shellgallery.com/packages/MicrosoftTeams.

For Microsoft's guide to managing M365 with PowerShell, visit docs .microsoft.com/en-us/microsoft-365/enterprise/manage-microsoft-365-with-microsoft-365-powershell.

Policy Management

Teams uses policies to control what features and functionality are available to users and devices. These policies are usually grouped by category, for example calling, messaging, or app integrations (see Figure 1.14). Unlike with Windows Group Policy where policy objects are merged to produce the desired outcome, in Teams each user or device takes their settings from only one policy of each type.

FIGURE 1.14 Policy list for a user in the TAC

Assigned policies ∥ Edit

Meeting policy
Global (Org-wide default)

Messaging policy
Global (Org-wide default)

Live events policy
Global (Org-wide default)

App permission policy
Global (Org-wide default)

App setup policy
Global (Org-wide default)

Call park policy
Global (Org-wide default)

Calling policy
Global (Org-wide default)

Caller ID policy
Global (Org-wide default)

Teams policy
Global (Org-wide default)

Update policy
Global (Org-wide default)

Emergency calling policy
Global (Org-wide default)

Emergency call routing policy
Global (Org-wide default)

Dial plan
Global (Org-wide default)

Voice routing policy
Global (Org-wide default)

You can typically assign policies directly to users (either individually or in bulk) or auto-apply them based on group memberships. If no specific policies are assigned, the org-wide policy (this will be called *global* if you are using PowerShell) will apply. This gives good flexibility when deciding how best to apply policies, but does mean that you need to carefully consider what settings you want to place in the org-wide versus individual policies and weigh the administrative overhead of managing/assigning policies. For example, do you put the most restrictive settings into the org-wide policy and then remove these restrictions as required with individual policies, or vice versa? This will mostly depend on your company culture and what the risks might be of having a user picking up the wrong policy by mistake. The best rule of thumb is to try to keep things simple and not make things too complex, which usually means putting the most common settings into the org-wide policies and then only modifying them as required for users after that.

As a user can have only one effective policy, there is an order of precedence applied to determine which settings a user will get. They are applied as follows:

1. Policy directly assigned to a user

2. Policy inherited from groups (by rank order)

3. Policy inherited from org-wide policy

This is great until you realize that you can have a user who is a member of more than one group that you are using to apply policies. Fortunately, when you assign policy objects to groups, you have to specify a policy ranking. The rankings are a numerical value with number 1 being the highest rank. If a user who does not have an individual policy assigned is a member of more than one group with a group policy assignment configured, they will take their settings from the highest rank (but lowest number!) policy. Group assignments for policies are dynamic, so as users are added or removed from the groups, their settings will be modified, but these changes will be subject to O365 replication delays, so they are unlikely to apply immediately. The TAC will show you what policies are being applied to a user if you look up their specific user account and find the Policy tab.

To learn more about assigning policies, visit docs.microsoft.com/
en-us/microsoftteams/assign-policies.

Summary

In this chapter, while we have not covered any specific exam content, we have looked at some of the basic principles behind what Teams does and how you can manage it. It is essential that you have a good grasp on the fundamentals of how Teams operates and where it can add value to an organization so that you can understand the context for the chapters to come.

We started by looking at why Teams is a product that is seeing such rapid growth across many organizations today and how you can split its functionality into two broad categories of collaboration and communications.

Next we covered how Teams relies on some of the other O365 services and uses them to store its own information, as well as how it is licensed as part of the different O365/M365 offerings.

Then we covered some of the management fundamentals. You should have a good idea of how and where you can configure different elements of Teams, which is the knowledge you will need to follow along with the rest of the book as we delve deeper into all of the configuration options that you will need to be aware of.

Exam Essentials

Understand how and why an organization would benefit from using Teams.   Understand what benefits a product like Teams can bring to a company by improving both its collaboration and communication capabilities. These benefits can apply equally for internal and external users.

Understand how Teams fits into the O365/M365 offerings.   You should understand how Teams is positioned at the heart of Microsoft's O365 and M365 offerings and that it works by drawing a lot of other components together under one umbrella. For example, understand Team's use of SharePoint to support file sharing inside channels.

Understand the principles of Microsoft licensing plans.   While no one could accuse Microsoft's licensing plans of being simple, you should have an understanding of the differences between the Personal, Business, and Enterprise plan options available. At the least, be familiar with the differences between the E1, E3, and E5 licensing types.

Know about the Teams management interfaces.   Know about the Teams admin center, how to access it, and broadly what sort of configuration options are available—do not worry about specifics at this point as we will cover them as needed in the subsequent chapters. You should also be familiar with the basic workings of PowerShell and how it works by manipulating objects.

Understand the basic principles of Teams policies.   Most Teams functionality is controlled through policies; be aware that you can apply policies at multiple levels (user, group-based, or org-wide) and what happens when a user has more than one applicable policy configured.

Exercises

EXERCISE 1.1

Opening the Microsoft 365 Admin Center

In this exercise, you will log into the M365 admin center and check your user licensing status just to familiarize yourself with the portal.

1. Open your browser and navigate to `portal.office.com/adminportal`.

2. Log in with an account that has tenant admin permissions.

3. Expand Users and select Active Users.

4. Use the search box on the right side to find your user account.

5. Select the user and look through the tabs in the pop-out window.

6. Under the Licenses and Apps section, view what licenses are assigned to your account.

7. If you are not licensed for Teams, enable it.

EXERCISE 1.2

Opening the Teams Admin Center

In this exercise, you will log into the TAC and check your user licensing status just to familiarize yourself with the portal.

1. Open your browser and navigate to `admin.teams.microsoft.com`.

2. Log in with an account that has Teams administrator permissions.

3. Select Users from the left menu.

4. Use the search box on the right side to find your user account.

5. Select the Policies tab and look at what policies you have configured for the account.

EXERCISE 1.3

Connecting to Teams PowerShell

In this exercise, you will set up and connect to the Teams PowerShell management interface.

1. Open a PowerShell window with administrative permissions.

2. Install the Microsoft Teams module using this:

   ```
   Install-Module -Name MicrosoftTeams
   ```

3. Connect to the Teams PowerShell interface using this:

   ```
   Connect-MicrosoftTeams
   ```

4. Return a list of teams in your environment using this:

   ```
   Get-Team
   ```

5. Now connect to Skype for Business Online using this:

   ```
   $SfBOnlineSession = New-CsOnlineSession
   Import-PSSession $SfBOnlineSession
   ```

6. Return a list of online users using this:

   ```
   Get-CsOnlineUser
   ```

Review Questions

1. In the Teams client, where would you see a list of recently made calls?

    A. Calendar

    B. Calls

    C. Meetings

    D. Files

2. Which of the following is not a presence state?

    A. Away

    B. Do Not Disturb

    C. Available

    D. Idle

3. When sharing a file with another user in a one-to-one chat, where will that be stored?

    A. Azure AD

    B. OneDrive for Business

    C. SharePoint Online

    D. Exchange Online

4. Which of the following license types would be the cheapest option for a user who just needs access to Teams in your company?

    A. O365 E1

    B. O365 E3

    C. O365 E4

    D. O365 E5

5. Which management portal would you need to change a user's O365 license allocation?

    A. Teams admin center

    B. Microsoft 365 admin center

    C. Azure Active Directory admin center

    D. Call Quality Dashboard

6. Which management portal would you need to view your call-quality trends?

    A. Teams admin center

    B. Microsoft 365 admin center

    C. Azure Active Directory admin center

    D. Call Quality Dashboard

7. Which management portal would you use to view a user's configured Teams policies?

   A. Teams admin center

   B. Microsoft 365 admin center

   C. Azure Active Directory admin center

   D. Call Quality Dashboard

8. Which management portal would you use to configure a new domain for your tenant?

   A. Teams admin center

   B. Microsoft 365 admin center

   C. Azure Active Directory admin center

   D. Call Quality Dashboard

9. What would you need to install to manage Teams via PowerShell?

   A. Skype for Business Management Shell

   B. Skype for Business Online PowerShell Connector

   C. Microsoft Teams PowerShell Module

   D. PowerShell Core

10. You want to test a PowerShell script that will update one of your user's configuration settings. Which PowerShell commonly available switch would you use to test your code?

   A. `-Test`

   B. `-Confirm`

   C. `-Try`

   D. `-WhatIf`

11. You create a new Teams policy and use group-based assignment to push it out to some of your users. A user who is in the group and also has a different Teams policy configured will receive settings from where?

   A. Group-based assignment policy

   B. Org-wide policy

   C. User-assigned policy

   D. Most restrictive policy

Chapter

2

Getting Teams Up and Running

MICROSOFT EXAM OBJECTIVES COVERED IN THIS CHAPTER:

✓ **Plan and configure a Microsoft Teams environment**

- Upgrade from *Skype for Business* to *Microsoft Teams*

- Plan and configure network settings for Microsoft Teams

- Deploy and manage Microsoft Teams endpoints

Now that we have covered the what and why of Teams, let's start to think about the how. This chapter covers three main topics required to get started.

- Migrating from (and integrating with) Skype for Business

- Preparing your network for Teams

- Deploying clients required for Teams

Migrating from Skype for Business

Skype for Business and Teams have several overlapping features, especially for the communications type of workloads that we discussed in the previous chapter. As Microsoft is pitching Teams as the de facto replacement for Skype for Business, it is important that we look at how the two products overlap so that you can understand how they work alongside each other.

This is important to help plan migrations from Skype for Business to Teams, but even if you do not have Skype for Business deployed, this topic is important to understand (not least because it is an exam topic!) because it can affect other behavior such as federation between users/organizations. For example, if you have Teams fully deployed to all of your users but they are communicating with people at another company who are still running Skype for Business, not all the Teams functionality will work.

Let's start by looking at the core workloads and how they sit across the two products (see Table 2.1).

TABLE 2.1   Skype for Business vs. Teams Workloads

Workload	Skype for Business	Teams
Presence	Yes	Yes
Text chat	Yes, Instant Messaging	Yes, Chat
Audio/Video (A/V) calling	Yes	Yes
Meetings	Yes	Yes
Telephony	Yes	Yes
Collaboration	No	Yes, Teams, Channels, Apps, and Bots

You will note that while both Teams and Skype for Business have "chat-like" functionality, I like to differentiate between the experiences they provide. In Skype for Business, which originated in a "pre-mobile-first" world, chat messages were transient, and they were sent between endpoints (via the server). However, you usually read and responded to them at a moment in time, and when you closed the chat window or moved to a new device, the message thread was lost. While the later versions of Skype for Business did introduce features like conversation history, this was a bit hit-or-miss and didn't always work the way it was intended. On the other hand, Teams was built from the ground up to fully support a cross-device experience where you are using multiple devices, possibly at the same time; therefore, conversations follow you seamlessly from device to device, and the full context is maintained between them. This is what provides Teams with a more rounded "chat" experience.

To help with this overlap of features, Microsoft provides a number of coexistence modes (these are referred to as Teams *upgrade policies* in the Microsoft documentation and *Power Shell* cmdlets) where you can control which features are handled by what product. Which coexistence mode a user is in determines how the two products work together, for example which product is providing *presence*. This is referred to as *interoperability* (see Figure 2.1).

FIGURE 2.1   Coexistence versus interoperability

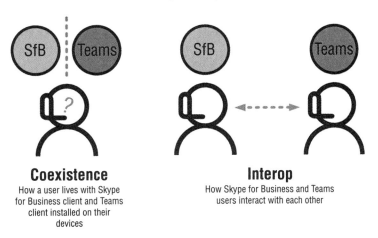

Coexistence
How a user lives with Skype
for Business client and Teams
client installed on their
devices

Interop
How Skype for Business and Teams
users interact with each other

Note that in all of these scenarios, when we talk about Skype for Business, we are assuming that it is either Skype for Business Online or Skype for Business Server configured for *Hybrid* with O365. Without Hybrid enabled, the O365 service is not able to "interact" with Skype for Business users.

Coexistence Modes

There are several coexistence modes in Teams and we are going to look at each of them in turn, starting with the default.

Islands Mode (Islands)

Islands mode (see Figure 2.2 and Table 2.2) is the default, and it lets both products run alongside each other without any sort of integration or interoperability between the two. Each product is operating in its own space—or "island" if you will (see what they did there!).

FIGURE 2.2   Islands mode

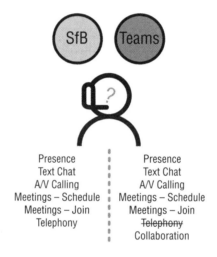

TABLE 2.2   Teams vs. Skype for Business Workloads: Islands

Workload	Skype for Business	Teams
Presence	Yes	Yes
Text chat	Yes	Yes
Audio/video (A/V) calling	Yes	Yes
Meetings: schedule	Yes	Yes
Meetings: join	Yes	Yes
Telephony	Yes	No
Collaboration	N/A	Yes

Messages and calls started from Teams will be received in Teams, and messages and calls started from Skype for Business will be received in Skype for Business. The two main exceptions to this are public switched telephone network (PSTN) calling and federation (inbound messages from external parties), which will still require Skype for Business.

Having Islands as the default is both a blessing and a curse. It can be great when you are first experimenting with Teams, as it lets you access all of the available features with no restrictions or complications. However, users will need to still run both clients, as they will only receive Teams messages in Teams and Skype for Business messages in Skype for Business. See the later section "Islands Mode Trap" where we also cover interoperability.

Islands mode can also be a user adoption headache with two products that, on the surface, serve the same purpose. Imagine a large organization with both Skype for Business and Teams deployed across all users: if you want to send someone a message, which platform or client should you use? What if you need to call them? Teams presence shows they are busy in a call, but Skype for Business shows that they are green and available. Which do you believe?

This is where upgrade planning and the rest of the coexistence modes come into play.

Skype for Business Only (SfbOnly)

In this mode (see Figure 2.3 and Table 2.3), users "stay" in Skype for Business and use this for all communications and meetings. If a user in this mode signs into Teams, they will still see teams and channels, as these are not explicitly disabled; however, they can be removed if required via an App permission policy to hide them from view (but remember to remove the policy as you start the migration).

FIGURE 2.3   SfbOnly

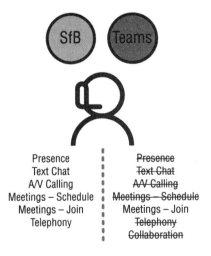

TABLE 2.3   Teams vs. Skype for Business Workloads: SfbOnly

Workload	Skype for Business	Teams
Presence	Yes	No
Text chat	Yes	No
Audio/video (A/V) calling	Yes	No
Meetings: schedule	Yes	No
Meetings: join	Yes	Yes
Telephony	Yes	No
Collaboration	No	No—remove via app permission policy

When would you use this mode?   You would generally use this mode at the start of a migration when you don't want users starting to use Teams before you have provided proper training.

Are there any catches?   It does not let users experiment with Teams at all, so it might not be helpful if you are trying to get users excited about this new software that you are rolling out soon.

Skype for Business with Teams Collaboration (SfBWithTeamsCollab)

This mode (see Table 2.4 and Figure 2.4) starts to light up Teams functionality by enabling Teams' collaboration feature set (teams and channels), but it does not enable any of the Teams communication or meeting (scheduling) functionality.

TABLE 2.4   Teams vs. Skype for Business Workloads: SfBWithTeamsCollab

Workload	Skype for Business	Teams
Presence	Yes	Yes (driven by Skype for Business)
Text chat	Yes	Yes (channel chat only)
Audio/video (A/V) calling	Yes	No
Meetings: schedule	Yes	No

Workload	Skype for Business	Teams
Meetings: join	Yes	Yes
Telephony	Yes	No
Collaboration	No	Yes

FIGURE 2.4   SfBWithTeamsCollab

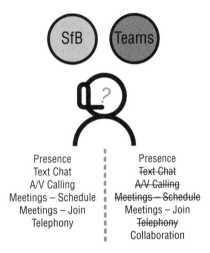

Presence
Text Chat
A/V Calling
Meetings – Schedule
Meetings – Join
Telephony

Presence
~~Text Chat~~
~~A/V Calling~~
~~Meetings – Schedule~~
Meetings – Join
~~Telephony~~
Collaboration

When would you use this mode?   This mode can be helpful in the early stages of a migration when you are not ready to move away from Skype for Business and do not want to confuse users with having to make decisions about which product to use when, but you do want to start benefiting from the Teams collaboration features.

Are there any catches?   It does not provide the full Teams workflow experience for users; where you have provided training for users, they may find that those features are not available in Teams, so their ability to explore and self-teach is reduced.

Skype for Business with Teams Collaboration and Meetings (SfBWithTeamsCollabAndMeetings)

This mode (see Figure 2.5 and Table 2.5) is similar to SfBWithTeamsCollab, but this time, you've guessed it, we've added the ability to schedule Teams meetings. This mode may sometimes be referred to as Meetings First.

FIGURE 2.5   SfBWithTeamsCollabAndMeetings

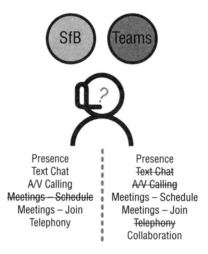

TABLE 2.5   Teams vs. Skype for Business Workloads: SfBWithTeamsCollabAndMeetings

Workload	Skype for Business	Teams
Presence	Yes	Yes (driven by Skype for Business)
Text chat	Yes	Yes (channel chat only)
Audio/video (A/V) calling	Yes	No
Meetings: schedule	No	Yes
Meetings: join	Yes	Yes
Telephony	Yes	No
Collaboration	No	Yes

When would you use this mode?   Teams provides a much better meeting experience than Skype for Business and can be one of the main drivers behind an organization's desire to upgrade. By putting users into this mode, users are able to use teams, use channels, and run "modern" meetings in Teams. Private chat (not in a channel) and non-meeting calling remains in Skype for Business.

This mode can be a popular choice when a company is using Skype for Business Server for PSTN calling (Enterprise Voice). Migrating PSTN calling to Teams in this scenario might require extra planning and preparation time (see Chapter 5, "Adding Telephony"), so this mode lets users benefit from Teams meetings sooner rather than later.

Are there any catches?   As with Skype for Business with Teams Collaboration, you are not giving users a full Teams experience.

Teams Only (TeamsOnly)

Teams Only (see Figure 2.6 and Table 2.6) is essentially the "destination" coexistence mode if you are performing a migration. It means that all workloads are being handled by Teams and that Skype for Business isn't available for active use by a user any longer. For this reason, you may see this mode sometimes referred to as an *upgraded user*.

FIGURE 2.6   TeamsOnly

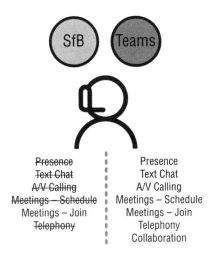

TABLE 2.6   Teams vs. Skype for Business Workloads: TeamsOnly

Workload	Skype for Business	Teams
Presence	No	Yes
Text chat	No	Yes
Audio/video (A/V) calling	No	Yes
Meetings: schedule	No	Yes

continues

TABLE 2.6   Teams vs. Skype for Business Workloads: TeamsOnly *(continued)*

Workload	Skype for Business	Teams
Meetings: join	Yes	Yes
Telephony	No	Yes
Collaboration	No	Yes

When would you use this mode?   The main difference and important thing to remember is that this mode is the only mode where Teams can be used for PSTN calling, so if you are performing any sort of Teams telephony deployment, you must remember to include a step to change a user's coexistence mode to Teams Only; otherwise, PSTN calling will not work.

Are there any catches?   If you have a mix of users who are configured for TeamsOnly alongside users in Islands mode, be aware that you could end up with some messages not being noticed or acknowledged unless all of your Islands mode users are active Teams users. This is because any conversation initiated by a TeamsOnly user with someone in Islands would not be processed through the interop service and so would be delivered to the Islands mode user's Teams client. If they are only an occasional Teams user, it is possible that they would need see these messages or receive incoming calls.

To learn more about Microsoft Teams and Skype for Business coexistence and interoperability, see https://docs.microsoft.com/en-us/microsoftteams/teams-and-skypeforbusiness-coexistence-and-interoperability.

Interoperability

As mentioned, a user's coexistence mode governs the technical interoperability between Teams and Skype for Business, both for decisions taken inside the O365 service (i.e., how to route messages between users) and for how the clients operate. Interoperability is what lets users interact between the two different products.

To fully benefit from the interoperability Microsoft provides, you need to have Skype for Business Server configured in Hybrid mode if you have it deployed on-premises, and you should be running an up-to-date version of the Skype for Business client, ideally a recent release of the Click-to-Run version.

The client version is important, as the Skype for Business client was originally released before Teams was available, and some of the interoperability features have minimum client version requirements to work. With Teams, Microsoft can frequently update the client to support any new interoperability features; however, the Skype for Business client is a more "traditional" installation package and isn't usually serviced as regularly. There are generally two forks of the Skype for Business client. One is the MSI version that is a traditional-style installer—a fixed product version (i.e., Office 2016 16.0.4266.1001) is installed, and then patches are applied manually (or through an automated updating tool). The other is referred to as Click-to-Run. This installer can still be managed and automated like an MSI deployment but is designed to self-update more regularly. Organizations can select how frequently they receive updates by selecting which "channel" they are deploying from (see `docs.microsoft.com/en-us/deployoffice/overview-update-channels`).

Here are some examples of the different types of interoperability available:

- Service-side interop
  - Presence provider
  - Incoming message routing
  - Default meeting scheduler
- Client-side interop
  - Which client responds to headset button presses (USB HID support)
  - Hiding UI elements
  - Notifications and prompts to guide users
- Presence provider

As a rule of thumb, presence is "pushed" from the client that is responsible for chat and calling (so for all modes except Islands and Teams Only, this will be coming from Skype for Business). This works for most scenarios; however, there are some complications where presence won't be accurately represented. For example, because users with Teams deployed, configured in any coexistence mode, are always able to join a Teams meeting, you can encounter situations where a user is available in Skype for Business despite them being actively in a Teams meeting. See Table 2.7 for what comes from which platform in each mode.

TABLE 2.7   Presence Interoperability

Coexistence mode	Skype for Business	Teams	Notes
Islands	Independent	Independent	
SfBOnly	Reflects activity	Pushed from SfB	Teams unable to manually change presence
SfBWithTeamsCollab	Reflects activity	Pushed from SfB	Teams unable to manually change presence
SfBWithTeamsCollabAnd-Meetings	Reflects activity	Pushed from SfB	Teams unable to manually change presence
TeamsOnly	Pushed from Teams	Reflects activity	

Message Routing

Message routing is used to determine where a user will receive inbound chat messages and calls. The behavior here is similar to that seen with presence in that generally Skype for Business will "take the lead" when any of the Skype-based coexistence modes are used, but it can get more complicated as you have multiple potential initiating clients as well as both user coexistence modes.

You will see three basic types of routing methods.

- **Native:** A "full" Teams-to-Teams interaction between users in the same tenant
- **Interop:** A Teams/Skype for Business conversation between users in the same tenant
- **Federated:** A Teams or Skype for Business conversation between users in different tenants. (Before Q4 2019, any Teams-to-Teams interaction across tenants still relied on the Skype for Business interop gateway in O365, so conversations were limited to rich text only.)

Again, you can apply a rule of thumb here that if the recipient is configured for any of the Skype for Business Interop coexistence modes, then the incoming messages will be received by them in the Skype for Business client regardless of which client they originated from. The main exception here is when the recipient of a message coming from Teams is homed on Skype for Business Server, interoperability is not possible, and the message will fail.

Meeting Scheduler

Meeting scheduling is perhaps one of the most straightforward interop scenarios and determines which service should be the default for creating meetings. Both Skype for Business and Teams install plugins into Outlook that provide quick access to scheduling meetings. These icons will obey a user's coexistence mode and will be displayed only if the user is allowed to create scheduled meetings on the relevant platform. Refer to Table 2.8 to see which is displayed where.

Remember that regardless of a user's coexistence mode, the user will always be able to join meetings on either platform if they have been scheduled by someone else (provided they still have the client installed).

TABLE 2.8   Default Meeting Scheduler

Mode	Default Meeting Platform	Note
Islands		Outlook will show both icons.
SfBOnly	Skype for Business	
SfBWithTeamsCollab	Skype for Business	
SfBWithTeamsCollabAndMeetings	Teams	
TeamsOnly	Teams	

Source: docs.microsoft.com/en-us/microsoftteams/teams-add-in-for-outlook

Interoperability Limitations

With both platforms being based on slightly different technologies, Skype for Business and Teams are not always able to "speak the same language," which means some features from either platform are not supported in a direct interop interaction. Fortunately, to work around some of these scenarios that can fail, Microsoft has introduced the ability to "escalate" interactions from one platform to another.

- Chat
  - Only basic text supported
  - Advanced formatting, emoticons, Markdown, Giphys, etc. not supported
- Multiparty chat/IMs
  - Supported only across the same platform
  - Can trigger escalation
- Screen sharing
  - Not natively supported
  - Will trigger escalation
- Voice/video
  - Supported for one-to-one calling
- File transfers
  - Not supported
- Other Skype for Business workloads
  - Not supported (for example, persistent chat, Extensible Messaging and Presence Protocol [XMPP] interop, etc.)

Escalation

To work around this interop gap, Teams and more recent releases of the Skype for Business client (since the July 2019 Click-to-Run build) are capable of *escalating* a chat conversation into a meeting when the previous triggers are hit. Escalation creates a meeting on whichever platform the "triggering" user is running and prompts both participants to join. Each party will receive a meeting join URL to click, and the interaction will then pick up in the meeting space.

While this isn't an ideal scenario, as users receive a notification and have to manually join the new meeting, it does at least place both parties onto the same platform so they can continue their activities with the full native feature set of either Teams or Skype for Business. It is better than either client just generating an error message and not letting the interaction continue.

On the Skype for Business side, this escalation behavior is automatic (provided the client version is new enough) and does not require any backend configuration.

In Teams, because escalation works by generating an ad hoc meeting, this setting must be enabled for your user. This is controlled by the `-AllowPrivateMeetNow` switch in the `CSTeamsMeetingPolicy` PowerShell cmdlets (see Chapter 3, "Teams Core Functionality" for more information about managing meeting policies).

NOTE To learn more about coexistence with Skype for Business and how messages are routed, see docs.microsoft.com/en-us/MicrosoftTeams/coexistence-chat-calls-presence.

Coexistence Modes and Migration/Upgrade Paths

The primary reason for all these coexistence modes and the available interoperability is to help support a company's migration from Skype for Business to Teams. In an ideal world, you might want to move all of your users at once so that you receive full functionality in one go, but this might not be possible for a number of reasons.

- Volume of users
  - Too many people to train in one go
  - Care to not overwhelm a support desk with any issues
- *Enterprise Voice*
  - Teams' *PSTN* connectivity does not use all the same connection methods as Skype for Business, so migrating PSTN calling workloads may require work per location.
- Hardware/equipment
  - Upgrading physical equipment may require visits to each location, i.e., meeting room hardware or desk phones.
- Pilot phases
  - Checking Teams functionality and behavior for parts of the business

Staged Migrations

With the available coexistence options, you might think that an ideal migration would let you plan a nice progression from "left to right," starting in SkypeOnly mode and working through to TeamsOnly, taking users through each mode one at a time, but the reality is that you will likely skip some of the phases.

For example, you might jump straight to SfBWithTeamsCollabAndMeetings before completing any PSTN planning and moving to TeamsOnly. Or perhaps you need to pause in SfBWithTeamsCollab while waiting for Teams support with your particular meeting room devices (or while deploying a video interop gateway).

Islands Mode Trap

With Islands being the default mode for Teams, it can be easy to get carried away with deploying Teams to your user base before carrying out proper migration planning. Figure 2.7 shows the Islands behavior.

FIGURE 2.7   Islands mode interactions

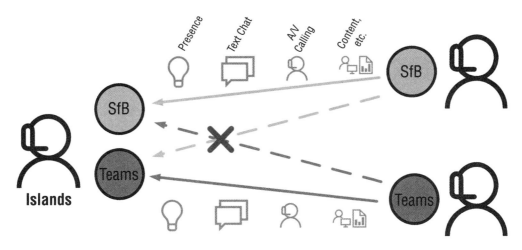

Before you know it, you can have a large portion of your user base running Teams in (almost) full functionality mode using rich chat and advanced meeting features. Then when you start to realize that you might have issues with interoperability or coexistence between users in parts of the organization where Teams usage hasn't become as prevalent, you might start looking at how to employ the coexistence modes to force Skype for Business and Teams to use the interoperability service in escalation scenarios. However, if you now push your Teams users into one of the coexistence modes, they will lose functionality, and it will actually be a backward step for them:

- SfBWithTeamsCollab
  - They would lose Meetings along with the newer one-to-one chat and calling experience.
- SfBWithTeamsCollabAndMeetings
  - They would still be missing the improved one-to-one chat and calling experience from Teams.

You can see how you might have to end up making the best choice out of some bad options. Do you remove functionality from Teams that they might already be using by enabling an SfB-based coexistence mode that will improve interop to other internal users? Or should you let them keep "full" functionality in Teams but at the expense of a poor experience talking to departments where Teams uptake hasn't been as good (or to external federated users)?

There isn't, strictly speaking, a right or wrong answer here. It will always depend on the specific circumstances of the company, their migration goals, and what users will and won't find acceptable.

If customers have a good saturation of Teams already running in Islands mode, my preference here when advising them is usually to not "remove" Teams functionality and to move forward as quickly as possible with both with the saturation of the Teams client (so that the scenarios requiring interoperability are reduced) and whatever migration planning activities they need to get into TeamsOnly mode ASAP.

It is important to be aware that these coexistence modes exist, know what their limitations are, and understand how you can apply them as necessary to help manage the experience for your users.

You won't see Microsoft referring to an "Islands mode trap" (and therefore it is not something on the exams), but it is common with real-world deployments.

Meeting Migration Service

When talking about migrating users from Skype for Business to Teams, one of the workloads we have been considering is online meetings. Meetings can be the lifeblood of a company, with people often having many meetings scheduled far into the future (especially if they are using recurring meetings). If you have had a successful adoption of Skype for Business, it is likely that many of these meetings will have been created as online meetings containing Skype for Business join details. The last thing we want to do as part of migrating a user to Teams is to force everyone to delete and re-create these meetings with new Teams coordinates instead. This isn't something that would win you a Systems Administrator of the Year trophy!

Fortunately, Microsoft has us (mostly) covered with something called the *Meeting Migration Service* (MMS). This is a service that runs in O365 and when triggered can "look inside" a user's mailbox (assuming they are in Exchange Online) and scan for any meetings that the user has scheduled in the future that were originally created with either Skype for Business or Teams join details. The service will then automatically regenerate and replace the joining details with updated ones (usually Teams).

MMS will never replace a Teams meeting with Skype for Business details, so you cannot use it as part of any rollback migrations (again, another issue that can form part of our Islands mode trap!).

What MMS Does

When activated, MMS will search through the target mailbox for all meetings where the target user is the host and they are scheduled for a future time. For each meeting that is discovered, the service will check the body of the appointment to identify if it contains an "online meeting block." If it does, then it will generate new online meeting information (i.e., a join URL and any dial-in details per the target user's policy) and replace this portion of the message. The updated meeting is then saved, which triggers each recipient to receive a standard Exchange "Meeting update" information message. It does not matter if the recipients are internal or external; they will receive the same standard update notification.

It is important to understand the timing behind MMS, as it is not an instantaneous process. There will always be a delay of at least 90 minutes after triggering MMS before anything changes, as the request to run it is placed in a queue to avoid overloading. MMS will usually complete within two hours but can take much longer if the target user has a lot of meetings that need processing. If any errors are encountered, it will try again up to nine times over a period of 24 hours.

Here are a few things to consider:

- Only online meeting invites created either by the relevant Outlook plugin or via the Outlook on the Web plugin are updated. If a user has copy/pasted the online meeting section between invites from somewhere else, those invites will not be updated.

- While the contents of the meeting invite are usually retained (i.e., any included attachments or additional text outside of the meeting block), if the user has updated anything inside the online meeting section, it will be deleted.

- Any content that the user might have uploaded into the meeting in advance is not migrated, only the invitation itself, and only for meetings with fewer than 250 listed participants.

Triggering MMS

MMS is usually triggered in the following scenarios:

- Migrating a user from Skype for Business Server either to Skype for Business Online or to Teams
- Adding or updating a user's audio conferencing settings
  - For example, adding an Audio Conferencing license
- Coexistence mode changes for an individual user to either TeamsOnly or SfBWithTeamsCollabAndMeetings
- Manually run by an administrator
  - Via the Start-CsExMeetingMigration PowerShell cmdlet

The MMS service was originally designed to help with user migrations from Skype for Business Server to Skype for Business Online because, once migrated to O365, the server environment would have lost references to any meetings that had been scheduled for a user.

When migrating a user from Skype for Business Server, you can migrate them straight to Teams by specifying the MoveToTeams switch as part of the Move-CsUser PowerShell cmdlet. When you do this, the user will be automatically assigned the TeamsOnly coexistence mode, which should then trigger MMS to run.

When updating a user's coexistence policy to one of the two modes listed earlier, MMS will also be triggered, but only if the settings are applied to specific users. If the tenant-wide policy is updated to either of these modes, it will not trigger MMS! You must remember to take this into account as part of any bulk migrations; if you need MMS to run after updating the tenant policy, then you can still trigger it manually against each user with a Power-Shell script.

To run MMS manually for specific users, you can use the `Start-CsExMeetingMigra-tion` PowerShell cmdlet as follows:

```
Start-CsExMeetingMigration -Identity <User> -TargetMeetingType <Teams/Current>
```

The following are the main parameters for the cmdlet:

Identity: Specifies either the user principal name (UPN), Session Initiation Protocol (SIP) address, or display name to target.

SourceMeetingType: Specifies what meeting type should be updated; usually this is left at the default of All.

TargetMeetingType: Specifies what the target platform for update meetings will be. Acceptable values are either Current (only update conferencing information) or Teams (migrate all meetings to Teams meetings).

Confirm: Specifies `$true` or `$false` value (not required by default) used as a check before running the cmdlet.

Monitoring MMS

As you can see, MMS is a useful solution provided by Microsoft but isn't something that you have precision control over, especially the timings for when to schedule its execution. If you need to rely on MMS as part of your Skype for Business to Teams migrations, it can make sense to perform your migration tasks outside business hours so that O365 replication and MMS all happen and can "apply" while users are not active and trying to use the services. For MMS as well, it can be wise to make sure you notify users about what to expect if you are doing large-scale migrations, as some of them could receive a large quantity of updated meeting requests in their mailboxes as colleagues are migrated to Teams and MMS diligently sends out updated meeting invites!

If you need to check how MMS is progressing, you can use the `Get-CsMeetingMigra-tionStatus` PowerShell cmdlet to see the status of what it has been doing (see Figure 2.8).

FIGURE 2.8   MMS results

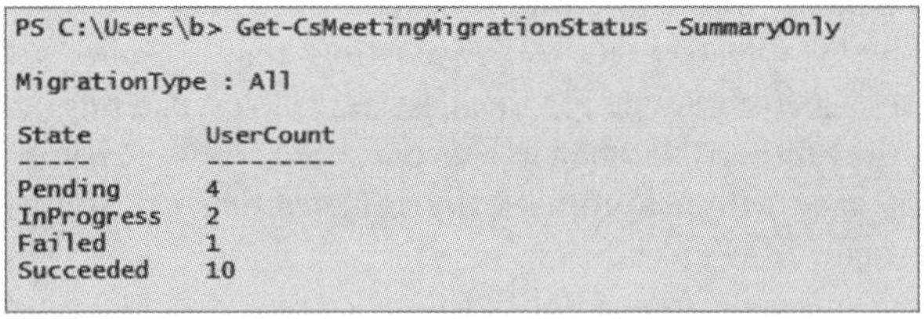

```
PS C:\Users\b> Get-CsMeetingMigrationStatus -SummaryOnly

MigrationType : All

State        UserCount
-----        ---------
Pending      4
InProgress   2
Failed       1
Succeeded    10
```

The following are the main parameters you will need:

SummaryOnly: Shows a summary table of the migrations broken down by Pending, InProgress, Failed, and Succeeded

StartTime/EndTime: Specifies dates over which to return details

Identity: Specifies either the UPN, SIP address, or display name to target

Combining these switches with some standard PowerShell tricks, you can create the following command to check the status of any failed MMS listed by user:

```
Get-CsMeetingMigrationStatus | Where {$_.State -eq "Failed"} | Format-Table
UserPrincipalName, LastMessage
```

Ideally, this will give you no results because everything will have worked!

MMS is enabled by default for tenants, but you can choose to disable it either permanently or temporarily. Check the current status for your tenant using the `Get-CsTenant-MigrationConfiguraiton` PowerShell cmdlet, which will return either a `True` or `False` value for `MeetingMigrationEnabled`.

If you need to change the value, you can run the "set" version of this command to either turn on or off MMS globally.

```
Set-CsTenantMigrationConfiguraiton -MeetingMigrationEnabled <$True/$False>
```

Remember to take O365 replication delays into consideration when applying this setting; if you need to change things, make sure to apply it well in advance of when you plan to migrate user accounts.

> To learn more about the Meeting Migration Service, see docs.micro-soft.com/en-us/skypeforbusiness/audio-conferencing-in-office-365/setting-up-the-meeting-migration-service-mms.

Managing Skype for Business to Teams Migrations

Now that we have covered how Skype for Business and Teams can coexist and how you might approach migrating users between them, we will cover how you control it.

A user's Teams upgrade policy (or coexistence mode) is configured either specifically for their account or at an organizational level. You cannot apply these policies by department, region, or based on other filters automatically (but that doesn't mean you can't create PowerShell scripts to do that for you).

As with all Teams policies, if a user has a specific policy applied to them, this overrides whatever "global default" or "tenant level" policy is configured.

Configuring a Teams Upgrade Policy for All Users

In the *Teams admin center* (TAC), you can find the organization-wide setting currently configured for your tenant under Org-wide Settings ➤ Teams Upgrade (see Figure 2.9).

FIGURE 2.9 Teams Upgrade options

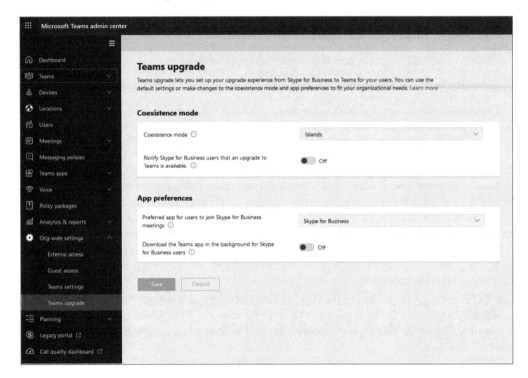

Here you can see two sections. The Coexistence Mode section lets you choose one of the modes we discussed (see Figure 2.10). The second thing you will see here is a toggle switch that will cause the Skype for Business client (subject to being a new enough version) to display a banner notification advising users that "Skype for Business will be upgraded to Microsoft Teams."

This notification (see Figure 2.11) can be a good way to generate some buzz or excitement about the upcoming deployment for Teams, but make sure you have planned your coexistence migration path correctly before encouraging more users to get Teams installed and running.

The App Preferences section in the Teams Upgrade options covers application behavior. You can configure the default client used by a user when joining Skype for Business meetings and set whether the Teams client is to be automatically downloaded and installed by the Skype for Business client.

FIGURE 2.10   Coexistence Mode options

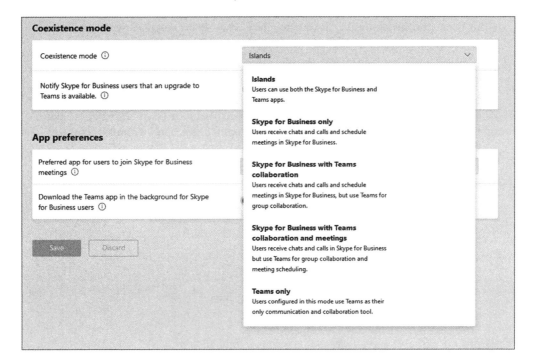

FIGURE 2.11   Skype for Business notification

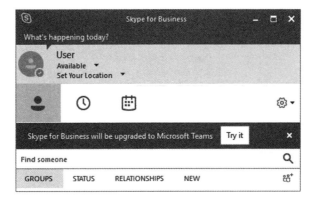

Preferred Skype for Business Meetings Application   This can be set to Skype for Business (default client), or you can force the use of the Skype Meetings app, which is the browser plugin-based solution. This option can be helpful after you have completed your migration to Teams and want to think about removing the Skype for Business client from your install base and want to check whether users have any issues joining Skype for Business meetings just from the browser. However, unless you have a good reason not to, it is probably recommended to leave the Skype for Business client installed, as it will usually provide a better meeting join experience.

Note that once a user has been placed in TeamsOnly mode, the Skype for Business client can detect this and will open in a reduced functionality mode (see Figure 2.12) where users are only able to join meetings and access contact lists. They cannot initiate any new conversations or start calls using the client.

FIGURE 2.12   Skype for Business reduced functionality mode

Download Teams App   This setting will make the Skype for Business client attempt to download and install the Teams application in the background. This setting will only apply to Windows clients and may not be possible because of network restrictions or install rights, etc. In theory, this setting sounds like a good idea, and it might work for organizations that do not have heavily managed desktops, but in reality most companies are likely going to want to manage the deployment of the Teams client independently. However, if you do start getting some odd behavior regarding the Teams client, make sure you come and check what has been configured in here!

Configuring an Individual User Policy

While it is essential that you configure these global policies for your organization to make sure that you are controlling what you want the default behavior to be, there will be scenarios where you have to control the policies on a per-user basis. These can include the following:

- Testing interop behaviors
- Enabling pilot users for TeamsOnly
- Migrating users through the coexistence modes

In the TAC, we can override the organization-wide policy for specific users to set them into any of the modes that we need.

Open TAC and select Users from the left menu, select the user that you want to modify, and on the main account tab that will open you should see near the bottom a Teams Upgrade section. The settings here should appear the same as for the org-wide settings for the coexistence mode, allowing you to select any of the same options. If you choose one of the Skype for Business interop modes, you will also see the option to notify via the Skype for Business client as well.

Configuring via PowerShell

Any of these settings can also be configured programmatically using PowerShell, which is handy if you need to update settings for users en masse, i.e., as part of a bulk migration program.

The PowerShell cmdlets that you might need are split over two "families." `CSTeams-UpgradePolicy` controls the upgrade policies being used, and `CSTeamsUpgradeConfiguration` controls the Skype for Business client meeting join and Teams client download behaviors.

For the Teams upgrade policy, the cmdlet is fairly straightforward, as the only variant we need to use is `Grant-CsTeamsUpgradePolicy` (see Table 2.9) because we can choose only one of the predefined options. You cannot make your own upgrade policy modes.

This PowerShell cmdlet has four important switches:

Global: Use this when not specifying a user to update the "global" tenant-wide policy.

Identity: Alternatively, use this to update only the specific user; it can be either the UPN or SIP address (note that the Display Name option is missing here).

MigrateMeetingsToTeams: This specifies whether MMS should be triggered to run and update the user's meetings. This will work only when moving to TeamsOnly or SfBWith-TeamsCollabAndMeetings modes and when targeting a specific user. Remember, we can't run MMS against all users automatically.

PolicyName: This specifies the name of the specific TeamsUpgradePolicy that we want to apply to our target.

TABLE 2.9   Grant-CsTeamsUpgradePolicy PolicyName Choices

PolicyName	Coexistence Mode Used	Trigger Skype for Business Notification
SfBOnly	SfBOnly	No
SfBOnlyWithNotify	SfBOnly	Yes
SfBWithTeamsCollab	SfBWithTeamsCollab	No
SfBWithTeamsCollabWithNotify	SfBWithTeamsCollab	Yes
SfBWithTeamsCollabAndMeet-ings	SfBWithTeamsCollabAnd-Meetings	No
SfBWithTeamsCollabAndMeet-ingsWithNotify	SfBWithTeamsCollabAnd-Meetings	Yes
UpgradeToTeams	TeamsOnly	No
"Islands" or "Global"	Islands	No
IslandsWithNotify	Islands	Yes
$Null	Reset to default	n/a

Source: docs.microsoft.com/en-us/powershell/module/skype/grant-csteamsupgradepolicy

Here are some examples of using this cmdlet:

```
Grant-CsTeamsUpgradePolicy -PolicyName SfBWithTeamsCollab -Identity
Ben@LearnTeams.info
```

This would give that specific user the UpgradePolicy of SfBWithTeamsCollab, i.e., Teams running in collaboration-only mode.

At the start of my migration path to Teams, you might want to run the following to set the global policy to Skype for Business Only mode:

```
Grant-CsTeamsUpgradePolicy -PolicyName SfBOnly -Global
```

To "reset" a user to the global policy, you can specify a "nothing" value using the PowerShell `$null` variable:

```
Grant-CsTeamsUpgradePolicy -PolicyName $null -Identity Ben@LearnTeams.Info
```

To control the Skype for Business client behavior, we have the `Set-CsTeamsUpgrade-Configuration` PowerShell cmdlet with the following switches:

SfBMeetingJoinUX: You can use either `SkypeMeetingsApp` to use the browser-based plugin or `NativeLimitedClient` to allow the Skype for Business client to open in limited functionality mode to join meetings.

DownloadTeams: You can use `$True` or `$False` to control if the Skype for Business client should attempt to download and install Teams.

For example, if we wanted the client to install Teams and for Skype for Business to still be available for meetings after migration, we would run the following:

```
Set-CsTeamsUpgradeConfiguration -DownloadTeams $true -SfBMeetingJoinUx
NativeLimitedClient
```

To check, you can use the `get-` variant of the cmdlet.

```
Get-CsTeamsUpgradeConfiguration
```

This will return the current values configured. Always remember to check when you change something to make sure it is correct!

Preparing Your Network for Teams

To have a good user experience in Teams, especially when using it heavily for communications (think voice, video, and PSTN calling), you need to make sure the network is operating as efficiently as possible. Any hiccups or interruptions will be noticeable to end users and will affect their perception of the platform.

In this section, we will take a look at what you can do to help check and optimize your network to give Teams the best possible chance of succeeding. In Chapter 6, "Review Usage and Maintain Quality," we will cover how you can proactively monitor the real-world calling experience of your users.

As a basic rule of thumb, you should aim to get the traffic from the Teams device out of your network and into Microsoft's as quickly and cleanly as possible. Once the traffic is on Microsoft's network, managing the quality and capacity is Microsoft's problem and (ideally) not yours. With O365, and especially Teams, Microsoft is doing a lot of clever things behind the scenes to make sure there are entry points to its network in lots of locations around the world.

The Microsoft networking guidance for Teams is available here: docs .microsoft.com/en-us/microsoftteams/prepare-network.

Broader networking guidance for M365 is available here: docs.microsoft .com/en-us/microsoft-365/enterprise/microsoft-365-network-connectivity-principles.

Internet Breakout

Figure 2.13 shows the common perception of how traffic will travel between a user and Teams (in the O365 cloud). It goes over some portion of the company network before reaching some sort of Internet breakout and then crosses the Internet to the O365 servers before returning.

FIGURE 2.13   Networking perception

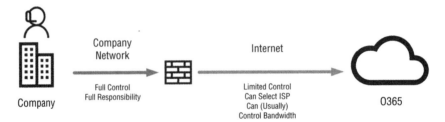

The reality is that with Microsoft having these entry points (or Azure Front Door) to their network around the world, you can have a shorter Internet path than you might expect (see Figure 2.14).

FIGURE 2.14   Networking reality

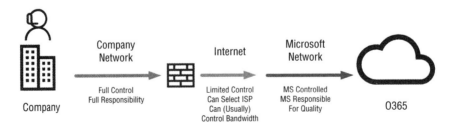

The goal is to try to reduce and optimize as many parts of the connection chain as you can, as shown in Figure 2.15. The area that you have most influence over is the "Company Network" leg. Here you can make sure that you reduce processing and transit time by minimizing things like proxy servers, not forcing the use of virtual private network (VPN) tunnels, and disabling firewall tricks such as deep packet inspection for Teams traffic.

FIGURE 2.15   Networking goal

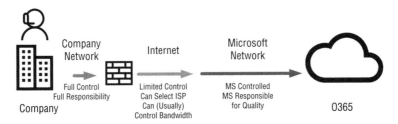

When considering how to prepare your network for Teams, there are two main areas that you need to check:

Connection Quality   Is the performance of the network fundamentally able to meet the requirements needed by real-time media? In other words, is the connection reliable and sufficiently speedy?

Connection Capacity   It's all well that the connection might be of a suitable quality to support calls, but can it do that at scale? When you have an office full of users all trying to make and receive calls at the same time, can you maintain that quality without everything getting too congested?

Networking Best Practices

You can find the official list of what ports and protocols Teams requires to have open through a firewall at docs.microsoft.com/en-us/microsoft-365/enterprise/urls-and-ip-address-ranges. Even if you have scripts or canned firewall configurations, it is recommended that you regularly check back to this table, as the IP ranges (and sometimes ports) are subject to change as the platform evolves.

Table 2.10 lists the main ports and protocols from that list (this table is not a comprehensive list; please refer to the table source for the full list).

TABLE 2.10   Microsoft Teams Primary Ports/Protocols (Snippet)

Category	Express Route	Address	Port/Protocol	Notes
Optimize	Yes	13.107.64.0/18, 52.112.0.0/14, 52.120.0.0/14	UDP: 3478, 3479, 3480, 3481	Used for Teams media traffic
Allow	Yes	`*.lync.com`, `*.teams.micro-soft.com`, `teams.micro-soft.com`, 13.107.64.0/18, 52.112.0.0/14, 52.120.0.0/14, 52.238.119.141/32, 52.244.160.207/32, 2603:1027::/48, 2603:1037::/48, 2603:1047::/48, 2603:1057::/48, 2620:1ec:6::/48, 2620:1ec:40::/42	TCP: 443, 80	Primary destinations for sign-in and most critical client operations

Source: As the ports and protocols used can change frequently, please see the current list at docs
.microsoft.com/en-us/microsoft-365/enterprise/urls-and-ip-address-ranges?view=o365-
worldwide.

> You may see references to a large port range (50,000–59,999) that was used for media. This is no longer required, as traffic has been migrated to use the UDP range 3478–3481.

The User Datagram Protocol (UDP) port ranges are what Teams "should" be using for making calls, as UDP is the preferred protocol (lower networking overhead), but it will fall back and send media over Transmission Control Protocol (TCP) 443 if something is blocking UDP. Most organizations will have the firewall configured to allow TCP 443 outbound, so Teams can tunnel this way if needed. This is one of the reports you should be checking when we get to Chapter 6 for monitoring quality (TCP versus UDP), as chances are good that while a call over TCP will succeed, it will not be great quality.

> A full list of M365 ports and protocols is available here: docs.microsoft .com/en-us/microsoft-365/enterprise/urls-and-ip-address-ranges.

Understanding Traffic Categories

In the official networking tables, Microsoft assigns one of the following categories against each entry in the table:

- Optimize
  - High volume and/or latency sensitive
  - Microsoft-owned and managed endpoints

- IP address provided
- URLs endeavor to not be updated too frequently
- Allow
  - Not as sensitive to networking conditions
  - URLs/IPs will change more frequently than the Optimize category
  - Lower bandwidth/volume of traffic
- Default
  - Does not require special treatment
  - May be resources not in Microsoft-hosted datacenters

The following are recommendations about how to treat each category:

- Optimize
  - Use local Internet breakout
  - Use local/regional DNS lookup
  - Bypass proxy servers
  - Bypass packet filtering
  - Bypass SSL inspection
  - Bypass VPN tunnels
  - Do not "hairpin" traffic
  - Prioritize traffic through any upstream devices (top priority)
- Allow
  - Use local Internet breakout
  - Use local/regional DNS lookup
  - Bypass packet filtering
  - Bypass SSL inspection
  - Prioritize traffic through any upstream devices (above default priority)
- Default
  - Treated as standard Internet traffic

As you can see, there are some common themes of things that you should try to avoid in order to help optimize Teams traffic. Let's look at the key ones:

Local Internet Breakout   A common networking topology is to have all your company sites connected to a private network, usually via some sort of Multiprotocol Label Switching (MPLS) network (see Figure 2.16). The onward connection to the Internet would then either also connect directly into the MPLS cloud or be accessed via a datacenter also connected to the MPLS. This model makes sense in a world where most services are hosted inside company locations, but as more services move outside the company boundaries and are delivered directly from the Internet, the trend is now toward replacing expensive MPLS connections with commodity Internet links. These links let traffic break out from the site directly to its destination and removes some of the length (or unnecessary hops).

FIGURE 2.16   Centralized versus local Internet breakout

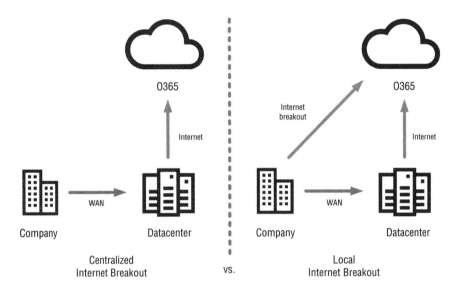

Local/Regional DNS Lookup   *Domain Name System* (DNS) lookups help devices work out the server IP address where they need to send their network requests. O365/ Teams uses geo-DNS for some of its services, whereas the DNS servers on Microsoft's side will attempt to check the geographical location of incoming requests and respond with the IP address of a service local to the requesting server (seeing as Microsoft has multiple parts of its service split around the world). In other words, if Microsoft determines that the incoming DNS request comes from the United States, respond with the address of a U.S. server. If the request comes from the European Union, respond with the IP address of the same service but in the EU. You can help with this process by making sure that any company DNS responders are not being centralized to a single worldwide breakout point but are at least being resolved in the same region as the original client device.

Proxy Servers/Packet Filtering/SSL Decryption   These are all services that can help monitor and manage Hypertext Transfer Protocol Secure (HTTPS) traffic on a company network. However, for Teams traffic, especially for our optimize category, the need to filter/inspect it is reduced, as we can tell from the destination IP and port ranges that it is traffic required for O365. Anything we do that will slow down the transit of packets can introduce latency and deteriorate the experience for users. The only scenario where we might want to use proxy servers is in locations that have poor local Internet breakout and we want to force the routing of those connections somewhere else on the network to a breakout that has better upstream connectivity, but this should be the exception, not the rule. For *Secure Sockets Layer* (SSL) inspection, it is worth noting that it is actually against the terms of service that organizations agreed to when they signed up to O365; included in these terms is a stipulation that traffic shall not be decrypted to/from the service.

VPN Tunnels   *Virtual private network* (VPN) tunnels are quite common in corporate networks; they provide a private, encrypted connection over a public network, so they are commonly used to protect connections between company locations or, probably more commonly, between individual user computers and the company datacenters. While VPN tunnels have their place, they can really interfere with real-time media traffic in Teams. First, they can force our traffic to take a "longer route" similar to the local Internet breakout issue, and second, because of what VPNs are designed to do, they add an encryption wrapper to each packet that is being sent. This then must be removed at the far end. This has two impacts: increasing processing time taken to add/remove the encryption wrapper and making the packets larger. This can cause them to be split into multiple parts to transit the network (especially if the connection is over a wireless network). These two things together introduce extra latency/jitter to our connection that we do not want. All traffic that Teams puts on the network is encrypted, so this extra VPN wrapper is not required. (Sure, there are some small exceptions; see Secure Real-time Transport [SRTP] headers per RFC 3711, for example, but anything sensitive is certainly encrypted by default, unlike other similar services—Zoom, I'm looking at you!) Most VPN solutions will allow for something called either *selective* or *split* tunneling where they allow some traffic (based on destination) to not be included in the corporate VPN tunnel. When setting up your network to support Teams, you should aim to exclude just the Teams media traffic from any VPN connections, if nothing else (see Figure 2.17).

FIGURE 2.17   VPN split tunnels

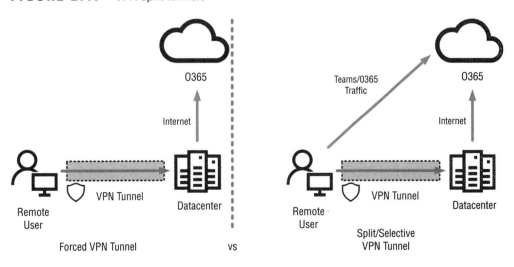

Forced VPN Tunnel   vs   Split/Selective VPN Tunnel

Traffic Prioritization   Where you have congestion points in your network, your devices might have the ability to prioritize some traffic based on a set of rules. The most common solution is known as *quality of service* (QoS) and will be covered in more detail in the section "Network Capacity."

Network Quality

Reviewing network quality is a way that we can gauge the basic performance of the network and its suitability to carry Teams traffic. Remember that just because you have a high bandwidth connection, that does not mean that it is suitable for carrying real-time media needed in calls.

Network Metrics

Having established how to help give Teams a fighting chance at a good connection, let's now consider what that good connection looks like. Microsoft provides some clear guidance (shown in Table 2.11) about the network conditions you need to meet (and ideally exceed) to have good-quality calls.

TABLE 2.11   Network Quality Metrics

Metric	Target (from Client to Microsoft)	Target (from Internet Edge to Microsoft)
Latency (one way)	< 50ms	< 30ms
Round-trip time (latency both ways)	< 100ms	< 60ms
Burst packet loss	< 10% in 200ms	< 1% in 200ms
Packet loss	< 1% in any 15s	< 0.1% in any 15s
Jitter	< 30ms in any 15s	< 15ms in any 15s
Packet reorder	< 0.05%	< 0.01%

Source: docs.microsoft.com/en-us/skypeforbusiness/optimizing-your-network/media-quality-and-network-connectivity-performance

Microsoft provides two sets of metrics here because your expected values can vary depending on where you are measuring from. If you are measuring the connection quality from the edge of your network right where it starts to travel over the Internet, you should look at the right column ("From Internet Edge to Microsoft"), and you will notice that these values are "tighter" than those in the middle column. This is because it is expected that you will lose some quality between wherever your Internet breakout is and the client. However, if you are testing the connection quality from whatever location the client is situated in, then you should use the middle set of metrics as your benchmark.

Latency/Round-Trip Time   Latency is the time taken for a packet to get from A to B, and *round-trip time* (RTT) is the time taken for a packet to go from A to B and then back to A. You should expect the RTT to be double the value of one-way latency, but this might not be the case if traffic is taking different routes for some reason. If you have high latency/RTT during a call, this will be noticeable as delays, or lag, in the audio streams.

Packet Loss   *Packet loss* is when packets are lost along the way to the destination. Teams is able to cope with a small amount of lost data before quality starts to degrade, as it can employ tricks like Forward Error Correction (FEC) where audio snippets are overlapped when sent over the network. This means that, for example, if a sample of audio is split over packets A, B, and C but packet B is lost, Teams can reconstitute some of the missing audio from the data it received in packets A and C. If you are on a network suffering from high packet loss, you will get garbled or "robot"-style audio as some of the fidelity is lost.

Jitter   *Jitter* is differences in the rate at which packets arrive at their destination. Ideally, we would want/expect a steady stream of data for our call so that they can be processed smoothly without any delays. If Teams detects that data is arriving in bursts, it will create a buffer to try to smooth out the stream, but obviously the larger any buffer gets, then the bigger the delay in the audio/video streams will be. As this buffer dynamically expands/contracts, it may be noticeable as glitches or squeaks in the stream.

Packet Reorder   *Packet reorder* has a similar impact to Jitter and can be common on wireless networks. Teams will ideally be using UDP for calls, and while UDP is a "fire-and-forget" protocol, each packet is numbered so that the remote end can play them back in the correct order. If Teams is receiving packets out of order, it will use a buffer to give packets a chance to arrive before playing the stream. This has the same impact/downsides as it does for Jitter.

You can see from earlier that Teams has a few tricks up its sleeve to try to maintain an acceptable level of quality for calls across a wide range of network conditions, and this only covers tricks down at the bottom of the networking stack. Teams also uses several different codecs for voice/video that help it optimize for different network conditions, and it can swap between them if needed to help maintain quality. If Teams finds itself on a poor-quality connection, it will notify the user (via an on-screen banner) and will prioritize the voice stream over everything else so that you should be able to least hear the other party. As network conditions improve, so will the capabilities in your call.

Measuring Quality

To help see what quality you can expect from your network, Microsoft provides some tools that you can run to generate some "Teams audio-like" traffic that will then be scored against the previous metrics. While this isn't a definitive or perfect way to check your network connection quality, it does give you a decent (and free) way to check how things are looking. If you get a pass on these tools, you can likely proceed with your deployment, but if they highlight any problems, you know that you have some work ahead of you to investigate and fix the network.

Skype for Business Network Assessment Tool

This tool is available from `www.microsoft.com/en-us/download/details .aspx?id=53885`. Don't be put off by the name here; this command line–based tool is equally valid for both Skype for Business Online and Teams traffic. It works by sending a small sample of audio (18 seconds) to the Microsoft network edge, where it is then relayed back to the endpoint. For this interaction, the tool gathers metrics for packet loss, round trip time, jitter, and packet reorder ratio and saves the results into a local TSV file.

The tool has a configuration file that can be edited to make it run multiple iterations back to back; however, be careful, as each time you execute the tool, it will overwrite any existing results without prompting. Having gathered your results, there is then a second command-line tool that will parse them and give you some pass/fail scores against the two sets of recommended values (network edge versus client network).

The tool also has a specific switch that can be used to perform port checks out to O365 and report if any combinations of IP and port are being blocked. This can be invoked with the `/connectivitycheck` switch.

As shown in Figure 2.18 and Figure 2.19, this tool isn't very user friendly and probably is not something you would want end users to be running by themselves. However, there are several unofficial scripts available aimed specifically at helping automate the process of running the test, capturing its data, and helping to process them. Using this tool, it is possible to build up a decent picture of the quality on your network across multiple locations, but remember that as it is only using a small sample audio size, it might not reflect real-world conditions.

Network Testing Companion

The *Network Testing Companion* tool is available from `www.powershellgallery.com/ packages/NetworkTestingCompanion/`. This is a Microsoft-provided PowerShell-based GUI/wrapper for the Network Assessment Tool but is packaged up in a much neater way.

As this tool is part of the PowerShell gallery, you can invoke its installation directly from inside PowerShell (using an elevated window). (If it is the first time you have installed something via the PowerShell gallery, you may be asked to trust code from this repository for installation [see Figure 2.20]):

```
Install-Module -Name NetworkTestingCompanion
```

FIGURE 2.18   Network Assessment Tool running

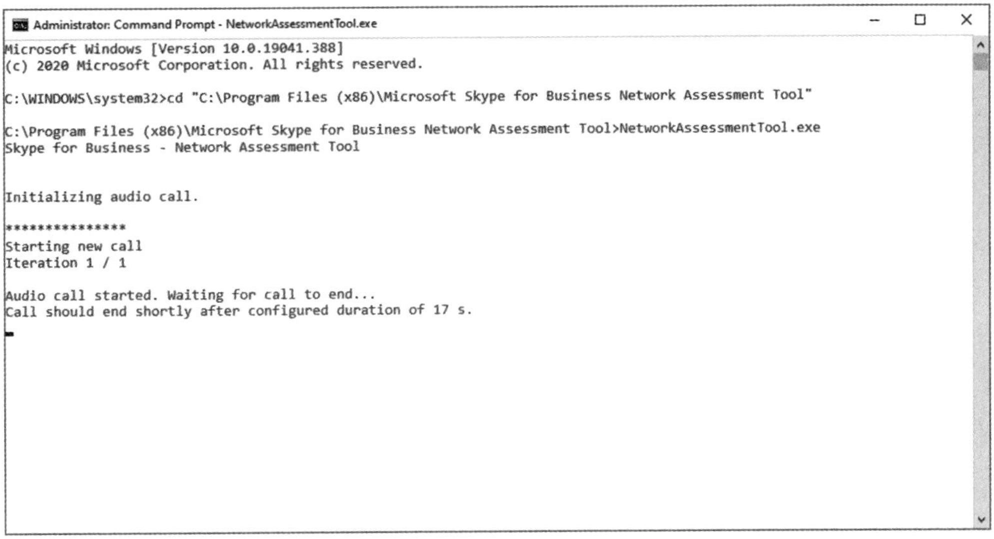

```
Administrator: Command Prompt - NetworkAssessmentTool.exe                              —    □    ×
Microsoft Windows [Version 10.0.19041.388]
(c) 2020 Microsoft Corporation. All rights reserved.

C:\WINDOWS\system32>cd "C:\Program Files (x86)\Microsoft Skype for Business Network Assessment Tool"

C:\Program Files (x86)\Microsoft Skype for Business Network Assessment Tool>NetworkAssessmentTool.exe
Skype for Business - Network Assessment Tool


Initializing audio call.

***************
Starting new call
Iteration 1 / 1

Audio call started. Waiting for call to end...
Call should end shortly after configured duration of 17 s.
```

FIGURE 2.19   Network Assessment Tool results

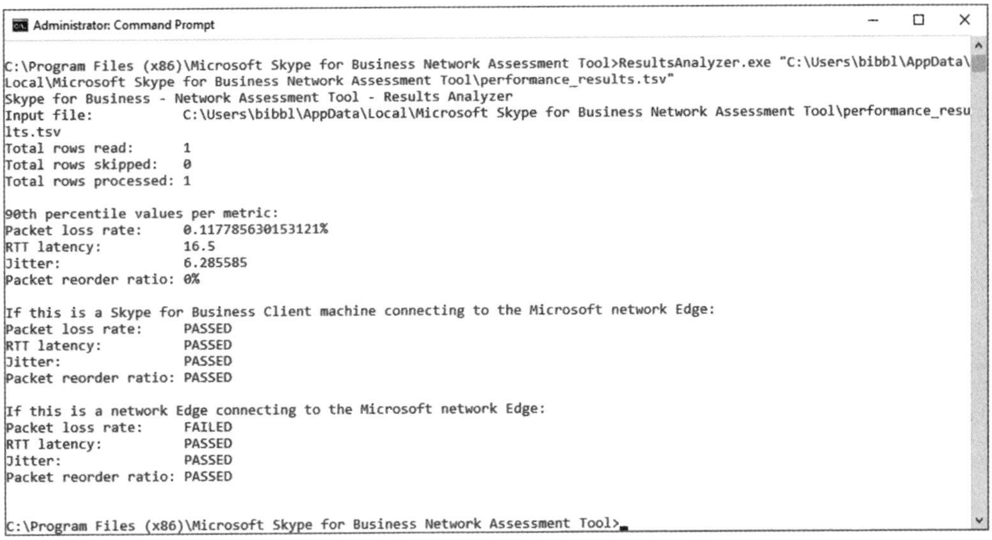

```
Administrator: Command Prompt                                                          —    □    ×
C:\Program Files (x86)\Microsoft Skype for Business Network Assessment Tool>ResultsAnalyzer.exe "C:\Users\bibbl\AppData\
Local\Microsoft Skype for Business Network Assessment Tool\performance_results.tsv"
Skype for Business - Network Assessment Tool - Results Analyzer
Input file:          C:\Users\bibbl\AppData\Local\Microsoft Skype for Business Network Assessment Tool\performance_resu
lts.tsv
Total rows read:     1
Total rows skipped:  0
Total rows processed: 1

90th percentile values per metric:
Packet loss rate:    0.117785630153121%
RTT latency:         16.5
Jitter:              6.285585
Packet reorder ratio: 0%

If this is a Skype for Business Client machine connecting to the Microsoft network Edge:
Packet loss rate:    PASSED
RTT latency:         PASSED
Jitter:              PASSED
Packet reorder ratio: PASSED

If this is a network Edge connecting to the Microsoft network Edge:
Packet loss rate:    FAILED
RTT latency:         PASSED
Jitter:              PASSED
Packet reorder ratio: PASSED


C:\Program Files (x86)\Microsoft Skype for Business Network Assessment Tool>
```

FIGURE 2.20   Installing Network Testing Companion

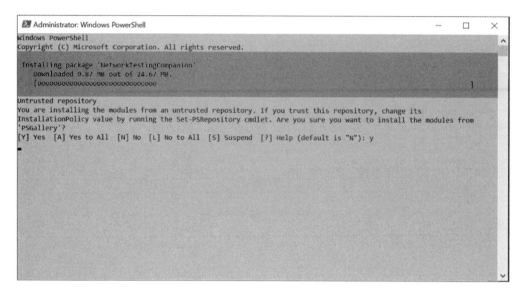

After installation, you need to run another command to set up the shortcuts so that you can run it (see Figure 2.21):

```
Invoke-ToolCreateShortcuts
```

FIGURE 2.21   Network Testing Companion shortcut

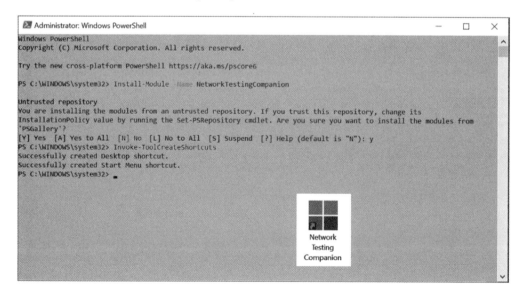

Once you have the shortcuts created, you can now run the tool, which will do some initial checks behind the scenes. As this is a wrapper for the Network Assessment Tool, it will check whether it can find the tool. If not, you will see a warning along with a large green Install button (see Figure 2.22) that will download and install the tool for you (you may get a UAC prompt for administrative access).

FIGURE 2.22   Networking Tool not found

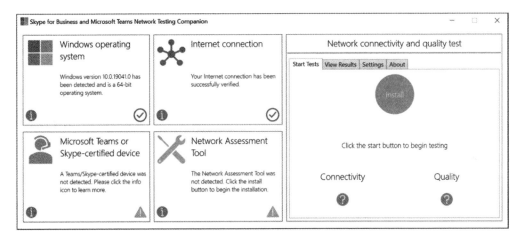

When the tool is installed, click Start (see Figure 2.23); if this is the first time running the Network Assessment Tool, you may get a Windows Firewall prompt confirming that you want to allow network access for the tool. If everything is good, you should now see a progress bar on the right side of the window while the tests are running in the background. Testing should take between 5 and 10 minutes, and when completed, you should have some information displayed on the View Results tab for both the connectivity and quality tests (shown in Figure 2.24). You can click either of the blue file icons to see the exact output from the Network Assessment Tool if you need to get more information on any issues detected.

At the time of writing (late 2020), this version of the tool is the one that is currently referenced on the Microsoft exam. However, a new browser-based connectivity checker that covers Teams along with other O365 services was recently released. It will be worth using and understanding this service too.

Microsoft 365 Network Connectivity Test

A browser-based tool is available at `connectivity.office.com/`. This tool aims to give you an overview of where your traffic for O365 is being routed (see Figure 2.25) and lets you download an `.exe` tool to perform more detailed tests. These are then uploaded back to the service where you can see a report of the findings. You can choose to run the tests without being signed in to an O365 account, but if you are, the results can be saved and shared to help build up a picture of connectivity for different locations.

FIGURE 2.23   Networking Tool installed

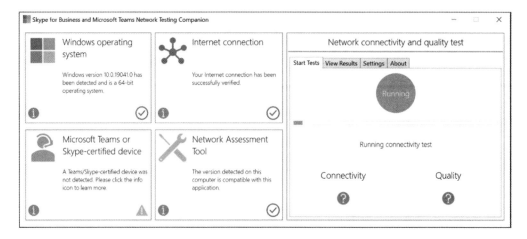

FIGURE 2.24   Network results

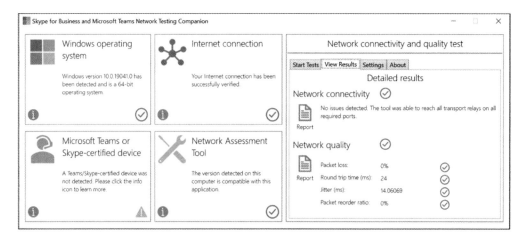

You can let the service auto-detect your physical location, or you can manually specify it (see Figure 2.26). You can also specify your main O365 domain so that the tests can be tailored to check your actual URLs.

Once it has completed some basic tests (see Figure 2.27), you should see a prompt in the browser to download/run a customized executable file. This file will, when executed, run several more detailed tests from your client machine and upload the results to the service.

Once the results have uploaded, you can switch to the Details tab and scroll down a bit to see the Teams section (see Figure 2.28). The results here should be similar to those seen when using either of the previous two tools.

FIGURE 2.25   M365 network connectivity test

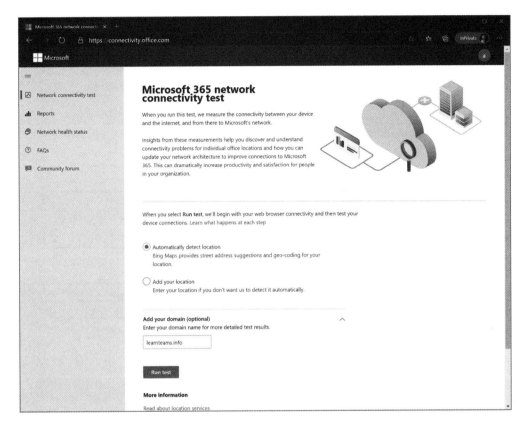

The nice thing about this browser-based tool is that it can give you an idea of the connectivity to all the O365 services and not just for Teams.

You can see that there are a few options available for helping gauge the quality of your network connections, but remember that these synthetic tests may not accurately represent conditions you experience during real-world usage. There are many other factors that could influence quality; this is another reason that we will be looking at tools such as the Call Quality Dashboard (CQD) in later chapters to gauge the actual performance. Choosing how and when to test can make a big difference in your results. The following are some things to consider:

- Are you testing wired versus wireless?

- Are you testing at 9 a.m. when the network is busy versus 1 a.m.?

- Is a network backup running at 1 a.m. that might impact capacity?

- If testing wireless performance, should you be close to or far away from the access point?

FIGURE 2.26   M365 network connectivity test: initial run

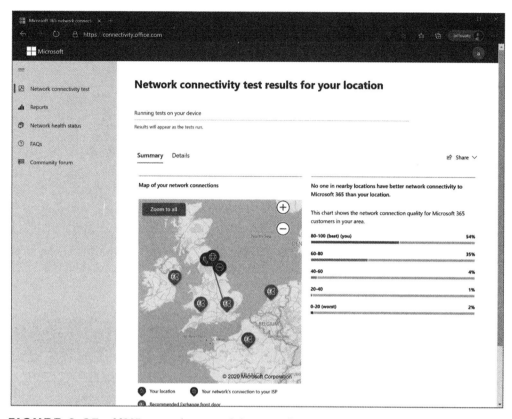

FIGURE 2.27   M365 network connectivity test: client executable

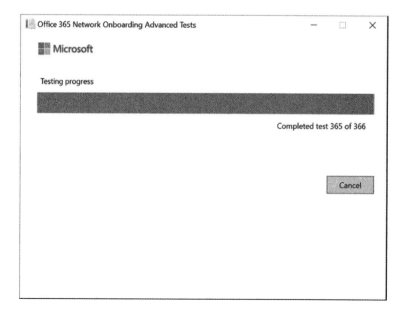

FIGURE 2.28   M365 network connectivity test: Teams results

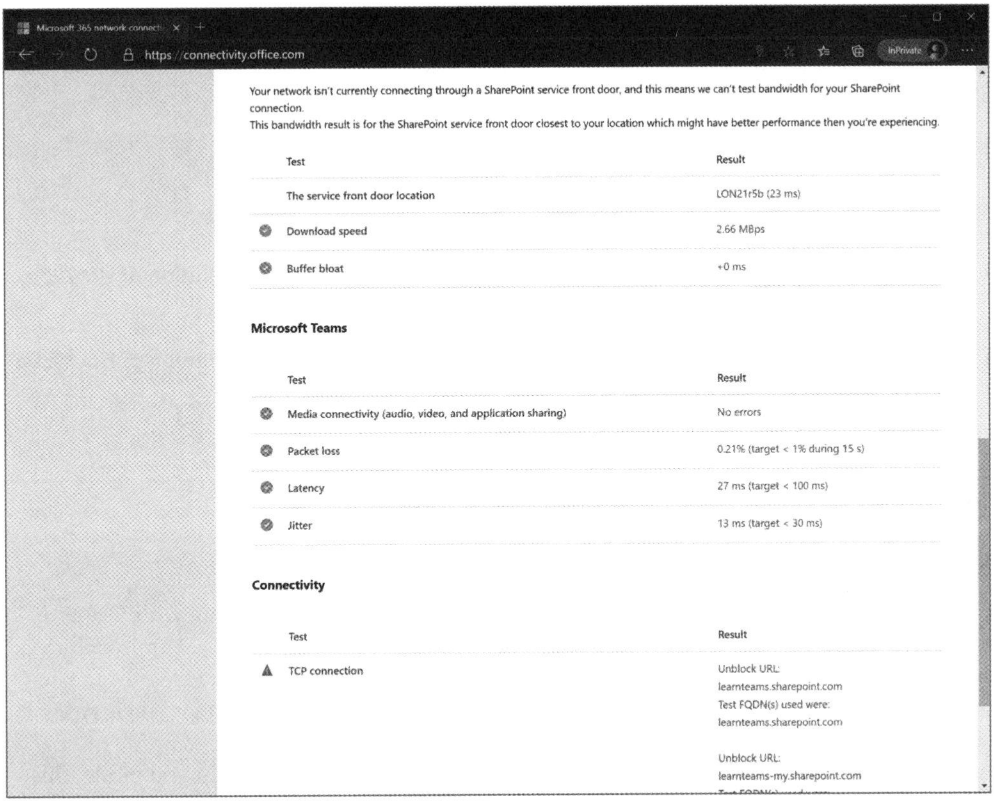

Your network isn't currently connecting through a SharePoint service front door, and this means we can't test bandwidth for your SharePoint connection.
This bandwidth result is for the SharePoint service front door closest to your location which might have better performance then you're experiencing.

Test	Result
The service front door location	LON21r5b (23 ms)
⊘ Download speed	2.66 MBps
⊘ Buffer bloat	+0 ms

Microsoft Teams

Test	Result
⊘ Media connectivity (audio, video, and application sharing)	No errors
⊘ Packet loss	0.21% (target < 1% during 15 s)
⊘ Latency	27 ms (target < 100 ms)
⊘ Jitter	13 ms (target < 30 ms)

Connectivity

Test	Result
⚠ TCP connection	Unblock URL: learnteams.sharepoint.com Test FQDN(s) used were: learnteams.sharepoint.com Unblock URL: learnteams-my.sharepoint.com

> **NOTE** You can find the Skype for Business Media Quality and Network Performance documentation at docs.microsoft.com/en-us/skypefor-business/optimizing-your-network/media-quality-and-network-connectivity-performance. The same principles apply for Teams.

Network Capacity

Having looked at one of two networking factors (quality), it is time to talk about capacity. Capacity is what will let you make sure that the "size" of network connections can sustain the volume of Teams traffic that you are anticipating creating.

Table 2.12 shows you the estimated bandwidth used in some common scenarios; however, there are far too many possible permutations to be able to precisely calculate the amount of bandwidth you might use, and this will also vary over time. This is where network modeling will need to come into play.

TABLE 2.12   Teams Bandwidth per Workload

Bandwidth (Both Directions)	Workload
30Kbps	Peer-to-peer audio calling
130Kbps	Peer-to-peer audio calling and screen sharing
500Kbps	Peer-to-peer quality video calling 360p at 30fps
1.2Mbps	Peer-to-peer HD quality video calling with resolution of HD 720p at 30fps
1.5Mbps	Peer-to-peer HD quality video calling with resolution of HD 1080p at 30fps
500kbps/1Mbps	Group video calling

Source: docs.microsoft.com/en-us/microsoftteams/prepare-network

Network Modeling

Given the multitude of different workloads that a user could be performing with Teams at any one time, such as voice, video, screen share, and more, the only practical approach to anticipating network capacity requirements is to perform a version of modeling using personas. Personas allow us to group users into categories where we can estimate their type of usage and concurrent usage.

Fortunately the days of complicated spreadsheets are behind us. To help you model this type of information, Microsoft has some web-based tooling provided as part of the Teams admin center that you can use to build a representation of your network topology and user *personas*.

To access the network planner, log into admin.teams.microsoft.com/ and then expand Planning ➤ Network Planner. Here you will see a list of any plans and personas that you have created in the tenant.

By default you will have three personas already created for you: Teams Room System, Remote Worker, and Office Worker. Microsoft suggests that in a "normal office" environment you would expect a split of 80 percent office workers to 20 percent remote workers. (Guess they didn't see 2020 coming either!) While you cannot modify or delete these defaults, you are able to create up to three custom entries (see Figure 2.29). To do this, click Add and then select the workloads you want to model. Here's an example:

- Audio only user
  - Audio: on
  - Everything else: off

- PSTN phone
  - PSTN calling: on
  - Everything else: off

FIGURE 2.29 Creating a persona

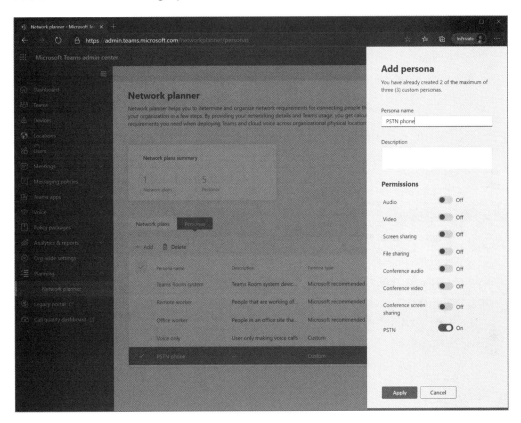

This can be helpful when you know that a group of your users will not be performing any particularly intensive workload; in other words, they do not have a webcam or laptop and so will only make PSTN calls.

Having created the personas that we want to use in our plan, go ahead and make a plan (you can have more than one plan at a time to help you model things like planned network upgrades or "what if" scenarios). A network plan consists of a list of network sites/locations and reports that are generated by assigning personas against the sites.

Start by adding some sites to your network plan and add as much information as you have (see Figure 2.30):

- Site name
- Site description
- Site address
- Network users
  - Total number of "users" that will be allocated against this site
- Network
  - Subnet and subnet mask used at the site
- Express Route
  - Toggle this if the site is directly connected to Microsoft via Express Route (for O356 services; not if it is just connected for Azure)
- Connected to WAN
  - Does traffic from this site have to pass through another location to get to the Internet?
  - WAN capacity
    - Total connection capacity
  - WAN audio queue
    - Capacity reserved for audio traffic
  - WAN video queue
    - Capacity reserved for video traffic
- Internet egress
  - Local or via another site
- Internet egress site
  - Only available if you have more than one site already set up and also connected to the WAN
- PSTN egress
  - VoIP only
    - No PSTN calling
  - Local
    - Lets you choose a PSTN connection method
- PSTN connectivity type
  - Only active when Local is selected
  - Direct routing
    - Calling via gateway (assumed to be local)
  - Calling plans
    - Calling via Microsoft

FIGURE 2.30   Creating a site

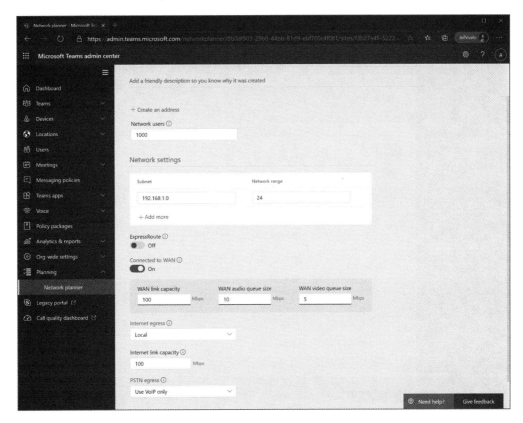

It makes life easier if you create sites with a local Internet breakout first, which may need to include some "zero user" locations if you have breakout via datacenters with no actual users (the planner will not let you save a site with 0 users, so just choose 1).

Once you have all your sites set up, you can hop over to the Report tab and select Start Report. Here you can then map your personas against the total number of users for each site (see Figure 2.31).

You can select personas from the drop-down menus and allocate them up to the total number of users per location. When you are happy, click Generate Report to see the expected bandwidth allocations required by location. Where the tool detects that you may go over your current connection values, they will be highlighted (see Figure 2.32). Here you can also adjust the total percentage (for the whole network plan) of bandwidth that should be allocated to Teams media traffic.

Find the Microsoft Network Planning Guidance at docs.microsoft .com/en-US/microsoftteams/network-planner.

FIGURE 2.31   Allocating personas to a site

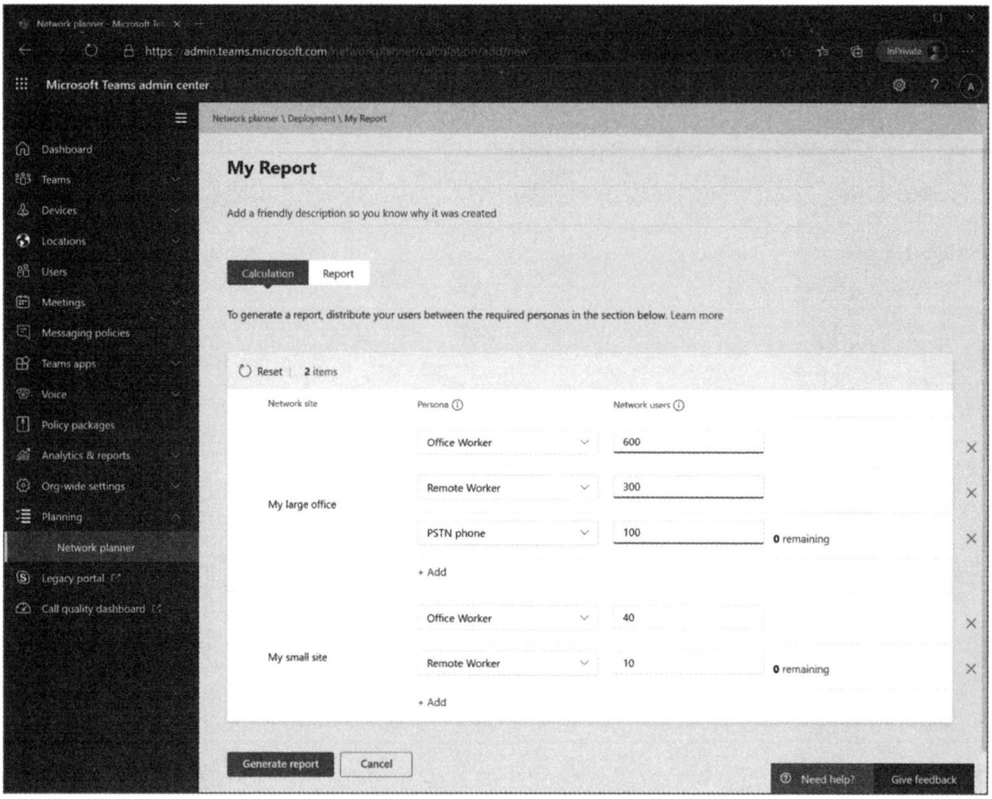

Quality of Service

Quality of service (QoS) is a networking feature that allows you to prioritize some traffic over other traffic. If you have any points in your network that are acting as a bottleneck (i.e., too much data is trying to flow through them), then other than increasing capacity, deploying QoS is what you should do to help make sure that Teams calls are able to maintain a suitable level of quality.

QoS works by identifying traffic that meets a particular fingerprint and then assigning it to a queue. Different queues have different levels of priority (see Table 2.13) and can "skip ahead" when passing through devices. Think of it as having a bus/taxi lane alongside normal traffic on a route into a busy town. Things that get to use the extra lane can still travel at the same speed as they would normally because they get to bypass all the standard traffic that is being held up, but it only makes a difference during rush hour. Any other time of the day, they are still traveling at the same speed as everything else.

With Teams you can identify traffic for QoS in two ways, either by getting the client to tag traffic as it is put onto the network with the appropriate QoS markers (but the network devices must be configured to "trust" these tags) or by getting the network to identify the traffic itself using a combination of source/destination ports and IP addresses.

FIGURE 2.32   Site warning

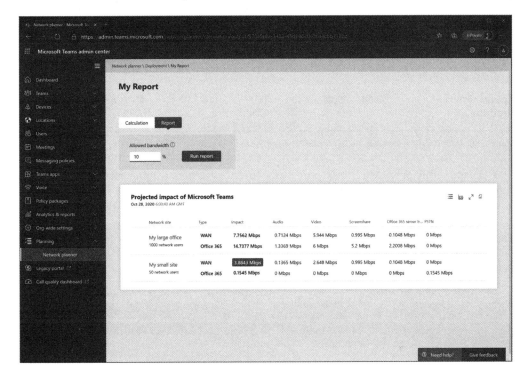

TABLE 2.13   Suggested QoS Markers

Traffic Type	Suggested QoS Queue
Audio	Priority Queue
Video	BW Queue + DSCP WRED
Everything else (web, email etc.)	Best Effort Queue

Source: docs.microsoft.com/en-us/microsoftteams/qos-in-teams

Best practice means that generally if you are deploying QoS, use a combination of both methods to make sure you catch and tag as much traffic as you can.

Defining Network Port Ranges

Table 2.14 lists the default port ranges used by the Teams client.

TABLE 2.14   Suggested Port Ranges/QoS Tags

Media Traffic Type	Client Source Port Range	Protocol	DSCP Value	DSCP Class
Audio	50,000–50,019	TCP/UDP	46	Expedited Forwarding (EF)
Video	50,020–50,039	TCP/UDP	34	Assured Forwarding (AF41)
Application/screen sharing	50,040–50,059	TCP/UDP	18	Assured Forwarding (AF21)

Source: docs.microsoft.com/en-us/microsoftteams/qos-in-teams

You can modify or increase these port ranges from the Teams admin center under Meetings ➢ Meeting Settings. Here you will see a Networking section where you can turn on QoS tagging and manually specify the port ranges. While it is recommended that you leave the values at the defaults listed earlier, unless you have a good reason to change them, it is still suggested that you select Manually Specify Ports and then save the settings (see Figure 2.33).

FIGURE 2.33   Teams Admin Center QoS settings

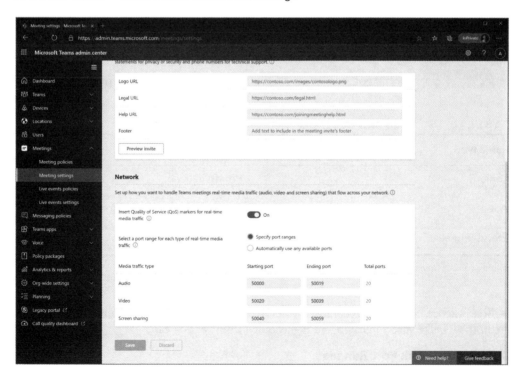

These port ranges cannot overlap, so if you need to allocate more ports for, say, the Audio range, you would also need to update the others at the same time.

Network Tagging

Once you have defined the port ranges you want your client to use, you should then configure, according to your networking vendor instructions, the appropriate QoS tags and identifiers (using source port ranges). This means that you can then prioritize traffic as it is leaving your network.

One thing often overlooked with network-based QoS tagging is that all the tags will be lost when traffic goes over the Internet. This means you will want to retag and classify the returning traffic on whatever device gets data back from Microsoft first (probably either your edge firewall or datacenter core router); otherwise, you will only be prioritizing half of the journey! As this traffic will be inbound, not outbound, you should reverse the ports to be destinated based, not source based (This catch will also apply to returning traffic that was originally tagged on the client side—another reason to use both network- and client-based tagging.)

Client-Side Tagging

Client-side tagging can be controlled via *Group Policy* (GPO) for your domain-joined Windows machines, but it is hard-coded into the Mac client and cannot be changed. To create a GPO-based policy, follow these steps:

1. Create a new GPO in your domain, or edit an existing one.

2. Expand Computer Configuration/Windows Settings.

3. Right-click Policy-Based QoS and then Create New Policy.

4. Give your policy a name, i.e., **Teams Audio** (see Figure 2.34).

5. Specify the DSCP value per Table 2.14 and then click Next.

6. Specify Only Applications With This Executable Name, enter **teams.exe**, and click Next (see Figure 2.35).

7. Allow any source/destination IP (we will control it on a port/application match only), and click Next.

8. Change the protocol to TCP/UDP and enter the ports from Table 2.14 in the source port box, i.e., **50000:50019** (see Figure 2.36).

9. Click Finish and repeat the process for the other workloads (video and desktop share).

Now that you've created your GPO policy, go to your test machine (after making sure it has been placed in an OU where your new GPO applies) and force an update of Group Policy (run `gpupdate /force` from an elevated CMD window). If the policy has been applied correctly, you should have some values in your registry under `HKEY_LOCAL_MACHINE\Software\Policies\Microsoft\Windows\QoS` that match the settings configured previously.

FIGURE 2.34 GPO QoS settings

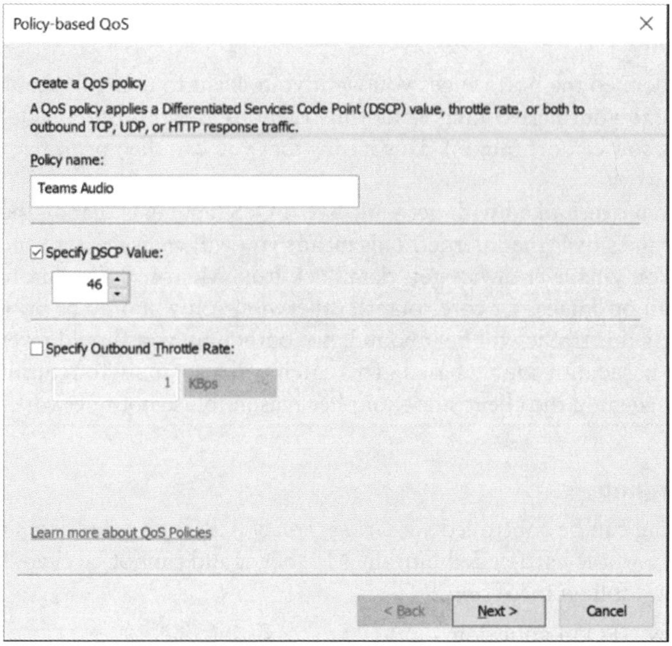

FIGURE 2.35 GPO QoS settings, applications applied to

FIGURE 2.36 GPO QoS Settings, source port box

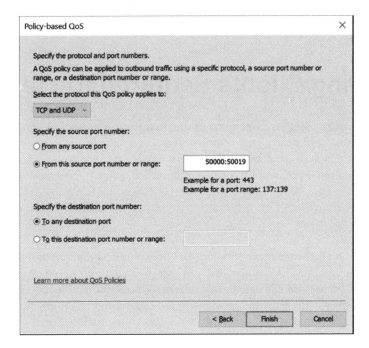

You can also create or update QoS settings with the following PowerShell cmdlets:

```
new-NetQosPolicy -Name "Teams Audio" -AppPathNameMatchCondition "Teams.exe" -
IPProtocolMatchCondition Both -IPSrcPortStartMatchCondition 50000 -
IPSrcPortEndMatchCondition 50019 -DSCPAction 46 -NetworkProfile All

new-NetQosPolicy -Name "Teams Video" -AppPathNameMatchCondition "Teams.exe" -
IPProtocolMatchCondition Both -IPSrcPortStartMatchCondition 50020 -
IPSrcPortEndMatchCondition 50039 -DSCPAction 34 -NetworkProfile All

new-NetQosPolicy -Name "Teams Sharing" -AppPathNameMatchCondition "Teams.exe" -
IPProtocolMatchCondition Both -IPSrcPortStartMatchCondition 50040 -
IPSrcPortEndMatchCondition 50059 -DSCPAction 18 -NetworkProfile All
```

Now that you've defined your QoS tagging and applied it to either your clients or your network (or both if you are doing it right!), then you need to check that the tags are being maintained as they pass through your network from device to device. You can do this by either checking in your networking vendor's management software or doing a packet capture in at least two locations, from close to the client itself and again from a location near the Internet breakout. You should be able to find in the captured packets the correct networking flags to show what QoS tags are being applied at both ends of the conversation.

NOTE   Here is where you can find the Microsoft guidance for QoS: `docs.micro-soft.com/en-us/microsoftteams/qos-in-teams`.

Deploying Clients Required for Teams

In this section, we are going to cover some of the things that you need to know about where you can run Teams. Unlike Skype for Business, Teams is available on pretty much every major platform (including an official Linux release) and is also supported by most modern web browsers, so even if you don't have a client installed, you can probably still get what you need done.

Clients

Microsoft provides clients for most popular platforms. For desktop and mobile these are software packages that need to be installed, but there is also a web-based client that can run in most modern browsers, meaning that nearly anybody should be able to access Teams when they need to. You do get some variation in the capabilities of the clients depending on what platform limitations may exist, but generally speaking core functionality, such as access to shared content and messaging, is the same across them.

Desktop Clients

While Teams supports a wide number of platforms, it is likely that your users' primary interaction with the service will be through some kind of personal computer with Teams installed. Microsoft provides clients for the three main operating system variants available today.

Windows

The windows client is the most common client deployed and generally sees new features and updates ahead of either the Mac or Linux variants. The key things to know about it are these:

- Provided as either a 32-bit or 64-bit installer and supported on Windows 8.1/Server 2016 or later.
- There is also an ARM64 edition available for Windows 10 on ARM.
- The installation version is independent of the Office architecture (i.e., a 64-bit client is supported alongside the 32-bit Office).
- This is installed into the user's `AppData` profile folder (`%userprofile%\AppData\Local\Microsoft\Teams`).
- Administrator rights are not required to install it due to the install location (which is not a protected system location).
- MSI versions are provided for installation via platform automation tools, i.e., Endpoint Configuration Manager.

When deploying via MSI, this doesn't actually install the Teams client; it places an installer into Program Files that is activated when a new user logs in to the machine and makes sure that Teams is installed in that profile folder. If it detects Teams is already installed, it skips. The MSI should not be used as a way to deploy client updates, as once installed into a user's folder, the client will update itself.

As the application is installed into the user's `AppData` folder, they will receive a Windows Firewall notification (see Figure 2.37) the first time they make/receive a call. It is not possible to remove this prompt directly via a GPO, but it can be prevented from appearing with scripts (see the Microsoft reference for this section for more information).

FIGURE 2.37   Teams Windows Firewall prompt

Mac

Microsoft provides a fully supported and feature-rich version of the Teams client for Mac. While the core functionality will be in line with the Windows client, there may be some differences in appearance and behavior where Microsoft has tailored the application to match the look and feel of macOS. Key things to note about the Mac client include the following:

- Provided as a PKG file
- Administrator credentials required during installation
- Can be deployed via platform automation tools
- Supported on the last three versions of macOS (this is Microsoft official wording about version support, meaning that as Apple introduces new major versions of macOS, Microsoft will update support in Teams to match).

Linux

Instead of having to rely on a web version of Teams, Microsoft does provide an installable version of the client for Linux. Here are the key things to know about it:

- Provided in both .deb and .rpm formats
- Will allow automatic updating
- Supported on Ubuntu, Fedora, RHEL, and CentOS
- Supported under GNOME and KDE desktop environments

 Find the Microsoft list of supported clients here: docs.microsoft.com/en-us/microsoftteams/get-clients.

Hardware Requirements

Teams has the following hardware requirements:

- CPU
  - 1.6GHz dual core (quad core recommended for calling)
- RAM
  - 4GB minimum
- Display
  - 1024 × 768
- Disk
  - 1.5GB on Windows/macOS
  - 3GB Linux
- Other
  - USB 2.0 webcam for video
  - Microphone/speakers for audio (ideally a certified headset)

 Here are the Teams hardware requirements: docs.microsoft.com/en-us/microsoftteams/hardware-requirements-for-the-teams-app.

Updates

The Teams client is usually subject to a two-week release cycle and will take care of the update process in the background. It has recently been optimized to reduce the amount of bandwidth being taken up when downloading updates to reduce issues caused by all clients potentially updating at the same time.

To check the version of your client or force an update, right-click your profile icon and select either About ➤ Version Information or Check For Updates. You may sometimes see

TAP (Technology Adoption Program) or IT superimposed over the profile icon here. This means the user is subject to an earlier preview release of the Teams client and is on an earlier deployment ring.

Management

Teams was originally not included alongside the rest of the Microsoft 365 Apps installer packages (think Office from an O365 subscription) but was recently added. This means it can be maintained and serviced alongside the other Office 365 applications.

Users can configure things such as notification behavior and other client-side options for themselves; there is no specific client-side configuration that you can control via Group Policy, PowerShell, the registry, or the tenant itself (Teams admin center).

Other Clients

While the full Teams client usually provides the best end-user experience, it is not always practical to have access to your computer. For use on the go or to cover flexible scenarios, Microsoft also provides clients for mobile platforms and one that can run in web browsers.

Mobile

For mobile devices Microsoft supports the main two platforms of Android and iOS, and the Teams app can be installed from the relevant mobile vendors' app stores. As mobile platforms are frequently updated with new revisions coming out frequently, Microsoft commits to support a fixed number of previous major releases:

- **Android:** The last four major versions of Android are supported.
- **iOS:** The last two major versions of iOS are supported.

Microsoft did originally have a Windows mobile client for its platform, but this is no longer available or supported (much like the platform itself). RIP Windows Mobile.

Web Client

When you are not able to, or perhaps choose not to, install the full Teams client you can access most functionality through the web browser. Support for Teams functionality will vary from browser to browser and OS to OS, especially with regard to making/receiving calls. Fortunately Microsoft supports the webRTC standard in the Teams web client, which allows most modern browsers to do plugin-free voice/video calling. This is supported on the following browsers:

- Chrome
- Edge
- Partially on Safari (one-to-one calling is not supported)

Other browsers can still use the collaboration feature set of Teams but need the user to either dial in, install a desktop client, or change browsers if they want to join meetings or make/receive calls.

Teams on VDI

Virtual desktop infrastructures (*VDIs*) have previously proved difficult for products like Teams for two reasons. First, this is because they are installed into the user's application data folder so are "transient." In a VDI environment, this can cause problems where profiles need to be kept as light as possible so they can move around between installations freely. Second, this is because it increases the complexity of making calls via the platform, as there is now an abstraction layer between where the user is generating audio and where it needs to be processed/sent to Microsoft.

Fortunately, with Teams, Microsoft has put a lot of time and effort into trying to resolve these issues, and Teams is supported in the most popular of these environments:

- Windows Virtual Desktop
- Citrix Virtual Apps and Desktops
- VMware Horizon

Each of these vendors provides its own set of instructions and information about how to correctly install Teams for their platform, but the summary is as follows:

- Check if you need to install Teams in "per machine" or "per user" mode.
- Make sure you have any media optimization plugins configured per the manufacturer's policies.

VDI Media Optimization plugins let media travel direct from the user's client device (usually some sort of thin client device) to the Teams service without having to take extra hops to get to Microsoft.

Note that with VDI you might find the Teams experience is slightly different or reduced. In other words, only a single video stream is supported during a call. You will not get tiled video or a gallery view.

Here is some Teams VDI information: docs.microsoft.com/en-us/microsoftteams/teams-for-vdi.

Devices

Teams is supported across a wide variety of third-party devices, some aimed at meeting rooms and others at desk phones or even companion-style devices. You can see the full list of currently certified and available hardware at www.microsoft.com/en-us/microsoft-365/microsoft-teams/across-devices/devices.

Teams Phones

Teams has a wide range of third-party physical handsets available that can be deployed. They come in two broad categories:

Third-Party Integration Phones (*3PIPs*)

These were devices manufactured by third parties for use with Skype for Business Online. The functionality will vary from device to device as each manufacturer decides how/what functionality to implement (i.e., limited calendar integration). These devices are supported for connection to Teams, as they leverage a Microsoft Interop Gateway running in O365. This gateway, which relies on Skype for Business, is exempt from the "shuttering" notice for the service and will be supported until "beyond 2023."

Here you can find information about Teams and 3PIP phones: tech-community.microsoft.com/t5/microsoft-teams-blog/skype-for-business-phones-3pip-support-with-microsoft-teams/ba-p/789351.

Native Teams Devices

Referred to as Teams phones, these devices run a variant of Android and a fork of the Microsoft Android Teams client. The hardware and form factors will vary by device type, but the user experience should remain fairly consistent across the devices and be rich (i.e., full dialing, calendar integrations, etc.), as Microsoft is responsible for the software. It also means that as Microsoft adds new features/functionality to the platform, these devices should receive them in a timely manner as, again, the software platform is the same. Microsoft has a certification program for Teams devices to make sure they meet the minimum standards of quality but also manageability and user experience.

Here is the Teams phone feature set:

- Support for modern authentication sign-in
  - Using multifactor, for example
  - Conditional access
- Speed dial/call history
- View schedule for meeting/calls
- Group calling management
- Delegated calling support
- Hot desking (sign out to clear down the device ready for the next user)
- Video where hardware supports it
- Better together
  - Integration of lock/unlock with user's PC
- Standard accessibility
- Dynamic/enhanced E911 support
- Ability to enroll in InTune via Android Device Administrator (DA)

If you are deploying Teams to a greenfield site (one with no previous deployment) and need to purchase new phones for your office (assuming you have pushed users toward headsets where possible!), then native Teams devices are the way forward. If you are coming from a Skype for Business Enterprise Voice environment and have phones deployed that are still operational, then absolutely continue to use them with Teams (after making sure the functionality is acceptable, of course).

At the time of writing (late 2020), Microsoft has also announced that it will be bringing direct support to the platform for standards-based SIP devices. This means that where you have basic requirements to just have a handset, you should be able to configure low-cost generic devices to register as endpoints into Teams for calls. How this will operate in practice remains to be seen, especially what the server-side management platform will look like; still, it's going to be a nice platform addition.

Meeting Room Devices

As well as phones to live on people's desks (or in kitchens, cupboards, or server rooms), there are many devices aimed at delivering great in-room meeting experiences.

Officially these types of devices are split into two categories, those for small/medium rooms and those for medium/large rooms.

The reality is that whichever device you choose, you should make sure that you have mapped the requirements from users (e.g., do they need digital inking capabilities, such as a virtual whiteboard, to collaborate on something or just good voice/video?) along with choosing appropriate hardware for the size of the room (a small phone in a giant boardroom will probably not cut it!).

> **Microsoft Teams Rooms**   The main category of larger meeting room hardware is called *Microsoft Teams Rooms*. These devices are the latest evolution of what started out as Lync/Skype Room Systems, which took "best-of-breed" components from vendors and combined them with a central display/computer that powered the in-meeting experience. You can find Teams Rooms hardware designed to cater to different room scenarios from small "huddle"-style spaces to as large a room as you can provide suitable cabling for. These devices run a variant of the Windows 10 Enterprise edition, so managing and updating them is relatively simple. The main vendors that currently produce Teams Rooms hardware include the following:
>
> - Poly (formerly Polycom)
> - Yealink
> - Microsoft
> - Logitech
> - HP
> - Lenovo
> - Crestron
>
> An interesting feature that is starting to roll out to Teams Rooms is the ability for them to interop with other conferencing providers like Zoom and WebEx. While this does not

provide the full native experience, it is a good way to maintain some cross-compatibility when your users are invited to meetings on other platforms.

Microsoft Teams Rooms on Android   Formerly known as Collaboration Bars, this form factor was recently designed for use in a small to medium-sized room where a lower-cost option was required compared to some of the heavy-hitting Teams Rooms equipment. They were originally designed to run another fork of the Teams Android client (like the desk phone) and were a "single unit" where the hardware was combined into a form factor that looks not unlike a TV soundbar but with a webcam stuck in the middle. When they were originally released, they had a fairly limited feature set, but this is rapidly changing.

Teams Displays   This is a new category of device that is not currently released and is currently produced by only two vendors. They are an interesting form factor and look like a sort of Google Home/Echo Show type of device combined with a Teams phone. Again, they run Android and are designed to sit alongside the user's main PC. They then act as a kind of "smart" Teams companion offering quick access to see upcoming meetings, answer calls, join a meeting PC-free, or supplement the activities on the main PC. While this category of device is not currently part of MS-700, it is worth knowing the name, as you will see it in the Teams admin center.

Table 2.15 provides an overview of some differences between the device types.

TABLE 2.15 Teams Rooms Feature Comparison

Feature	Teams Rooms on Android	Teams Rooms
OS	Android 9.x	Windows 10 Enterprise
Supported displays	One	Two
Maximum video resolution	720p	1080p
Skype for Business support	No	Yes
Guest join access (Webex/Zoom)	No	Yes
Meet Now	Yes	Yes
Whiteboard support	Yes	Yes
Content camera (Magic Whiteboard)	No	Yes
HDMI content input	No	Yes
Raise hand	Yes	Yes
Pin video feed	No	Yes

continues

TABLE 2.15   Teams Rooms Feature Comparison *(continued)*

Feature	Teams Rooms on Android	Teams Rooms
One-touch join meetings	Yes	Yes
Proximity join (Bluetooth)	Yes	Yes
USB connectivity of cameras/audio	No	Yes
Center of room console	Basic	Advanced
Teams Admin Center management	Yes	Yes
3 × 3 gallery layout	No	Yes
Coordinated meetjings	No	Yes

Licensing

Let's talk about licensing for a moment. The previous hardware devices need to have a license assigned to the account they are signed into. For Teams phones and Teams displays, this will usually be the account of the user to whom they are normally assigned. However, there might be some scenarios where you need a phone to be logged in with a generic user account, e.g., in a break room. You could allocate and license the account for this device using a standard user, but it can be expensive to assign an E3/E5 (plus any add-ons for calling) just for use on a device.

Fortunately, Microsoft has a license SKU for this purpose called the *Common Area Phone* (CAP) license. When allocated to an account, this gives the user Microsoft Teams and Phone System capabilities, so the only thing you need to add is either your own calling minutes via Direct Routing or a Calling Plan license if you want to allocate numbers and minutes via Microsoft.

This CAP license, however, probably does not include what you want if you need to license a meeting room device, as it does not include any Exchange Mailbox support (used for meeting bookings and coordination, etc.). Again, Microsoft has us covered with the Meeting Room SKU, which includes management capabilities as well as free Exchange calendaring capabilities.

Table 2.16 summarizes the differences between the two license types.

TABLE 2.16   CAP vs. Meeting Room Licenses

Feature	CAP License	Meeting Room License
Skype for Business	Yes	Yes
Teams	Yes	Yes
Phone system	Yes	Yes
Audio conferencing	No	Yes
Intune	No	Yes
Exchange calendar	No	Yes

Source: docs.microsoft.com/en-us/MicrosoftTeams/rooms/rooms-licensing; docs.microsoft.com/en-us/microsoftteams/set-up-common-area-phones

Managing Devices

Management for these devices is primarily carried out using the Teams admin center, where you can view the devices enrolled in your organization, create and assign configuration profiles, and manage individual devices.

Phone/Teams Rooms on Android/Teams Display Configuration

Most of the configuration for these happens via the admin portal (see Figure 2.38). Once a device has been signed in, it is registered into the TAC and can be managed further from there. Initial sign-in should happen automatically following the same process that would apply for a user signing into the Teams application.

After the device has been registered, either you can manually configure it through the right-click menu or you can assign it a preconfigured configuration profile.

Without using a configuration profile, you can control/apply the following commands:

- Device information
  - View and edit details such as asset tag, name, etc.
- Manage updates for the device
- Assign a configuration policy

- Restart the device
- Assign any management tags to help organize your view
- Filter the view using management tags
- View device history
- View diagnostic logs

FIGURE 2.38   Phone management in TAC

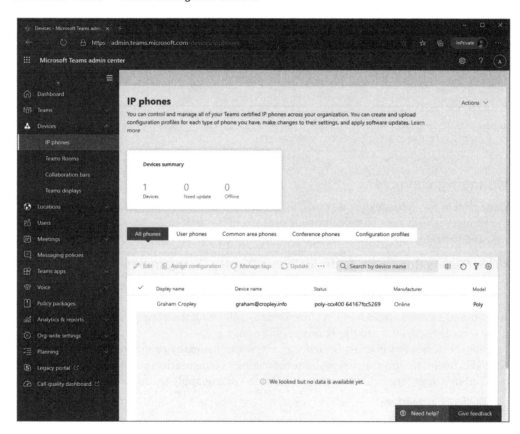

Profiles are a quick way to apply settings to either a single device or a group of devices. They can contain the following settings (see Figure 2.39):

- General
  - Device lock
    - On/off and timeout value
    - Device lock PIN

- Language profile
- Time zone
- Date format
- Time format
- Device settings
  - Screensaver
    - Timeout
  - Backlight brightness
  - Backlight timeout
  - High-contrast mode
  - Silent mode
  - Office hours
  - Power saving
  - Allow screen capture
- Networking
  - DHCP enabled
  - Network-level logging
  - Host name
  - Domain name
  - IP information
    - IP address
    - Subnet mask
    - Default gateway
    - Primary/secondary DNS
  - Admin password
  - PC network port
    - Enable/disable any passthrough port if it exists

Find out more information about Teams device management via TAC here: techcommunity.microsoft.com/t5/microsoft-teams-blog/one-place-to-manage-all-your-teams-devices/ba-p/1527766.

FIGURE 2.39   Device configuration profile

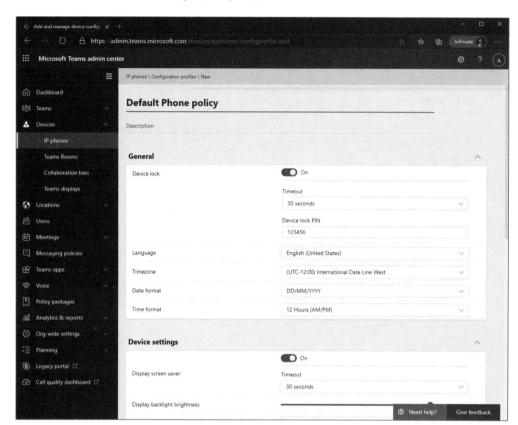

Microsoft Teams Account Configuration

As a Teams Room offers more functionality than the other device types and it runs Windows 10, there are a few more hoops to jump through to get them up and running. This is especially true for Exchange, where they need to have some special configuration applied to let them automatically process incoming meeting requests.

First, you should create the account you want to use for the meeting room (either on-premises or online, provided that it is synchronized) and assign it the correct licenses (see Table 2.16). Once the account has replicated successfully, you need to create and then set up the mailbox:

1. Connect to Exchange Online.

2. Run the following command:

```
New-Mailbox -Name "<Our Account>" -Alias <Friendly Name> -Room -
EnableRoomMailboxAccount $true -MicrosoftOnlineServicesID < Account UPN> -
RoomMailboxPassword (ConvertTo-SecureString -String '<Password>' - AsPlainText -
Force)
```

3. Apply the automatic calendar processing:

```
Set-CalendarProcessing -Identity "<Our Account>" - AutomateProcessing AutoAccept
-AddOrganizerToSubject $false -DeleteComments $false -DeleteSubject $false -
RemovePrivateProperty $false
```

If the account comes from on-premises, you probably should configure the Never Expire Password flag for the account, or you need to make a note of when the account will expire so you can update devices as necessary. You can do this against Azure AD if the account is cloud only via PowerShell:

```
Set-MsolUser -UserPrincipalName <Our Account> -PasswordNeverExpires $true
```

If you want to assign a phone number from Teams to the device, don't forget that you might need to manually set the account to TeamsOnly mode so that it has native Teams PSTN functionality available, and then configure it per any standard user (see Chapter 5 for more details).

Now that the account is correctly configured, you can proceed with the rest of the hardware deployment steps for the device.

Find information about configuring accounts for Microsoft Teams Rooms here: docs.microsoft.com/en-us/microsoftteams/rooms/with-office-365.

Teams Rooms Options

Once the device has been configured and connected, it should show up in the TAC under the Devices ➢ Teams Rooms menu. From here, similar to what you have done for phone devices, you can perform management tasks and view the status of the different devices.

Device settings:

- Supported meeting mode
  - Skype for Business (default) and Microsoft Teams
  - Skype for Business and Microsoft Teams (default)
  - Skype for Business only
- Modern Auth
  - On/off
- Account details
  - Email address
  - Exchange address
  - Domain/username
  - Domain

- Meeting features
  - Automatic screen sharing
  - Show meeting names
  - Auto-leave if last in meeting
- Device
  - Dual screen mode
  - Bluetooth beaconing
    - Used for "finding nearby rooms feature"
  - Auto-accept proximity meeting invites
  - Send logs with feedback
  - Email address for logs
- Peripherals
  - Conferencing the mic
  - Conferencing the speaker
    - Volume
  - Default speaker (device noises)
    - Volume
  - Content camera
    - Camera to use
    - Rotate 180
- Theme

From here you can also choose to restart the device either right away or on a schedule (specific point in time or routinely overnight).

If you have had a device fail and need to remove it from the organization, you can block/remove the device from operating or appearing in the list. However, if a device still has a valid username/password combination, it will show up if it attempts to reconnect in the future.

The dashboard gives you a status of how all your Teams Rooms devices are performing. If you click into any device, you can then get more information about the calls it has made and the connection quality. This report will be similar to what we will cover in Chapter 6 when we cover quality reviews.

You can find more information about Teams device management here: docs.microsoft.com/en-us/microsoftteams/devices/device-management.

Summary

This chapter covered a lot of ground, looking at what you need to understand and get in place for your Teams deployment. There was a lot of time given in this chapter to how Teams and Skype for Business work together, and you might be thinking that this isn't going to be relevant for your deployment; however, it is something that is critical to a large number of organizations and can be a big stumbling block for their adoption of Teams. As such, it is an important topic for the exam. Also, remember that even if you do not have Skype for Business deployed, you may run into interop issues when federating with users from other organizations, so a good understanding of the expected behavior and how escalation works will help you troubleshoot any problems.

Next, we looked at some of the networking requirements for Teams. Because real-time communications plays such a key part in what makes Teams Teams, the network quality is particularly important. It can be easy to assume that because you have a super-fast connection everything will be fine, but speed isn't the same thing as quality. You should always perform at least some sort of quality check before any large-scale migrations because fixing network issues can sometimes be a lengthy, time-consuming process and you want to be ahead of any issues your users might have.

For clients and devices, it is likely that your deployment will consist mostly of Windows or Mac full client deployments, but it is good to know where else you can install Teams. If you have VDI deployed in your organization, make sure you have looked into any vendor-specific recommendations to help optimize calling and meeting experiences (and note that they will be slightly different for non-VDI clients). Teams is also available on a wide variety of hardware devices to cover the majority of meeting room and common area requirements. Microsoft has a certification program to ensure that devices and hardware perform to a certain minimum standard and guarantee compatibility with the platform. Teams has a rapidly evolving management portal for devices that provides a good window into the devices deployed in your environment and a simple way to apply common configurations across devices.

Exam Essentials

Understand the coexistence modes available for Skype for Business and Teams.
Make sure that you remember the different coexistence modes and understand where you might use each one in different circumstances, such as using Skype for migrations, then or Skype for Business with Teams Collaboration modes while you plan migrations, then using Skype for Business with Teams Collaboration and Meetings while migrating some PSTN workloads from Skype for Business. Before finally moving to Teams Only mode at the completion of migration. Business, and Teams Only mode is required if you want to use Teams for any sort of PSTN calling.

Understand how Teams and Skype for Business interact with each other (interoperability). You should be able to anticipate which product becomes the primary source for presence and understand how messages are routed between users on the two platforms. Remember that this will change depending on what coexistence mode is applied to the users (or at a tenant level). Understand that the feature sets in Skype for Business and Teams do not match up exactly, and some scenarios will result in escalation where meetings are generated to continue the interaction. Remember that the escalation will occur on whatever platform the initiating user is using.

Understand what the Meeting Migration Service does and how to trigger and troubleshoot it. The Meeting Migration Service can be a great help when moving users between modes or upgrading them from Skype for Business to "full" Teams (or at least a mode with Teams Meetings enabled). You should understand the limitations of the tool (i.e., it will not migrate meetings from Teams to Skype for Business) as well as how to check its status (via PowerShell) and manually trigger it for specific users.

Know where and when to apply coexistence modes to your tenant and users. Be able to apply the first three essentials (coexistence, interop, Meeting Migration Service) to decide the best approach to migrating users and which coexistence modes you want to use.

Know how to control Skype for Business upgrade notifications and meeting platform selection. Understand how you can control the behavior of the Skype for Business client with Teams upgrade notifications and the ability to install the Teams client for you.

Be able to determine what behavior you would like with Skype for Business after your migrations are complete (i.e., desktop app remains in limited mode or force use of browser plugin for meeting joins).

Understand the best practices for Teams networking. Having a good-quality network for Teams is really important. Understand the best practices for how to handle network traffic for Teams. This includes things like local Internet breakout and bypassing proxy servers and other inspection devices where possible.

Know how to check the quality of a network. Network capacity isn't the only factor that affects Teams behavior on a network; the connection quality is just as (if not more) important. Understand what metrics your connections are expected to meet (depending on if you measure from the client or network edge) and how you can use the Network Testing Companion to measure your connection.

Know how to model network capacity requirements for Teams. Understand how you can model your expected network usage via the Teams admin center using the Network Planning tool.

Know that you can create personas for your users that show what features you expect them to be using (i.e., voice or video calls).

Create a virtual plan of your sites and their connectivity where you can assign your user personas and view the expected impact of your Teams deployment.

Identify the key ports used by Teams clients. Remember the key ports Teams uses on the network: TCP 443 for most operations, while UDP 3478–34781 are preferred for media. Remember that UDP is by far the preferred protocol for media traffic.

Understand how you would configure and apply QoS to support Teams. Understand where QoS can be applied to help prioritize Teams traffic on the network. Determine how you would choose to enable QoS (either client side via the GPO or on the network at a device level).

Know what clients are available for Teams. Know where native clients are available for Teams (Windows, Linux, macOS) and that Teams can operate just in a browser when required (with limited functionality, depending on browser). Know that Teams can be supported running on virtual desktops, but that will likely require additional configuration depending on the solution in use. Know that Teams is available on a range of device types from personal to large-scale meeting rooms. Understand how you can license these devices via the dedicated Meeting Room/Common Area Phone licenses or whether it's not required when they are logged in as end users.

Understand where and how you would apply configuration policies for devices. Remember that you can use the Teams admin center to get an overview of the devices logged into your tenant. From here you can configure policies for device behavior and apply updates.

Understand how to configure a Microsoft Teams Rooms system. Microsoft Teams Rooms require special configuration outside of Teams to make sure that they can process and accept incoming meeting requests. You should also know how to use the `Set-CalendarProcessing` PowerShell cmdlet.

EXERCISE 2.1

Reviewing Tenant Coexistence Mode

In this exercise, you will review the global coexistence mode set for your tenant.

1. Log into the Teams admin center (requires at least Teams Administrator permissions).

2. Browse to Org-Wide Settings/Teams Upgrade.

3. Review the Coexistence Mode setting.

4. Review the App Preferences settings.

EXERCISE 2.2

Configuring a Custom Coexistence Mode for a Test User

In this exercise, you will override the global policy for a test user and configure them into Teams Only mode. (You will only be able to update this for users in a tenant that has Skype for Business Online enabled.)

1. Log into the Teams admin center (requires at least Teams Service Administrator permissions).

2. Browse to Users.

3. Use the search box to find your test user account.

4. Select the user.

5. Under Account, modify the coexistence mode.

EXERCISE 2.3

Triggering the Meeting Migration Service for a User

In this exercise, you will trigger the Meeting Migration Service for a test user.

1. Identify the UPN for a test user account.

2. Connect to PowerShell Online using either the Microsoft Teams PowerShell Module or the Skype for Business PowerShell Connector (requires at least Teams Service Administrator permissions).

3. Run the following cmdlet where <userUPN> is the name of your test account:

```
Start-CsExMeetingMigration –Identity <userUPN> –TargetMeetingType Teams
```

EXERCISE 2.4

Reviewing the Meeting Migration Service Status

In this exercise, you will view a report showing the status of the Meeting Migration Service.

1. Connect to PowerShell Online using either the Microsoft Teams PowerShell Module or the Skype for Business PowerShell Connector (requires at least Teams Service Administrator permissions).

2. Run the following cmdlet:

```
Get-CsMeetingMigrationStatus –SummaryOnly
```

3. Run the following command for a given date range:

```
Get-CsMeetingMigrationStatus –StartTime "01/01/2021" –EndTime "02/01/2021"
```

4. Run the following cmdlet for your test user:

```
Get-CsMeetingMigrationStatus –Identity <userUPN>
```

EXERCISE 2.5

Configuring Custom Coexistence Mode for a Test User via PowerShell

In this exercise, you will override the global coexistence policy for a test user via Power-Shell. We want to set up the user so they can use Teams for meetings and have the Skype for Business client show an upgrade notification banner.

1. Identify the UPN for a test user account.

2. Connect to PowerShell Online using either the Microsoft Teams PowerShell Module or the Skype for Business PowerShell Connector (requires at least Teams Service Administrator permissions).

3. Run the following cmdlet where <userUPN> is your test user:

```
Grant-CsTeamsUpgradePolicy -PolicyName SfBWithTeamsCollabAndMeetings WithNotify -
Identity <UserUPN>
```

EXERCISE 2.6

Testing Your Network Connection Using the Network Testing Companion

In this exercise, we will test your network connection's ability to support Teams real-time media traffic.

1. Run a PowerShell window with administrative permissions (on the local machine).

2. Run the following cmdlet to install the companion:

```
Install-Module -Name NetworkTestingCompanion
```

3. Answer Y to the prompts.

4. Next add shortcuts to your desktop with the following command: `Invoke-ToolCre-ateShortcuts`.

5. Close PowerShell and start the Network Testing Companion via the new Start menu or desktop shortcuts.

6. If the Network Testing Tool is not installed, click the green "install" button and wait for it to complete.

7. There should now be a large green "start" button on the right side of the window. Click Start to run the test.

continues

8. Allow the test to complete and then open the View Results tab and see how your connection performed. Is your connection good enough to support Teams?

9. Try running the test a few times during the day or from wired and wireless connections to understand how it may change.

EXERCISE 2.7

Modeling Your Network Capacity

In this exercise, we will create some personas and site locations and generate a bandwidth calculation for Teams usage.

1. Log into the Teams admin center (requires at least Teams Service Administrator permissions).

2. Browse to the Planning/Network Planner.

3. Open the Personas tab.

4. Create a new persona called Voice Only with only the Audio permissions selected.

    a. Create a new persona called "Heavy user" with Audio, Video, and Screen Sharing selected.

    b. Switch to the Network Plans tab and add a new plan called Deployment.

5. Select the plan you just created.

6. Add a new network site called Site 1 with 50 users connected to the WAN (10Mbps) and with local Internet breakout (20 Mbps).

7. Add a second site called Site 2 with 10 users connected to the WAN (10Mbps) and Internet breakout configured through Site 1.

8. Move to the Report tab and create a new report.

9. Give the report a name and divide the user personas between the two sites, making sure to include some of the specially created personas.

10. Generate the report and see what the impact on the network will be.

11. Try rerunning the report with different combinations of personas and site types to understand how these change the bandwidth estimates.

EXERCISE 2.8

Creating a Configuration Profile for Teams Phones

In this exercise, you will create a policy to control Teams IP phones for your organization.

1. Log in to the Teams admin center (requires at least Teams Service Administrator permissions).

2. Browse to Devices/IP Phones.

3. Open the Configuration Profiles tab.

4. Add a new profile called Site 1 Phones. Configure the device with your time zone, language, and correct date/time format.

5. Configure Power Saving so that the devices turn off their screens between 6 p.m. and 9 a.m. with a 60-second screensaver timeout.

6. Save the policy.

7. If you have any test devices in your tenant, find them on the All Phones tab and assign your new policy to these devices by selecting them and clicking the Assign Configuration button.

8. Search for your policy and click Apply.

EXERCISE 2.9

Configuring an Account to Auto-Accept Meeting Requests

While it is unlikely that you will have a Microsoft Teams Rooms system that you can use for testing, in this exercise you will configure an account to auto-accept incoming meeting invites in the same way that you would need to do for a Microsoft Teams Rooms account.

1. Identify or create a test account that is configured with an Exchange Online mailbox.

2. Log into Exchange Online PowerShell.

3. Run the following PowerShell cmdlet to configure these options on the account: auto-accept invites where not busy, maintain privacy for a meeting when configured, and respond with a notification telling users that the meeting room has Teams hardware.

   ```
   Set-CalendarProcessing -Identity <userUPN> -AutomateProcessing AutoAccept -
   AddOrganizerToSubject $false -RemovePrivateProperty $false -DeleteSubject $false -
   DeleteComments $false -AddAdditionalResponse $true -AdditionalResponse "This
   meeting room has Teams capabilities."
   ```

Review Questions

1. A user running Skype for Business reports that they are unable to share their desktop with a user running in Teams Only mode. What settings should you check?

   A. If the Skype for Business user is running in Islands mode

   B. The version of the Teams client

   C. The version of the Skype for Business client

   D. If port 4568 UDP is open on the firewall

2. A user complains that their Skype for Business meetings have not been updated to Teams when you migrated them last night. What would you do next?

   A. Check if the user created the Skype for Business meeting in Outlook Desktop.

   B. Check if the user is configured for Audio Conferencing.

   C. Assign the user the correct geographical region.

   D. Check if the user was the original creator of the meeting.

3. A user complains that their Skype for Business meetings have not been updated to Teams when you migrated them last night. You have ascertained that the meeting in question was created correctly and should have been updated. What else could be stopping the update?

   A. The Meeting Migration Service is still processing the user's mailbox.

   B. The meeting occurred in the past and has no future instances.

   C. The user's Outlook is running in offline mode.

   D. All of the above.

4. A user running Teams reports that they are unable to share their screen with a Skype for Business user. What settings should you check?

   A. Check if –AllowPrivateMeetNow in the user's CsTeamsMeetingPolicy is $True.

   B. Configure AllowIPVideo in the user's CsTeamsMeetingPolicy.

   C. The Teams user presence status is set to DND.

   D. The tenant is not configured for Teams Only mode.

5. You have completed your migration to Teams for all users and are in Teams Only mode. You would like to stop the Skype for Business desktop application from being used to join external meetings. How could you achieve this?

   A. From the Teams admin center, set the preferred app for Skype for Business to Skype for Business.

   B. From the Teams admin center, set the preferred app for Skype for Business to Skype Meetings App.

   C. Reinstall Office, and Skype for Business will be automatically uninstalled.

   D. Disable the Skype for Business Outlook plugin.

6. You have 50 Windows 10 computers deployed across your organization, all users are running Skype for Business, and you need to prepare for an upcoming Teams deployment. How can you easily deploy the Teams client to these computers?

    A. Configure a GPO with an app install package and apply it to the computers.

    B. Place `teams.exe` on a file share and email users asking them to run the file.

    C. Invite all users into a team so they will receive an invitation email.

    D. In the Teams Admin Center, set the organization-wide policy to download Teams in the background.

7. Users are reporting poor call quality. When running a packet capture during a call, you only see traffic on TCP port 443. What should you do to remediate the issue?

    A. Apply a QoS policy to the computers via a GPO.

    B. Verify if the required UDP ports are open for Teams on the network edge.

    C. Run the Network Assessment Companion tool.

    D. Apply a network persona to your site in the network planner.

8. You have a user using Skype for Business with Enterprise Voice (PSTN calling) configured, and you are not ready to migrate PSTN calling to Teams; however, you do want them to stop using Skype for Business for meetings. Which PowerShell cmdlet would you run?

    A. `Grant-CsTeamsUpgradePolicy -`
    `PolicyName`
    `SfBWithTeamsCollabAndMeetings -`
    `Identity <user>`

    B. `Grant-CsTeamsUpgradePolicy -`
    `PolicyName SfBWithTeamsCollab -`
    `Identity <user>`

    C. `Set-CsTeamsUpgradePolicy -PolicyName`
    `SfBWithTeamsCollabAndMeetings -`
    `Identity <user>`

    D. `Grant-TeamsUpgradePolicy -`
    `PolicyName SfBwithTeamsMeetings -Identity`
    `<user>`

9. After updating the tenant-wide coexistence mode to Teams Only, users are complaining that their meetings are still Skype for Business. What else do you need to do to make sure user meetings are updated?

    A. Also change each user's coexistence mode to Teams Only.

    B. Run a PowerShell script against each user to trigger the Meeting Migration Service.

    C. Give each user a Communication Credits license.

    D. Disable and reenable each user's account.

10. A user complains that they are unable to schedule a meeting in a room where a Microsoft Teams Rooms system is located. What should you run to check that automatic processing of meeting invites is configured?

    A. In the Teams admin center under Devices ➤ Teams Meeting Rooms, add a new configuration policy to auto accept invitations.

B. Log into Outlook as the meeting room account and create an auto-forward rule to process the meeting requests.

C. Run the following cmdlet against Exchange Online PowerShell: `Set-CalendarProcessing -Identity "<Meeting Room Account>" -AutomateProcessing AutoAccept`.

D. Run the following cmdlet against Exchange Online PowerShell: `Set-CalendarProcessing -Identity "<Meeting Room Account>" -Enabled $True`.

11. A user complains that when working at home they have had a lot of poor-quality calls. What should you get them to check or test? (Select all that apply.)

A. Try using a wired connection to their router.

B. Add their home subnet to your QoS GPO.

C. Make sure Teams traffic is exempted from using the company VPN.

D. Contact their ISP for assistance tracing the connection.

12. You have purchased some Teams devices that need to be used in shared areas around the office (e.g., the kitchen). What is the best way to license these devices?

A. They do not need a license; each user can sign into the device when they want to make a call.

B. Create an account for each device and assign it an E5 license with Calling Plans.

C. Create an account for each device and assign it a Common Area Phone license.

D. Create an account for each device and assign it a Meeting Room license.

13. Your company is in the process of moving offices, and you are taking the opportunity to deploy new hardware into meeting rooms. There are some small meeting rooms (four people) that you want to enable for video calling. What device type might you select?

A. Microsoft Teams Rooms on Android (Collaboration Bars)

B. Teams desk phone

C. Microsoft Teams Rooms

D. Desktop computer running Windows 10 with an account that auto-logs in

14. You need to decide on a plan for how to best implement QoS. Which of the following actions should you take? (Select all that apply.)

A. Configure a GPO for your Windows 10 devices to mark traffic for `teams.exe`.

B. Create source port–based tagging rules on your network routers.

C. Create destination port–based tagging rules on your network routers.

D. Configure Teams client port ranges in the Teams Admin Center.

15. When testing an office's Internet connection (local breakout) in preparation for deploying Teams, you run the Network Testing Companion and see the following results. Which of these metrics might cause call issues?

A. Packet Loss: 0.01% burst

B. Round Trip time: 55ms

    C. Jitter: 25ms

    D. Packet reorder ratio: 0.001%

16. You have a number of Teams Phone devices that have just been deployed, and you need to make sure they immediately pick up any new firmware updates. Where would you configure this for the devices?

    A. From the Teams admin center

    B. From PowerShell

    C. From the user's Teams client

    D. From the O365 admin portal

17. After completing a Skype for Business Online migration, you are not sure that your QoS is applying correctly to Teams. You had previously deployed QoS using GPOs. What might you have forgotten to update?

    A. The ports used by Teams

    B. The QoS GPO to now apply to `teams.exe`

    C. The QoS GPO to now apply to `msteams.exe`

    D. Also enabled QoS in the user configuration policy

18. For your standard x64 Windows desktops, you have deployed the x86 Click-to-Run edition of Office. Which edition of Teams can you deploy successfully on the machine?

    A. Teams x64 `.exe` installer

    B. Teams x64 `.pkg` package

    C. Teams x86 `.deb` package

    D. Teams x86 `.exe` installer

19. You have deployed Teams via SCCM using the MSI installer. Where would you check for the Teams client files for a logged-in user?

    A. In the `C:\Program Files` folder

    B. In the user's `%userprofile%\AppData\Local\Microsoft\Teams` folder

    C. In the `C:\Program Files x86` folder

    D. In the user's `%userprofile%\AppData\Roaming\Microsoft\Teams` folder

20. You have completed your migration from Skype for Business Online to Teams and have changed the tenant-wide coexistence policy to Teams Only; however, some users are still not able to make/receive PSTN calls. You have verified their PSTN configuration is correct. What else might be the issue?

    A. You have not decommissioned the Skype for Business environment.

    B. DNS needs to be updated to point at Teams.

    C. The Teams client must be re-installed to pick up the new mode.

    D. The users have a manually specified coexistence policy that is not Teams Only.

Chapter

3

Teams Core Functionality

MICROSOFT EXAM OBJECTIVES COVERED IN THIS CHAPTER:

✓ Manage a team

✓ Manage chat and collaboration experiences

✓ Configure and manage guest access

✓ Manage meeting experiences

Having covered the groundwork of preparing to upgrade from Skype for Business (if you have it), getting your network ready to support Teams traffic, and deploying clients to your users and devices, we are now going to look at how you will actually use Teams. This chapter and the next one are going to contain the bulk of the tasks and activities that you as a Teams administrator will need to be dealing with on a day-to-day basis.

This chapter will focus more on the more bread-and-butter activities such as the types of teams available, how you can control what features and functionality are available, and how to share content with guests. Chapter 4, "Advanced Teams Functionality and Management" will then look at the more advanced side of things such as enforcing compliance rules and protecting your data.

Let's get started and make some teams for your users to use.

Creating Teams

A *team* is what sits at the heart of the collaboration workload inside Teams; it is designed to pull people who need to work closely together into one place and provide them with access to all the resources they might need to get their work done. Teams can be created in a structured way, or they can be created dynamically as work requirements flex and shift.

Each team that you create is actually based on an M365 group. This is essentially a special type of security group, created in Azure AD. It contains the users associated with the team and controls access to all the resources needed when using the team, such as the Share-Point document library created to store any channel files. You cannot have a team without an M365 group, but you can have M365 groups that are not Teams enabled (more on this to come).

Once you have created your team, it will contain channels. *Channels* are a way to keep discussions organized into sections. There will always be a General channel created by default, and it cannot be removed. By default, channels are visible to all members of the team and can be extended through the use of tabs and apps to enhance their usefulness.

Figure 3.1 shows an example of how you might structure teams and channels for an organization.

You can create private channels inside a team should they be required, but first let's look at the basic types of permissions inside a team.

FIGURE 3.1   Teams logical layout

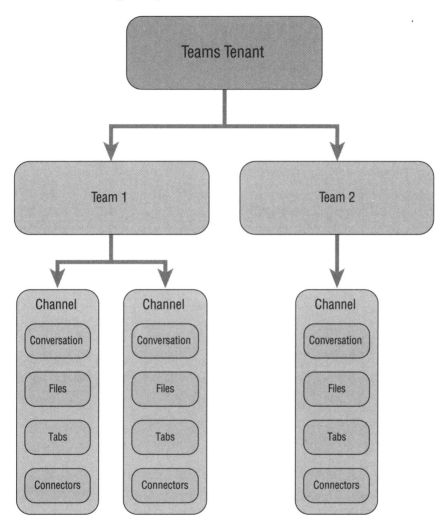

 For Microsoft's overview of teams and channels, see docs.microsoft.com/
en-us/microsoftteams/teams-channels-overview.

Teams Memberships

Each member of a team will be assigned one of three different permissions that control what they can do inside the team, as shown here:

Owner: Owners of a team can control certain settings for a team, as well as being able to control membership and perform administrative tasks for the team. Each team has to have at least one owner but can have more than one, and a user may be an owner for more than one team.

Member: This is the default permission type for someone inside the organization who has been added to a team. A member can participate in all things that have been enabled/allowed inside the team and can usually view and upload file content.

Guest: A guest is a user from outside of your organization who has been invited to participate in your team. Guests only have the ability to interact with teams that they have been specifically invited to participate in. Guest access requires its own set of considerations and settings to manage and will be covered in more detail later in the chapter.

Table 3.1 gives an overview of what the different team permissions allow you to do.

TABLE 3.1   Permissions Inside a Team

Capability	Owner	Member	Guest
Create a channel	Y	Y	Y
Private chat and channel conversations	Y	Y	Y
Share a channel file	Y	Y	Y
Share a chat file	Y	Y	
Add apps to a channel (tabs, bots, connectors)	Y	Y	
Can be invited via external Microsoft 365 account			Y
Create a team	Y	Y	
Delete or edit posted messages	Y	Y	Y
Discover and join public teams	Y	Y	
View org chart	Y	Y	
Manage team membership (including adding guests)	Y		
Perform team maintenance (edit, delete, renew, archive, restore)	Y		
Set team permissions for channels, tabs, and connectors	Y		

TABLE 3.1   Permissions Inside a Team

Capability	Owner	Member	Guest
Change the team picture	Y		
Auto-show channels for the whole team	Y		
Allow usage of emojis, GIFs, memes, and @mentions	Y		

You can view and change these permission types inside Teams (see Figure 3.2) by using the Manage Team menu (click the . . . next to the team name in the team list and then Manage Team) or by modifying the M365 group itself directly in Azure AD or the M365 Admin Center. The two primary membership types of owner and member are native properties of M365 groups, so you manage them the same way as you would any other type of group membership. Figure 3.3 shows the Azure AD group interface.

FIGURE 3.2   Teams memberships

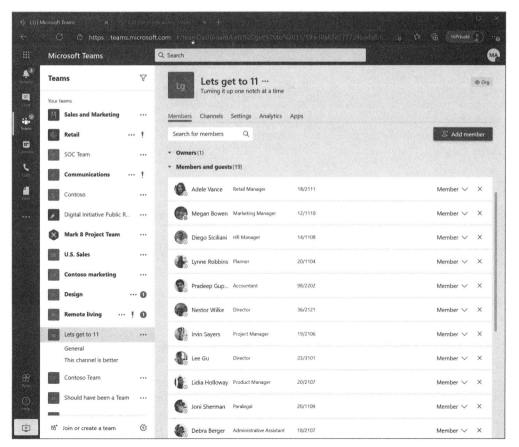

FIGURE 3.3   M365
group membership in M365
Admin Center

Types of Teams and Discoverability

Teams themselves come in a few varieties that control the ability of users to automatically join them.

Public: Users can find and join the team from the team directory screen.

Private: Only an owner of the team can add new users.

Org-wide: This is a special kind of team to which all normal users in the tenant are automatically added.

In addition to these privacy levels, there is a setting that governs the discoverability of a team; this is the ability to find a team using the built-in directory from the Teams client.

By default, private teams are created to be discoverable and users are allowed to search for them. However, both of these settings can be controlled independently so you can block certain groups of users from searching for private teams, or you can specifically mark teams as being hidden from the directory.

An example might be that you want to prevent contractor accounts from searching for private teams, or you might have a private team created to support a new company merger where even the name of the team could be a giveaway, so you want to make sure no one can stumble across it.

You could well be wondering why you would want private teams to be discoverable, and why is this now the default setting? The answer has to do with trying to reduce team duplication. If you have two groups of people working on similar ideas or themes in your company, it is possible with discovery disabled that they create more than one team for the same task and you end up with a duplication of resources.

Control Discoverability in PowerShell

To change the discoverability for a single team with PowerShell, use the `Set-Team` cmdlet with the `ShowInTeamsSearchandSuggestions` switch. The `Set-Team` cmdlet doesn't take a friendly name as an input, so it is best to combine it with `get-team` to first find the team you want to update:

```
Get-Team -DisplayName "Hidden Team" | Set-Team -ShowInTeamsSearchandSuggestions
$false
```

To change the user policy to control whether they can search for private teams, we need to use the `CsTeamsChannelsPolicy` family of PowerShell cmdlets (see "PowerShell Cmdlet Families Used in Teams PowerShell").

PowerShell Cmdlet Families Used in Teams PowerShell

When working with PowerShell cmdlets, especially for managing policies in Teams, it is common to have a standard verbiage set of Get-<policy type>, Set-<policy type>, New-<policy type>, Grant-<policy type>, and Remove-<policy type>.

Once you understand how these cmdlets generally operate, you will find it easy to pick up the specific behavior for the family of cmdlets you need to work with.

Get- will return a list of the policy objects requested.

Set- and New- will create or update settings for the policy object (they usually share the same switches/options).

Grant- will let you assign the policy object to a user or group.

Remove- will delete the policy object (if a policy is in use and you try to remove it, depending on the cmdlet you may get an error, or any users who had the policy will be reverted to the global policy). You can also use this to reset the global policy to the defaults.

You can read more about Teams PowerShell at docs.microsoft.com/en-us/MicrosoftTeams/teams-powershell-managing-teams.

So if we want to make a contractor policy to prevent searching for private teams, we could run this:

```
New-CsTeamsChannelsPolicy -Identity ContractorPolicy -AllowPrivateTeamDiscovery
$false
```

Or to make sure that employees can search for private teams, you might choose to do this:

```
New-CsTeamsChannelsPolicy -Identity StaffPolicy -AllowPrivateTeamDiscovery
$true
```

This is where you might want to consider how you set the default global policy to be either the most or least restrictive policy. Think what the worst-case scenario might be—if you want to push caution, perhaps make the default to not allow private search, but then this might lead to team duplication.

Having created your policy, now assign it to your user:

```
Grant-CsTeamsChannelsPolicy -Identity Ben@LearnTeams.Info -PolicyName
StaffPolicy
```

The same policy object (`CsTeamsChannelsPolicy`) can be used to control the ability to create private channels using the `-AllowPrivateChannelCreation` switch. We will be covering private channels later in the chapter.

Making a Team from Scratch

By default, all Teams licensed users in the company can create new teams, but this can be restricted so that only Global Administrators or Teams Service Administrators have the access to do so.

New teams can be created via the following:

- Teams client
- Teams Admin Center
- PowerShell

Using Teams Client

To make our first team, open the Teams client, and from the left bar select Teams; then choose Join Or Create Team from the bottom of the left panel to get to the Teams discovery screen. From here you can start making a new team (see Figure 3.4).

FIGURE 3.4   Team discovery and creation screen

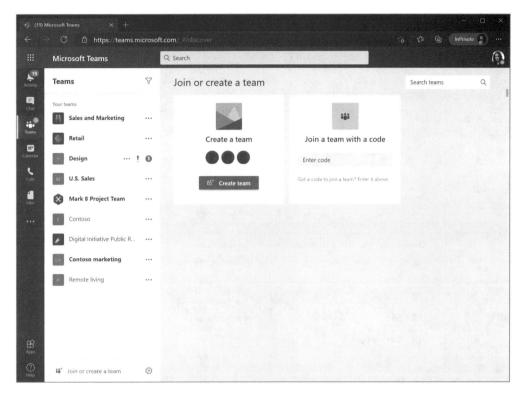

When using the Teams client, you can make new teams either from scratch, from a template, or from an existing resource (existing team or M365 group). If you select to copy an existing team, you get a choice of which elements you bring over into your new team (see Figure 3.5).

FIGURE 3.5   Copying existing team options

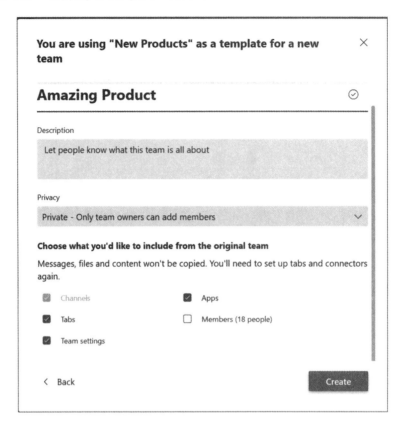

If you select to create one from scratch, you will next have to choose what type of team you want. You will see Org-Wide here only if you are signed in with an account that has tenant admin permissions (see Figure 3.6).

FIGURE 3.6 Choosing your team type

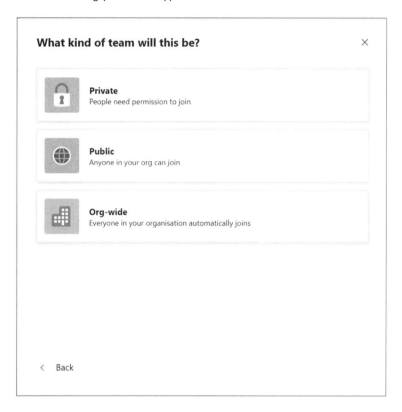

Give your new team a sensible name and click Create (see Figure 3.7).

Think carefully about if you need to have a naming convention for teams in your organization, as it can help bring structure to your team deployment. For example, I like to use the suffix "-EXT" where I know a team will have external customers invited to join so that it is obvious to anyone who joins. In Chapter 4, we will cover some O365 features that let you apply naming conventions to your team creation, but this requires extra licenses to work.

FIGURE 3.7 Entering a team name

Next the wizard will give you an option to start adding members to your new team; you can skip it at this point or select individuals or groups of users to add. If you select groups, Teams will pull out the individual members of that group (expand) and place them into the team; it does not upgrade or create a relationship between the source group and your new team. It's a one-time thing (see Figure 3.8).

FIGURE 3.8   Adding members at creation

 With your new team now created, you might want to consider making sure that it has more than one owner; it is generally considered best practice to make sure that a team always has more than one owner to reduce the likelihood of teams becoming orphaned (where all the owners' accounts have been disabled or deleted).

To view the options for your new team, click the three dots next to your team name and then select Manage Team. Here you can manage settings for your team including membership, permissions, and channels (see Figure 3.9).

FIGURE 3.9   Managing a team

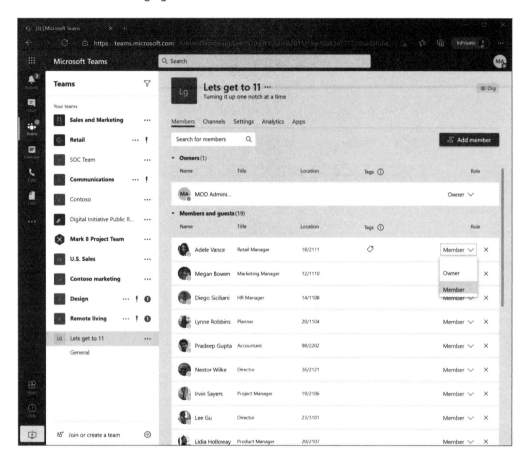

Creating in PowerShell

Having now created a team via the Teams interface, it is good to know that if you need to bulk-create a lot of teams in one go, you can automate it using PowerShell with just a line or two of code.

The cmdlet that you need to use is called New-Team. Table 3.2 shows the main options you might need.

TABLE 3.2   New-Team Cmdlet Main Options

Parameter	Description	Required?
DisplayName	Name given to the team	Yes
Description	Team description	No
Visibility	Private/public visibility	No (defaults to Private)
Owner	Set an owner	No (defaults to account running the cmdlet)
Template	Use a template if one exists	No

docs.microsoft.com/en-us/powershell/module/teams/new-team

Open a PowerShell window and connect to your Teams tenant (see Chapter 1, "Teams Introduction and Background"), and then you can use the following code to make your new team (see Figure 3.10):

```
New-Team -DisplayName "12 beats 11" -Visibility Private -Owner <User Account>
-Description "12 is 1 more than 11"
```

When you create the team you can also control some permissions for the team, such as the ability to use Giphys, memes, channel messaging settings, and certain guest permissions. See the source link of Table 3.2 for a full list of what can be configured at the time of creation.

If you do not specify an account to be the owner for your new team, it will default to the account that you used to run the PowerShell cmdlet. It can also take a bit of time after running before the team is visible inside your Teams client.

FIGURE 3.10   Creating a team in PowerShell

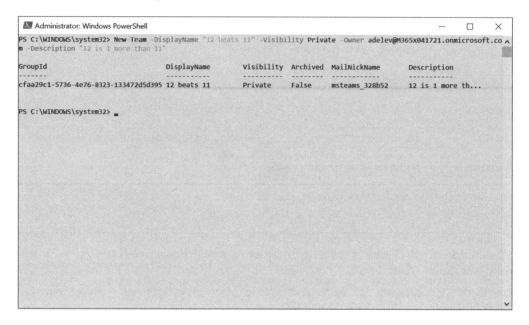

Creating from the Teams Admin Center

You can also manage/add new teams to your organization from the Teams Admin Center (TAC).

Log in to the TAC and from the left menu select Teams and then Manage Teams. Here you should now see a list of all the teams along with some useful stats about membership (such as the number of owners, members, and guests). To create a new team, select Add from just above the Teams list and enter the details for what you want to create (see Figure 3.11).

FIGURE 3.11   Creating a team via the TAC

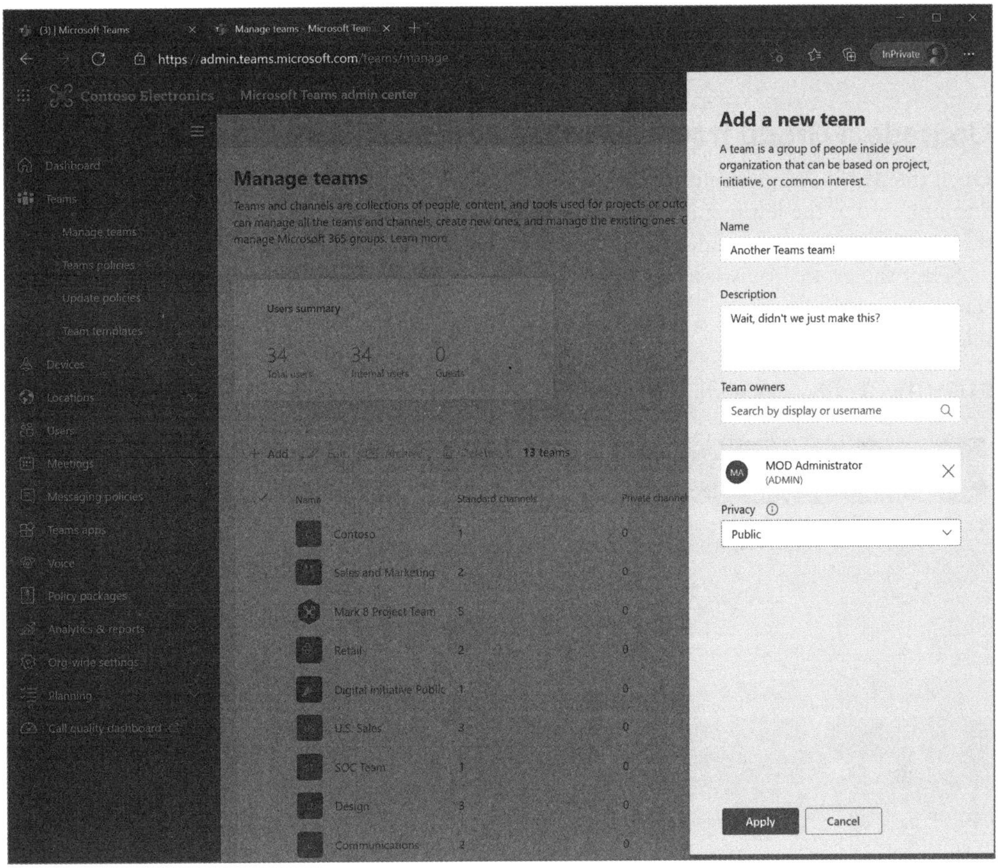

Upgrading an Existing Resource to a Team

You might already have groups in your organization that it would make sense to convert into teams rather than duplicating them. Fortunately, you are able to do that fairly simply, especially when the existing resource is already an M365 group.

As you can also create an M365 group from an existing distribution list, you have a few options for converting existing resources into teams:

- M365 group → team
- Distribution list → M365 group → team
- SharePoint team site → team

This link has information about converting a distribution list into an M365 group: docs.microsoft.com/en-us/microsoft-365/admin/manage/ upgrade-distribution-lists.

Upgrade a Group from the M365 Admin Center

Open the M365 Admin Center, making sure you are logged in with a tenant administrator account, and in the left menu expand Groups ➢ Active Groups. Here in the table you should see a visual indication (small Teams logo) of what groups are already Teams enabled.

Select the group you want to convert, and an overlay should appear on the right of the screen. Select the Teams tab, click Create A Team (see Figure 3.12), and then confirm your selection.

FIGURE 3.12 Converting an M365 group via the Admin Center

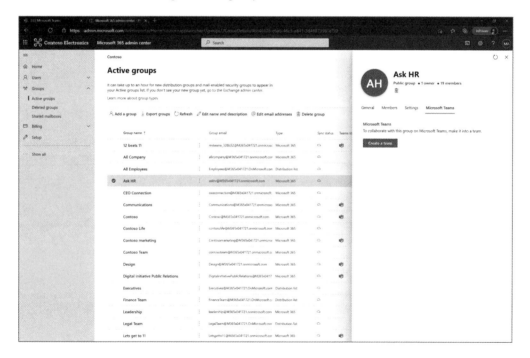

Once the group has been Teams enabled, you can manage it from inside the TAC.

Upgrade a Group from the Teams Client

This is essentially the same process we used when we created a brand new team from the Teams client, so, in the Teams client, choose Teams from the left menu bar and then Join Or Create Team, but now instead of creating one from scratch, we want to select From A Group Or Team (see Figure 3.13).

FIGURE 3.13   Creating a team from a group or team

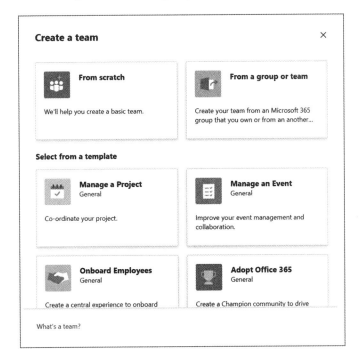

Now select Microsoft 365 Group (see Figure 3.14), and you will see a list of all eligible groups that you can convert (see Figure 3.15).

Read more about updating existing resources to work with Teams at docs
.microsoft.com/en-us/microsoftteams/enhance-office-365-
groups.

FIGURE 3.14 Options
for creating teams

FIGURE 3.15 Eligible
M365 groups

Upgrade a Group via PowerShell

As PowerShell is a little magical, we can combine two cmdlets to upgrade an M365 group for us from the command line.

First we need to use `Get-UnifiedGroup` to find the M365 group object that we enabled for Teams, and then we pass it along to the same cmdlet that we used earlier, `New-Team`, which will then enable it for us.

The good news with it being the same cmdlet is that you can then still apply the same controls that we learned earlier to perform any additional configuration in one pass.

The bad news is that the `Get-UnifiedGroup` cmdlet that you need to find the M365 groups is not currently included in the Teams PowerShell module, so you also need to connect to the Exchange Online management shell. See the reference link from Microsoft for the detailed steps of how to connect.

Learn more about the `Get-UnifiedGroup` cmdlet at docs.microsoft.com/en-us/powershell/module/exchange/get-unifiedgroup.

To connect to the Exchange Online PowerShell, see docs.microsoft.com/en-us/powershell/exchange/connect-to-exchange-online-powershell.

There are several ways in PowerShell to achieve the same thing, so either you can create a single line that finds the group and then uses the PowerShell pipeline to pass the group object to our `New-Team` cmdlet:

```
Get-UnifiedGroup -Identity "Contoso Team" | New-Team
```

or you can first find the group and store it in a variable to then use in the `New-Team` cmdlet. Either approach is acceptable as the result is the same (see Figure 3.16):

```
$M365Group = Get-UnifiedGroup -Identity "Contoso Team"
New-Team -GroupID $M365Group.ExternalDirectoryObjectId
```

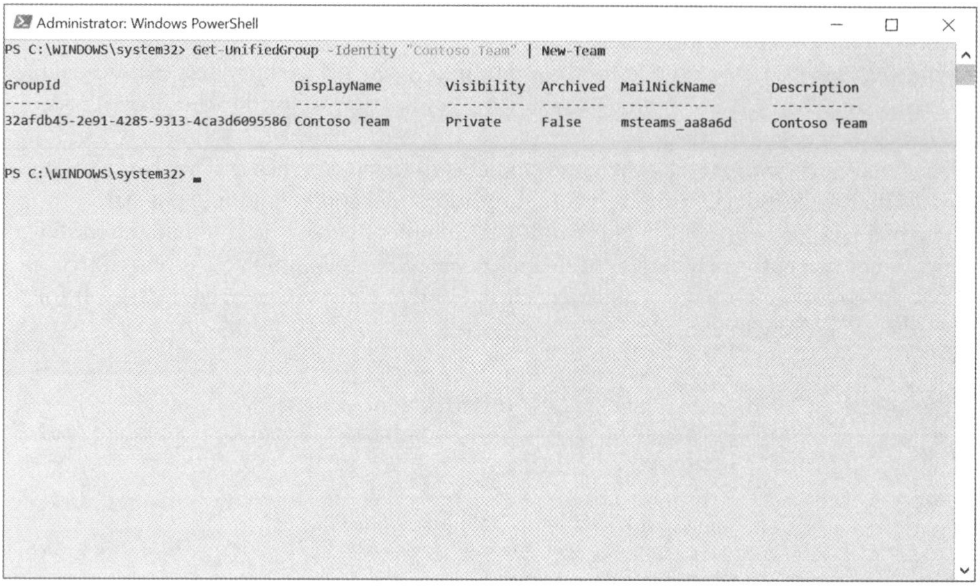

FIGURE 3.16   Converting an M365 group via PowerShell

Upgrade a SharePoint Team Site

It is also possible to upgrade a SharePoint team site to a Teams team. This is possible because team sites share the same back-end requirement to be based on an M365 group. Other SharePoint site types may not be based on an M365 group so would not be eligible to upgrade.

To convert a SharePoint team site, log in to the M365 Admin Center and navigate to the SharePoint-specific management portal (you may have to click Show All on the left menu to find it). Then expand Sites ➢ Active Sites, find the site you want to use for the new team, and click the URL column to navigate to the site. When the site opens (make sure your account has permission to access the site), you should see a link on the left side of the page offering to add Microsoft Teams for the site (see Figure 3.17).

FIGURE 3.17   A SharePoint team site ready to add Teams

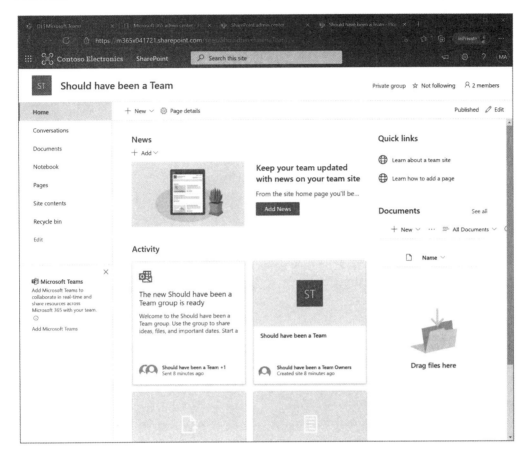

Wait for the process to finish and then refresh the page; you should now have a new menu item for Teams in the left menu for the site (see Figure 3.18). This link will push you over to the newly created team inside Teams.

FIGURE 3.18 SharePoint team site also enabled for Teams

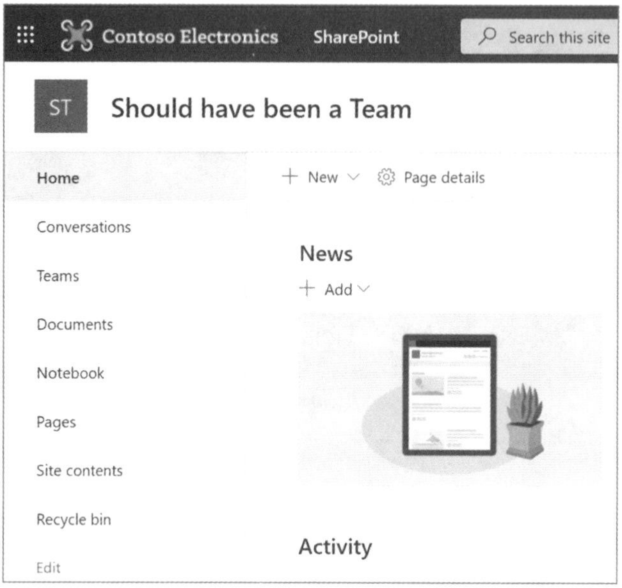

![SharePoint team site screenshot showing "Should have been a Team" site with navigation menu including Home, Conversations, Teams, Documents, Notebook, Pages, Site contents, Recycle bin, Edit, and News/Activity sections]

Org-Wide Teams

As mentioned in the section "Types of Teams and Discoverability," there is a special type of team called *org-wide*. This type of team will automatically update its membership as users join or leave your organization.

> **NOTE** While org-wide teams may seem like a great idea to keep everyone up to date on company news and developments, their usage should be carefully considered. Sometimes it might be more appropriate to use another tool such as Yammer to communicate with all the people in your org.

There are a few constraints to be aware of when considering whether to create org-wide teams:

- Only global administrators can create them.
- They can be created only from inside a Teams client (desktop or web).
- The maximum membership is 10,000, so you cannot create them if you have more users than this.
- Only five can be created per tenant.

When the team is created, the following accounts will not be automatically added:

- Accounts blocked from logging in
- Guest accounts
- Special account types
  - Resource/service accounts (i.e., used in call queues)
  - Room/equipment accounts
- Accounts backed by a shared mailbox

 Microsoft's documentation for org-wide teams is at docs.microsoft.com/en-us/microsoftteams/create-an-org-wide-team.

Creating a New Org-Wide Team

To make your org-wide team, start the same process used for making a team from scratch inside the Teams client, but on the What Kind Of Team selection page choose Org-Wide. Enter a suitable name for your team and click the Create button (see Figure 3.19).

FIGURE 3.19 Creating an org-wide team

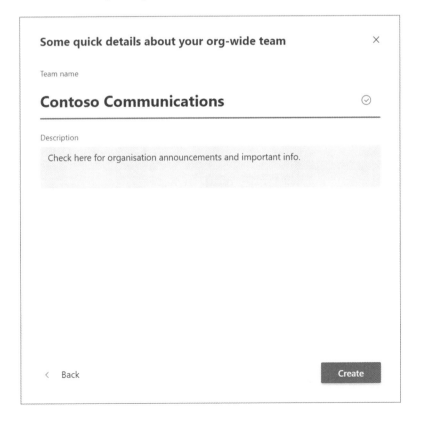

Once the team is created, it looks and acts like a normal team, but there is a small visual indicator in the top menu showing that everyone in the organization will be able to see what is posted (see Figure 3.20).

FIGURE 3.20 An org-wide team

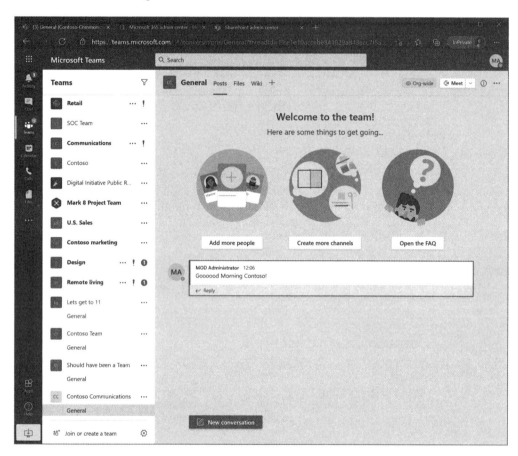

Change an Existing Team to an Org-Wide Team

You can also change the status of an existing team to turn it into an org-wide team in the same way that you can change the status from public to private. You can also do the reverse if you need to demote an org-wide team.

Inside the Teams client, open the team that you want to modify by selecting Teams in the left menu and then choosing the team that you want to work with. Click . . . next to the team name, and from the menu choose Edit Team. From here you can view and change the privacy status for the team (see Figure 3.21). Click Done to apply any changes you make.

FIGURE 3.21   Team privacy status

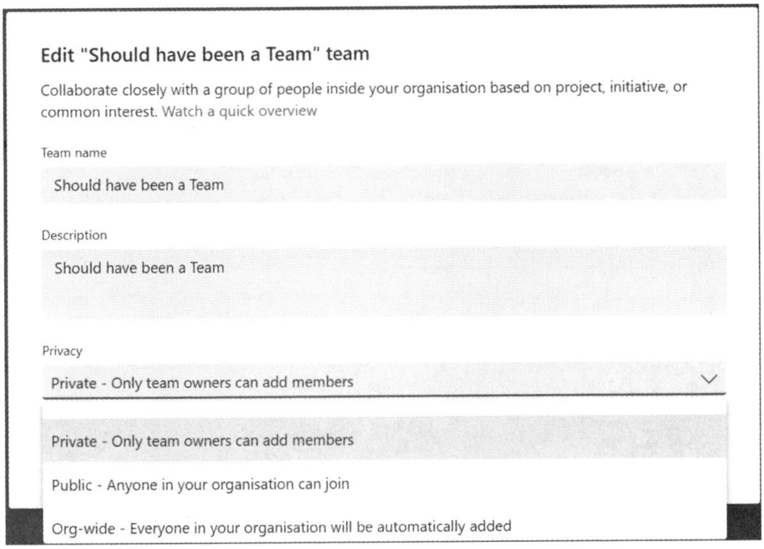

Edit "Should have been a Team" team

Collaborate closely with a group of people inside your organisation based on project, initiative, or common interest. Watch a quick overview

Team name

Should have been a Team

Description

Should have been a Team

Privacy

Private - Only team owners can add members

Private - Only team owners can add members

Public - Anyone in your organisation can join

Org-wide - Everyone in your organisation will be automatically added

Best Practices When Using Org-Wide Teams

As org-wide teams, once they are created, look and behave the same as any normal team, there are a few things you might want to consider changing to stop things from getting messy in the channel, causing too many notifications for your users.

Turn off @mentions: Consider turning off mentions under the . . . menu; select More Options ➤ Manage Team ➤ Settings ➤ @mentions (see Figure 3.22).

FIGURE 3.22   Changing @mentions

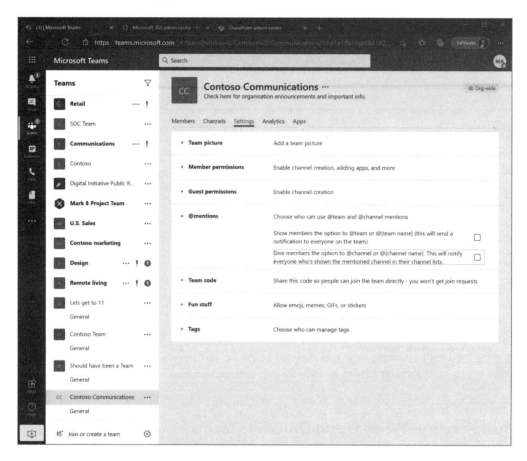

Only allow team owners to post in the General channel: Found under . . . next to the channel, select Manage Channel. Change the permissions to Only Allow Owners To Post Messages (see Figure 3.23).

Configure channel moderation: Delegate permissions to certain members in the team who can post in the channel to apply some form of control over what is allowed to be posted.

Check membership and remove accounts that do not belong: While end users are not able to remove themselves from an org-wide team, team owners can remove any users or accounts that should not have access to the team. You must use Teams to remove users from the org-wide team; otherwise, they may be automatically added back in.

FIGURE 3.23   Restricting posting to owners

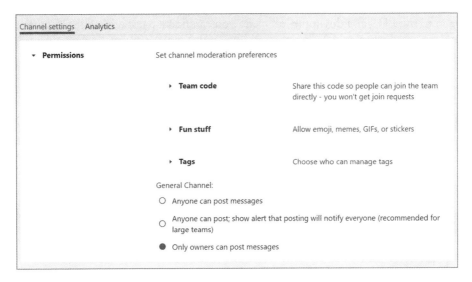

Create suitable channels for subconversations: Consider creating channels under the org-wide team to help keep relevant topics together. These channels can also be favorited so that they automatically show for all users. You'll learn more about this and other channel features in the next section.

Managing Features Inside Teams

Now that we have gotten up and running with some teams created and users ready to go, we need to look at what features and functionality we might want to control. Some of the settings will be inside teams themselves and relate to things you can do with channels, and others will be global Teams features that have to do with controlling chat and other collaboration workloads.

Messaging Policies

Messaging policies control users' core chat and collaboration functionality, such as modifying messages, using memes or stickers, or adding users to existing chats.

As mentioned in Chapter 1, each user will by default have an org-wide (global) policy applied, but you can create and apply custom user policies to change features for individuals (or apply the same policy to more than one user). However, each user can have only a single policy applied at any time.

While you can manage messaging policies from either PowerShell or the TAC, it makes sense to start by looking in the TAC, as you can see everything laid out.

Log in to the TAC, and down the left menu you can find a Messaging Policies button at the top level (see Figure 3.24). Click this, and you will see an overview of the policies that have been created in your tenant.

FIGURE 3.24   Messaging Policies overview screen

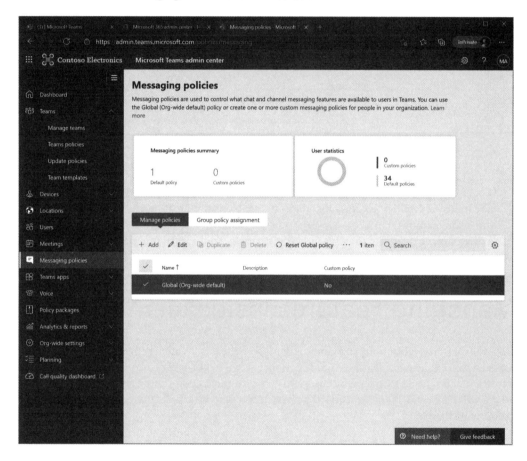

Select a policy (the org-wide one is fine), and it will open a screen so you can change its settings.

Owners can delete sent messages: Lets a team owner delete a message from another user in the channel chat.

Delete sent messages: Lets a user delete one of their own messages that they have posted in the chat.

Edit sent messages: Lets a user edit a chat message after they have sent it.

Read receipts: Allows read receipts to be shown for one-to-one (and one-to-many—up to 20 users) chats. This setting has three choices including some badly named "for everyone" choices; remember that in reality the choice will only apply to the users covered by the policy.

User Controlled: Lets a user configure their own read receipts.

On for everyone: Forces them on.

Off for everyone: Forces them off.

Chat: The button turns on or off chat functionality (not channel chat, but conversations).

Use Giphys in conversation: Giphy is a third-party service that contains popular animated GIFs that can be included in chats to help get the point across (even if that is just a bit of humor). When used correctly, they can really help improve engagement and interaction in conversations. Each Giphy has a content rating applied to it.

Giphy content rating: Controls what rating of Giphys users are allowed to select to include in chat. This setting has multiple options:

> **No restriction:** No filtering is applied, so adult content may be selectable.
>
> **Moderate:** Filtering is applied, but some adult-related content may still be accessible.
>
> **Strict:** No adult-related material should be accessible.

Use Memes in conversations: Teams has a set of built-in images that can help illustrate your points in chat. Memes are images onto which users can overlay their own text. The setting is either on or off.

Use Stickers in conversations: Turn on or off the ability to use the static (not customizable) set of built-in sticker images.

Allow URL preview: When a user enters a URL into a conversation, their Teams client can request and display a small preview of the destination URL into the message. This can be turned on or off.

Translate messages: Allows a user to automatically translate chat text into their native language using Microsoft's cloud-based translation services.

Allow immersive reader: Immersive reader is a special mode where the text is presented in a format designed to be easier to read or can be read aloud using a built-in narration tool. This setting can be turned on or off.

Send urgent messages with priority notifications: Messages sent with a priority notification will alert the recipient every 2 minutes for 20 minutes unless the message is viewed. This setting can be turned on or off.

Create voice messages: Allows users to record and upload small audio messages. Note that these are not accessible via eDiscovery so are not auditable. This might be a reason to consider disabling them for certain users. The setting has the following options:

> **Allowed in chats and channels:** Recordings can be added to both types of chat.

> **Allowed in chats only:** Recordings only allowed in nonchannel chats.

> **Disabled:** Recordings not allowed.

Display favorite channels above chat for mobile: Provides better visibility of favorite channels in the mobile application. This can be turned either on or off.

Remove users from group chat: Lets you remove users from a one-to-many chat message without having to set up a new group. This is handy as sometimes you can add a user to a group call, and it will automatically add users to the chat as well. This can be turned either on or off.

Suggested replies: Suggested replies attempts to provide users with some quick responses when more detail is not needed. This is similar technology to that found in more recent versions of Outlook for email. This can be turned either on or off.

As you can see, the messaging policy configuration manages settings for a few different areas. Some of them, such as Giphy support, can be further controlled at a team or channel level by a team owner.

Managing Messaging Policies in the TAC

To make a new policy, go to the Messaging Policies section of the TAC (Messaging Policies is a top-level item on the TAC left-hand menu). From here you can see what policies exist for your organization and see some stats about how many users have custom policies applied versus using the default.

To create a new policy, click the +Add button and give your new policy a name and description (to help understand its purpose when you, or someone else, returns in future). Change your settings from the list presented and then save the new policy (see Figure 3.25).

You can edit existing policies in the same way by first selecting them and then choosing the Edit button from the menu above the display list. You can also quickly duplicate an existing policy or reset the global policy to its default values if you need to roll things back (see Figure 3.26).

FIGURE 3.25   Creating a new messaging policy

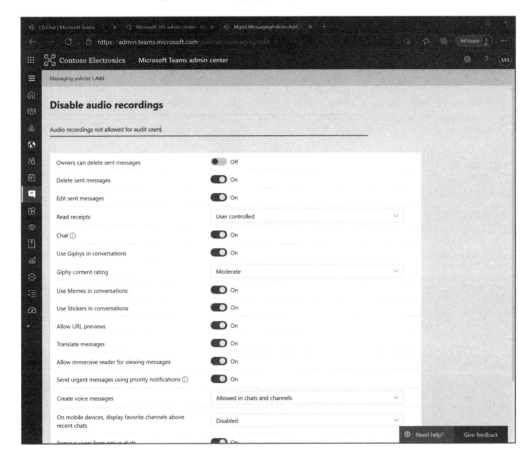

FIGURE 3.26   Messaging policy options

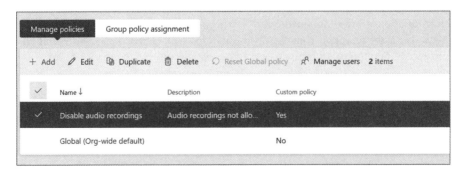

When you are ready to assign a policy to users, there are three choices: you can either assign it to a user from the messaging policy screen, assign it directly against the user from the user object itself, or use group policy assignment to assign it based on group memberships.

Assign from the messaging policy screen: In the messaging policy screen in the TAC, select the policy you want to apply to a user and then choose Manage Users from the menu. This will open a pop-out menu on the right side of the page where you can enter a username to search the company directory. Select your user and click Apply (see Figure 3.27).

FIGURE 3.27   Messaging policy being applied to a user

Apply directly to a user: Open the TAC and from the left menu select Users. Search for and click the user you want to target. This will open the user information page where you can select Policies to view all the different types of policies applied to this user. Select Edit next to the "assigned policy" title, and under Messaging Policy pick the policy you want to apply from the drop-down list (see Figure 3.28). Note that changing policies can take up to 48 hours to apply but usually takes a couple of hours.

FIGURE 3.28   User policy list

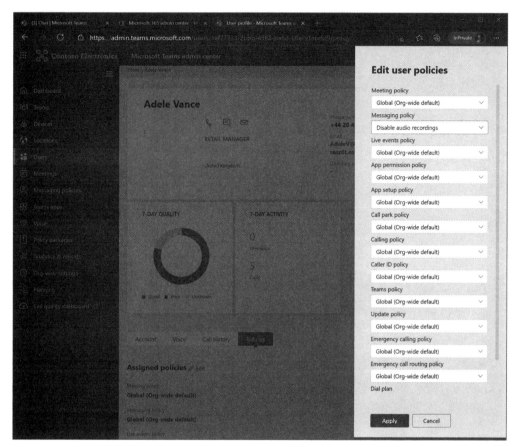

Using Group policy assignment: Back on the Messaging Policies screen in the TAC, navigate to the second tab called Group Policy Management. Here you can see a list of any existing policies applied automatically based on group membership. To add a new assignment, click +Add Group, and then from the right pop-out screen select the group you want to use to assign the policy against. Change the rank as appropriate (where the lowest number takes priority if a user is covered under more than one policy) and then choose the policy you want to use and apply your selection (see Figure 3.29).

FIGURE 3.29   Group policy assignment

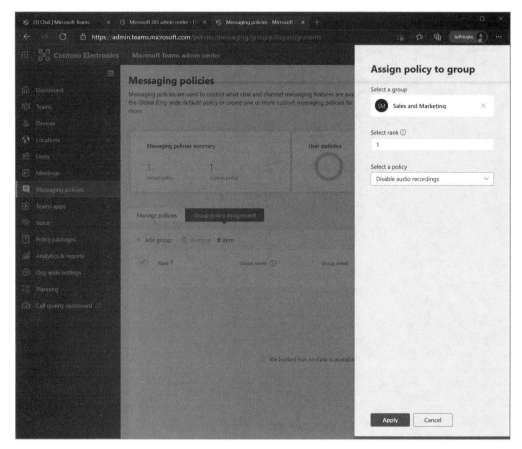

Managing Messaging Policies in PowerShell

You can also work with messaging policies using PowerShell. The cmdlet family we want to use is the CsTeamsMessagingPolicy family, so the cmdlets in question we'd need are as follows:

Get-CsTeamsMessagingPolicy: Return a list of messaging policies. This can be filtered with wildcards.

New-CsTeamsMessagingPolicy: Create a new messaging policy with the supplied inputs.

Set-CsTeamsMessagingPolicy: Update an existing messaging policy with the supplied inputs.

Grant-CsTeamsMessagingPolicy: Assign the specified messaging policy to the specified user.

Remove-CsTeamsMessagingPolicy: Delete the specified messaging policy.

Most of these cmdlets just require basic input to perform their operation (such as the name of the messaging policy you are looking for), but it's worth looking at the parameters for both the `New-` and `Set-` cmdlets, as shown in Table 3.3.

TABLE 3.3   New- and Set- `CsTeamsMessagingPolicy` Cmdlet Main Options

Parameter	Description	Options
AllowGiphy	Use of Giphys	$True/$False
AllowImmersiveReader	Use of the immersive reader	$True/$False
AllowMemes	Use of memes	$True/$False
AllowOwnerDeleteMessage	Owners can delete any message	$True/$False
AllowPriorityMessages	Use of priority notifications	$True/$False
AllowRemoveUser	Able to remove user from group conversation	$True/$False
AllowSmartReply	Suggested replies	$True/$False
AllowStickers	Allow stickers	$True/$False
AllowUserChat	Use of chat (private, group, and meeting)	$True/$False
AllowUserDeleteMessage	Able to delete own messages	$True/$False
AllowUserEditMessage	Able to edit own messages	$True/$False
AllowUserTranslation	Enable translation services	$True/$False
AudioMessageEnabledType	Control audio messaging	ChatsAndChannels ChatsOnly Disabled
ChannelsInChatListEnabled-Type	Mobile display for favorite channels	DisabledUserOverride EnabledUserOverride
GiphyRatingType	Control rating of Giphys that can be searched	STRICT MODERATE NORESTRICTION

docs.microsoft.com/en-us/powershell/module/skype/new-csteamsmessagingpolicy

Managing Channels

Channels are a way of breaking up or sectioning off areas within a team. This can help to group conversations and resources into similar areas. For example, you might create a team for a customer but then use channels for the specific projects that are being worked on. This way anyone can quickly check and find out what else is going on with a customer while only having to focus on the channel specific to the project that they are working on.

Each team will always include a General channel that cannot be deleted or modified, but a team owner can add up to 200 channels inside the team. By default, channels are created as public, so any member of the team can view their content. There is another special type of channel, called a *private channel*, where membership and visibility can be independently managed. A team can have up to 30 channels (in addition to the 200 public type), and a private channel can support a membership of 250 users.

Private Channels

Private channels have a separate membership list (but members must also be members of the parent team in the first place) of who can see and participate in the channel. You cannot change the channel type after it has been initially created. While private channels may seem like a great way to go, you should consider each use case, as it may be more appropriate to create a separate team for the task and remove some of the administrative overhead of managing permissions.

Imagine you need to provide a way for people to work on a secret ProjectX. The following questions could be helpful in deciding if you should create private channels or a new team:

- Does a team already exist for the same group required by ProjectX? (Perhaps you can reuse that team instead of creating more.)

- Does ProjectX have multiple topics or areas that need to be covered? (Multiple channels could work here.)

- Do any of the ProjectX topics need to be kept independent of each other? (Private channels could keep things separate.)

 Microsoft's documentation for private channels is at docs.microsoft.com/ en-us/MicrosoftTeams/private-channels.

Private Channel Permissions

Permissions for a private channel are handled independently of the parent team, and ownership of a team does not grant access to any child private channels. The user who creates a private channel is automatically assigned as the channel owner and can then add other users to the channel.

Settings for a private channel are also independent of the parent channel, so settings such as @mentions, stickers, and Giphys can be controlled separately.

If the private channel owner leaves the parent team, then another user who has access to the private channel will be automatically promoted to owner status. See Table 3.4 for a list of the permissions that can apply to private channels.

TABLE 3.4   Private Channel Permissions

Item	Team Owner	Team Member	Team Guest	Private Channel Owner	Private Channel Member	Private Channel Guest
Create private channel	Controlled by policy	Policy and team owner controlled	No	N/A	N/A	N/A
Delete private channel	Yes	No	No	Yes	No	No
Leave private channel	N/A	N/A	N/A	Yes	No	Yes
Edit private channel	No	N/A	N/A	Yes unless no other owners	Yes	No
Restore private channel	Yes	No	No	Yes	No	No
Add members	No	N/A	N/A	Yes	No	No
Edit members	No	N/A	N/A	Yes	No	No
Manage apps and tabs	No	N/A	N/A	Yes if installed in team	Channel owner controlled	No

docs.microsoft.com/en-us/MicrosoftTeams/private-channels

Private Channels and SharePoint Sites

It is worth knowing what happens behind the scenes when you create a private channel in SharePoint. By default each public channel inside a team shares resources from the same SharePoint site. For example, a channel has its own folder in the SharePoint site document library that is used for any file uploads.

In a private channel this wouldn't work, as users could simply browse the SharePoint site directly and find materials that they should potentially not be able to see. For this reason, when a private channel is created, this actually makes a new SharePoint site to ensure that the permissions are handled correctly. These private channel sites are created using a lightweight site using a custom template with the ID of TEAMSCHANNEL#0 if you ever needed to manipulate them using PowerShell.

Managing Channels via the TAC

You can manage channels inside your teams directly from the TAC. First log into the TAC, and then from the left menu select Teams ➤ Manage Teams. This will give you an overview of all the teams in your organization (see Figure 3.30).

FIGURE 3.30   Full list of teams

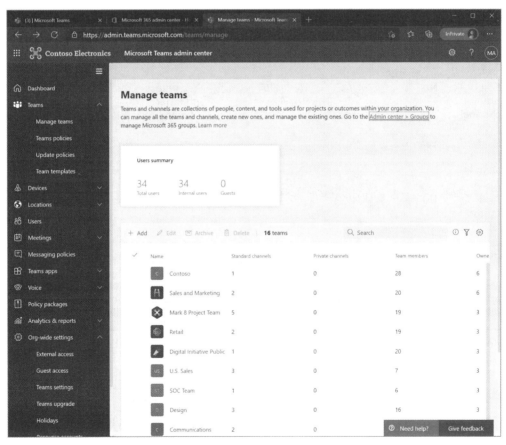

Click the name of the team you want to work with, and you will go into the team-specific page. By default this will show you the team membership list, but you can move to the Channels tab. Here you can choose to add a new channel to your team by filling out the pop-out panel on the right. To make a channel private, change the Type option. When you're happy, click Apply to save the new channel (see Figure 3.31).

FIGURE 3.31 Adding a new private channel

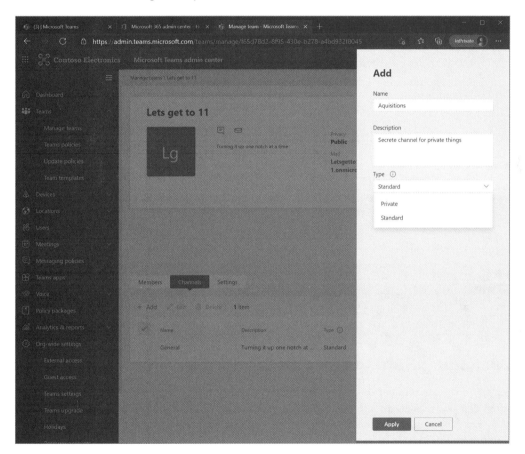

You can also edit a channel (change its name or description) or flag a channel for deletion (remember, you cannot change the privacy type for an existing channel).

Channel deletion in Teams is a soft delete—the channel will be hidden for 30 days before being deleted. At the time of writing, it is only possible to restore a deleted team from the Teams client; it is not an option in either the TAC or PowerShell.

Managing Channels in PowerShell

For managing team channels in PowerShell, the cmdlet family we want is `TeamChannel`, made up of the following:

Get-TeamChannel: Returns a list of channels in a team. This requires the GroupID property (its GUID) for the team you want to work with, so it's probably easier to pipe into this cmdlet from the `Get-Team` one.

New-TeamChannel: Creates a new channel with the following parameters: channel name, description, membership type (Standard or Private), and owner (if the administrator account is not to be the default owner).

Set-TeamChannel: Updates an existing team channel with a new name or description.

Remove-TeamChannel: Deletes the specified channel.

So to view a list of channels inside our team, we could run the following:

```
Get-Team -DisplayName "Lets get to 11" | Get-TeamChannel
```

Or to make a new channel as we did in the TAC, we could run the following:

```
Get-Team -DisplayName "Lets get to 11" | New-TeamChannel -DisplayName
"Acquisitions" -Description "Secret channel for private things" -MembershipType
Private -Owner Ben@LearnTeams.Info
```

At the time of writing (early 2021), there seems to be an issue with using the -MembershipType parameter, which is still preview functionality. It had been working in earlier releases of the PowerShell connector, but as of release 1.1.6, it has stopped working again.

Managing Settings in a Team

Each team has a number of settings for the availability of features inside a team. These settings can be accessed directly from the Teams client and can be modified by any team owner. Any settings configured here do not override any policies configured at a global or user level. For example, if a user is disabled from using Giphys, then the team setting will not apply, and the user will still not be able to use them.

Controlling Team Settings from Teams

To view or update the settings for a team, open the Teams client, select Teams from the left menu, and then find the team you want to work with. Click . . . next to the team name and select Manage Team. Here you should now see the membership list of the team (we will cover how to manage Teams memberships in Chapter 4) and can select Settings from the top tab (see Figure 3.32).

FIGURE 3.32   Settings for a team

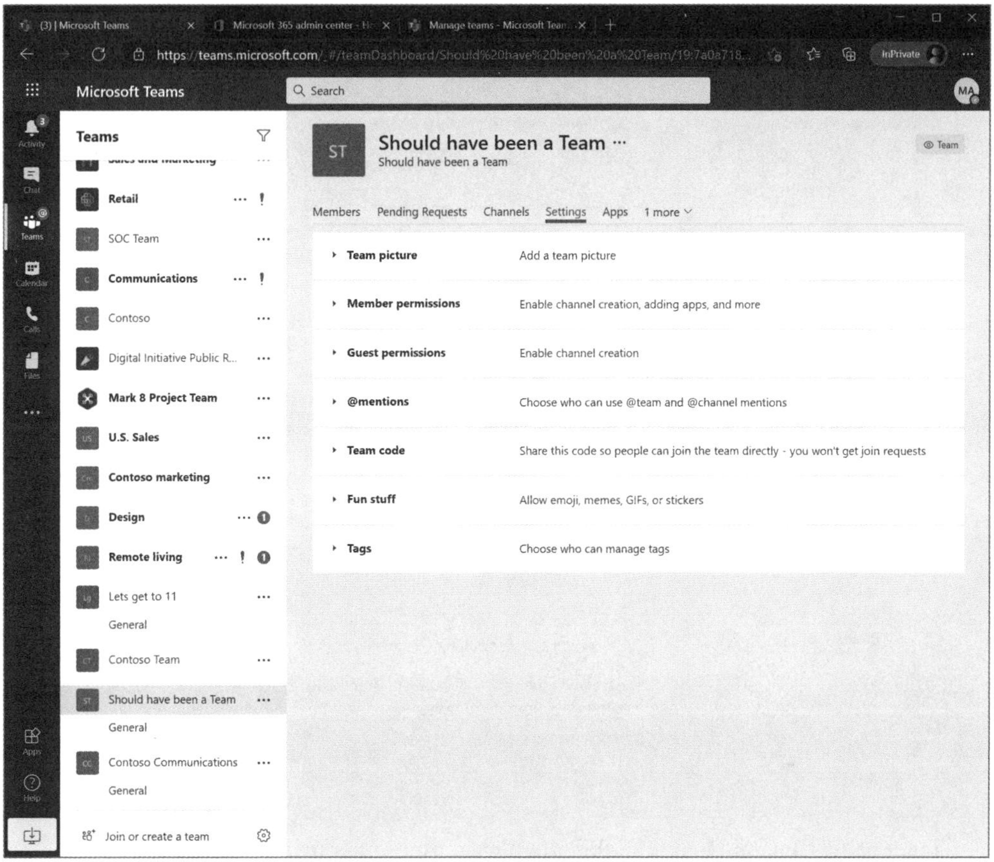

The settings are broken up into the following sections:

Team picture: Change the picture or icon displayed for the team.

Member permissions: Control what features are available for standard members inside the team. Features include managing channels (add/delete/create private); managing tabs, apps, and connectors; as well as the ability to edit messages (see Figure 3.33).

Guest permissions: Control if guest accounts can create/update/delete channels (see Figure 3.33).

@mentions: Control who can use @team or @channel mentions to generate notifications in the client (see Figure 3.33).

FIGURE 3.33 Member, guest, and @mentions settings for a team

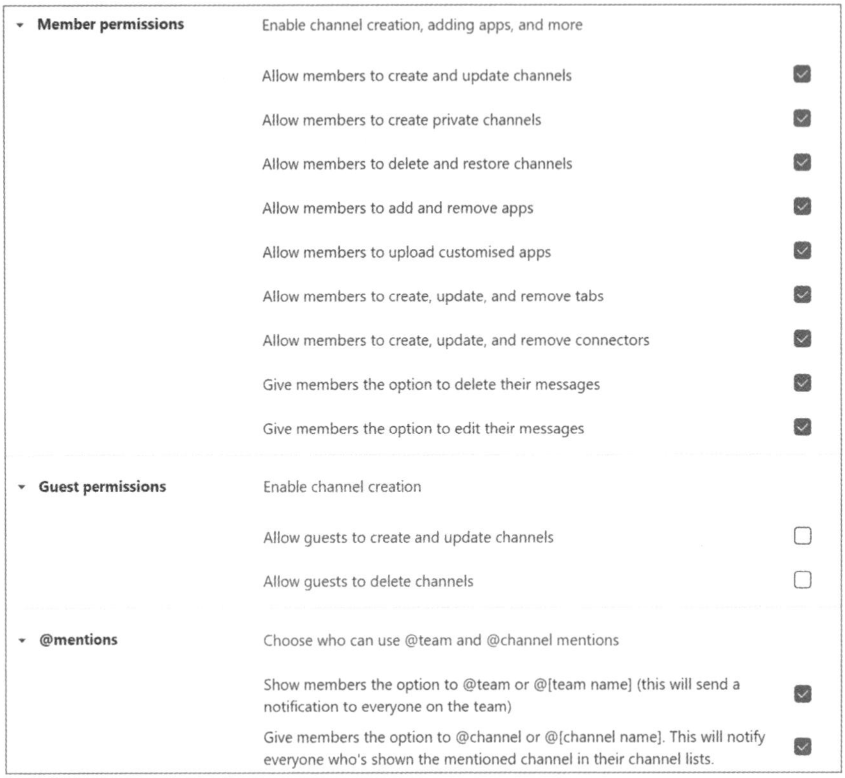

▾ **Member permissions**	Enable channel creation, adding apps, and more	
	Allow members to create and update channels	☑
	Allow members to create private channels	☑
	Allow members to delete and restore channels	☑
	Allow members to add and remove apps	☑
	Allow members to upload customised apps	☑
	Allow members to create, update, and remove tabs	☑
	Allow members to create, update, and remove connectors	☑
	Give members the option to delete their messages	☑
	Give members the option to edit their messages	☑
▾ **Guest permissions**	Enable channel creation	
	Allow guests to create and update channels	☐
	Allow guests to delete channels	☐
▾ **@mentions**	Choose who can use @team and @channel mentions	
	Show members the option to @team or @[team name] (this will send a notification to everyone on the team)	☑
	Give members the option to @channel or @[channel name]. This will notify everyone who's shown the mentioned channel in their channel lists.	☑

Team code: Generate a unique code that lets a user join a team directly if they have the code.

Fun Stuff: Control the use of Giphys, the Giphy filter, and the ability to upload/use stickers and memes.

Tags: Control who can manage tags for a team.

Channel Moderation

Moderation allows you to control who is allowed to participate in channel conversations (moderation is not available for private channels). This can be particularly useful when you are using org-wide teams or other teams that have a large membership (for example, if you wanted to create an "announcements" channel where only marketing can post content).

Moderation applies only at a channel level and does not apply automatically to the whole team. It also operates independently of the owner or member permissions roles in a team, but it can feed from these permissions. Channel moderation needs to be configured, at least initially, by a team owner.

Managing channel moderation is done from the Teams client. Find the channel you want to manage by selecting Teams in the left menu and then expand the team where the channel you want to work with is. Click the . . . option next to the channel name and select Manage Channel (see Figure 3.34).

FIGURE 3.34   Channel moderation preferences

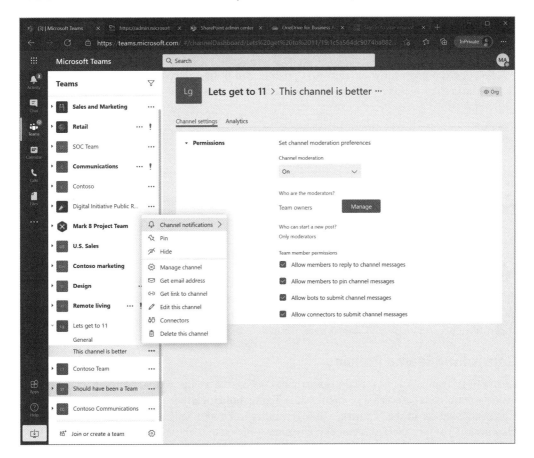

Here you can enable channel moderation and configure the main settings you might need:

Who can start a new post: When moderation is enabled, only the moderators specified can start a new conversation.

Allow members to reply to channel messages: You might want to allow members to reply to a conversation that a moderator started.

Allow bots/connectors to submit channel messages: Control whether Teams automatic agents are allowed to make posts into the channel, such as a bot configured to generate IT service alerts.

To select new moderators, use the Manage button to search for users from the team who will be assigned moderator privileges.

The General channel has its own special kind of moderation where you can configure only one of three options:

Anyone can post messages: This is the same as moderation being disabled in a channel.

Anyone can post; show an alert that posting will notify everyone: This is recommended for large channels, as it shows the user about to post a new message how many people will see it.

Only owners can post: Only owners are able to post new content; this is a type of enforced moderation.

 For more information about channel moderation, see `docs.microsoft`
`.com/en-us/microsoftteams/manage-channel-moderation-in-`
`teams`.

Manage Settings for Teams

In this section, we will look at controlling a number of settings that relate to how Teams handles different integrations and features. Some we have covered a little bit already (such as controlling private channels), but others are new.

Controlling Teams Policies

Currently a Teams policy is used primarily to control the ability to make private channels inside a team. You can create or manipulate Teams policies either using PowerShell (which we covered earlier in the "Control Discoverability in PowerShell" section) or using the TAC. However, if you use the TAC, you can currently only change the setting that controls the ability to make private channels inside a team.

You can view Teams policies from inside the TAC. They can be found on the Teams ➤ Teams Policies screen, where you can use the interface to create or edit a new policy using the top menu buttons (see Figure 3.35).

FIGURE 3.35   Adding a new Teams policy

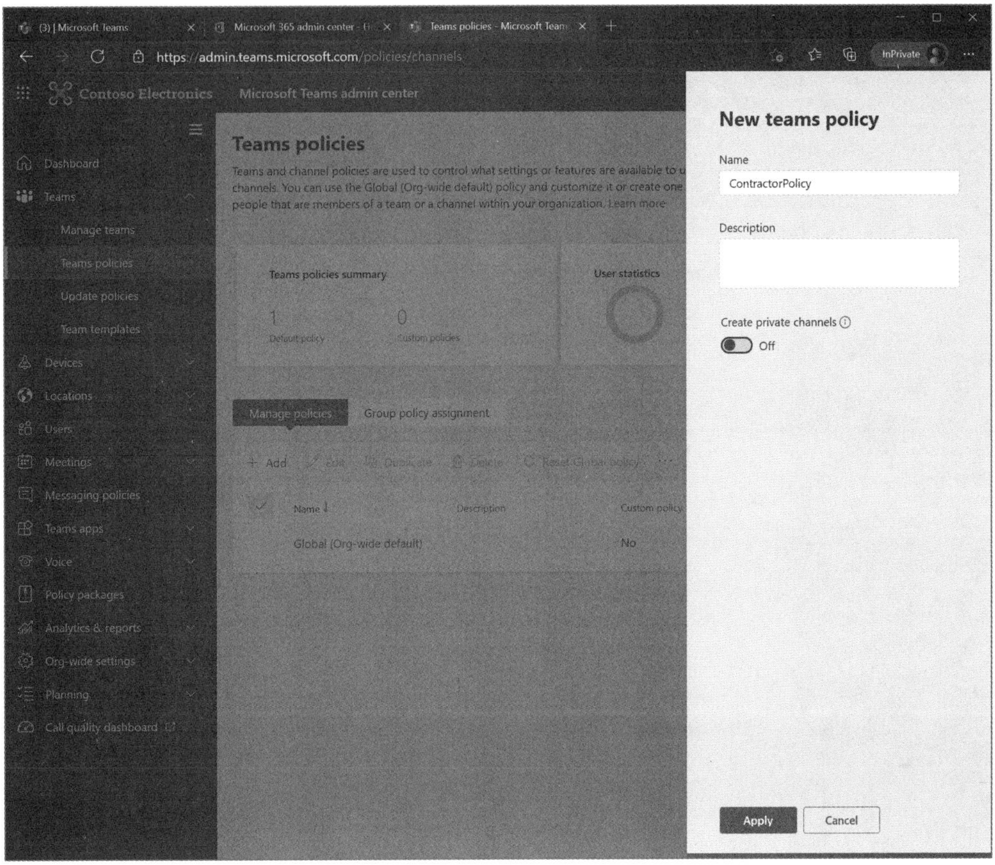

Org-Wide Teams Settings

As the name suggests, the settings that can be configured here will apply uniformly across all users and teams in the organization and cannot be overridden. These settings control basic features in Teams such as email integration, cloud storage providers, and tagging.

These settings can be all found in the TAC under Org-Wide Settings ➢ Teams Settings (see Figure 3.36). The following is an outline of some of the key settings you may want to look at configuring.

> **NOTE** For more details on how to manage Teams settings, see `docs.microsoft.com/en-US/microsoftteams/enable-features-office-365`.

FIGURE 3.36 Org-wide Teams settings

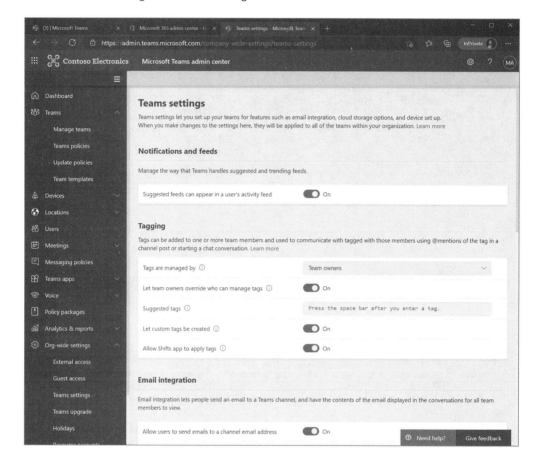

Notifications and feeds: The Activity feed area of the Teams client provides quick access to activity the user might be interested in. Suggested feeds can help improve discoverability inside your organization, especially between users who might not have worked together before.

Tagging: Tags can be used similarly to how @mentions work; they can be a way to mark conversations against a particular theme or topic.

> **Tags managed by:** The default is team owners, but you can allow members to also create them. Alternatively, you can choose to disable the feature entirely.

> **Suggested tags:** This lets you supply a basic list of terms that can be suggested when users are configuring tags for a channel (you can supply up to 25).

Email integration: Each team channel can be configured with its own email address (generated by Teams) so that users can forward emails to the channel for further discussion or reference.

> **Allow users to send email to the channel email address:** Enable or disable the feature.
>
> **Accept channel email from these SMTP domains:** Limit what domains can send email into the channel.

Files: Teams can integrate with a number of different (non-Microsoft) storage providers. You can choose to enable or disable the different vendors here (each one has their own toggle). Providers currently include the following:

> Citrix Files
>
> Dropbox
>
> Box
>
> Google Drive
>
> Egnyte

Organization: Show the organization chart tab when hovering the mouse over a user in Teams.

Devices: Some settings specific to Surface Hub devices when joining meetings to control access to meeting content.

Search by name: When searching inside Teams for users, by default the entire Exchange Global Address List will be used. If you need to use a filtered address book, you can enter it here.

Managing Email Integration

From the list of settings available in the org-wide settings list, there are two features that we should cover in more detail. The first of these is email integration.

I find email integration more frustrating than helpful because of my particular use case. When you forward an email into a channel, it is saved to the channel, but any further replies will generate their own conversation inside the team with no link to the original conversation.

However, you may find your usage differs and that being able to forward an email to save it on the record is a useful feature.

When you forward an email to a channel, unless it is small it will be saved as an EML attachment with the first few lines of the message visible as the chat header.

When this is enabled, any member of a team can view the email address associated with a channel. You will notice that apart from being unique, each channel email address does not actually send email to your tenant, but rather to an email address based on the region in which your Teams tenant was created.

Inside the Teams client, open the team and then the channel that you want to find the email address for. From the . . . menu on the channel, select Get Email Address, and the email will be displayed. You will notice that the format of the email address is similar to the following:

`uniqueID.TenantName.Onmicrosoft.com@<tenantregion>.teams.ms`

If you delete email integration and then later reenable it, the address will be different because of the unique ID that is generated. Once it is deleted, an email address will not be available again.

As this email address is not very user friendly, you could choose to add contact objects into your Exchange environment to act as easy-to-remember forwarders for the channel email addresses.

Managing File Sharing

The second integration that we will cover has to do with file sharing. File sharing is one of the most common features that you are likely to use when collaborating with someone on the platform. We have talked previously about how Teams leverages SharePoint and One-Drive for Business, but let's have a quick recap on which service is used where:

Sharing a file in one-on-one or group chat: Gets placed in the sending user's OneDrive for Business in a folder called Microsoft Teams Chat Files. Any recipients are then given individual permissions on the individual file.

Sharing a file in a conversation in a channel: File is uploaded to the team's document library contained in the team's SharePoint site. Permissions are then applied based on the configured team's policy.

Copy a link feature used inside Teams: Generates a SharePoint link directly to the specific file where permissions can be applied to the specific file (see Figure 3.37).

FIGURE 3.37   Sharing a file link options

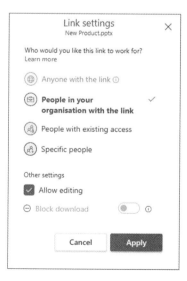

As you can see, with Teams using SharePoint and OneDrive for Business to handle permissions for shared files, it is important to make sure that any organization-level sharing permissions do not limit what you might want to achieve inside Teams.

To check the permission levels being applied, first open the Microsoft 365 Admin Center, expand Show All, and then select the SharePoint Portal link (we are not there yet!). Then in the left menu open the OneDrive Admin Center (the direct URL is `admin.onedrive.com`). Choose Sharing and scroll partway down the page to see a slider showing the maximum level of permissions that can be applied (see Figure 3.38).

FIGURE 3.38   OneDrive external sharing permissions

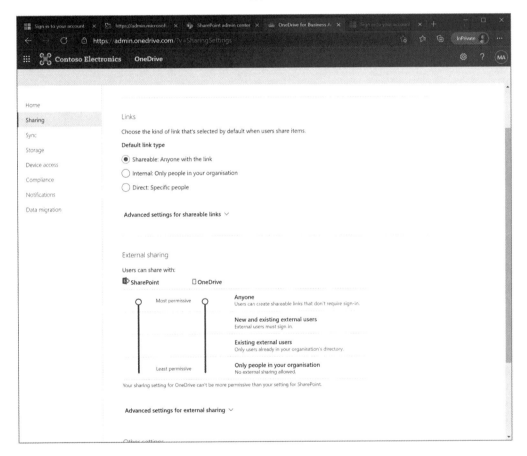

The options are as follows:

Anyone: Sharing links can be freely created and shared.

New and existing guests: Users can send invitations (subject to domain restrictions). Recipients must sign in with an account recognized by Azure AD (that is, another AD tenant or Microsoft account), and a new guest object will be created for the user.

Existing guests: Only existing guests (those who have previously been invited to the tenant) can redeem file share invitations.

Only people in the organization: External sharing is blocked.

Managing Guests and External Access

At varying points through this book so far, we have talked about permissions relating to guests and external users. In this section, we are going to explore what happens behind the scenes to support this, that is, how Azure AD plays an important part in guaranteeing the security of what is happening.

External Access vs. Guest Access

There are two ways to interact with users from outside of your organization, and it can be easy to confuse the two, especially when you can also invite external users into a Teams meeting.

As a rule of thumb, an external user can access a team via guest access and can be communicated with in their home tenant via external access. Oh, and external users can still join a Teams meeting you host without needing to have either of them configured.

Guest Access

First up we have guest access. This is where you invite a named user from an external organization to work with you inside a team. That user needs to be able to authenticate against Azure AD through either their own work or school account, another Microsoft account provider, or a supported authentication federation provider (such as Google); failing that, if none of those options is available, they can verify their identity using an email-based one-time passcode interaction.

Once the invited user has accepted the invitation and verified themselves with Azure AD, an account is created in your tenant and given a special type of license (at no cost) to enable them to interact with the required Teams services, such as SharePoint to access channel files.

If that user is also configured for Teams in their home organization, they may need to swap their client between tenants, as Teams does not currently support being signed in to more than one tenant at a time.

There is no limit inside Teams to the number of guest accounts, but this is managed at a tenant level, where five guest licenses can be assigned per paid Azure AD license in the tenant (effectively you can have five guests for each normal user in your tenant).

Guest users, while they have access to most Teams functionality (permissions allowing), they do not have access to these features:

- User calendaring functionality
- PSTN calling
- Browsing, creating, or editing teams
- Uploading files in a chat (one to one, one to many)
- Searching for people outside of Teams

When a team contains guest accounts, there are clear visual indicators that external users are part of the team and any guest accounts are clearly labeled with "(Guest)" after their names.

 Read more about guest access at docs.microsoft.com/en-us/Micro-softTeams/guest-access.

External Access

The second type of access is referred to as *external access*, which if you have come from a Skype for Business background is similar to what we would have called *federation*. It is where you can find, chat, call, and invite to meetings users from another company.

The users need to have a different email domain from the one used in your own tenant; otherwise, Teams will not see them as being from a separate organization. External access is controlled at the domain level; it is not possible to grant access to named users.

External access users are not able to partake in any team's functionality. (To clarify, that's a small *t* on the teams, so there are no collaboration features available to them inside a team! But they can use Teams functionality such as joining a Teams meeting). Named users can be invited into a team; however, this would be through the guest access process described earlier.

It is possible to use external access to invite users into a Teams meeting that you have created; however, both organizations must have mutual external access enabled. Otherwise, the remote user will be blocked by their policy from joining the meeting. If you do run into this, the other party should still be able to join your meeting as an unauthenticated guest user.

This also means you can invite external users into your Teams meetings without specifically enabling external access, as the mechanism for guests in meetings is handled separately.

 Read more about external access at docs.microsoft.com/en-us/micro-softteams/manage-external-access.

Summary of External User Capabilities

Table 3.5 shows the functionality your users will have when communicating with either an external or guest user.

TABLE 3.5   Native User Functionality

Native User Functionality	External Access User	Guest User
Chat with someone in another org	Yes	Yes
Call someone in another org	Yes	Yes
See presence from another org	Yes	Yes
Search for people in another org	Yes	No
Share files	No	Yes
See out of office notifications	No	Yes
Block someone	No	Yes
Use @mentions	Yes	Yes

docs.microsoft.com/en-us/microsoftteams/communicate-with-users-from-
other-organizations

Table 3.6 shows the functionality available to people from another organization.

TABLE 3.6   External Access Capabilities by Access Type

External User Functionality	External Access User	Guest User
Access Teams resources	No	Yes
Be added to a group chat	No	Yes
Be invited to a meeting	Yes	Yes
Make private calls	Yes	Yes
View the phone number for dial-in meeting participants	No	Yes
Use IP video	Yes	Yes
Use screen sharing	Yes	Yes

TABLE 3.6   External Access Capabilities by Access Type

External User Functionality	External Access User	Guest User
Use meet now	No	Yes
Edit sent messages	Yes	Yes
Delete sent messages	Yes	Yes
Use Giphy in conversation	Yes	Yes
Use memes in conversation	Yes	Yes
Use stickers in conversation	Yes	Yes
Presence is displayed	Yes	Yes
Use @mentions	Yes	Yes

`docs.microsoft.com/en-us/microsoftteams/communicate-with-users-from-other-organizations`

Managing External Access

Now we know the differences between guest and external access, let's look at how to control them. We will start with external access, as it is native Teams functionality and does not rely on any other components, so it is simpler to configure.

It operates in three basic modes:

Open federation: This is the default setting and allows external users to be discovered dynamically based on their email addresses (using specific DNS records associated with the domain). When a user has been discovered, you can IM, chat, and call the user.

Allow list: This lets you create a list of specific domains that are allowed for external access. If you put any domain name in here, it will block access to all other domains!

Block list: This creates a list of domains that your users are not able to interact with; all other domains will remain accessible.

You can configure these settings from the TAC under Org-Wide Settings ≻ External Access. Here you will see two toggle switches, one to allow external access for Skype for Business (federation) and Teams users, the other to allow communications with Skype (consumer) accounts. Simply adjust the toggles to enable or disable access.

Underneath the toggle boxes is a list of domains that have been allowed or blocked. If the box is empty, you are currently configured for open federation. To add a new domain, click the Add Domain button, enter the domain name suffix, for example, `learnteams.info`, and then select if you want to allow or deny that domain.

While you can mix both blocked and allowed domains in the table, there is probably little point. Remember that as soon as you add an explicit domain to the Allow list, you effectively block all other domains from external access, so be careful when you add an allowed domain that this is actually what you want to achieve.

Managing Access for Guest Users

Management of guest users is controlled in four different locations, so make sure when you are troubleshooting or planning for guest access that you understand how each one is responsible for the overall experience:

Azure AD: Azure AD Business-to-Business (B2B) is the platform behind the scenes that controls authentication of guest users.

M365 Groups: This controls membership for guest users, both for the group itself and for Teams.

Teams: This controls the capabilities inside Teams for a guest user account.

SharePoint Online and OneDrive for Business: This controls the guest experience for file sharing and access.

For example, if you wanted to allow guest access inside Teams but guest users were turned off in Azure AD, no guest user accounts could be created. Or perhaps you want to disable guest access just inside Teams but not prevent sharing links from SharePoint directly—you could just turn off guest access at the Teams level only. Figure 3.39 shows how some of the permissions are required to line up to grant access.

FIGURE 3.39   Showing the multiple stages required to allow guest access

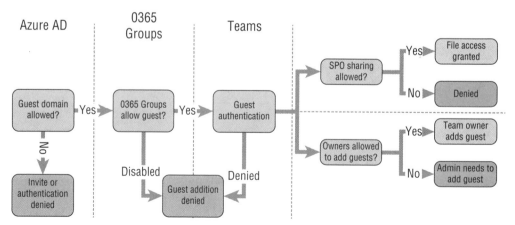

External Collaboration in Azure AD

To be able to create objects in your Azure AD tenant, external collaboration must be configured in Azure AD. Any restrictive settings here would limit your ability to have guest users inside Teams (and other O365 applications).

To view/change your Azure AD settings, first log into the Azure portal (`aad.portal .azure.com`) and then from the left menu select Azure Active Directory ➢ Users ➢ User Settings. Partway down the page should be a Manage External Collaboration Settings option (see Figure 3.40).

FIGURE 3.40 User settings in the Azure AD portal

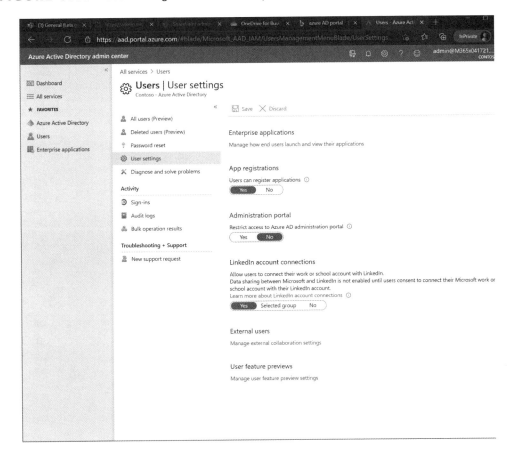

From here you can see the settings applied to your tenant (see Figure 3.41).

FIGURE 3.41   External collaboration settings in the Azure AD portal

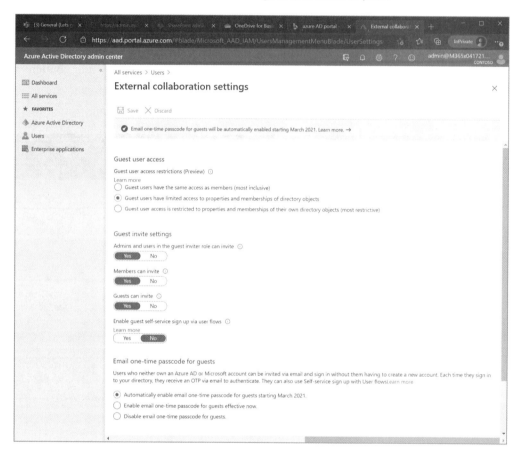

The following are the main settings to look at:

Guest user access

> **Same as member users:** Guests can see the same Azure AD objects as normal users.
>
> **Limited access (default):** Guests can see membership of all nonhidden groups.
>
> **Restricted access:** Guests cannot see membership of any groups.

Guest invite settings

> **Admins and users can invite:** Users with the special role of "guest invite" can initiate an invitation request.
>
> **Members can invite:** Normal user accounts can initiate the invitation.
>
> **Guests can invite:** Guest accounts can initiate the invitation.
>
> **Enable one-time passcode for guests:** This lets guests who do not have their own Azure AD tenant (or supported third-party authentication service) perform authentication by confirming receipt of a code via email. This means in theory you can validate any external party with an email address for guest access.
>
> **Collaboration restrictions (see Figure 3.42)**
>
> **Allow invitations to any domain:** Any domain can be used to invite a guest user.
>
> **Deny invitations to specific domains:** You can block specific domains from receiving guest invitations.
>
> **Allow invitations only to specified domains:** Create a list of allowed domains who can become guest accounts.

FIGURE 3.42   Guest access domain controls

Collaboration restrictions

○ Allow invitations to be sent to any domain (most inclusive)
● Deny invitations to the specified domains
○ Allow invitations only to the specified domains (most restrictive)

🗑 Delete

☐ **Target domains**

example.com or *.example.com or example.*

The last setting for collaboration restrictions is important, as this is how you can control if any domain can be invited to your tenant or if you want to use allow/blocklists, which contain specific domain names that are allowed or denied from accessing your tenant. To configure these in the browser, simply enter the domains and save the setting (see Figure 3.42).

Read more about how blocking external access works at docs.microsoft.com/en-us/azure/active-directory/external-identities/allow-deny-list.

Control Azure AD Guest Access Allow/Blocklists via PowerShell

Alternatively, you may want to use PowerShell to automate the management of the domain allow/blocklist. Unfortunately for us the process is a little convoluted in PowerShell, but once you have done it and saved the code, it should be simple to reproduce.

You may need to make sure you have the AzureAD PowerShell module installed before running these commands, and you will have to build up your command using a few components because of the way the cmdlets operate.

First create some JSON-style code that you will use to build the domain you want to deny:

```
$policyValue =
@("{`"B2BManagementPolicy`":{`"InvitationsAllowedAndBlockedDomainsPolicy`":{`"A
llowedDomains`": [],`"BlockedDomains`": [`"learnteams.info`"]}}}")
```

Then make the new policy with the settings that you want:

```
New-AzureADPolicy -Definition $policyValue -DisplayName B2BManagementPolicy -
Type B2BManagementPolicy -IsOrganizationDefault $true
```

Before you can apply it, you need to find the policy ID:

```
$currentpolicy = Get-AzureADPolicy -All $true | ?{$_.Type -eq
'B2BManagementPolicy'} | select -First 1
```

Lastly, you can then set the policy that you just created and got the identity for:

```
Set-AzureADPolicy -Definition $policyValue -Id $currentpolicy.Id
```

Guest Access Settings in Teams

Having made sure that you have guest access allowed inside Azure AD, you can take a look at what controls and restrictions are being applied at the Teams layer.

To do this, you need to open the TAC and check under Org-Wide Settings ➤ Guest Access. Here you can control settings to do with Teams-specific features at a tenant level (see Figure 3.43).

The main settings in here are as follows (they are similar to the type of settings we covered earlier for "normal" users):

Allow guest access in Teams: Does what it says; can be either on or off.

Make private calls: Allow peer-peer calls.

Allow IP video: Allow video in calls and meetings.

Screen sharing mode: Permit screen sharing in a meeting and either allow full screen or allow only application-based sharing.

Allow Meet Now: Allow the creation of ad hoc meetings.

Edit sent messages: Allow editing of sent messages.

FIGURE 3.43 Org-wide guest features in Teams

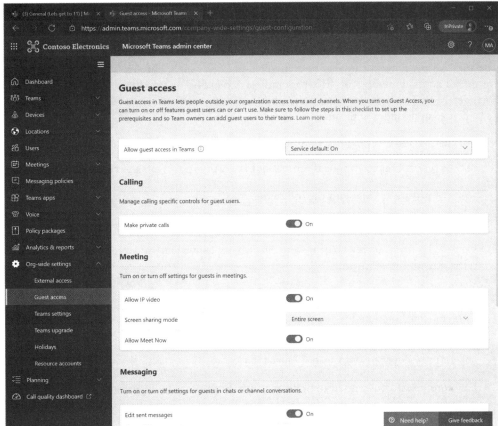

Delete sent messages: Guests can delete messages after they have been sent.

Chat: Enable chat functionality for guests.

Use Giphys: Allow the use of animated gifs from the Giphy service.

Giphy content rating: Select what level of filtering is applied when searching Giphy for content to include.

Use memes: Allow memes to be added to conversations.

Use stickers: Allow the use of stickers in conversations.

Allow immersive reader: Allow the immersive reader application to open messages to improve readability.

Control Guest Access via PowerShell

The guest access settings can also be controlled in PowerShell, but annoyingly the settings are spread across a number of different cmdlets depending on what you want to achieve. Fortunately, they all follow our cmdlet family rules so you can review the configuration with `get-` before updating it with `set-`.

Toggle the global setting in Teams to allow guest access using the following:

```
Set-CsTeamsClientConfiguration -Identity Global -AllowGuestUser $true
```

Control private calling with the following:

```
Get-CsTeamsGuestCallingConfiguration
```

Control IP video, screen sharing, and Meet Now as well as transcriptions and caption settings with the following:

```
Get-CsTeamsGuestMeetingConfiguration
```

Control chat functionality (editing, deleting, stickers, memes, Giphys) with the following:

```
Get-CsTeamsGuestMessagingConfiguration
```

For example, if you wanted to prevent guests from using video in calls and only be allowed to share an application and disable the use of Giphy, stickers, and memes, you could run the following (see Figure 3.44):

```
Set-CsTeamsGuestMeetingConfiguration -Identity Global -AllowIPVideo $false -ScreenSharingMode SingleApplication
Set-CsTeamsGuestMessagingConfiguration -Identity Global -AllowGiphy $false -AllowMemes $false -AllowStickers $false
```

FIGURE 3.44   Configuring guest settings in PowerShell

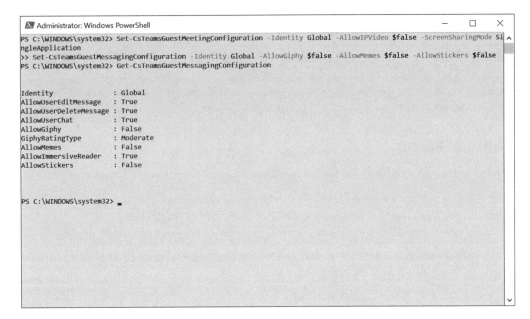

```
Administrator: Windows PowerShell                                    —  □  ×
PS C:\WINDOWS\system32> Set-CsTeamsGuestMeetingConfiguration -Identity Global -AllowIPVideo $false -ScreenSharingMode Si
ngleApplication
>> Set-CsTeamsGuestMessagingConfiguration -Identity Global -AllowGiphy $false -AllowMemes $false -AllowStickers $false
PS C:\WINDOWS\system32> Get-CsTeamsGuestMessagingConfiguration


Identity               : Global
AllowUserEditMessage   : True
AllowUserDeleteMessage : True
AllowUserChat          : True
AllowGiphy             : False
GiphyRatingType        : Moderate
AllowMemes             : False
AllowImmersiveReader   : True
AllowStickers          : False


PS C:\WINDOWS\system32> _
```

Reviewing Guest Access

As there are so many settings relating to guest access, it is good practice to make sure you regularly perform reviews of guest activity to check where guests have been added to Teams. The act of adding a guest user into a team, as it is actually adding a user to the underlying M365 group, is something that is logged under the Azure AD group administration item called Added Member To Group.

You can also get more information about what guests are invited to your organization through the Azure AD Access Review feature and the Analytics and Reporting part of the TAC. These will be covered in more detail in Chapter 6, "Review usage and Maintain Quality".

Meetings with Teams

Lastly in this chapter we are going to look at the meeting workload and how you can deploy and optimize the experience for your end users. The meeting experience in Teams is so good. If you remember from Chapter 2, "Getting Teams Up and Running," where we discussed the different migration modes when coming from Skype for Business, you know there is a mode specifically dedicated to moving the meeting workload away from Skype for Business and into Teams (Skype for Business with Teams Collaboration and Meetings), as many organizations prefer the Teams experience here.

When we are talking about meetings inside Teams, it would be normal to assume we mean just the standard online meetings where you generate an invite, distribute the link, and people join from their devices, but actually in Teams there are two categories of meetings.

Those in the first category are as described earlier, Teams Meetings, and they are the standard type of meeting that you might think of. The meetings in the second category are *Teams live events*. These are a special kind of meeting designed for large broadcast-style events where you want to share content to a significant number of people in one go (like an "all-hands" company update or perhaps a product announcement).

Teams Meetings

There are three different kinds of normal meetings that you can create in Teams:

Meet Now (ad hoc): Creates a meeting on the spot; you can then invite people to the meeting or share the join link with whomever you want to participate.

Channel meeting: Created by scheduling a meeting in a team channel; all members of the channel are automatically invited and will see any meeting chat and uploaded files and will be able to view the recording if it is activated.

Private meeting: A meeting created outside of a channel, for example, from the Outlook calendar.

While you may see references to these types of meetings under the hood, they are all essentially the same thing, a meeting space created on the Teams platform where users can join with voice and video, chat, and share files and their screens.

In theory, anyone can join a Teams meeting even if they do not have a Teams client installed or an account in your organization. All they have to do is click the Join URL link that is generated when the meeting is created (or scheduled). If they do not have Teams installed, they can join the meeting using a modern web browser. The Teams web-based meeting experience is pretty solid.

You may be able to join the meeting even if you do not have access to a computer. There is a special type of license that can be purchased and allocated to your users that creates dial-in coordinates for each meeting that the user creates. Using these details, you can then join a meeting from any normal PSTN phone by dialing a conference access number and entering the meeting information when prompted. This license is called the Audio Conferencing license.

Audio Conferencing

The Audio Conferencing license is included in the standard E5 licensing bundle or can be purchased and allocated separately to your users. When this license is assigned, any meeting that the user creates will have dial-in detail associated with it. You do not have to allocate an Audio Conferencing license to every user in the organization, but remember that only users with the license will be able to create meetings with dial-in details.

By default you will have access to a shared set of toll numbers (standard numbers) in approximately 70 countries. It is possible to add more numbers to your tenant, including toll-free numbers, if you want coverage in specific countries or cities. By default these numbers are available only from Microsoft, but you can transfer, or port, your own numbers to Microsoft so that you can use them with your tenant.

When adding toll-free (freephone) numbers to your tenant, you do need to have another license type called Communications credits enabled for your tenant. Communications credits act like a pot of money that billable PSTN functionality can draw from to cover the cost. This covers a few scenarios such as the following:

- Calls to toll-free numbers associated with the tenant. (These could be used for dial-in meetings, call queues, or auto attendants.)
- A user with a calling plan license, making calls outside of their bundle. (These could be international calls or minutes that exceed the included volume.)

Dial-in numbers are managed through a conference bridge, the conference bridge can be configured with more than one number, and you can specify a default one.

You can find Microsoft's explanation for audio conferencing at docs .microsoft.com/en-US/microsoftteams/audio-conferencing-in-office-365.

Conference Bridge Settings

The following settings are available to configure for a conference bridge:

Default number: This number will be displayed by default inside a meeting invite when created. There will also be a Find A Local Number link where all the numbers associated with the bridge (and their language) can be found (see Figure 3.45)

Meeting entry and exit notifications: This will play a notification when users join or leave the meeting.

Entry/exit announcement type: If notifications are configured, they can be set to either play just a tone or play the name or number of who has joined. If set to names or phone numbers, you can prompt the person to record their own name instead of just having the system read it out loud. Be careful if you enable entry notifications as they can become frustrating to users in the meeting, especially if you have large meetings!

Pin length: Specify the length of PIN that will be used. A PIN is needed only if a meeting has not been started by a user in the Teams client. If everyone has joined by dialing in, then the meeting organizer can start the meeting by entering their allocated PIN.

Automatically send emails to users when their dial-in settings change: The system will email users when dial-in settings are updated.

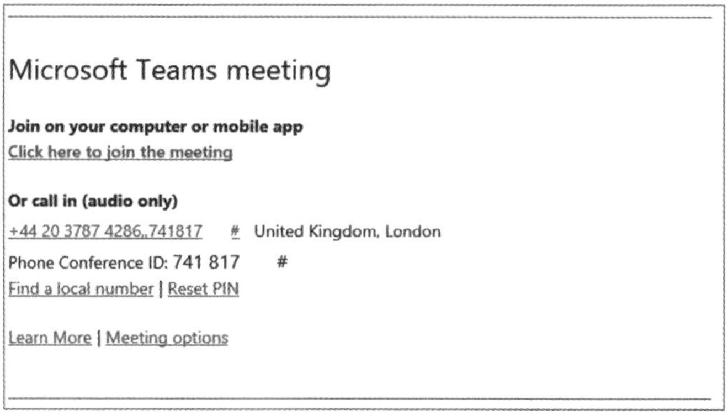

FIGURE 3.45   Default number shown in an invitation

Microsoft Teams meeting

Join on your computer or mobile app
Click here to join the meeting

Or call in (audio only)
+44 20 3787 4286,,741817   #   United Kingdom, London
Phone Conference ID: 741 817   #
Find a local number | Reset PIN

Learn More | Meeting options

Read more about PIN settings here: docs.microsoft.com/en-US/
microsoftteams/set-the-pin-length-for-audio-conferencing-
meetings-in-teams.

Managing Conference Bridge via the TAC

You can view the current conference bridge settings in the TAC; from here you can add new numbers to your tenant, select a global default dial-in number that is used in meeting invites, and modify the global settings for the bridge.

To find your conference bridge settings, first open the TAC and then look for Meetings ➤ Conference Bridges from the left menu (see Figure 3.46).

Here you can then make changes to the bridge as required:

Add new numbers: Select Add and pick either toll or toll-free numbers to associate with the conference bridge. For any numbers to display here, you need to have first added them to your tenant ready for selection (and they must not already be allocated to another PSTN function). This will be covered in more detail in Chapter 5, "Adding Telephony".

FIGURE 3.46   Conference bridge numbers

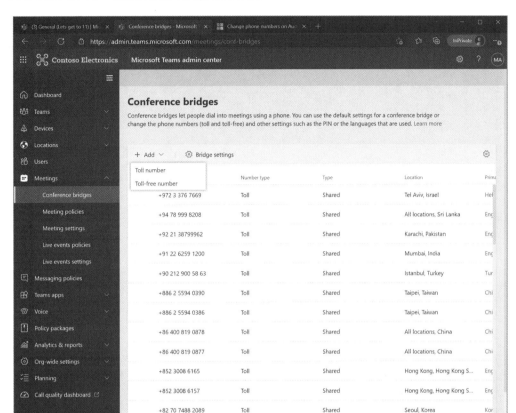

Set as default: Select a number in the table and then choose the Set As Default option that appears in the table header.

Bridge settings: This changes settings relating to the conference bridge as we just covered (see Figure 3.47).

FIGURE 3.47 Conference bridge settings

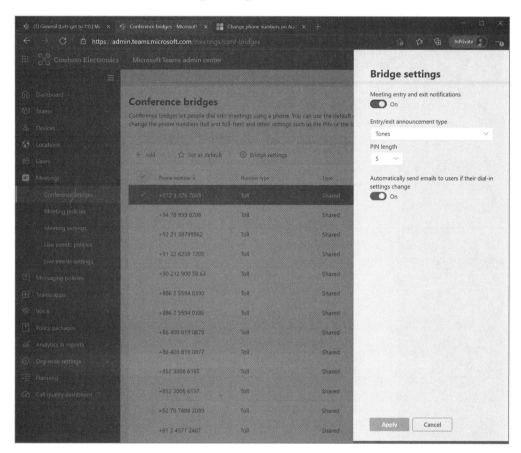

Managing Audio Conferencing Settings per User via the TAC

As well as applying global settings at a conference-bridge level (think default), you can specify settings at a per-user level. This is managed inside the TAC by finding the user you want to change and then editing the section for audio conferencing:

1. Open the TAC and select Users from the left menu.

2. Search for the user you want to work with and click their name.

3. Scroll down the account page for the user (for some reason at the time of writing a large amount of white space is shown on the page!) until you find the Audio Conferencing section (see Figure 3.48).

FIGURE 3.48   User audio conferencing settings

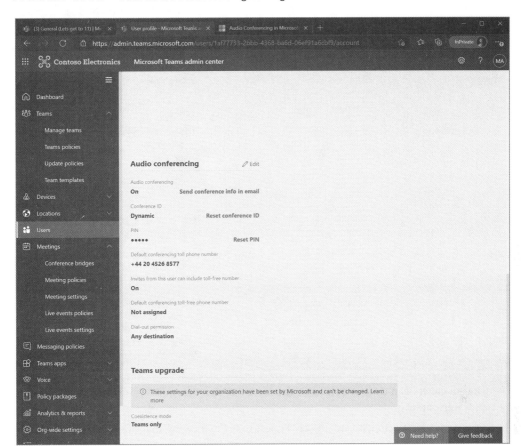

4. To change the settings for this user, click Edit next to the title, and a pop-out menu will appear on the right side (see Figure 3.49).

    Audio Conferencing: Enable or disable audio conferencing entirely (without having to remove the associated license).

    Toll number: Specify the default number shown when the user creates a Teams meeting invite.

    Include toll-free numbers in meeting requests: Should any toll-free numbers that you have manually associated with the tenant be included in invites? (Remember, you need to have a communications credits license associated with your tenant to absorb any call charges.)

    Toll-free number: If you have any toll-free numbers, which one should be included as default?

FIGURE 3.49 Audio conferencing settings options

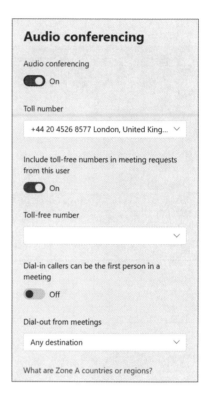

Dial-in callers can be first person in the meeting: Can the meeting start when a dial-in user joins first?

Dial-out from meetings: Can a user request that the meeting dial out to them on a number? This may have its own associated costs depending on the configuration of the user for PSTN calling, so there are further options available:

> Any destination
>
> In same region as organizer
>
> Zone A countries (countries that do not have large costs associated with them)
>
> Don't Allow (disabled)

For the exam, don't get too caught up on things like dial-out capabilities and costs or the detail behind how communications credits work, as you will not be tested to this level of detail. Instead, you should just know that such functionality exists and how you can enable it.

Read more about dial-out charges at `docs.microsoft.com/en-US/microsoftteams/complimentary-dial-out-period`.

Meeting Settings

Teams (confusingly) splits some meeting configuration options between meeting settings and meeting policies. In this section, we will look at what is classed as a meeting setting. These are configuration items that apply at a global level and cannot be customized on a per-user basis.

You can find these settings in the TAC under the Meetings ➤ Meeting Settings menu on the left side (see Figure 3.50).

FIGURE 3.50 Meeting settings list

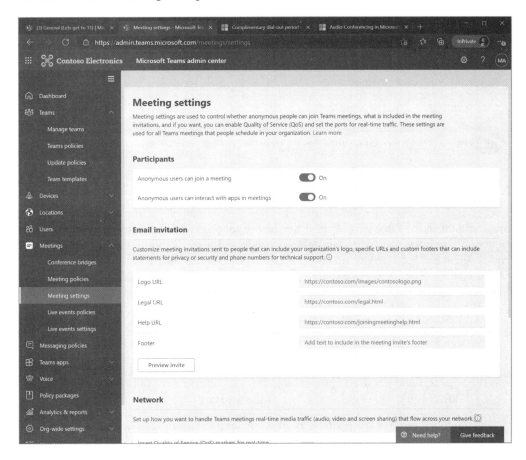

These settings are broken into three main categories:

Participants: This controls how anonymous users can interact with one of your user's meetings.

Email invitation: This lets you customize portions of the invitation that is generated when a user creates a meeting invitation. You can specify images, help links, and text to include.

Network: We used this section in Chapter 2 to help define whether QoS was deployed for our network.

Here we have yet another term for an external user in a Teams context with "anonymous." This isn't a guest user who has authenticated in some way (via Azure AD) but rather is a user who is not known and where no authentication is attempted.

Read more about meeting settings in Teams: `docs.microsoft.com/en-us/microsoftteams/meeting-settings-in-teams`.

Meeting Policies

The remaining settings regarding Teams meetings are configured via meeting policies. These operate in much the same way as the other Teams policies that we encountered earlier in the chapter. There is a global (org-wide default) policy, and then custom policies can be created and assigned either directly to users or via group policy assignment.

The settings inside a meeting policy can be applied in one of three ways:

Per user: This only affects a user who is participating in a meeting, for example the Allow Meeting Now In Channels setting.

Per organizer: This affects the user who created the meeting. For example, the Automatically Admit People setting only applies to the user who created the meeting invitation.

Per organizer and per user: Some settings are a combination of both, such as Allow Cloud Recording where either the user or the organizer can permit recording to start.

The following settings are available to be configured via meeting policies:

General

Allow Meet Now In Channels (per user): Controls who can create an unscheduled meeting inside a channel.

Allow the Outlook add-in (per user): Allows meetings to be scheduled via the Teams add-on that is installed into Outlook.

Allow channel meeting scheduling (per user): Lets users create scheduled meetings inside a channel.

Allow scheduling private meetings (per user): Lets users create meetings outside of a channel.

Audio and Video

Allow transcription (combination): If the user's language is set to English, Teams can attempt to automatically transcribe the meeting recording using Microsoft's language processing technology.

Allow cloud recording (per user): This controls if a user is allowed to start recording a meeting. Only authenticated users from the main tenant can start recording.

Mode for IP audio (per user): This controls if computer audio is allowed in a meeting.

Mode for IP video (per user): This controls if video can be used during a meeting (inbound and outbound) (see Table 3.7).

Allow IP video (combination): This is used to disable outbound video (see Table 3.7).

Media bit rate (Kbs) (per user): This controls the maximum bit rate that is used across the modalities in the call (voice, video, and screenshare). The minimum value is 30 Kbps. This can be used as a rudimentary way to help limit the bandwidth used by Teams, but remember that the value is only the maximum that the client can use. If it detects a low-bandwidth connection, it will scale things back automatically.

Content Sharing

Screen sharing mode (combination): This controls what type of screen sharing is allowed, if at all.

Allow a participant to give or request control (per user): This controls if an internal user can take control or give access to the screen when being shared.

Allow an external participant to give or request control (per user): This controls if an external user can take control or give access to the screen when being shared.

Allow PowerPoint sharing (per user): This controls if PowerPoint slides can be shared into a meeting.

Allow whiteboard (per user): This controls if the whiteboard can be accessed.

Allow shared notes (per user): This controls if shared notes can be created during the meeting (supported for sub–100–user meetings).

Participants & Guests

Let anonymous people start a meeting (per organizer): This requires an authenticated user to start the meeting. With this setting, disabled users not from your company wait in the lobby.

Automatically admit people (per organizer): This controls who can bypass the lobby when the meeting is open.

> **Everyone:** There is no lobby for most users.

> **Everyone in your organization and federated orgs:** Known and trusted users can bypass the lobby.

> **Everyone in your organization:** Authenticated users (including guests) can bypass the lobby.

> **Organizer only:** Everyone other than the organizer will wait in the lobby.

Allow dial-in users to bypass the lobby (per organizer): This controls if dial-in users can bypass the lobby.

Enable live captions (per user): This controls if Teams will attempt to present live captions using language transcription services during the meeting.

Allow chat in meetings (per user): This controls if the meeting chat is accessible to users in the meeting.

> Learn about meeting policies here: docs.microsoft.com/en-US/micro-softteams/meeting-policies-in-teams.
>
> Find out more about live captions here: support.microsoft.com/en-gb/office/use-live-captions-in-a-teams-meeting.

TABLE 3.7   IP Video Policy Overlap

Allow IP Video Setting	Mode for IP Video Setting	Meeting Result
Organizer: On Participant: On	Participant: Disabled	The Mode For IP Video setting takes precedence. The user who is assigned this policy can't turn on or view videos shared by others.
Organizer: On Participant: On	Participant: Outgoing and incoming video enabled	The user who is assigned this policy can turn on or view videos shared by others.
Organizer: On Participant: Off	Participant: Outgoing and incoming video enabled	The Allow IP Video setting takes precedence. Users can only see incoming video and not send outgoing video.
Organizer: On Participant: Off	Participant: Disabled	The Mode For IP Video setting takes precedence. The users will not see any video.
Organizer: Off		The Allow IP video setting takes precedence because it is turned off for the organizer, so video is disabled entirely for the meeting.

Work with Meeting Policies in the TAC

Teams includes a number of default policies that you can assign to your users or you are able to create your own. You can view the policies configured for your organization by logging into the TAC and selecting Meetings ➤ Meeting Policies on the left menu; you should be able to see all the policies you have available (see Figure 3.51).

FIGURE 3.51   Meeting policies list

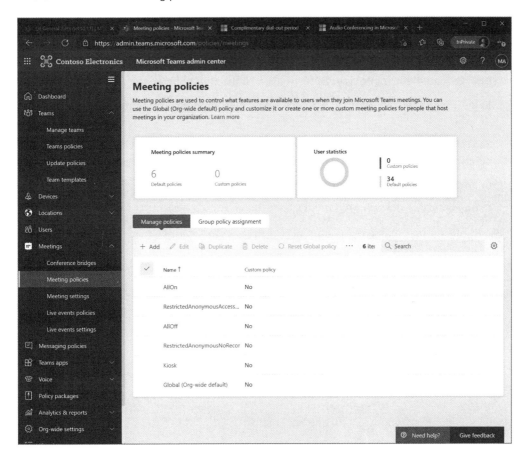

To edit a policy (only if it is the global policy or a custom policy), highlight it and select Edit. You will then see a screen with the options available outlined earlier.

Assign from the meeting policy screen: In the messaging policy screen in the TAC, select the policy you want to apply to a user, and then choose Manage Users from the menu. This will open a pop-out menu on the right of the page where you can enter a username to search the company directory. Select your user and click Apply.

Apply directly to a user: Open TAC and from the left menu select Users. Search for and click the user you want to target. This will open the user information page where you can select Policies to view all the different types of policies applied to this user. Select Edit next to the assigned policy title, and under Meeting Policy pick the policy you want to apply from the drop-down list.

Work with Meeting Policies in PowerShell

I hope with PowerShell policy management you have started to notice the patterns of how this works.

To work with meeting policies via PowerShell, the cmdlet family we want is the CsTeamsMeetingPolicy family, made up of the following:

Get-CsTeamsMeetingPolicy: Returns a list of meeting policies

New-CsTeamsMeetingPolicy: Creates a new meeting policy using the options shown in Table 3.8

Set-CsTeamsMeetingPolicy: Updates an existing meeting policy with a new name or description

Grant-CsTeamsMeetingPolicy: Assigns a policy to the specified user

Remove-CsTeamsMeetingPolicy: Deletes the meeting policy

See Table 3.8 for a list of the main PowerShell cmdlet options.

TABLE 3.8 New- and Set- CsTeamsMeetingPolicy Cmdlet Main Options

Parameter	Options
AllowChannelMeeting-Scheduling	$true/$false
AllowMeetNow	$true/$false
AllowPrivateMeetNow	$true/$false
MeetingChatEnabledType	Disabled, Enabled
LiveCaptionsEnabledType	Disabled, DisabledUserOverride
AllowIPVideo	$true/$false
IPAudioMode	EnabledOutgoingIncoming/Disabled
IPVideoMode	EnabledOutgoingIncoming/Disabled
AllowAnonymousUsersTo-DialOut	$true/$false

TABLE 3.8   New- and Set- `CsTeamsMeetingPolicy` Cmdlet Main Options

Parameter	Options
AllowAnonymousUsersToStart-Meeting	$true/$false
AllowPrivateMeetingScheduling	$true/$false
AutoAdmittedUsers	EveryoneInCompany, Everyone, EveryoneInSameAndFederatedCompany, OrganizerOnly
AllowCloudRecording	$true/$false
AllowOutlookAddIn	$true/$false
AllowPowerPointSharing	$true/$false
AllowParticipantGiveRequest-Control	$true/$false
AllowExternalParticipantGiveRe-questControl	$true/$false
AllowSharedNotes	$true/$false
AllowWhiteboard	$true/$false
AllowTranscription	$true/$false
MediaBitRateKb	Number
ScreenSharingMode	SingleApplication, EntireScreen
AllowPSTNUsersToBypass-Lobby	$true/$false
DesignatedPresenterRoleMode	EveryoneInCompany, Everyone, EveroneInSameAndFederatedCompany, OrganizerOnly
AllowIPAudio	$true/$false
AllowOrganizersToOverrideLob-bySettings	$true/$false

docs.microsoft.com/en-us/powershell/module/skype/set-csteamsmeetingpolicy

Teams Live Events

Live events are a special kind of meeting geared toward running large meetings at scale where you don't want equal participation between all attendees. Live events can host up to 10,000 attendees and can last up to four hours in length. At any one time in a tenant there can be 15 events running at one time. (If you require more attendee capacity, you can request dedicated support from the Microsoft live-event assistance program that can help schedule live events for up to 100,000 people! Sign up at `resources.techcommunity.microsoft.com/live-events/assistance/`.)

Live events use yet another aspect of the O365 offering called Microsoft Stream. Stream is used for processing and presenting video content in an efficient way (a bit like a corporate YouTube).

Live events require a bit of special planning and can be especially heavy on network bandwidth if you are not careful. For that reason, there are a number of configuration settings you might want to set up to control who can create live events for your organization.

There are also a number of specialized roles used during a live event:

Organizer: This role can control all aspects of a live event including creating it, setting attendee permissions, configuring settings such as Q&A, and managing reports after the event has completed.

Producer: A user is given access to help manage the live event stream. They can start and stop the stream, share content into the stream, and select what layout is being displayed.

Presenter: This role can share audio, video, and a screen (desktop or specific window) into the live event.

Attendee: This is a user who is simply participating in the live event, either through the Teams client or through a browser.

To be able to create a live event, the following conditions must be true of the user and the client:

- The user must be a native tenant user (have an authenticated account).
- The user must be allocated an E1, E3, or E5 license (or the educational equivalents: A3, A5).
- The user must be allowed to create live events by policy in Teams.
- The user must be allowed to create live events in Microsoft Stream (if using external broadcasting hardware).
- Private meetings, screen sharing, and IP video must be allowed in the meeting policies.
- The user must have a coexistence mode that allows scheduling Teams meetings.

Live events either can be produced through Teams itself or can be produced using external hardware and software encoders directly inside Stream. This can have an impact on the behavior of a live event as well as the licenses required to participate.

When creating live events, you can specify that they are either public or private. When a live event is set to private, all attendees must log in to be able to access the meeting using their company credentials. If the event has been produced in Teams, each attendee must have a Teams license, or if it was produced directly inside Stream, they need to have a Stream license.

For more information about prepping for live events, see `docs.microsoft.com/en-us/MicrosoftTeams/teams-live-events/plan-for-teams-live-events`.

To control live events, in the same way that we had for normal Teams meetings, there are both settings and policies, so let's dig in.

Live Event Settings

There are only two things we can configure in settings for live meetings. The first is a customized support URL if someone needs to access help during a live meeting. The second is the ability to specify if any third-party video CDN providers are deployed in your network (eCDN stands for enterprise content delivery network).

eCDNs are used to help reduce the amount of bandwidth required for a large broadcast-style meeting. Without one of these systems each attendee for the meeting is downloading their own copy of the meeting streams (video, audio, screen share) even though a lot of those users are probably all in the same physical location (office building). An eCDN acts as a local cache for this data so that it is downloaded once and then distributed to all the local clients that are participating in the feed.

If you have a supported eCDN solution deployed in your organization, you can configure live events to take advantage of it. Configuration is pretty straightforward with just a few details of your provider being added into the TAC. Only one eCDN provider is supported for use at any one time, and the current list of products is as follows:

- Hive
- Kollective
- Riverbed

Manage Event Settings in the TAC

To view or update your live event settings, open the TAC and then select Meetings ➤ Live Events Settings from the left menu. You should see a screen with the two options available to configure (see Figure 3.52).

If configuring an eCDN, you can select your vendor from the drop-down box and then enter the license key provided to you as well as an API template URL and an SDN API template URL (again, this will be provided to you by the eCDN vendor).

FIGURE 3.52   Live events settings

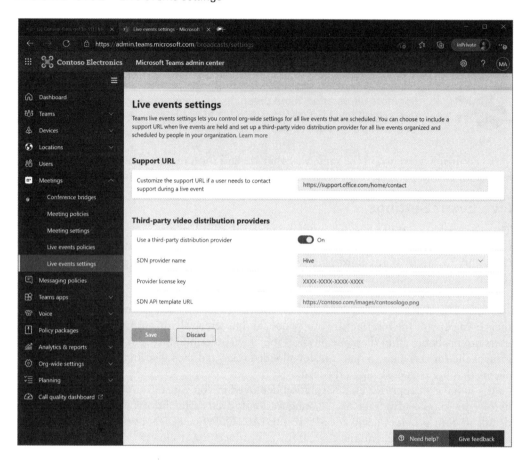

Manage Event Settings in PowerShell

Both of these settings can also be configured in PowerShell with the following cmdlets:

Configure Support URL:

```
Set-CsTeamsMeetingBroadcastConfiguration -SupportURL "{your URL}"
```

Configure eCDN:

```
Set-CsTeamsMeetingBroadcastConfiguration -AllowSdnProviderForBroadcastMeeting
$True -SdnProviderName <provider> -SdnLicenseId <License key provided by
vendor> -SdnApiTemplateUrl "<SDN API URL provided by vendor>"
```

Live Event Policies

Having looked at the global settings, now we can see the policies that control the actual use of live events in the organization. As with the other policy items, the core behavior for the policies themselves should by now be familiar. There is a global default policy, and then we can create custom policies to assign against users, either directly or using Group Policy assignment.

There are four main items that can be controlled through Group Policy:

Allow scheduling: Enable and disable live meetings (they can only be scheduled and not ad hoc).

Allow transcription for attendees: Allow transcriptions to be produced for the meeting.

Who can join scheduled live events?

> **Everyone:** Essentially a public event, no authentication required to view the stream.

> **Everyone in the organization:** Any authenticated user in your tenant.

> **Specific users or groups:** Lets you scope attendees to a specific group if you need.

Who can record an event?

> **Always record:** Automatically record and save the live event.

> **Never record:** Do not record the event.

> **Organizer can record:** The organizer can choose.

Normally I don't advocate limiting features inside Teams as I find that it can inhibit user adoption and uptake; however, as live events are such a specialist function, it can make sense to disable scheduling of live events at a global level and then create two policies that can be assigned to users as required when they want to run events. The first would only allow the creation of company live events, and the second would be for events that need to be open to anonymous users as well.

Live Event Policies in the TAC

You can view the live event policies configured for your organization by logging into the TAC and selecting Meetings ➤ Live Event Policies on the left menu. You should be able to see all the policies you have available.

To edit a policy, highlight it and select Edit. You will then see a screen similar to Figure 3.52 with the options outlined earlier available.

Assign from the meeting policy screen: In the meeting policy screen in the TAC, select the policy you want to apply to a user and then choose Manage Users from the menu. This will open a pop-out menu on the right of the page where you can enter a username to search the company directory. Select your user and click Apply.

Apply directly to a user: Open the TAC, and from the left menu select Users. Search for and click the user you want to target. This will open the user information page where you can select Policies to view all the different types of policies applied to this user. Select Edit next to the assigned policy title, and under Meeting Policy, pick the policy you want to apply from the drop-down list.

Live Event Policies in PowerShell

To work with meeting policies via PowerShell, the cmdlet family you want is the `CsTeams-MeetingBroadcastPolicy` family, made up of the following:

Get-CsTeamsMeetingBroadcastPolicy: Returns a list of channels in a team. This requires the GroupID GUID, so it's probably easier to pipe into from the `Get-Team` cmdlet.

New-CsTeamsMeetingBroadcastPolicy: Creates a new channel with the following parameters: channel name, description, membership type (standard or private), and owner (if the administrator account is not to be the default owner).

Set-CsTeamsMeetingBroadcastPolicy: Updates an existing team channel with a new name or description.

Grant-CsTeamsMeetingBroadcastPolicy: Updates an existing team channel with a new name or description.

Remove-CsTeamsMeetingBroadcastPolicy: Deletes the specified channel.

See Table 3.9 for a list of the main PowerShell cmdlet options.

TABLE 3.9   New- and Set- `CsTeamsMeetingPolicy` Cmdlet Main Options

Parameter	Options
AllowBroadcastScheduling	$true/$false
AllowBroadcastTranscription	$true/$false
BroadcastAttendeeVisibilityMode	Everyone EveryoneInCompany InvitedUsersInCompany EveryoneInCompanyAndExternal InvitedUsersInCompanyAndExternal
BroadcastRecordingMode	AlwaysEnabled AlwaysDisabled UserOverride

docs.microsoft.com/en-us/powershell/module/skype/new-csteamsmeetingbroadcastpolicy

User Experience in a Live Meeting

Now that we have created policies to allow live meetings to be scheduled if you log in to the Teams client as a user who is allowed to create a live meeting, you should have a new option show in the top left of the calendar screen (see Figure 3.53).

FIGURE 3.53 Live event creation, part 1

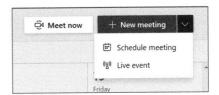

Fill in the details of your event including adding in any users who you want to help manage the event as producers and presenters (see Figure 3.54). On the next screen, select the permissions you want to apply to the event (subject to your policy restrictions being applied) (see Figure 3.55).

FIGURE 3.54 Live event creation, part 2

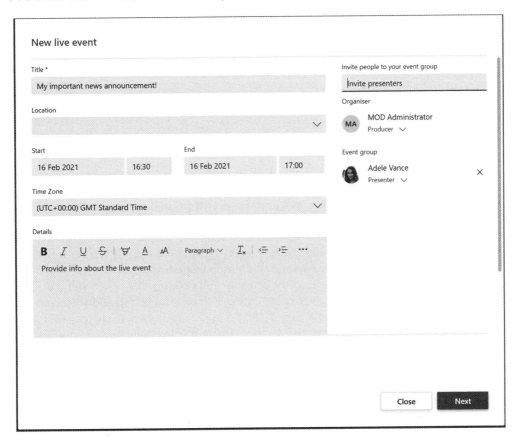

FIGURE 3.55   Live event creation, part 3

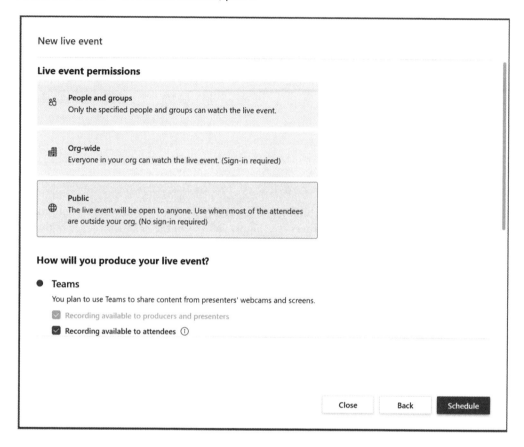

When the event has been created, it will show in your calendar, and you can view the details (see Figure 3.56). You will notice in the display that there are two links available: One is for you to use to join the live event, and the other is for the attendees to use to join the event.

It is important that you do not just treat this invitation as a normal calendar invite, because of the special permissions assigned to presenters and producers. If you want to edit the invite to add new helpers, use the special edit button from this screen.

When it is time to start your event, join it using the full desktop client (web and mobile clients do not support the presenter/producer experience), and you should see Teams kick into a new live event mode (see Figure 3.57). From here you can manage the event by starting and stopping, changing presented content, managing Q&A questions, and so forth.

FIGURE 3.56   Live event invitation

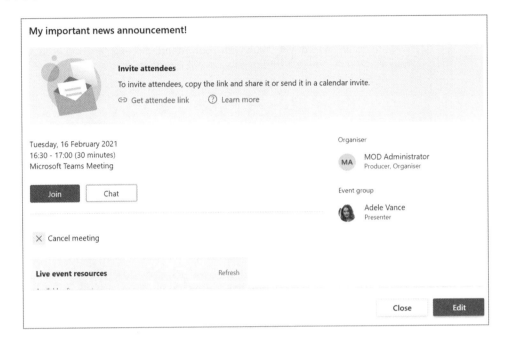

FIGURE 3.57   Live event in progress

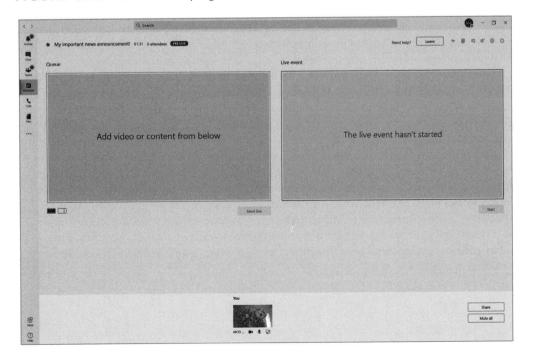

One thing to be careful about when using live events is that, unlike normal Teams meetings, they are time sensitive, so once you have started a meeting, even if it is just for testing, you cannot use it again! This means that if you want to do any sort of a test run with your intended presenters and producers, make sure they create a separate live event for the dry run.

Summary

In this chapter, we covered a mixture of basic functionality from both of Teams' core collaboration and communications workloads. By this point you should now have a good understanding of how you might approach using Teams in your organization and how you can start controlling the features and functionality available for your users. There were a lot of new configuration items added as you got a lot of granular control over the availability of specific features enabled. You should also now have a good idea about how the principles of managing configuration work in Teams (checking global settings, creating policies, and applying them to users), both from the TAC and using PowerShell.

For collaboration we looked at how you can approach creating teams for your users to work with and how there are different controls available to deal with the visibility and automatic membership (org-wide) of a team. We talked about how you can migrate or upgrade existing resources that you might already have deployed in the organization (such as other M365 groups or SharePoint team sites) and turning them into Teams teams.

We then showed how you can further add structure to your team by subdividing them using channels to help group conversations. Channels brought with them their own layer of options and controls, allowing the experience to be further refined. We also covered private channels and how they can offer separation of content from a regular channel.

Teams provides several ways to work with users outside of your organization. We talked about the differences between guest users and external access, how each can be used, and where they apply. With Teams leveraging many other O365 services, we showed what other components also need to be configured to let guest access in Teams operate the way that you require.

Finally, we covered meetings in Teams, both Teams meetings and Teams live events. Teams meetings are the native meeting experience where you can either schedule or run them ad hoc and invite users from inside and outside your organization to participate. We showed how you can make these meetings truly universal by adding dial-in functionality using the Audio Conferencing license of Teams. Where you have special requirements for large-scale meetings, you can support those through Teams live events. We showed how you can allow their use and covered the different permission types (owner versus producer versus presenter).

Exam Essentials

Understand how the structure of teams and channels works inside Teams. Know that teams sit at the heart of the collaboration features of Teams and that these can be further subdivided into channels to help manage different conversations.

Know that each team that is created is based on an M365 group. When you create a team, it is actually based on an M365 group that is created in your tenant. This M365 group controls all permissions and security relating to the team and its resources.

Know that there are three different permission types inside a team. Each team has owners, members, and guests who have different rights to perform actions inside a team. Best practice would be to make sure that each team has more than one owner.

Teams themselves also come in three different varieties. Teams can be created as either public, private, or org-wide. Make sure you remember the differences between public and private teams, as this controls if people are free to find and join teams without explicit permission. Know that you can use org-wide teams for specific business use cases, such as having company-wide news alerts or discussion forums.

Understand how to control the visibility/discoverability of a private team. Remember that just because a team is marked as private, that does not mean it is hidden. Consider this if you have any teams in your organization where the name itself could give away too much information (such as a team called LearnTeams Merger).

Know how to create and manage a team as well as channels in the Teams client, the TAC, and PowerShell. As with most things Teams, you can create and manage teams from both PowerShell and in the TAC. You can also make and manage teams through the client if you are logged in with an account that has owner rights to the team you want to work with. Be familiar with the PowerShell cmdlets for this and other management tasks.

Know how to upgrade existing resources to a team. As teams leverage M365 security groups, where you have preexisting groups created, you can turn them into teams to avoid duplicating existing resources.

Know that you can control chat features using messaging policies. Chat and messaging features are controlled through both messaging policies and some controls at the individual team level. Know what controls you have when using messaging policies and understand how they can be created in the TAC and PowerShell and are applied to either individual users or groups.

Understand how private channels differ from normal channels. If you need further privacy controls for a team, you can create private channels to restrict who can see messages and resources inside a team. Private channels need to be considered carefully as they may not be suitable for all requirements, and they create their own SharePoint site for document storage.

Know how to control settings for a team.   Each team can have specific settings relating to chat and other functionality if you need to lock things down more than you can using messaging policies. This is combined with a user's messaging policy to dictate what an individual is allowed to do in a specific team. An example might be an org-wide team where you do not want to allow Giphys to be used but are happy for them to be used in less formal teams.

Know how to control settings for Teams.   There is another layer of settings for Teams that can be configured only at an org-wide level. These cover the ability to email-enable channels (users still need to specifically enable it for a channel) and the ability to choose what file-sharing platforms can be selected for use inside a team.

Know that file sharing in Teams that uses OneDrive also relies on OneDrive for Business configuration settings.   While you can share files from inside a team, this capability will be overruled by the settings that are configured inside SharePoint or OneDrive. If external sharing is disabled in SharePoint or OneDrive, it will not work inside Teams.

Understand the difference between guest access and external access.   Guest access allows named users who, after authenticating via Microsoft in some way, have access to teams and resources inside a team. They can access a team at any time and work on projects alongside normal users (but usually subject to a stricter set of controls). Guest users create a special type of guest account in your Azure AD that is automatically licensed for use with Teams.

External access is the ability to communicate with users outside of your organization without them having to have any sort of account in your Azure AD. It is like federation from Skype for Business, where you can IM and voice or video call them.

Know that you can control external access using allow/blocklists.   Either you can choose to have open federation, where any domain is discoverable using DNS lookups, or you can add specific domains to be either allowed or blocked. However, as soon as you add any allowed domain, this disables open federation, and you will only be able to communicate with allowed domains. This is a change in behavior from Skype for Business.

Know that guest access relies on other M365 components to operate correctly.   As Teams sits over so many other components of O365, guest access can be configured the way you want to use it in Teams and yet not function correctly. Know that you need to check settings in Azure AD and SharePoint Online or OneDrive for Business.

Know that you can use the Azure AD access review feature to review guests in your tenant.   You should keep track of guest access in your tenant to make sure it is being used as you intend. You can do this using an Azure AD access review. We will be covering this in Chapter 4, "Advanced Teams Functionality and Management."

Understand that there are two basic types of meetings in Teams.   Meetings in teams come in two flavors: Teams meetings and Teams live events. The majority of the time your users will just need to use Teams meetings for their day-to-day interactions, as Teams live events are geared toward hosting large one-to-many broadcast-type meetings where there is not a requirement for lots of interaction.

Understand how you can add dial-in details to a Teams meeting.   Teams meetings can be enhanced with dial-in support provided by Microsoft if you have the Audio Conferencing license (usually included in E5 or can be purchased as an add-on for lower tiers).

Know how to control settings relating to meetings.   As with the rest of Teams, you can create policies to control the behavior and available functionality inside a meeting. Some policy items apply only based on the policy settings of the user who created the meeting, others apply to the users that participate in a meeting, and some are a combination of the two. Be aware of the type of controls available and that you can configure them either in the TAC or via PowerShell. Again, remember the core PowerShell cmdlet families that will be used to view and set these policies.

Know what a Teams live event is and when you might use one.   Even if it is something you would not use frequently, if at all, you should still know when you might choose to use a Teams live event for a meeting and understand the different roles you get inside them for organizer, producer, and presenter (as well as attendee).

Remember that once you have started a live event you cannot reuse it!

Understand why you might choose to use an eCDN partner for a Teams live event.   Teams live events can be bandwidth heavy if you have all your attendees in a shared location. By using an eCDN partner, you can help reduce the load by using a form of local caching to stop each client from downloading the video stream from the internet independently. You do not need to know the low-level detail of how these solutions work; just know that you can add them to your deployment if you need to.

Exercises

EXERCISE 3.1

Creating and Managing a New Team

In this exercise, we will create a new private team using the TAC.

1. Log into the TAC with a Teams administrator account.

2. Expand Teams ➤ Manage Teams.

3. Click Add and fill in the information on the right pop-out pane that appears.

4. Set the privacy for the team to be Private.

5. Hit Apply to create the team.

6. Open the team you just created and view the current membership list.

7. Use the Add button to search for and add a new user.

8. Select the new user, and under the Role column change their membership type to Owner.

EXERCISE 3.2

Change a Private Team to Be Not Discoverable Using PowerShell

Using PowerShell, we will now change the discoverability setting for our test team so that it will not show up in the main listing.

1. Open a PowerShell window and connect to the Teams service.

2. Use the following command to find the new team:

   `Get-Team -DisplayName <Team name>`

3. Confirm that the correct team is returned by the command and look for the ShowIn-TeamsSearchandSuggestions property; by default this should be $true.

4. Next, pipe this team to the Set-Team cmdlet as follows:

   `Get-Team -DisplayName <Team name> | Set-Team -ShowInTeamsSearchandSuggestions $false`

5. Rerun the Get-Team cmdlet from step 2 and confirm that the ShowInTeamsSearch-andSuggestions property is now $false.

EXERCISE 3.3

Convert a Team into an Org-Wide Team, Apply Moderation, and Enable Email Posts

If you are using a test tenant now, we will convert your team into an org-wide team (if you are only able to test using a live environment, this is probably an exercise to skip!) and then apply moderation so that only owners can post to the team. While we are in the channel configuration, we will also generate an email address we can use to post content into the channel.

1. Open the Teams client and browse to the team you created earlier (make sure you are added as a member).

2. Pick the . . . menu next to the team name and click Edit.

3. Under Privacy, change the option to Org-Wide and click Done.

4. Expand the team in the Your Teams list so you can see the General channel for your team. Click the . . . menu next to the General channel.

5. Under the Permissions section, change the moderation settings to Only Owners Can Post Messages.

6. If you have a normal user account that isn't an owner of the team, verify that they cannot post into the General channel.

EXERCISE 3.3

7. Bring up the same . . . menu for the channel, but this time select Get Email Address. There may be a pause here while the email address is generated.

8. Copy the email address.

9. Send an email to the address with some content.

10. Check that the email appears in the channel.

EXERCISE 3.4

Create a Messaging Policy to Disable Giphys and Apply It to a User

Using the TAC, we will create a new messaging policy that disables the use of Giphys in conversation and apply it to our test user.

1. Open the TAC and under the left menu open Messaging Policies.

2. Above the list of policies Click +Add and give your new policy a name (very top of the screen).

3. Browse through the list of options and find Use Giphys In Conversations.

4. Toggle the settings so that it is gray.

5. Save the policy.

6. In the left menu, pick Users and search for your test user account.

7. Click the name of your user and then click the Policies tab.

8. Under Assigned Policies, click Edit, and in the right pop-out menu under Calling Policy select the policy you just created.

9. Hit Apply to save the new policy settings.

10. Give it a bit of time and then sign in to a Teams client with your test user. Start a one-to-one conversation and verify that you do not have the option to insert a Giphy into the chat (the GIF icon will be missing from under the chat box).

EXERCISE 3.5

Block a Domain for External Access

We are going to block a domain from communicating with our users via external access. While you can do this with just a test domain, you won't be able to verify if the configuration has applied properly. To test that, you would need two accounts, or a friend who is allowed to use external access at another company (so you can try to communicate with them).

1. From the Teams client, using the search bar built into the top of the window, type in the name of an external contact. Skip to step 5 if you don't have someone you can IM from another organization.

2. Choose Search Externally from the options when available.

3. Double-click the name of the user, and when the chat window opens, send a message.

4. Confirm that the user gets the message.

5. Open the TAC, and under Org-Wide Settings, open the External Access menu.

6. Click the Add A Domain button and enter the domain name of the user you are testing with externally, for example, LearnTeams.info.

7. Select Blocked and click Done to save.

8. Allow some time to elapse; then repeat steps 1–4 and confirm that the message is blocked.

EXERCISE 3.6

Configure Guest Access and Invite a User

Now that we have checked external access, we will invite an external user directly into one of your teams. Again, you ideally need two accounts from different tenants—someone you can test with from another organization or an email address that you can validate with Teams to allow access.

1. Open the TAC, and under Org-Wide Settings, open the Guest access screen.

2. Make sure Allow Guest Access In Teams is set to either On or Service Default: On.

3. While we are here, let's update some settings like disabling Edit Sent Messages. You may want an auditable trail, for example.

4. Inside Teams open a test team, and from the . . . menu next to its name select Add Member.

5. Start typing the external address of your other test account (or friend, etc.).

EXERCISE 3.6

6.   Select the Add <email> As A Guest option and click Add.

7.   Verify that the remote party gets their email and can access your team.

8.   Check that any settings you configured in the Org-Wide policy are applied, such as disabling editing.

EXERCISE 3.7

Use PowerShell to Modify Guest Access

This time, using PowerShell we can undo the guest access restrictions we implemented in Exercise 3.6.

1.   Open PowerShell and connect to the Teams service.

2.   Run the following PowerShell cmdlets one after another to view the current guest configuration:

```
Get-CsTeamsGuestCallingConfiguration
Get-CsTeamsGuestMeetingConfiguration
Get-CsTeamsGuestMessagingConfiguration
```

3.   You should see the setting for editing that we changed earlier in the Messaging Configuration cmdlet. To update it, we would run the following:

```
Set-CsTeamsGuestMessagingConfiguration -AllowUserEditMessage $true
```

EXERCISE 3.8

Configure Audio Conferencing Settings

We are going to configure the default dial-in number for users in the tenant, as well as making sure that entry and exit notifications are turned off. (You may find you can only complete parts of this exercise if you have an Audio Conferencing license in your tenant.)

1.   Open the TAC, and under Meetings open the Conference Bridges screen.

2.   Select a number from the list in the region where most of your users are present.

3.   Choose Set As Default from the list.

4.   Next to that open Bridge Settings.

(continues)

EXERCISE 3.8 *(continued)*

5. Check your current bridge configuration and then use the toggle at the top to disable Meeting Entry And Exit notifications.

6. Allow some time for the settings to apply and generate a new meeting.

7. Check what dial-in details are included in the meeting, and if you join, verify that no join notifications are played.

EXERCISE 3.9

Create a Meeting Policy to Let Phone Users Start the Meeting

In Exercise 3.8 you might have found that your dial-in user was not able to start the meeting. Let's make a policy that lets dial-in users open a meeting and assign it to a group of users.

1. Open the TAC, and under Meetings, open the Meeting Policies screen.

2. Create a new policy by clicking the Add button.

3. Give the policy a sensible name like Dial In first.

4. Enter a description so we remember what it was for: "This policy is for people who join meetings frequently via dial-in."

5. Scroll through the list of settings and look for the Participants And Guests section.

6. Toggle the Let Anonymous People Start A Meeting option to On.

7. Save the policy.

8. Switch to the Group Policy Assignment tab in the main part of the window.

9. Choose Add Group to open the pop-out screen on the right.

10. Under Select A Group, enter the name of a group containing your test user and click Add when they come up in the filter.

11. Leave the rank as 1 or update it if you already have existing policy assignments.

12. Select your new policy from the drop-down list and click Apply.

13. Allow some time for the settings to apply and create a test meeting and only connect via dial-in to confirm the settings have been applied.

EXERCISE 3.10

Configure a Teams Live Event

We are going to update the org-wide policy to prevent everyone from creating meetings and then make a specific policy to allow our test user to schedule them.

1. Open the TAC, and under Meetings, open the Live Events Policies screen.

2. Click the name of the global policy to open it.

3. Toggle the Allow Scheduling option to Off and save the policy.

4. Click Add to make a new policy.

5. Give it a sensible name such as "Marketing events" and a description.

6. Make sure the Allow Scheduling option is enabled and save the policy.

7. Pause, and with your test user check that you do not have an option to schedule live events from the Teams client calendar screen (see Figure 3.53).

8. Back in the TAC, in the left menu pick Users and search for your test user account.

9. Click the name of your user and then choose the Policies tab.

10. Under Assigned Policies, click Edit, and in the right pop-out menu under Live Events Policy, select the policy we just created for Marketing.

11. Hit Apply to save the new policy settings for our user.

12. After some time (may require the Teams client to be restarted), check if you have the button to schedule a live event from the Calendar screen.

13. Give your test event a title and select a date/time.

14. If you have other test accounts, add some of them as presenters using the pick list on the right side of the screen.

15. In the drop-down under the names of added users, change their Type to Presenter.

16. Click Next and select who you want to view the live event. For testing, use Public so you can test the event from accounts outside of your test environment.

17. Hit Schedule to save the live event.

18. Review the information summary and close the event item.

19. Open the event and copy the Attendee Link; then click Join (requires Teams desktop).

(continues)

EXERCISE 3.10 *(continued)*

20. This will open the live event in "pre-live" mode. Here you can set up your voice, video, and content. Any content added will be displayed on the bottom of the screen and must be selected before it can be Sent live.

21. Add either video or a screen share to the meeting and then start it with the Send Live yellow button displayed on the screen.

22. In another browser, paste the Attendee link that you copied earlier and verify that you can see the content of your live event.

Review Questions

1. You recently added a domain to the external access domain list as allowed for a company that you communicate with frequently. No other domains are in the list. Users start to report that they are no longer able to message users at other companies. What should you do?

   A. Disable external access before reenabling it with the new configuration.

   B. Remove the allowed domain you just added.

   C. Make sure that Skype federation is configured.

   D. Update the user policies to allow guest access.

2. You allow guests in your tenant but need to make sure that they are not able to share their screens in a meeting. Where would you configure this in the TAC?

   A. Update the org-wide guest access settings.

   B. Against the guest user Azure AD object.

   C. Under meeting policy.

   D. Configure external access.

3. You have a user who needs to be able to create meetings with dial-in details. They currently have an O365 E3 license. What should you change? (Select all that apply.)

   A. Configure a default number for your tenant in the conferencing bridge section in the TAC.

   B. Change the user to an E5 license.

   C. Purchase an add-on Audio Conferencing license.

   D. Run `Grant-CsTeamsMeetingPolicy -identity <user> -PolicyName AllowDialInMeetings`.

4. Your user account is a Teams administrator, and your organization has 12,000 users already configured for Teams. You want to create an org-wide team to push out information for upcoming IT changes, but when you try to make a new team, the org-wide option is missing. Why?

   A. You need to configure a channel moderation policy first.

   B. You need to be a tenant admin to create org-wide teams.

   C. Your organization already has too many org-wide teams.

   D. There are too many users in your tenant.

5. You need to disable the use of video for a group of audited users. The users are all members of an Azure AD group: AuditedTeamsUser. How can you achieve this and ensure that all audited users are always covered by the policy?

   A. Create new meeting policy that disables Allow IP Video and use group assignment applied to the AuditedTeamsUser group.

   B. Upgrade the AuditedTeamsUser group into an M365 group, create a new team option, and add the users to the team. Configure the team's policy settings to disable the use of video.

    C. Create a new meeting policy that disables Allow IP Video and assign it to each user. Update the new-starter process to ensure new users are assigned the right policy.

    D. Configure the global-meeting settings to manually change the number of allowed video ports to 2.

6. When gathering information from your company ready to deploy Teams, you pick up on the following requirements: Sales leaders must be able to send urgent messages but cannot edit them. Marketing must not be allowed to send urgent messages but are allowed to edit their messages. The solution should only affect users in these departments; what should you configure?

    A. Configure an org-wide Teams setting.

    B. Update the org-wide messaging policy and create one custom policy.

    C. Create and assign two messaging policies.

    D. Create and assign three permission policies.

7. An internal user creates a Teams meeting and invites two external parties to the meeting (User 1 and User 2). User 1 is able to join the meeting, but User 2 cannot. User 1 is also a guest in some teams. What should you do to fix the issue?

    A. Configure a meeting policy for the organizer to allow anonymous people to start a meeting.

    B. Update the meeting settings to allow anonymous users to join meetings.

    C. Ensure the user creating the meetings is licensed with an E5 license.

    D. Configure the default live event policy to allow everyone to join scheduled meetings.

8. Guest users in a team are unable to open the team's associated OneNote notebook, and they are able to chat and interact with users in the channel. Internal users report that they can access the notebook without any problems. Where should you change the sharing permissions?

    A. In the SharePoint Online Admin Center

    B. In the TAC

    C. In Azure AD

    D. In the team itself

9. You are rebranding the company, and the CEO wants to host an all-hands call to make the announcement. There are 9,000 users in the company split between two large offices. All users have been asked to come into their offices for the day to collect their new branded coffee mugs. What could you suggest to reduce the bandwidth required for the calls if they are to become a regular occurrence?

    A. Buy some projectors and set them up in the dining hall.

    B. Disable the use of video for the meeting.

    C. Deploy an SBC with media bypass enabled.

    D. Configure an eCDN solution compatible with Teams.

10. A user who is the owner of a team comes to you. They are missing a channel inside the team and insist that it was there last week. Where can you check and restore the channel from?

   A. Talk the user through restoring the channel in their Teams client.

   B. Find the team in the TAC, browse the channel list, and restore the channel.

   C. Run the following command in PowerShell: `Get-Team -identity <team> | Set-TeamChannel -deleted $false`.

   D. Create a new channel with the same name as the one that has disappeared.

11. You need to create a team for a group of users working on a new project together. There is already a distribution list in O365 for the group of users from before you deployed Teams. What should you do to create your team while making sure to reduce duplication of resources?

   A. Create a new team and use dynamic membership assignment to populate the group.

   B. Create a SharePoint Team site and then enable it for Teams.

   C. Convert the distribution list to an M365 group, and add Teams support to the M365 group.

   D. Create an M365 group, add the users, and then add Teams support to the M365 group.

12. You created a new org-wide team and want to enable channel moderation so that only owners can post to the General channel. How can you configure this?

   A. Change the org-wide messaging policy to require moderation.

   B. In the Teams client open the channel settings and enable moderation.

   C. In the Teams client disable "fun stuff" in the channel settings.

   D. In the Teams client open the team settings and configure moderation.

13. Users are complaining that they keep receiving urgent notifications from users in Finance. The notifications last for 20 minutes or until the message is acknowledged. What setting should you change to prevent Finance from doing this?

   A. Create a messaging policy for Finance that disables urgent/priority messages.

   B. Configure the global messaging policy to not allow receiving urgent messages.

   C. Disable tagging in the org-wide Teams settings.

   D. Change the Finance team settings to not allow @mentions.

14. When Teams was first deployed, you helped a team owner email-enable one of their channels. You also created a contact in the GAL with a friendly name for the channel email address. The owner comes to you saying that they accidentally disabled the channel email functionality. You help them email-enable the channel again, but emails from internal users that were previously working are now not appearing in the channel. What do you need to do?

   A. Modify the channel email address so that it matches the original email address.

   B. Wait 48 hours to allow replication to occur.

   C. Update the contact in the GAL with the current channel email address.

   D. Update the team setting to allow email integration to work.

15. You are asked to create a new team for a special project. Users must not be able to automatically join the team, and they should not be able to find it in the team directory. What should you do? (Select all that apply.)

    A. Create a new private team.

    B. Run the following in PowerShell: `Get-Team -DisplayName <team> | Set-Team -TeamDiscovery $false`.

    C. Create a new public team.

    D. Run the following in PowerShell: `Get-Team -DisplayName <team> | Set-Team -ShowInTeamsSearchandSuggestions $false`.

16. You have a team in the organization with 250 members, and a subset of the users (150 total) has a temporary requirement to work on a project that the other members should not be able to access information for. You want to minimize the administrative overhead in your solution. What should you do?

    A. There are too many users to create a private channel, so you make a new team for the project requirement.

    B. Create a private channel inside the existing team.

    C. Create a new channel and hide it from the directory.

    D. Configure a new SharePoint site using the TEAMCHANNEL# template.

17. You configure email integration for several channels but need to make sure that the channel will only accept email from internal users. Where would you configure the allowed domains?

    A. In the TAC under Org-Wide Settings, Teams Settings

    B. In the TAC under Org-Wide Settings, External Access

    C. In the team under the team settings

    D. In PowerShell using the `Set-TeamEmailSetting -AllowedEmailDomain <domains>`

18. Marketing has scheduled a Teams live event for a big upcoming event. They start the live stream when they are doing a practice run with the presenters. What should they do now before the start of the actual event?

    A. Make sure the owner starts the meeting at the right time.

    B. Remove and re-invite the presenters from the invitation.

    C. Add named guests to the attendee list.

    D. Schedule a new Teams live event and update the links with the new details (attended and presenter join).

19. A user is unable to create a new private channel in a team. What should you check? (Select all that apply.)

    A. If the user is an owner in the team

    B. That the team has fewer than 250 users

    C. If the team has guests in it

    D. That the Team setting allows members to create new private channels

20. You create a new org-wide team, and it automatically adds contractor accounts to the team. You remove the accounts from the M365 group using Azure AD but find that they are added back in. Where should you remove the accounts you do not want in the org-wide team?

   A.   Using the SharePoint Admin Center.

   B.   In Teams.

   C.   In on-prem AD and run a synchronization job.

   D.   Remove the users from the group using Outlook.

Chapter

4

Advanced Teams Functionality and Management

MICROSOFT EXAM OBJECTIVES COVERED IN THIS CHAPTER:

✓ Manage membership in a team

✓ Implement governance and lifecycle management for Microsoft Teams

✓ Manage security and compliance

✓ Implement policies for Microsoft Teams apps

This chapter will take us through some of the more advanced features in Teams, looking at things like how you can protect the data that your users are working with, as well as how you can control some of the lifecycle aspects around teams themselves (such as archiving or deleting them). We will also cover how you can use apps to integrate other services with your Teams deployment. Apps exist for other Microsoft or third-party services, or you can develop your own if you would like (don't worry, programing like that isn't in scope for this exam!).

A lot of the features that we are going to cover here are going to be configured outside of Teams (other than apps) using some new admin centers, as they are features that sit across the rest of the M365 suite. For some of them we will only be covering how to configure them through their respective admin portals and not going into detail about how to manage them completely through PowerShell. This is deliberate, as our goal here is to cover what should be required to pass the MS 700 exam, and while these features are very interesting, for the exam you are only expected to know about them at quite a high level. That doesn't mean, however, that you cannot supplement your learning by going off on a few tangents of your own if you find any of the features particularly interesting. Links have been included as much as possible to the full details of these features so that you can continue to explore on your own.

Before we get to the big stuff, let's start smaller and dig back into some alternative ways of handling administrative permissions and how you can manage team memberships.

In this chapter, we are going to come across the M365 compliance portal for the first time; this is a relatively new portal that consolidates some of the older portals. In the exam you may see references to the M365 Security and Compliance portal; while this still exists, it is being deprecated, so we are working with the new one here as much as possible.

Admin and User Management

We will start this chapter with some better ways of controlling who can administer our Teams deployment and how we can improve on controlling membership in the teams that we created in the previous chapter.

Teams Admin Roles

For all of the administrative tasks that we have performed so far, we have assumed that your account has been running with at least Teams Service Administrator permissions, which gives you access to all the settings related to Teams. However, as you can imagine, it is not good practice to give this level of access to everyone who needs to look after your Teams deployment, as they may be able to change (accidentally or deliberately) settings that you do not want updated. Industry best practice would be to use a system of "least privilege" where we make sure that users only have access to view or change settings that are relevant to their job roles. Fortunately, when Microsoft developed M365, it created a number of admin roles that we can use to apply the least privilege principle to your deployment. You will sometimes see this way of managing permissions referred to as *role-based access control* (RBAC).

This idea of least privilege/RBAC applies throughout the M365 service, with each product having its own set of restricted administrative roles (in Exchange and SharePoint, for example). The highest level of permission in a tenant is Global Administrator, and you want to make sure there are as few accounts as possible that have this permission, and that they are not used as day-to-day accounts, to minimize the risk of accidental configuration changes and to reduce the likelihood of access falling into the wrong hands.

The list of predefined admin roles is shown here, and fortunately, as you can see, the naming convention used is fairly descriptive of what access you can expect to have:

- Teams Service Administrator
- Teams Communications Administrator
- Teams Communications Support Engineer
- Teams Communications Support Specialist
- Teams Device Administrator

These roles only give permissions to the Teams-specific feature set. These roles will not give you access to configure other services as well, so it is likely that users who are given these roles will also hold delegated roles in other services too.

Table 4.1 gives a more detailed breakdown on what the intended job role for each one would be along with a summary of the access and tools available.

You can assign admin roles to users with the M365 admin center, with the Azure Active Directory admin center, or with PowerShell.

If you have an account that is used for administration purposes only, it does not require a license to be assigned as it will not actually use any services. This makes it easier to use separate "admin" accounts for higher-privilege roles without having to waste a license on functionality that will never be used, such as Teams calling or an Exchange mailbox.

TABLE 4.1   Teams Admin Roles

Role	Aimed at	Using These Tools
Teams Service Administrator	Managing all aspects of the Teams service, including M365 groups	Access to everything in the Teams Admin Center (TAC) and the associated PowerShell cmdlets Including: Managing all aspects of meetings (global configuration and policies) Managing all aspects of telephony in Teams Teams network planner tool Managing collaboration workloads Managing all org-wide settings including external access and federation, client upgrades Managing teams themselves including membership Managing any Teams devices Managing and publishing app integrations available for Teams Accessing all Teams-related reports Viewing user profile information inside the TAC, including call history and quality (for troubleshooting) Access to Call Quality Dashboard (CQD) to view calling trends

Role	Aimed at	Using These Tools
Teams Communications Administrator	Managing real-time communications workloads in Teams, such as calling and meetings	Access to parts of the TAC (and associated PowerShell cmdlets) relating to communications workloads
		Including: Managing all aspects of meetings (global configuration and policies)
		Managing all aspects of telephony in Teams
		Teams network planner tool
		Access to communications-related reports (PSTN blocked users, PSTN minute pools, and PSTN usage)
		Viewing user profile information inside the TAC including call history and quality (for troubleshooting)
		Access to Call Quality Dashboard (CQD) to view calling trends
Teams Communications Support Engineer	Troubleshooting communications workload issues with **advanced** tooling	Access to limited items in the TAC, only useful to help troubleshoot user calling issues:
		Viewing user profile information inside the TAC including full call history and quality information (for troubleshooting)
		Access to Call Quality Dashboard (CQD) to view calling trends (down to a user level)
Teams Communications Support Specialist	Troubleshooting communications workload issues with **basic** tooling	Access to limited items in the TAC, only useful to help troubleshoot user calling issues:
		Viewing user profile information inside the TAC including full call history and quality information (for troubleshooting) but only for the specific user (other participants in calls are obfuscated)
		Access to Call Quality Dashboard (CQD) to view calling trends (no specific user information shown)

continues

TABLE 4.1   Teams Admin Roles *(continued)*

Role	Aimed at	Using These Tools
Teams Device Adminis- trator	Managing devices that sign into Teams (e.g., phones and meeting room devices)	Can manage devices through the TAC Including (only for devices): Viewing status, applying updates, creating con- figuration policies Does not get access to any of the tools that allow viewing call quality information

`docs.microsoft.com/en-us/MicrosoftTeams/using-admin-roles`

Assigning Admin Roles in M365 Admin Center

To assign any of the Teams RBAC roles to a user in your organization, launch the M365 admin center with an account that has Global Administrator permissions in the tenant.

From the left menu, select Users ➤ Active Users, find the target user in the list, or search in the given box. Click the user's name to show a pop-out screen, and in the Roles section select Manage Roles. This will give you a list of the valid M365 RBAC roles. You can either pick Teams Administrator or, if you want to use one of the limited access roles shown in Table 4.1, expand the Show All By Category section and look under the Collaboration header (see Figure 4.1). Simply select the role you want and click Save changes.

Alternatively, you can view all of the roles available and assign them directly to users from the Roles option on the left menu (you may need to click Show All first as it is hidden by default). Scroll down the list or use the Search box to filter for Teams roles; from here you can view a list of assigned users and assign the role to a new user.

This interface also has two neat features where you can check what each admin role can access. If you select more than one role (but only up to three), you can then do a comparison to see exactly what parts of the system are accessible (see Figure 4.2). Alternatively, if you select just one role, you can choose something called Run As. When you do this, the Teams admin center will open but running under the role you selected so you can access settings with the level of permissions available to that role. It's a great way of confirming what level of access each role has, but be aware that you are still live and that any changes made will still apply (see Figure 4.3)!

FIGURE 4.1   Assigning Teams admin roles to a user

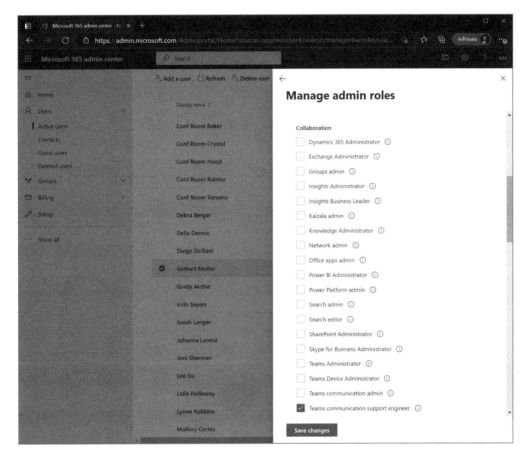

Assigning Roles Using Azure AD

You can also assign admin roles using the Azure AD interface. Log into the Azure AD portal (`aad.portal.azure.com`), again with an account that has Global administrator permissions.

From the left menu, select Azure Active Directory and then Users (or if you can see Users in the main left menu, you can just select that). Then choose the user you want to assign a role to, which will open the detailed user information screen. On the left click Assigned Roles, and you can then click Add Assignments to select which role you want to give the user (see Figure 4.4).

See docs.microsoft.com/en-us/azure/active-directory/funda-mentals/active-directory-users-assign-role-azure-portal for more information about assigning roles using Azure AD.

FIGURE 4.2 Comparing Teams admin roles in M365 Admin Center

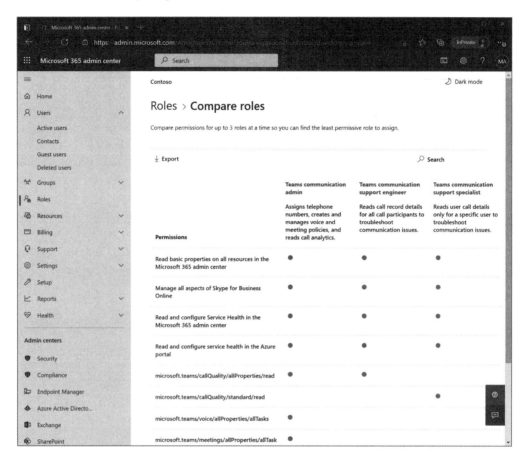

Assigning Roles in PowerShell

Lastly, you can also assign roles from PowerShell, but again there are two choices for how to do this: You can do it either using the Azure Active Directory PowerShell for Graph module or using the Azure Active Directory for Windows PowerShell.

We will use the Azure Active Directory PowerShell for Graph method as this is technically the newer set of cmdlets, but see the reference link in this section for the latest from Microsoft about how to operate either version.

See the following page for details of how to configure roles using either module: docs.microsoft.com/en-us/microsoft-365/enterprise/ assign-roles-to-user-accounts-with-microsoft-365- powershell.

FIGURE 4.3 Running M365 Admin Center as a different access role

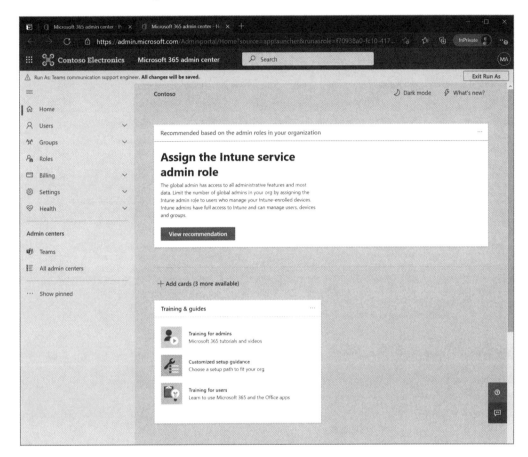

First run a PowerShell window as an administrator, and then run the following:

```
Install-Module -Name AzureAD
```

```
Connect-AzureAD
```

To install and connect to Azure AD, follow the prompts to enter the credentials of your Global administrator account.

Once up and running, you can view the full list of roles available (or filter it to only show Teams-related ones) by running this:

```
Get-AzureAdDirectoryroletemplate
```

```
Get-AzureAdDirectoryroletemplate | Where {$_.displayName -like "*Teams*"}
```

FIGURE 4.4   Assigning an admin role via Azure AD

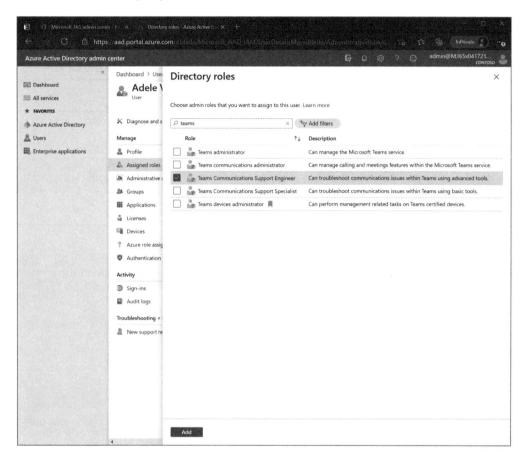

You may notice that the names in PowerShell do not exactly match the names used in the web-based portals. For example, in PowerShell, you will see "Teams Devices Administrator" instead of "Teams Device Administrator."

When using this Graph module, roles can be assigned only if they are also "enabled" in the tenant first, which is why this next code snippet may seem quite complicated. We first find the role and enable it; then we can assign it to the user. Replace the bits in angle brackets in the following code with your information to try it:

```
$userName="<UserID>"
$roleName="<Teams Role>"
$role = Get-AzureADDirectoryRole | Where {$_.displayName -eq $roleName}

if ($role -eq $null) {
    $roleTemplate = Get-AzureADDirectoryRoleTemplate | Where {$_.displayName -
eq $roleName}
```

```
    Enable-AzureADDirectoryRole -RoleTemplateId $roleTemplate.ObjectId
    $role = Get-AzureADDirectoryRole | Where {$_.displayName -eq $roleName}
}


Add-AzureADDirectoryRoleMember -ObjectId $role.ObjectId -RefObjectId
(Get-AzureADUser | Where {$_.UserPrincipalName -eq $userName}).ObjectID
```

Once this has been applied, you can check which accounts are assigned what role by running the following:

```
$roleName="<Teams Role>"
$role = Get-AzureADDirectoryRole | Where {$_.displayName -eq $roleName}
Get-AzureADDirectoryRoleMember -ObjectId $role.ObjectId
```

Manual Team Membership

Back at the start of Chapter 3, "Teams Core Functionality," we covered the types of memberships available in a team: Owner, Member, and Guest. However, this was before we had created any teams to work with. So now we are going to cover how to manually configure membership before looking at some smarter ways to do it.

Ideally, manually configuring team memberships for your organization will be an infrequent task for you because the team owners will be controlling who they want in their team. There are still some situations where you might have to modify memberships manually, however, such as if a team owner has left the company and you need to assign a new one.

Membership from the Teams Client

You might think that the quickest way to manage the membership of a team would be in the Teams client itself, but this is only the case for teams that you are a member of. You need to have joined the teams for them to show in your client to then manage.

In the Teams client, find the team you want to work with in the left menu and then click the three-dot menu next to the team name. From the list that appears, select Manage Team, and you will see a full list of who is currently a member and what their role is (Owner or Member). From here you can either change a user's role (remember that you cannot change a guest user as this is a special access type) between owner and guest, or you can add new users.

Membership via the TAC

Alternatively, if you need to manage teams where you are not or do not want to be a member, you can do it via the TAC.

Launch the TAC and from the left menu expand Teams ➤ Manage Teams. This will give you a list of all the teams in your organization. Select the name of the team you want to work with, and it will open the team's details. You should see a screen similar to the one shown in the Teams client where you can modify or add members as required; see Figure 4.5.

FIGURE 4.5 Teams membership in the TAC

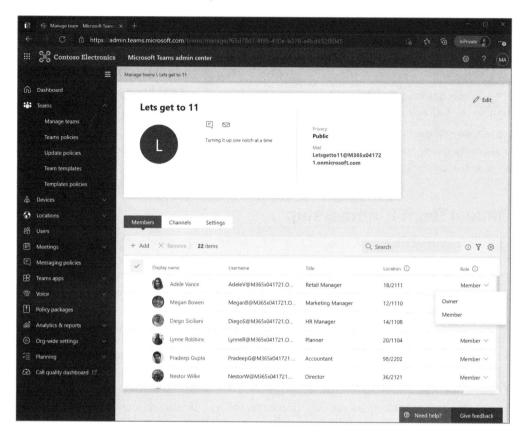

Membership via PowerShell

We can also manage membership using a bit of trusty PowerShell, and fortunately the cmdlets we need to use are fairly straightforward and ideally easy to remember. They are Add-TeamUser and Remove-TeamUser.

Table 4.2 shows the options for these cmdlets.

TABLE 4.2 Add- and Remove-TeamUser Cmdlet Options

Parameter	Description	Options
GroupId	Unique ID for the team you want to modify (GUID)	
Role	Role to allocate	Member/Owner
User	User principal name (UPN)	Username

docs.microsoft.com/en-us/powershell/module/teams/add-teamuser

The only slight trick here is that you wouldn't under normal circumstances know what the GUID for the team you want to manage would be, but we can string together another cmdlet `Get-Team`, which will find the team we want using a friendly name, with the previous one to make one user-friendly line of code that will update memberships for us:

```
Get-Team -DisplayName "<My Team>" | Add-TeamUser -User <Username> -Role Member
```

If you specify `-Role Owner` when using the `Remove-TeamUser`, it will demote the user in question to a member (assuming they are indeed an owner already) instead of removing them from the team altogether.

Dynamic Membership

Manually adding and removing users from a team is all very well and good, but I'm sure as an administrator you probably have better things you could be spending your time doing. That is why there is also a neat feature called *dynamic membership* that you can use to create rules in Azure AD that will automatically update group memberships (and therefore team memberships) for you.

These rules work by looking at attributes for the user objects and then processing them appropriately. For example, if a user has a particular job title or office location specified, they can be automatically added to a team of their co-workers.

While this sounds like a great feature, and it is, there is a downside: Each user you want to be covered needs to have at least an Azure AD Premium P1 license. While the specifics of this license type are beyond our scope for this exam, it is important to remember that it is required for this feature to operate correctly. Any user who doesn't have this license assigned, even if they meet the criteria of the dynamic membership rules, will not be processed.

 You can read more about the Azure AD Premium P1 and P2 license types at azure.microsoft.com/en-gb/pricing/details/active-directory.

Before rushing into using dynamic membership for all your teams, you should keep in mind the following considerations:

- Membership changes will take time to update automatically.
- Team owners cannot override the dynamic rules you create.
- Members will not be able to leave teams they are automatically included in.
- You cannot control who is a team owner dynamically.
- When applying dynamic rules to an existing team, all current memberships will be reset. Even if users meet the criteria, they may be removed and then added back into the team.

Dynamic membership is not something that can be configured directly inside Teams; strictly speaking it isn't really a Teams feature at all but rather is an M365 group/Azure AD feature that Teams can leverage, thanks to its use of M365 groups behind the scenes.

To get started with dynamic membership, you need to have an M365 group already created that you want to convert to dynamic control. It isn't important if the group is enabled for Teams at this point, but if you have made a new group, remember that you still need to Teams-enable it when you have set up the membership as you like.

Configuring Dynamic Membership in Azure AD

To get started we need to log into the Azure AD portal with an account that has either Global Administrator or User Administrator permissions to the tenant. From the left menu select All Services and then find Groups in the list. Scroll or search the list to find the group that you want to work with and click its name to open it. In the Membership Type drop-down you can choose between Assigned (manual control) and Dynamic User, as shown in Figure 4.6.

FIGURE 4.6   Group membership types

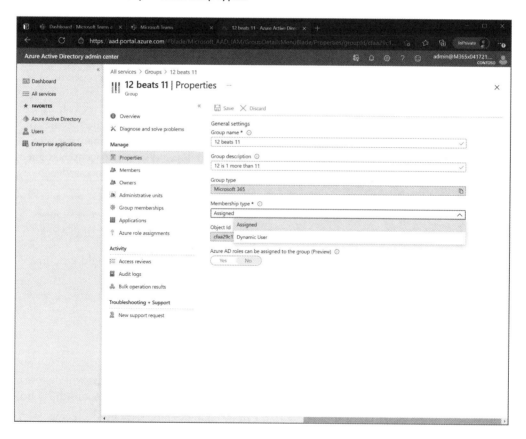

When you select Dynamic User, a new section will appear underneath where you can create your membership queries (rules). Click through to the query builder screen, where you can then use the selection boxes to build your query (see Figure 4.7).

FIGURE 4.7   Creating a membership rule

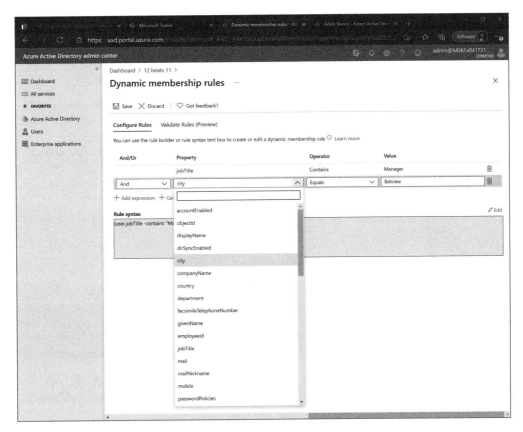

These queries can become quite complex as you can select from a range of AD attributes as well as combining them using AND and OR operators. If you need to construct a really complex query, you can also directly edit the syntax to update or paste in your own code selection.

When you have created your rules, you probably want to verify them before saving and applying them to your group. Thankfully, there is a feature (currently in preview) that lets you select some users to test your query against. To find this, click the Validate Rules button to move to that tab; here you can use Add Users to select users from your tenant to validate with. It would make sense to ensure you always pick at least two users, one that you would expect to be in your created group and one who will not. That way, you also test to make sure your rules are working as intended (see Figure 4.8).

FIGURE 4.8 User validation

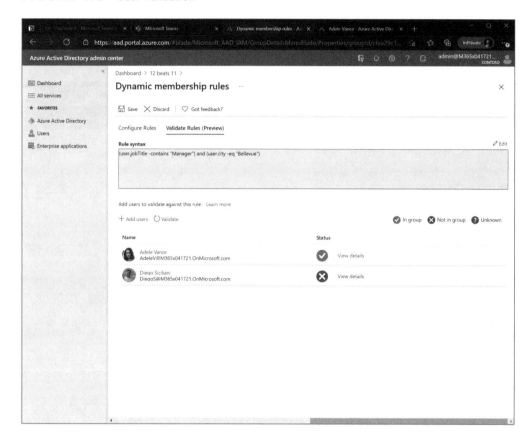

Once you are happy with the rules, you can then save the query and go back into the group overview page. You will now see a new option in the left menu for Dynamic Membership where you can view and update the queries being used.

The following list shows all the attributes that you can use to build your queries (you shouldn't need to memorize the list; just be aware what types of fields and data you can use to control dynamic membership):

- accountEnabled
- objectId
- displayName
- dirSyncEnabled
- city
- companyName
- country

- department
- facsimileTelephoneNumber
- givenName
- employeeId
- jobTitle
- mail
- mailNickname
- mobile
- passwordpolicies
- postalCode
- preferredLanguage
- sipProxyAddress
- state
- streetAddress
- surname
- telephoneNumber
- usageLocation
- userPrincipalName
- userType
- onPremisesSecurityIdentifier
- otherMails
- proxyAddresses
- assignedPlans
- extensionAttribute1 through to extensionAttribute15

Configuring Dynamic Membership in PowerShell

We can also deal with dynamic memberships through PowerShell, but unless you plan on doing this on a large scale, it is probably more complicated than it's worth, as you have to jump through a few hoops to make it work right.

First you need to use the Azure AD PowerShell module like we did earlier in this chapter, as well as the Exchange Online module (not necessary, but it lets us use friendly lookups to find out the group ID):

```
Import-Module -Name ExchangeOnlineManagement
Install-Module -Name AzureAD

Connect-ExchangeOnline
Connect-AzureAD
```

Then we need to set up a few variables that we are going to use, first for the group we want to work with and second to hold the dynamic rules that we want to configure for the group:

```
$TargetGroupId = (Get-UnifiedGroup <GroupEmail>).ExternalDirectoryObjectID

$DynamicMembershipRule =`(<Attribute> <Operator> <Value>)´
```

Then we need to check what GroupType properties are set on the group already and save them to a variable so that we can then add the one we need for dynamic membership if it doesn't exist:

```
$GroupTypes = (Get-AzureAdMsGroup -Id $TargetGroupId).GroupTypes
If ($GroupTypes -notcontains "DynamicMembership"){
    $GroupTypes.Add("DynamicMembership")
} else {
    Write-Output "Already a dynamic membership group"
}
```

Lastly, we can push our changes back to the group and save it:

```
Set-AzureADMSGroup -Id $TargetGroupId -GroupTypes $GroupTypes.ToArray() -
MembershipRuleProcessingState "On" -MembershipRule $DynamicMembershipRule
```

The following example modifies the group we have been working with, overwriting the existing membership rules with new ones (if the person is in the sales department):

```
Import-Module -Name ExchangeOnlineManagement
Install-Module -Name AzureAD

Connect-ExchangeOnline
Connect-AzureAD

$TargetGroupId = (Get-UnifiedGroup
msteams_328b52@M365x041721.onmicrosoft.com).ExternalDirectoryObjectID

$DynamicMembershipRule = `(user.department -eq "Sales")´

$GroupTypes = (Get-AzureAdMsGroup -Id $TargetGroupId).GroupTypes
If ($GroupTypes -notcontains "DynamicMembership"){
    $GroupTypes.Add("DynamicMembership")
} else {
    Write-Output "Already a dynamic membership group"
}


Set-AzureADMSGroup -Id $TargetGroupId -GroupTypes $GroupTypes.ToArray() -
MembershipRuleProcessingState "On" -MembershipRule $DynamicMembershipRule
```

Once that has run, you can check it against the group configuration in the Azure AD portal. You will notice that in the code we used brackets around the membership rule. This isn't strictly necessary, but if you didn't use them, then when you check in the portal, you would only see the query string and not be able to update the rules using the graphical builder.

If you want to add more than one condition, you can just concatenate them together using –and / –or operators like this:

```
(user.JobTitle -contains "Manager") -and (user.City -eq "Bellevue")
```

You can learn more about the syntax used by dynamic membership at docs.microsoft.com/en-us/azure/active-directory/enterprise-users/groups-dynamic-membership.

Access Reviews

In this section we are going to cover something that we talked about in Chapter 3 when we discussed guest access: access reviews.

Access reviews are a way of periodically checking up on who is currently a member of a particular group. This checking process can work either way, so you can request that group owners review and check who is a member of their groups, or you can ask users themselves to confirm that they still need to be members of their groups.

Remember that while access reviews are looking at group membership, in our Teams context that effectively means we are reviewing membership of the teams in our organization.

Similar to the dynamic membership feature we covered earlier, there is a licensing requirement associated with using access reviews. This time it is an Azure AD Premium P2 license: your tenant needs to have enough P2 licenses to cover the users who will be performing the reviews (either as owner or member).

Learn more about access reviews and their licensing at docs.microsoft.com/en-us/azure/active-directory/governance/access-reviews-overview.

Configuring Access Reviews

First, you have to onboard access reviews for your tenant, which can be done using the Azure AD portal. Launch the portal as a member of the Global Administrators group. From the left menu, select Active Directory and then select Identity Governance (see Figure 4.9).

FIGURE 4.9 Azure AD identity governance

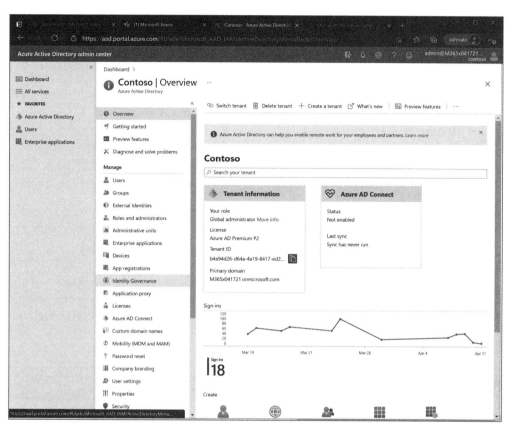

In the Identity Governance section, select Onboard under the section Access Reviews. Click the Onboard Now button. This process will then configure your tenant for use with access reviews; when the process is complete, you should get a notification in the upper right of the window.

Next we can start creating the kind of access reviews that we want, so make sure you are still in the same section, or come back to it, and you should now be able to click New Access Review (see Figure 4.10).

This will start the configuration form. First we want to specify that this access review will deal with Teams and Group memberships (see Figure 4.11).

Next you can choose to scope the access review just toward groups that have guest users as members or to any group in the organization (see Figure 4.12). This can be handy if you want to just gatekeep guest access, as it will automatically include new groups that have guests added over time.

FIGURE 4.10   Blank access review page

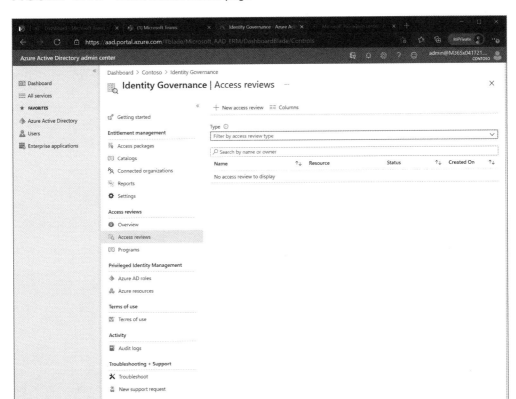

Under the review scope we can choose who will be responsible for carrying out the reviews, and we have the following options (see Figure 4.13):

Group Owners: Send the review request to the owner of the group in question.

Selected User or Group: Always send the review to the following person or group (e.g., Administrators).

Users review their own access: Ask users to review their own access.

Managers of users: This is whoever is defined in AD as the user's manager.

For some of these options you will need to specify a fallback reviewer. This is just a specified user or group that will be used if the primary review option is not available, for example if the user doesn't have a manager defined.

FIGURE 4.11   New access review form

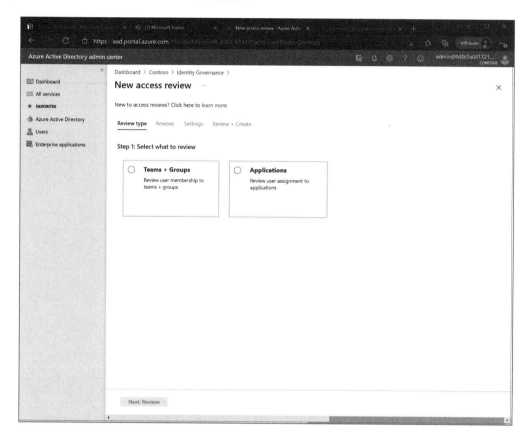

Underneath the reviews you can specify the frequency with which the reviews will occur; this can be anything from weekly to annually.

Duration: How long do people need to complete the review?

Start date: When should the first review be generated?

End: Should reviews stop being generated after a certain point?

On the next page, we can configure some advanced options (see Figure 4.14):

Auto Apply results: Applies the changes when the review is completed

No response: What to do if users don't respond (auto remove, approve, or recommendation)

Decision helpers (no sign-in): Flags users who have not been active

FIGURE 4.12   Access review scope

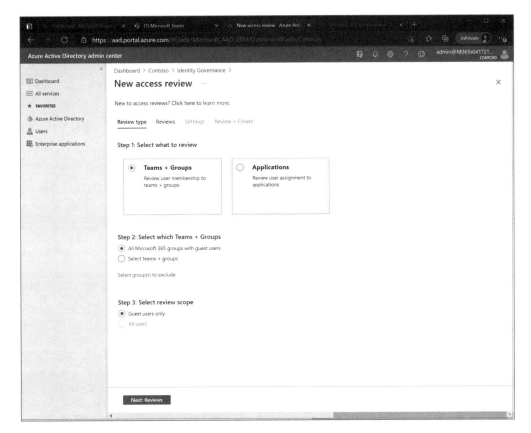

Justification: Requires input if approving the membership

Email notification: Email reminders of the review process

Reminders: Follow up during the review

Extra content: Add your own information to the generated emails

Then on the last page you can give your review a name and save it (see Figure 4.15).

That is it! Access reviews can be a handy feature to help make sure you are being responsible about controlling access to data in your Teams environment, especially where guests are concerned.

FIGURE 4.13   Access review type

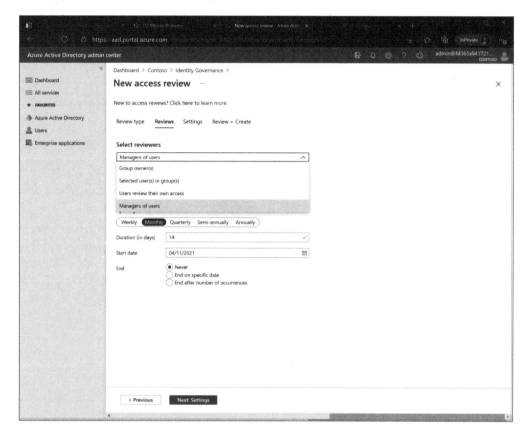

Lifecycle and Governance

Now we are going to look at some features that help us with how we can manage teams over their lifecycle, so in other words, stuff that helps us control how we set up and create teams in a more controlled manner (at the start of their life), as well as how we can deal with teams that are no longer required and need to be tidied up (the end of their life).

Team Templates

Once you have figured out how you can best use Teams in your organization and have got it up and running, you might find that a particular team structure works well for parts of your business, for example when using Teams to support customer projects. Each time a new project comes along you may find that you are creating a team and then customizing it the

FIGURE 4.14   Access review settings

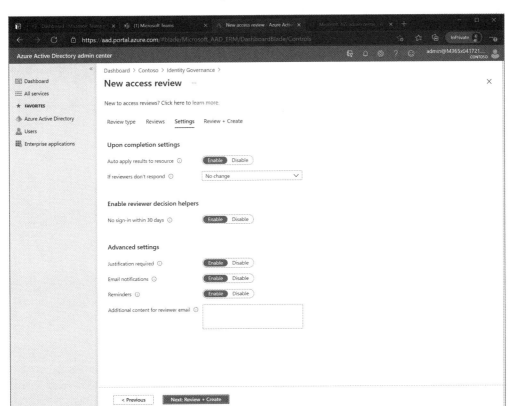

same way with specific channels and custom tab settings. Thankfully, with templates you can reduce some of that setup effort so that you can quickly and repeatedly, make new teams that are based around the same core layout.

You can manage templates through the TAC (or via the Graph API, but that is beyond the scope for MS 700); open it and then in the left menu choose Teams ➤ Team Templates. Here you can see a list of predefined templates provided by Microsoft (see Figure 4.16).

You are not able to delete or change these default templates, but you can create your own (from scratch or based on an existing team) or duplicate the default ones that can then be modified. Table 4.3 shows what can be controlled using a template.

You can see a full list of the default templates and what they contain at docs.microsoft.com/en-us/microsoftteams/get-started-with-teams-templates-in-the-admin-console.

FIGURE 4.15   Access review description

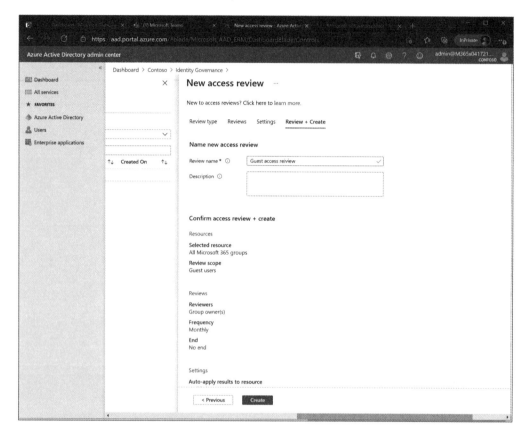

Templates also have the following size limit restrictions:

- 15 channels
- 20 tabs per channel
- 50 apps

Creating a Template in the TAC

Open the TAC and on the left choose Teams ➤ Team Templates. Select Add to start the new team template wizard. Here you will have three choices to either start from scratch, base a template on an existing team, or duplicate and modify one of the existing templates (see Figure 4.17).

FIGURE 4.16 Default team templates

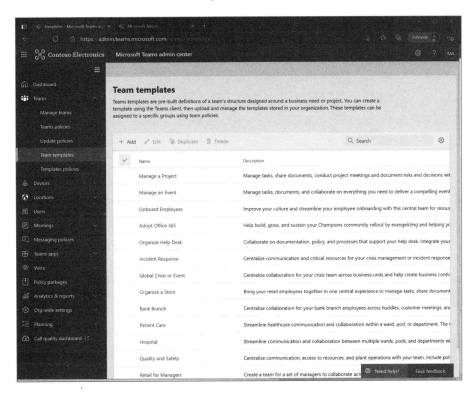

TABLE 4.3 Template Capabilities

Customizable	Not Customizable
Base template type	Team membership (this is where dynamic membership could help)
Team name	Team picture
Team description	Channel settings
Team type (public/private)	Connectors
Team settings	Files and content
Auto favorite channels	
Installed apps	
Pinned tabs	

docs.microsoft.com/en-us/microsoftteams/get-started-with-teams-templates-in-the-admin-console

FIGURE 4.17   New template screen

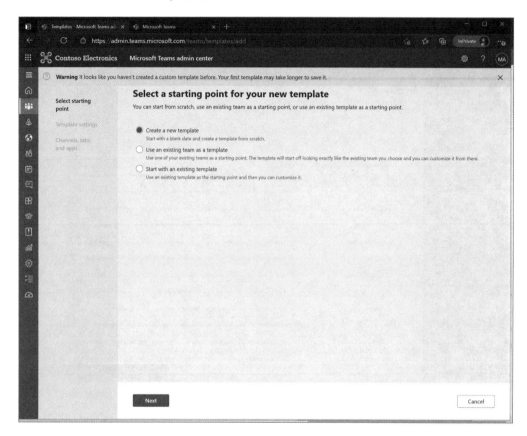

Choose to create one from scratch, as that will show you all of the options available. On the next screen you can name the template, give it a description (there is a requirement for both a short and long description!), and set the region and then move to the next screen (see Figure 4.18).

Here you can then lay out the channel structure that you want inside the team as well as adding any apps that are required. (We are going to learn about apps later in this chapter.) When adding a channel, you can choose if it is shown by default, as well as what other tabs to include (see Figure 4.19). When you're happy with the way the template looks, click Submit, and you will return to the main template screen.

Once the template has been saved, you should be able to use it when making new teams from the Teams client. Sign in to the client, and under the Teams menu if you select Join Or Create A Team and then Create A Team, you can now see your new template ready to go (see Figure 4.20).

FIGURE 4.18   New template settings

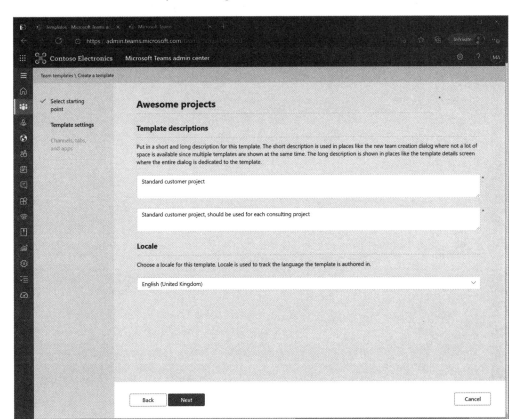

Be aware that when you create a new template, by default any user in the organization will have access to create a new team based on it.

Template Policies

Fortunately, we can control who has access to which templates using template policies. These policies work in the same way as the user policies that we covered in Chapter 3, so there is an Org-Wide policy, but we can override this for each user with a custom policy specifying which templates they will have access to.

To view and configure template policies, open the TAC, but this time go to Teams ➤ Templates Policy (see Figure 4.21).

Here you can add or edit the existing policy; there isn't much to do other than just select or deselect the available templates to hide them (see Figure 4.22).

Once you have saved or created your policy, you can then go into the user object, and in the long list of policy items you can specify the new template policy that you just created.

FIGURE 4.19 Template contents

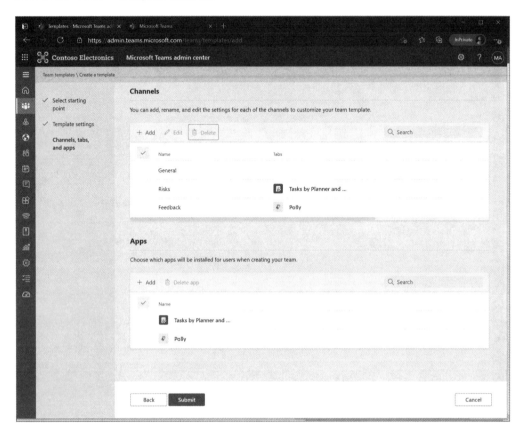

 At the time of writing, the TAC interface does not let you do batch policy assignment for templates policies; however, it is possible through Power-Shell. See docs.microsoft.com/en-us/powershell/module/teams/new-csbatchpolicyassignmentoperation.

Group Creation Policies

So far, we have assumed that anyone in your organization will have the ability to create new teams (and the associated M365 groups). This is what could be referred to as an *open* approach to group creation, but there may be situations where this might not be appropriate. Some alternative models are as follows:

IT lead: Only IT can create groups to ensure that there is always oversight about what groups are created and how they are configured.

FIGURE 4.20   Creating a team from template

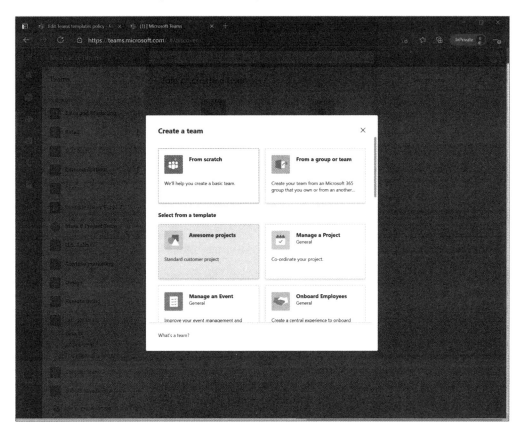

Controlled: Delegated users are allowed to create teams; this could be regional IT teams or managers/department heads.

Open (default): Anyone can create teams as they need.

These group creation models are just examples of how you might choose to limit group creation; they are not official models or referenced by Teams or M365 directly.

Configuring Group Creation

To restrict the ability to create new teams we need to control things at the M365 group layer. One downside to this is that unfortunately the Teams client will still show the Create Team

FIGURE 4.21   Templates policies

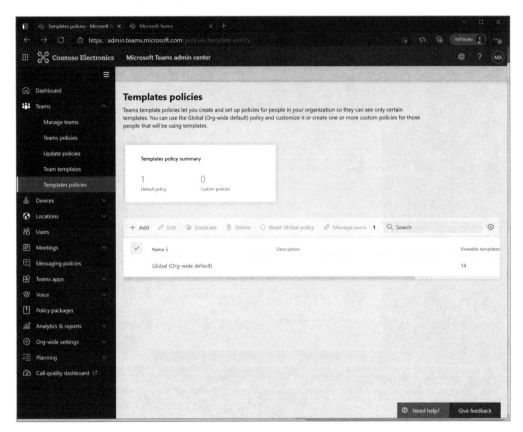

option in its interface, but the process will fail if someone not authorized attempts to make a group. So make sure that if you enable this setting, you inform your users so they don't think that Teams is broken.

Limiting group creation is done in PowerShell against Azure AD and uses a group itself! Essentially, we need to tell Azure AD which group (security or M365) contains users that are allowed to make new M365 groups and that we want to restrict it to only those users.

Also, the PowerShell cmdlets that you need to use are currently only available in the AzureAD Preview module, so if you have the release version installed, it needs to be removed and the preview version installed instead. At least the code for that is simple (will need administrative permissions on your local computer to run):

```
Uninstall-Module AzureAD
Install-Module AzureADPreview
```

FIGURE 4.22 Hiding templates in a policy

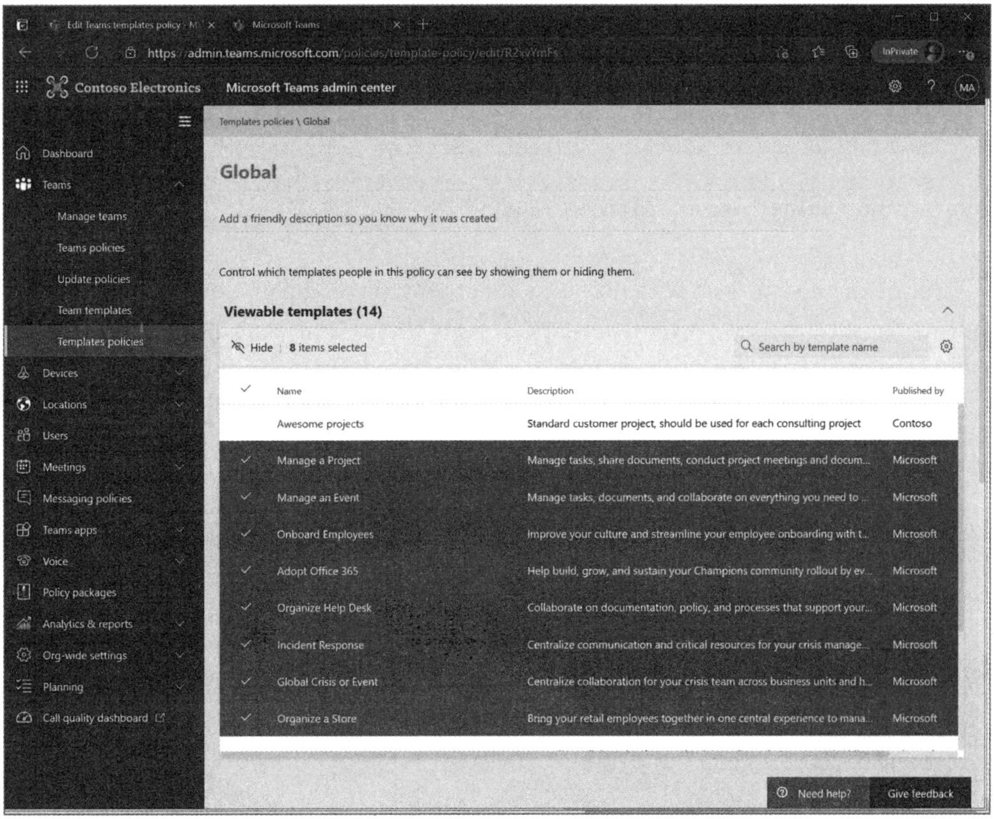

Once you have installed the connector, you can establish a connection to Azure AD, and we will set up two variables that we are going to use in our mini script. The first contains the name of the group that contains users allowed to make new groups, so make sure you have created this first. The second is a Boolean that we will toggle to restrict creation to only the specified group:

```
$GroupName = "<GroupName>"
$AllowGroupCreation = $False
```

```
Connect-AzureAD
```

The next part is a bit tricky, as we have to check if the settings for group creation have already been configured; if not, we copy them from a settings template:

```
$settingsObjectID = (Get-AzureADDirectorySetting | Where-object -Property
Displayname -Value "Group.Unified" -EQ).id
```

continues

(continued)

```
if(!$settingsObjectID)
{
    $template = Get-AzureADDirectorySettingTemplate | Where-object
{$_.displayname -eq "group.unified"}
    $settingsCopy = $template.CreateDirectorySetting()
    New-AzureADDirectorySetting -DirectorySetting $settingsCopy
    $settingsObjectID = (Get-AzureADDirectorySetting | Where-object -Property
Displayname -Value "Group.Unified" -EQ).id
}
```

Then we can update them with the new settings we want to apply:

```
$settingsCopy = Get-AzureADDirectorySetting -Id $settingsObjectID
$settingsCopy["EnableGroupCreation"] = $AllowGroupCreation

if($GroupName)
{
  $settingsCopy["GroupCreationAllowedGroupId"] = (Get-AzureADGroup -
SearchString $GroupName).objectid
}
 else {
$settingsCopy["GroupCreationAllowedGroupId"] = $GroupName
}
```

And then save them and check what we configured:

```
Set-AzureADDirectorySetting -Id $settingsObjectID -DirectorySetting
$settingsCopy

(Get-AzureADDirectorySetting -Id $settingsObjectID).Values
```

So, a full sample script would look like this:

```
$GroupName = "M365 Group Creators"
$AllowGroupCreation = $False

Connect-AzureAD

$settingsObjectID = (Get-AzureADDirectorySetting | Where-object -Property
Displayname -Value "Group.Unified" -EQ).id
if(!$settingsObjectID)
{
    $template = Get-AzureADDirectorySettingTemplate | Where-object
{$_.displayname -eq "group.unified"}
    $settingsCopy = $template.CreateDirectorySetting()
```

```
    New-AzureADDirectorySetting -DirectorySetting $settingsCopy
    $settingsObjectID = (Get-AzureADDirectorySetting | Where-object -Property
Displayname -Value "Group.Unified" -EQ).id
}

$settingsCopy = Get-AzureADDirectorySetting -Id $settingsObjectID
$settingsCopy["EnableGroupCreation"] = $AllowGroupCreation

if($GroupName)
{
  $settingsCopy["GroupCreationAllowedGroupId"] = (Get-AzureADGroup -
SearchString $GroupName).objectid
}
 else {
$settingsCopy["GroupCreationAllowedGroupId"] = $GroupName
}
Set-AzureADDirectorySetting -Id $settingsObjectID -DirectorySetting
$settingsCopy

(Get-AzureADDirectorySetting -Id $settingsObjectID).Values
```

After running the code and checking that the values look correct, you can then test using an account not included in your "creators" group to make sure they get an error message when trying to create a new team from the client. Be aware that this type of change may not apply immediately and can be subject to some lag before it kicks in.

 As the code here is based on the preview Azure AD PowerShell module, it is subject to change. This Microsoft page should be updated if the module changes: docs.microsoft.com/en-au/microsoft-365/solutions/manage-creation-of-groups.

M365 Group Naming Policy

Another weapon in your arsenal to make sure all of your teams are neat and tidy is the ability to enforce a naming policy that controls how your M365 groups are, well, named.

The policy comes in two varieties:

Prefix/suffix: Where you can enforce a string in front of or after the entered name of the team

Blocked words: Where certain words are not allowed in a group name

While using naming policies may seem like a great thing to do, unfortunately it isn't a free feature but instead requires each user who will be a member of the M365 groups to be covered by an Azure Active Directory Premium P1 license.

The naming convention will also only apply to any new groups that are created and will not retrospectively apply to any existing groups (although it will apply if someone attempts to edit the name of an existing group after a policy is in place).

Also anyone who is a member of the Global Administrator or User Administrator RBAC roles in Azure AD does not have the rules enforced, so they are able to create groups normally.

 Learn more about group naming policies at docs.microsoft.com/ en-us/azure/active-directory/enterprise-users/groups- naming-policy.

Prefix/Suffix

Strings added to a group's name can be either static or dynamic based on AD attributes:

Static (or fixed) strings: Such as "_Team," which can be used to help differentiate groups when showing up in places like the Global Address List (GAL)

Attributes: Dynamic information added based on who created the group, for example, a user's department

The following are supported attributes that can be used:

- Department
- Company
- Office
- StateOrProvince
- CountryOrRegion
- Title

You can combine both static and dynamic strings, but be aware that the maximum length for anything being added to the team name is 53 characters, so it is recommended to only use dynamic fields where you do not have long strings (for example if Office contains a full address).

Blocked Words

Blocked words can be helpful to make sure that users cannot create groups containing words that you might want to use for other purposes, such as if you wanted to make sure no one could create a group with the word "CEO" in it (which would also create an associated external email address by default).

There are some rules around how blocked words are handled:

- 5,000 words can be added to the block list.
- Words are not case sensitive.

- Substring matching is not used (that is, if Ben is on the block list, you can still use Benefit).

The block list is checked in real time when a user creates a team, so they will get some visual feedback in the Teams client if the name they are trying to use is not allowed.

Configure Naming Policy in Azure AD

As we are working with the M365 groups, the naming policy is configured in the Azure AD portal, so let's log in and take a look.

Launch the portal and log in; then select Groups from the All Services menu. Select Naming Policy on the left to open the settings page. By default this will show the Blocked Words configuration where you can download a CSV file containing the current list of blocked words, or you can upload a new file to apply it (see Figure 4.23).

FIGURE 4.23   Blocked word list in Azure AD

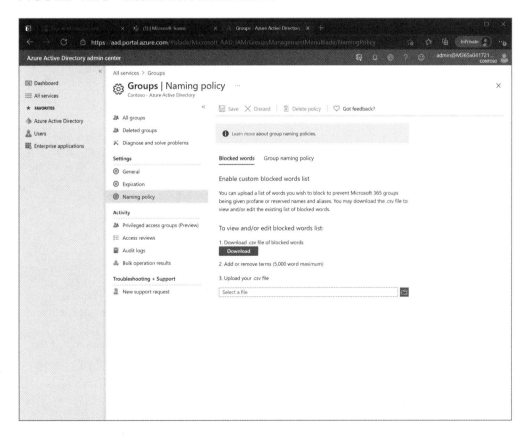

To configure a naming policy, move to the second tab called Group Naming Policy where you can see the current policy that is configured. You can then modify the policy using the selection boxes underneath (see Figure 4.24).

FIGURE 4.24   Group naming policy in Azure AD

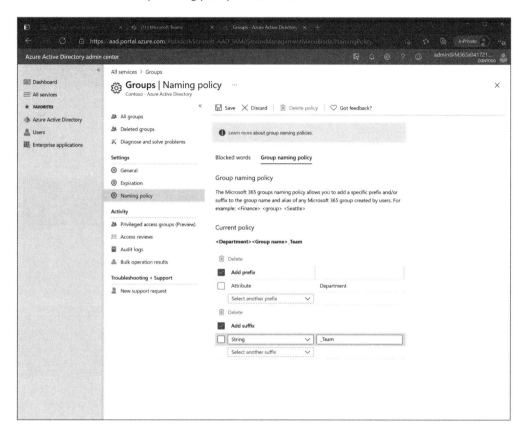

Here you can choose to apply any combination of dynamic or static strings before or after the chosen team name. The resultant policy is shown in the middle of the page where <Group name> is the name entered by the user at the time of creation.

To remove a naming policy, simply choose Delete Policy from the menu at the top of the page and accept the prompt. This will remove any naming policy configuration and return the settings to the defaults.

Configure Naming Policy in PowerShell

You can also modify or create these settings through PowerShell if the mood should take you. Similar to the group creation policy, you need to have the Azure AD preview PowerShell module installed to be able to work with naming policies (see the previous section).

To view the current configuration, connect to Azure AD, save the settings into a variable, and then display the values:

```
Connect-AzureAD

$Setting = Get-AzureADDirectorySetting -Id (Get-AzureADDirectorySetting | where
-Property DisplayName -Value "Group.Unified" -EQ).id

$Setting.Values
```

This should return a list of values; check the following two to identify what your current settings are: `CustomBlockedWorldsList` and `PrefixSufficNamingRequirement` (see Figure 4.25). There is another setting exposed here in PowerShell called `EnableMSStandardBlockedWords` that you can use to block a Microsoft-provided list of dodgy words. Interestingly, the MS documentation suggests you do not use this setting as it's assumed that users would not be creating groups with these words in them anyway.

FIGURE 4.25   Group naming policy in PowerShell

```
PS C:\WINDOWS\system32> $Setting.Values

Name                            Value
----                            -----
EnableMIPLabels                 false
CustomBlockedWordsList
EnableMSStandardBlockedWords    false
ClassificationDescriptions
DefaultClassification
PrefixSuffixNamingRequirement   [Department][GroupName]_Team
AllowGuestsToBeGroupOwner       false
AllowGuestsToAccessGroups       true
GuestUsageGuidelinesUrl
GroupCreationAllowedGroupId
AllowToAddGuests                true
UsageGuidelinesUrl
ClassificationList
EnableGroupCreation             true
```

Now that we have a variable with the settings, you can modify it with a change to the prefix or suffix configuration:

```
$Setting["PrefixSuffixNamingRequirement"]
="[Department]_[CountryOrRegion][GroupName]_Team"
```

 NOTE   If you use a property that is not supported, then it will just be applied as plain text! So you could have a group called My Group_[countryCode].

Or you can make a comma-separated list of blocked words to include:

```
$Setting["CustomBlockedWordsList"]="Ben,CEO,Marketing,Graham"
```

When you are happy with the settings, write them back to save them using the Set- version of the cmdlet:

```
Set-AzureADDirectorySetting -Id (Get-AzureADDirectorySetting | where -Property
DisplayName -Value "Group.Unified" -EQ).id -DirectorySetting $Setting
```

To remove the naming policy, simply set both settings to empty values and save the setting:

```
$Setting["PrefixSuffixNamingRequirement"] =""
$Setting["CustomBlockedWordsList"]=""
Set-AzureADDirectorySetting -Id (Get-AzureADDirectorySetting | where -Property
DisplayName -Value "Group.Unified" -EQ).id -DirectorySetting $Setting
```

M365 Group Expiration

So now you have a tidy and organized Azure AD with things locked down so that only trusted users can create new teams, and you have naming policies configured so that everything is appropriately named, but unfortunately that still doesn't mean you necessarily are on top of it all. By its very nature the usage of Teams can fluctuate as groups of people come together to work on projects and then when completed move on to something else. This can mean that slowly your Azure AD might be filling up with groups and teams that are no longer active. You might wonder what the harm is of just leaving groups alone that are unused as they do not technically take up any of your resources, but if you let it go unchecked for too long, then the job of tidying things up will grow exponentially.

Thankfully, there is another neat Azure AD feature that we can leverage (again this requires an Azure AD Premium P1 license) called *group expiration* that helps keep on top of unused groups. Expiration is turned off by default, but when enabled (by either a Global Admin or User Admin), the following cycle happens:

- Groups with activity are automatically renewed when near their expiry date.
  - In Teams just visiting a channel counts as activity, as well as things like users uploading files, etc.
- Owners of groups without activity receive an email notification asking them to renew the group.
- Groups that are not renewed are then deleted.
- Deleted groups can be restored for a period of 30 days after deletion (we will talk about this more in the following section).

So as you can see, while it is a handy feature to be aware of, you do need to consider how best to deploy it and perhaps consider making the group lifetime fairly long (for example, six months). You should also make sure that any team owners are aware of their responsibility to not ignore any renewal emails!

 When this feature was first deployed, it wasn't possible to automatically renew groups, so owners would receive renewal requests every time the renewal date was triggered. Thankfully, based on feedback, Microsoft updated the feature to operate how it does today, making it infinitely more helpful and less dangerous!

To configure an expiration, log into the Azure AD portal and then head to the Groups section (under All Services). This time instead of selecting Naming Policy in the left menu, select Expiration (see Figure 4.26).

FIGURE 4.26   Group expiration settings

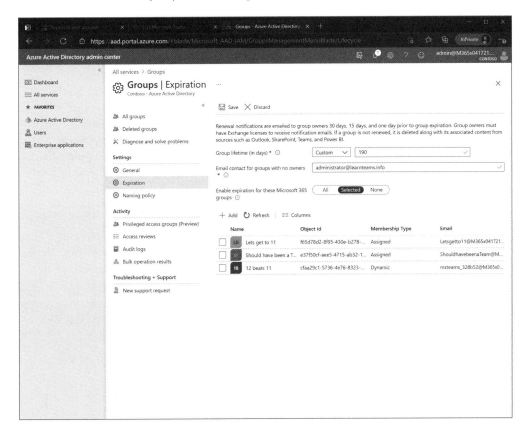

Here you can configure the following options:

Group Lifetime: Numerical value for how old a group can get with no activity; must be more than 30 days

Email contact: Who to send the renewal email to for orphaned groups with no owner

Enable expiration for these groups: Can choose to apply the policy to all groups, no groups, or a selection of groups

If you choose to apply the policy to only certain groups, you can pick them from a list up to a maximum of 500. Also, when you first apply the policy, the expiration date for any groups that are already past the expiry deadline are given 35 days to respond.

Several notifications are sent to remind the owner if no response is received: the first one at 30 days out from expiry, then again at 15 days, then the day before. The email will contain information about the group such as its description, expiry date, and links to last activity.

If the expiration date passes, the group is then deleted the following day, and another email is sent to the owner but this time with a link allowing them to self-service restore the group (if they were the original owner) if the group is still required.

> Read more about group expiration at docs.microsoft.com/en-us/ azure/active-directory/enterprise-users/groups-lifecycle.

Group Expiry in PowerShell

You can manage group expiration using PowerShell with two families of cmdlets: -AzureADMSGroupLifecyclePolicy and - AzureADMSLifecyclePolicyGroup.

When configuring them through PowerShell, you need to first create or configure a lifecycle policy object before and then add it into a policy group. The key cmdlets are as follows:

- `Get-AzureADMSGroupLifecyclePolicy`
- `New-AzureADMSGroupLifecyclePolicy`
- `Set-AzureADMSGroupLifecyclePolicy`
- `Remove-AzureADMSGroupLifecyclePolicy`
- `Get-AzureADMSLifecyclePolicyGroup`
- `Add-AzureADMSLifecyclePolicyGroup`
- `Remove-AzureADMSLifecyclePolicyGroup`
- `Reset-AzureADMSLifeCycleGroup`

So, to configure an expiration policy this way, we could use the following code (after connecting to Azure-AD PowerShell):

```
New-AzureADMSGroupLifecyclePolicy -GroupLifetimeInDays <days> -
ManagedGroupTypes All -AlternateNotificationEmails <email>
```

To check on the policies that are in the tenant, use this:

```
Get-AzureADMSGroupLifecyclePolicy
```

This will give you back an ID number along with the configured settings. We can then take this ID number and add it to the lifecycle policy that is applied to the tenant:

```
Add-AzureADMSLifecyclePolicyGroup -Id "<ID from previous step>" -groupId
"cffd97bd-6b91-4c4e-b553-6918a320211c"
```

The GroupID value that is shown here remains the same across tenants, so you should be okay using it as it stands.

Archiving, Deleting, and Restoring Teams

One of the last parts of the lifecycle management that we need to consider is what happens when a team is no longer required. This could be the deletion of the team that is automatically triggered through something like the expiration policy from the previous section, or it could be something that is either user or administrator initiated.

Archiving Teams

The first option that you might consider is the ability to archive a team. Archiving places the contents of the team into a read-only mode but the team itself is still visible in the client (subject to its original privacy and visibility settings, of course). This can be helpful if you need to retain the team or any content for future reference.

You can archive the team from the TAC if you are an administrator, or users can archive teams for which they are an owner (or in PowerShell, but this is covered in the following section about deleting a team).

To do this from the TAC, open the main list of teams from the left menu by selecting Teams ➤ Manage Teams. Select the team that you want to archive and then from the top menu pick Archive (see Figure 4.27). You will be presented with a confirmation dialog along

FIGURE 4.27 Archiving a team in the TAC

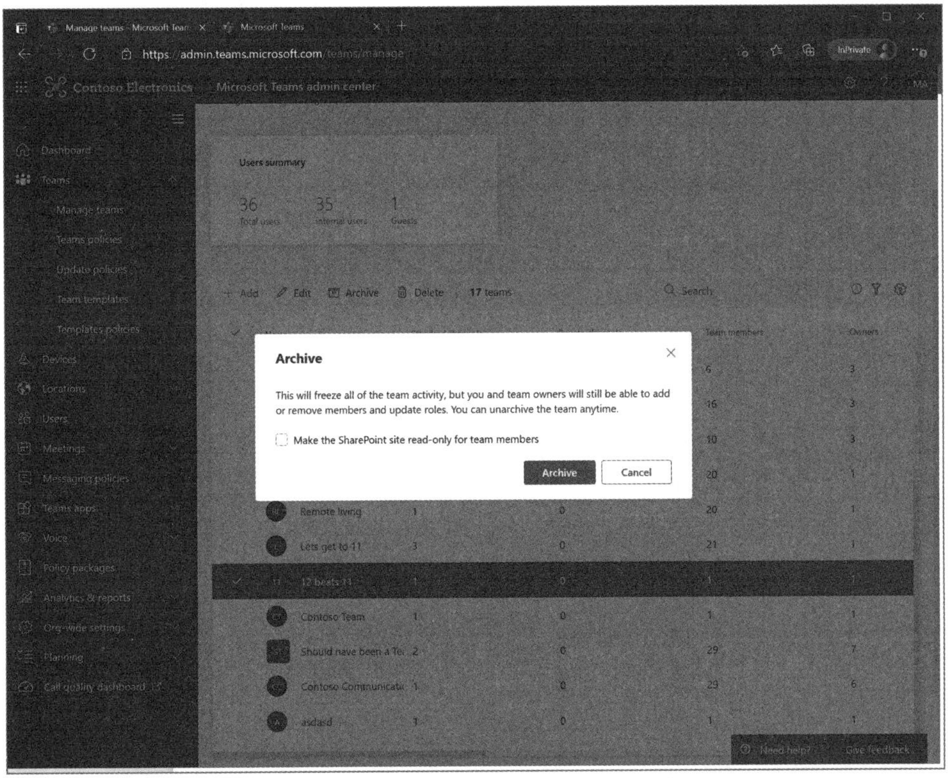

with a check box to also mark the associated SharePoint site for the team as read-only (do this to make any team files also read-only for members but owners can still edit).

The status shown for the team will now be Archived, and if you look in the Teams client, an archive icon will be visible next to the team name (see Figure 4.28).

FIGURE 4.28   An archived team in the Teams client

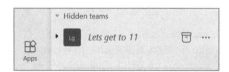

To archive a team from inside the Teams client, the setting is slightly hidden, which makes it harder to do it by accident. To find the setting, click the small cog shown at the bottom of the list of teams on the left menu. This will then show the Manage Teams screen with a list of teams. At the end of the line for the team you want to work with, click the . . . to open the options menu. Here you will find an option to archive the team (see Figure 4.29).

FIGURE 4.29   Archiving a team in Teams client

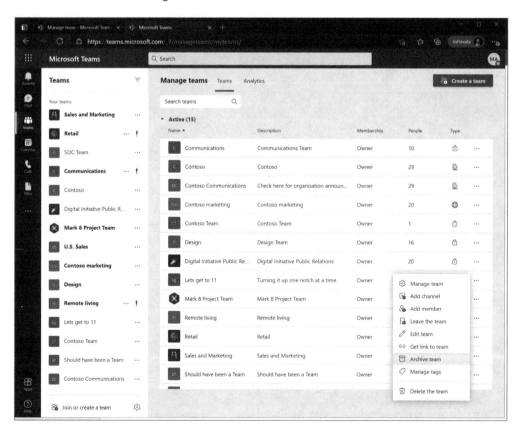

Restoring an Archived Team

If you need to make the team active again, you can easily reverse the process from either the TAC or the Teams client. If we start in the TAC this time, when you select a team that is already archived, the menu button at the top of the screen will change to Unarchive (see Figure 4.30). Click this, and within a few minutes the team status should be changed back to active.

FIGURE 4.30 Restoring an archived team from the TAC

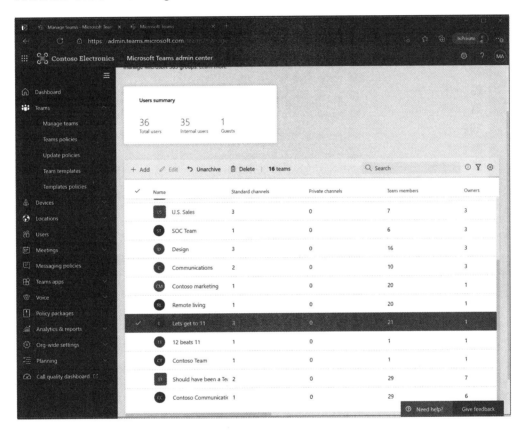

To reverse the process from the Teams client, head to the same Manage Teams screen by selecting the cog at the bottom of the team list. This screen will be split into two sections. The default is to show Active teams, but if you scroll down, you should see an expandable section where the Archived teams are hidden. Expand the arrow, find your team, and then from the . . . menu, you will now have an option to Restore Team (see Figure 4.31). Again, after a few minutes, the team should be restored and available for use again.

FIGURE 4.31   Restoring an archived team from Teams client

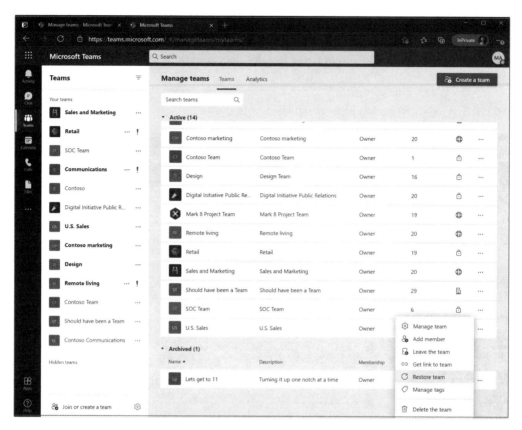

Deleting a Team

Instead of archiving teams, if you know that they are no longer required, you can choose to delete them. By default, when you delete a team, it is actually what is called a *soft delete*— this means that the team and its associated content are not really removed immediately but are hidden from sight; then after 30 days they are properly removed. This soft-delete process gives you a chance to restore the team and associated content with no negative impact (that is, all data and content are kept).

The process of deleting a team is the same as shown earlier for archiving it, except on each menu option select Delete instead of Archive.

For both archiving and deleting, you can also choose to use PowerShell using the `Set-TeamArchivedState` and `Remove-Team` cmdlets, respectively. Both of these cmdlets only accept the GroupID for a team, so in practice you would normally prefix them using `Get-Team` to find the team you want to work with and then pipe it to the respective cmdlet. For example, this code would archive the team for us:

```
Get-Team -DisplayName "Lets get to 11" | Set-TeamArchivedState -Archived:$true
-SetSpoSiteReadOnlyForMembers:$true
```

Or this code would delete the team:

```
Get-Team -DisplayName "Lets get to 11" | Remove-Team
```

You do not need to archive a team before deleting it this way; it is showing how the two cmdlets operate in a similar way.

In normal circumstances, you could sit back and let the soft delete work its way through and know that in time the team and content will be fully removed, but just in case you have to remove a team completely (for example, if you are testing some functionality or need to reuse the team name), then you can also choose to hard-delete a team, which will immediately remove the team, group, and content from the system.

To hard delete a team, you first soft delete it as shown earlier, and then it is recommended that you run the PowerShell cmdlets in a two-step process where you manually copy the GroupID between the cmdlets to identify the group you want to permanently delete just as a precaution. If you piped the output from one to the other, it is too easy to make an irreversible mistake! To get a list of the soft-deleted M365 groups, use (see Figure 4.32):

```
Get-AzureADMSDeletedGroup
```

FIGURE 4.32   List of soft-deleted M365 groups

```
PS C:\WINDOWS\system32> Get-AzureADMSDeletedGroup

Id                                           DisplayName         Description
--                                           -----------         -----------
cfccf516-6f74-45bc-996d-387540f34922 asdasd              asdasd
f65d78d2-8f95-430e-b278-a4bd932f8045 Lets get to 11 Turning it up one notch at a time
```

This will return a list of all the soft-deleted groups; copy the Group ID and use it in the next cmdlet to remove the group object from Azure AD:

```
Remove-AzureADMSDeletedDirectoryObject -Id <GroupID>
```

Restoring a Deleted Team

You can only restore a soft-deleted team through PowerShell, but remember if you used the previous steps to hard-delete it, or if you are past the 30-day retention period you are out of luck.

Use the following cmdlet to give you a list of deleted teams (this time shown using a filter):

```
Get-AzureADMSDeletedGroup -SearchString "<Team Name>"
```

If you are happy with the result, this can then be piped through to the `Restore-Azure-ADMSDeletedDirectoryObject` cmdlet as follows:

```
Get-AzureADMSDeletedGroup -SearchString "<Team Name>" | Restore-
AzureADMSDeletedDirectoryObject
```

If the command is successful, you should see the name of the team output in the window, and after a few minutes, the team will reappear in the client and the TAC.

Read more about archiving and deleting teams at docs.microsoft. com/en-us/microsoftteams/archive-or-delete-a-team.

Data Security and Compliance

In this section, we are going to look at how you can take steps to protect the data inside your teams as well as how you can make sure that your Teams deployment is compliant with any legal requirements that you may be subject to. For example, your organization, depending on where in the world it operates, may have a responsibility to retain certain types of data for a fixed period of time, or your company may be required to make data available in the event of legal proceedings, etc.

For example, if the company has offices or users in the European Union, then your company is likely going to be subject to the requirements around General Data Protection Regulations (GDPR), which control how personal data can be processed.

As with the lifecycle and governance requirements we just covered, Microsoft has a lot of neat features available as part of M365 that can be deployed together to help meet any requirements or obligations that your company has.

It almost goes without saying that really the first step toward deploying any of this into a real-world tenant is to make sure that you properly understand, agree, and sign off with the business what behavior is required and what would be nice to have.

Sensitivity Labels

The first feature to look at is something called *sensitivity labels*; this allows you to apply classifications against your data. Once classified, these labels can then be used either just as visual markers or reminders to end users about the type of data they are dealing with, or with other parts of the M365 suite to control how the data is processed. For example, data with a sensitive classification could be prevented from being emailed outside the organization.

For our scope here with Teams and for the MS 700 exam, we are going to look at how labels can be applied to teams and how this can be used to affect the privacy setting of a team.

Labels are generally applied at either the item level or the container level. With Teams, a team is considered to be a container, as it holds other items, such as documents, inside it.

To start using sensitivity labels, we need to have at least one Azure AD Premium P1 license in the tenant, and then we can enable their use for containers before configuring them and using policies to apply them to your users.

 You may see some references to classification labels; these were text-only strings that could be associated with an item but didn't then have any associated policies or controllable behavior. Sensitivity labels have effectively replaced them.

Enabling Sensitivity Labels for Containers

This is done inside PowerShell using the Azure AD module and is a similar process to that for configuring naming policies.

First connect to Azure AD:

```
Connect-AzureAD
```

Then get a list of the current group settings:

```
$Setting = Get-AzureADDirectorySetting -Id (Get-AzureADDirectorySetting | where
-Property DisplayName -Value "Group.Unified" -EQ).id
```

Now enable the use of sensitivity labels and write back the new configuration:

```
$Setting["EnableMIPLabels"] = "True"
Set-AzureADDirectorySetting -Id $Setting.Id -DirectorySetting $Setting
```

Once this has applied, you can kick off what is called a synchronization to make sensitivity labels available for use in your groups:

```
Execute-AzureAdLabelSync
```

Creating Sensitivity Labels

Once sensitivity labels have been enabled, we need to configure them, which is done through a portal we haven't used before: Microsoft 365 Compliance. This can be found at compliance.microsoft.com (see Figure 4.33).

FIGURE 4.33   M365 compliance portal

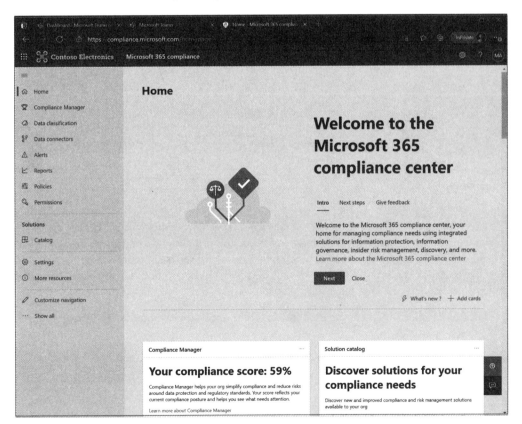

After logging in, click Show All at the bottom of the left menu and then select Information Protection to open the labeling interface (see Figure 4.34).

FIGURE 4.34   Sensitivity label management

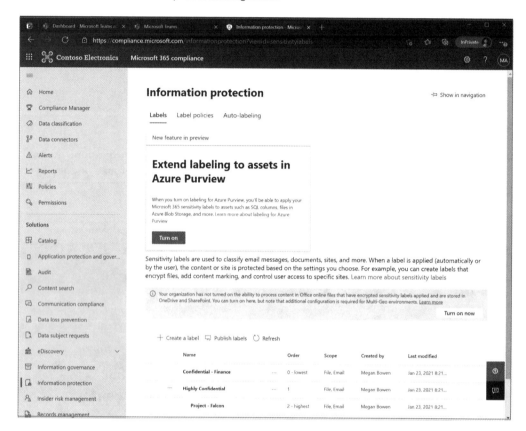

Here you can click Create A Label to start a new sensitivity label wizard. Give the new label a name, display name, and a brief description about its intended purpose. You can also provide an admin description that only administrators will see (see Figure 4.35).

Move to the next screen to choose where this label will be applied. There are two primary options (and one in preview that is out of scope for us):

Files & Emails: Labels can be used inside Office applications and files and can also be applied to emails.

Groups & Sites: Labels apply to M365 groups, SharePoint sites, and teams.

FIGURE 4.35   Naming a sensitivity label

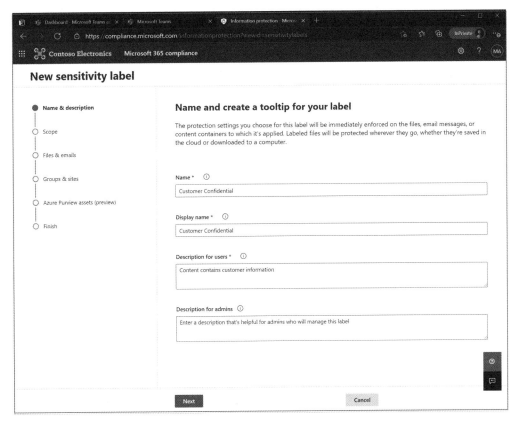

To use this inside Teams, select at least Groups & Sites (see Figure 4.36). You can choose to share sensitivity labels between documents and groups, or you can choose to have them as separate entities, which while giving extra control also increases the complexity of keeping track of things.

You can skip through configuring the settings for files and emails, if you would like, as they are outside of our scope here for MS 700, until you get to the section called Define Protection Settings For Groups And Sites (see Figure 4.37). Here the first option can apply to teams created using this sensitivity label; you can specify their privacy level and if they can have external users added as guests.

Click Next to then specify what privacy settings we want to control (see Figure 4.38):

Privacy: Can be set to Public, Private, or None (where the owner can decide)

External User Access: Controls if the team can have external (guest) users added as members

FIGURE 4.36   Scope for a sensitivity label

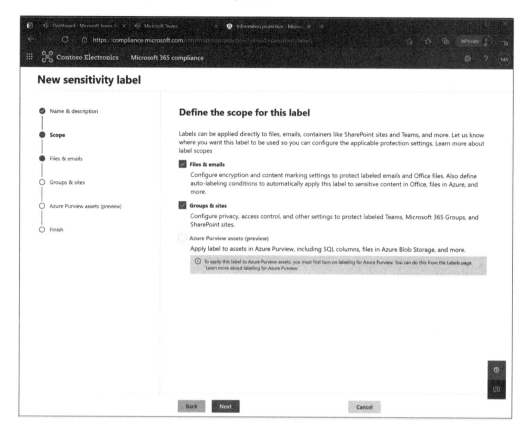

Finish the wizard and create the label. This will now show in the list, where you can edit the settings if you need to.

Once the label itself has been created, you need to publish it by specifying which group of users will have access to use and apply the label. From the menu just above the list of labels, click Publish Labels and follow the wizard by first selecting the sensitivity label that was just created (see Figure 4.39) and then choosing if you want all users, or only a certain group of users, to be able to apply it (Figure 4.40).

On the Policy Settings screen you can choose to make the label mandatory, but be careful here, especially if you have scoped this label so that all users in the organization have access to it (see Figure 4.41).

Lastly, name the policy and save it. When creating new sensitivity labels and policies, you can expect the change to apply roughly within an hour (subject to the usual "it could take up to 48 hours" caveat!), but if you are modifying an existing label or policy, plan for approximately 24 hours before the change kicks in.

FIGURE 4.37   Protection settings for groups and sites

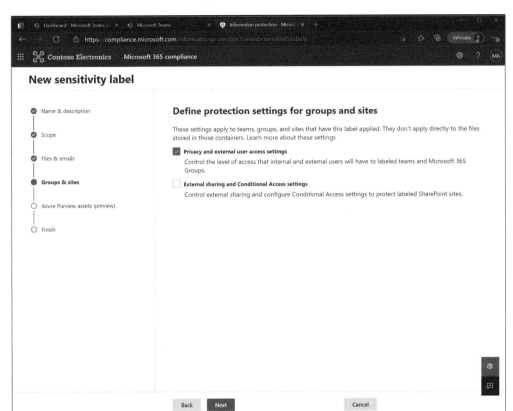

 To read more about managing sensitivity labels, as well as how to manage them through PowerShell (beyond our scope for MS 700), see docs.microsoft.com/en-us/microsoft-365/compliance/ create-sensitivity-labels.

Applying a Sensitivity Label to a Team

Once the change has taken effect, you will notice a slight change with the new option in any location that you used previously to create teams (that is, in the TAC or the Teams client). Figure 4.42 shows the updated interface in the Teams client, and you will notice that after the sensitivity label has been selected, the privacy level for the team is now enforced and cannot be changed.

FIGURE 4.38 Privacy and external access settings

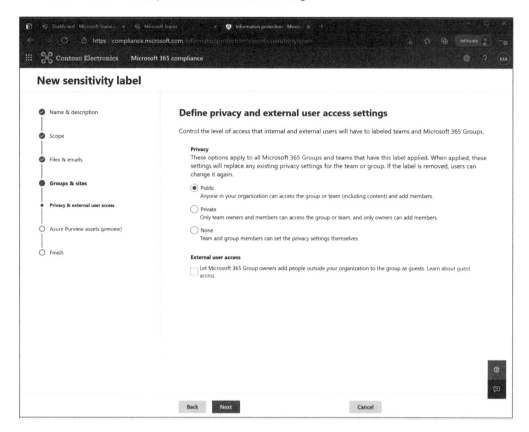

Once the team has been created, you will notice that there is a visual indicator showing the current sensitivity label that is being applied to the team (see Figure 4.43).

The owner of the team can change the sensitivity label at any time (assuming there is not a mandatory sensitivity label policy being enforced) from the usual Edit Team menu (see Figure 4.44).

When applying a sensitivity label to a team some of the labels settings, such as content marking and encryption settings, do not automatically apply to the content inside a team. For more information, see docs. microsoft.com/en-us/microsoft-365/compliance/sensitivity-labels-teams-groups-sites.

FIGURE 4.39 Selecting a label to publish

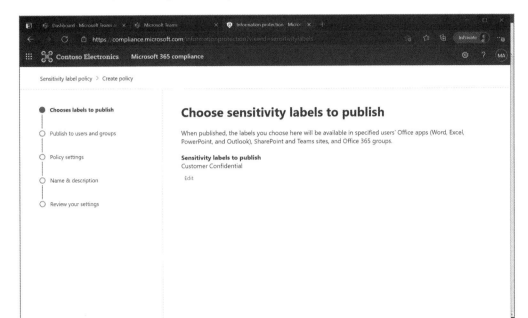

Retention Policies

Retention policies are used to enforce how long particular items of data should be kept. This can work both ways. You could create a policy to ensure that any data that you are required to keep cannot be deleted until enough time has passed that it is not considered relevant anymore, or perhaps you want to ensure that data that could be a liability but that you are not under any obligation to keep is deleted.

With that in mind, there are essentially three ways that you could choose to deploy a retention policy:

Retain: Make sure data cannot be deleted until a certain time frame has passed.

Delete: Make sure that data over a certain age is deleted.

Retain then delete: Prevent data from being deleted for a period of time and then make sure it is removed.

FIGURE 4.40 Selecting the scope of access

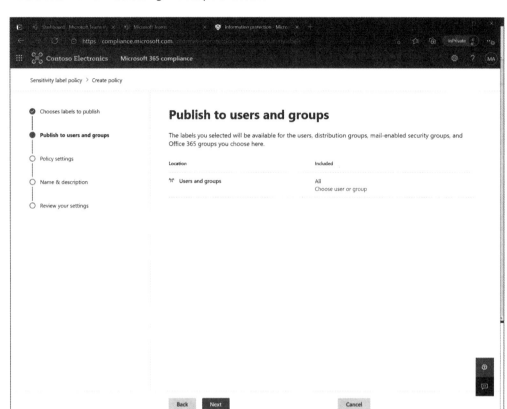

When creating a retention policy, you must define its scope or location. However, as by now you are more than aware, Teams covers multiple workloads (for example, keeping files inside SharePoint or OneDrive for Business). You will probably need to configure more than one retention policy to achieve the outcome you require.

When you see Teams referenced in a retention policy, it is referring to either chat messages (1:1 and 1:many) or channel messages (conversations in a channel).

To fully cover the Teams workload, you should also consider retention policies for the following areas:

M365 groups: Would catch any data in the group mailbox, etc.

Skype for Business: Would be needed if any users had not finished migrating to Teams and were still using Skype for Business to communicate (SfB messages are stored in the user's mailbox in a special folder)

SharePoint: Any files uploaded into a team channel

OneDrive for Business: Any files uploaded in a chat outside of a team

FIGURE 4.41   Policy Settings screen

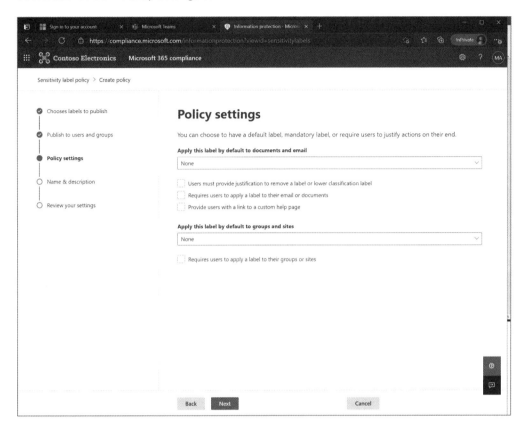

    Be aware that even if you apply a retention policy to a user's Exchange mailbox or an M365 group, this will not apply to Teams chat or channel messages even though they are stored inside a hidden folder inside the relevant mailbox.

Creating a Retention Policy

Creating a retention policy is carried out from the same compliance portal that we used for the sensitivity labels (or you can create them using PowerShell). This time from the left menu open Information Governance and then Retention from the top menu (see Figure 4.45).

Chose New Retention Policy to start the wizard. Here you can give the policy a name and description before moving to the next screen where you can select the locations (think scope) that the policy will cover (see Figure 4.46). You can further narrow down the scope if you choose by specifically including or excluding certain teams (for channel messages) or users (for chat).

FIGURE 4.42   Creating a team with a sensitivity label

FIGURE 4.43   Showing the sensitivity label in the team

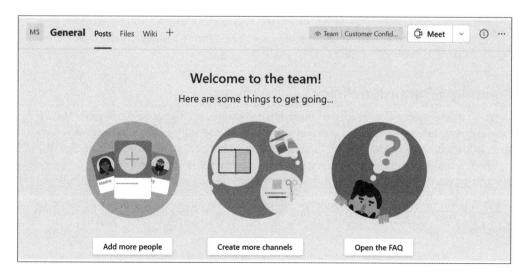

FIGURE 4.44   Showing the sensitivity label in the team

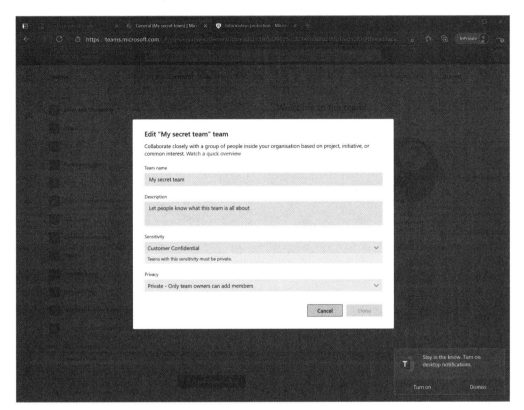

Next choose what behavior you would like to enforce through the policy; the default is to retain and then delete, but you can adjust it to meet your needs (see Figure 4.47).

Save the policy, and you are done! Be careful here when scoping the policy, especially if you are enforcing a deletion event, as you could easily apply the policy to the entire organization in one go, so make sure that is really what you would like to do!

When the policy has applied, if any chat messages are removed, users will simply see a placeholder with a note informing them that content has been removed due to an organizational retention policy.

You can also work with and create retention policies using PowerShell, but this is beyond the scope that you are required to know for the MS 700 exam. Instead, make sure that you are aware of the cmdlet families `-RetentionCompliancePolicy` and `-RetentionComplianceRule` that can be used to modify the policies, specifically the `New-RetentionCompliancePolicy` and `new- RetentionComplianceRule` cmdlets. These are part of the Security and Compliance Center PowerShell module.

FIGURE 4.45 Retention policy

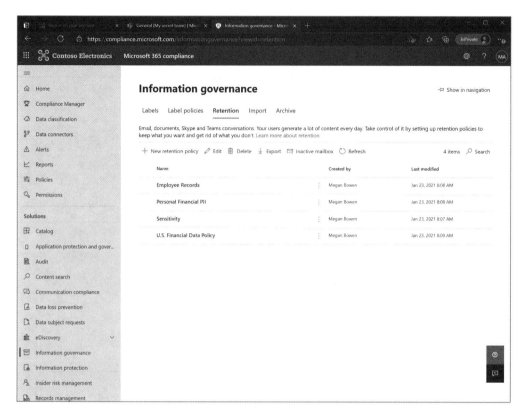

 You can read more about how retention policies apply in Teams at docs.microsoft.com/en-us/microsoftteams/retention-policies, and you can read up on using the Security and Compliance PowerShell module at docs.microsoft.com/en-us/powershell/exchange/connect-to-scc-powershell.

Data Loss Prevention Policies

Data loss prevention (DLP) is a way to identify and protect data from being shared where you do not want it. This would usually apply to sensitive data such as credit card numbers or healthcare-related information.

DLP policies will allow you to:

- Identify information (based on rules) across your environment (including Teams)
- Prevent users from being able to inappropriately share the identified information

FIGURE 4.46   Retention policy locations

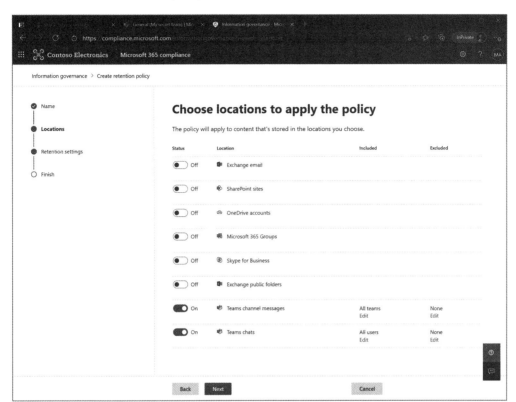

DLP does require additional licensing beyond a standard E3, but it is included in several higher-tier bundles and add-on SKUs:

- O365 E5
- M365 E5
- M365 E5 Compliance
- O365 Advanced Compliance (add-on)

As with the retention policies, you can configure DLP in Teams to support identifying and protecting information in messages as well as inside documents.

Fortunately, Microsoft provides a number of templates for different types of information (and by worldwide region) that you can call on to save you from having to start from scratch creating your rules. Some examples of the types of information identifiers available are:

- Social Security numbers
- Driving licenses

FIGURE 4.47   Retention policy actions

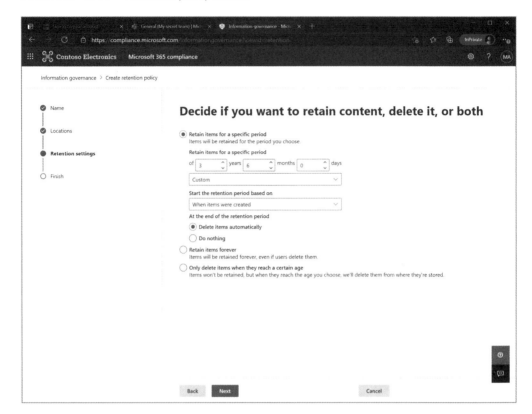

- Credit card numbers
- Bank account numbers
- Health records

 You can see a detailed list of what the built-in detection templates look for and how the confidence level of the detection is determined here: docs. microsoft.com/en-us/exchange/policy-and-compliance/data-loss-prevention/sensitive-information-types. For example, a valid credit card number in proximity to the word *creditcard* and an expiry date would have a higher confidence than just the number alone.

Creating DLP Policies for Use with Teams

To configure a DLP policy, open the same M365 compliance portal that we used earlier in this chapter and in the left menu select Data Loss Prevention (see Figure 4.48).

FIGURE 4.48   DLP management

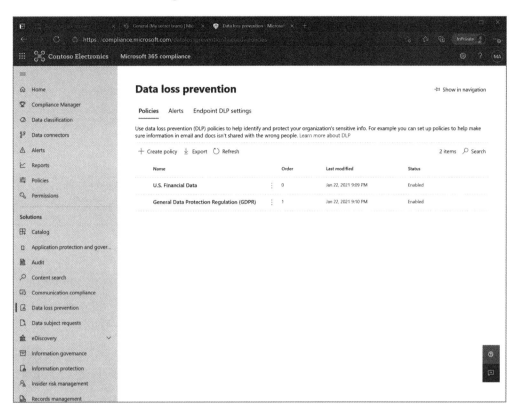

On the Policies page start the new policy wizard by clicking Create Policy. Here you can choose to start with a predefined identification template or start from scratch with a custom rule (see Figure 4.49).

On the next page give the policy a name and a suitable description so you can refer to it later. On the next screen you will note that this location configuration is similar to what we had previously for retention policies: you can choose where to apply the DLP rule. Remember that the Teams workload specifically covers chat and conversations and that SharePoint or OneDrive for Business would need to be used to cover files being uploaded. For this example, just stick with Teams (see Figure 4.50).

If you used a template, you can review and change the settings included in the template, or you can choose to customize things from scratch. Over the next few screens, you can control the following options (see Figures 4.51 and 4.52):

- Detect content shared to external users
- Detect content shared to internal users
- Adjust the confidence used when detecting values

FIGURE 4.49 DLP templates

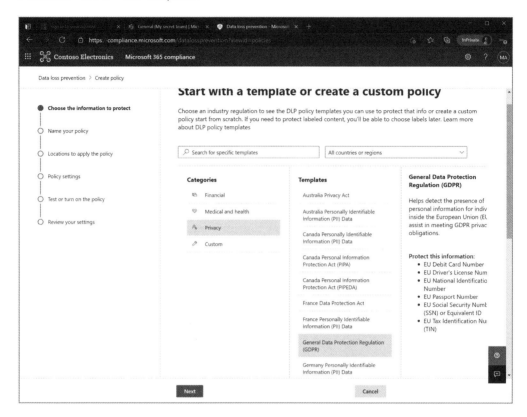

- Configure how users should be alerted to a policy breach
- Allow users to override or comment on the detected breach
- Look for high volumes of data being shared in one go
- Generate an incident report via email
- Generate an alert in the tenant
- Limit access or encrypt the file in question

The final screen of the wizard is important, as it gives you the opportunity to soft-enable the rule so that it will show informational tool tips when DLP has been activated without actually preventing users from communicating (see Figure 4.53). When enabling DLP for the first time, it would be recommended that you configure it for testing first and then come back later to enforce the policy when satisfied that it is working correctly.

FIGURE 4.50   DLP locations

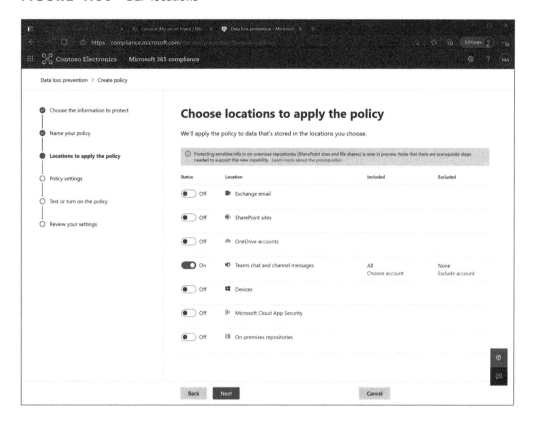

Again, you do not need to know how to configure DLP using PowerShell but the cmdlets you would use include:

- `New-DLpPolicy`
- `Get-DlpPolicy`
- `Set-DLpPolicy`
- `Remove-DLpPolicy`

DLP in Action

Once DLP has been configured and applied to the tenant (again due to replication, this can take about an hour for a new policy or 24 hours for a change), you should be able to test it from the Teams client. Messages are checked after the user has sent them, rather than while each message is being typed, so if something breaches the new policy, it will be detected within a second or so of being sent, and the message will change, depending on what settings you have configured.

FIGURE 4.51   DLP protection

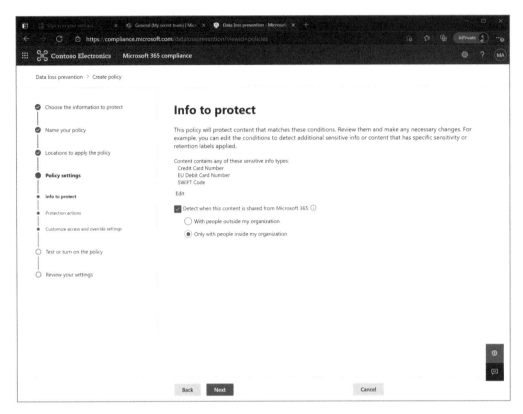

You can see in Figure 4.54 where a message containing a (fake) credit card number has been detected and flagged for attention.

Then, again depending on what settings you configured for the detection, the user can click the What Can I Do link. If you have allowed it, the user can override the detection and provide a justification for what they were attempting to do, or the user can flag it as a false positive (see Figure 4.55).

This message will be shown only to the sender; the recipient will only see a deleted message with a note saying that it was automatically deleted by the system due to sensitive content being detected.

It is important if you are going to deploy DLP to your users that you provide them with clear guidelines about what they can and cannot send in messages as well as how to deal with these messages that they will see in the client so that they know what to expect.

 You can read up more about DLP and applying it to other workloads at docs.microsoft.com/en-us/microsoft-365/compliance/data-loss-prevention-policies.

FIGURE 4.52 DLP actions

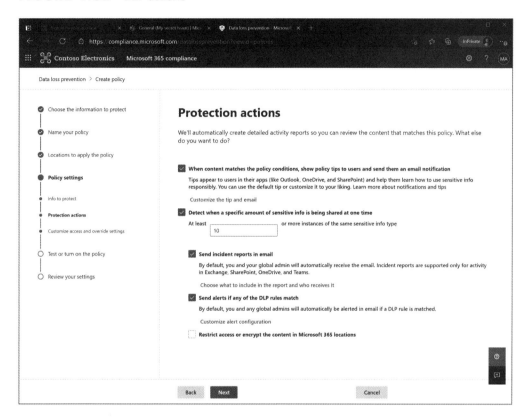

Segmentation and Information Barriers

You might find that you have a requirement to be able to segment off groups of your users from each other (so they cannot find each other in the address list), or you may need to actually prevent communications between groups of users. For example, imagine you work at a consultancy company that is running projects for two customers who are competitors with each other. You may be contractually obligated to ensure that the people working on these two contracts cannot collaborate and share information with each other!

Here we can use two features called *information barriers* and *scoped directory search* to create policies that will help keep everything nice and separate.

Scoped Directory Search

First we need to enable something called *scoped directory search* inside Teams at a global level. To do that, we need to return to the TAC and modify one of the org-wide policy settings.

FIGURE 4.53   DLP testing or enabling

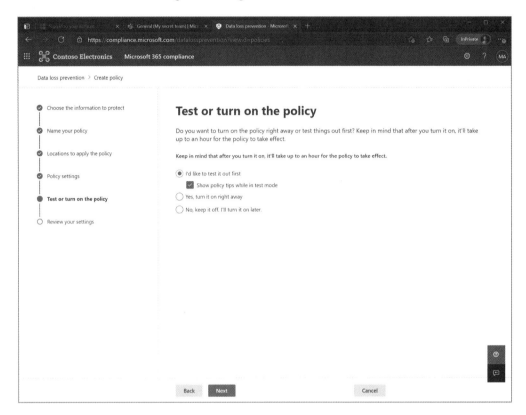

FIGURE 4.54   DLP warning flag

Open the TAC and in the left menu select Org-Wide Settings ≻ Teams Settings. Scroll down the page and at the very bottom should be a toggle in a section called Search By Name (see Figure 4.56).

By setting this to On, we are telling Teams that when users search for users in the Teams client, it is not to return results from the default Exchange Address Book but instead is to limit the scope based on a filtered version created via Exchange Online.

Read more about scoped directory search in Teams at docs.microsoft.com/en-us/MicrosoftTeams/teams-scoped-directory-search.

FIGURE 4.55 DLP justification message

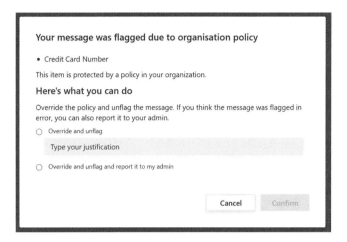

FIGURE 4.56 Scope directory search

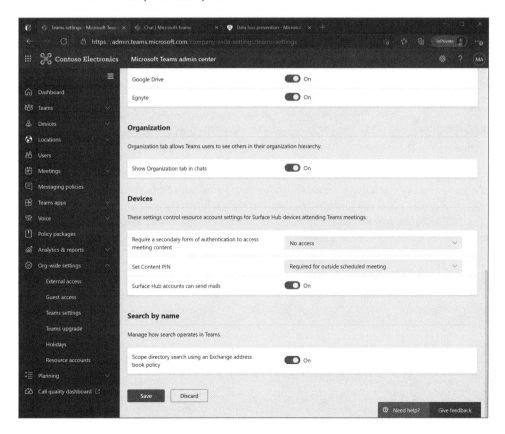

Information Barrier Requirements

Information barriers is another advanced compliance feature, so it has similar requirements to DLP from a licensing point of view, meaning that it is included in the higher-tier bundles and add-on SKUs:

- O365 E5
- M365 E5
- M365 E5 Compliance
- O365 Advanced Compliance (add-on)

To be able to configure and manage information barriers, your account needs one of the following RBAC roles:

- Global Administrator
- Compliance Administrator
- IB Compliance Management

There are also a few other catches or considerations to consider:

AD data: As information barriers rely on queries against user attributes, they will only be as good as the data in your AD.

Scoped directory search: This needs to be enabled (see the previous section).

Address book policies: You cannot have existing ABPs deployed as they are incompatible with information barriers.

Audit logging: This should be enabled.

Directionality: Policies are not bidirectional, so you need to create them in pairs or you cannot enable the service.

One other oddity about how information barriers work is that in order to allow the service to add or remove users from chats (as they move in or out of blocked groups), you need to explicitly give the information barriers application permissions into your Teams tenant. This is something that you do from the browser but only if the application is prepared.

The following code (which uses another Azure PowerShell module) will connect to your tenant, check if the information barriers app is ready to use, and if not add it in. Then it launches a browser session for you with the correct URL. All you need to do is then log in and authorize the permission request (see Figure 4.57):

```
Install-Module AZ

Connect-AzureAD

$appId = "bcf62038-e005-436d-b970-2a472f8c1982"
```

```
$sp = Get-AzADServicePrincipal -ServicePrincipalName $appId

if ($sp -eq $null) {
    New-AzADServicePrincipal -ApplicationId $appId
}

Start-Process
https://login.microsoftonline.com/common/adminconsent?client_id=$appId
```

FIGURE 4.57   Information barrier permissions request

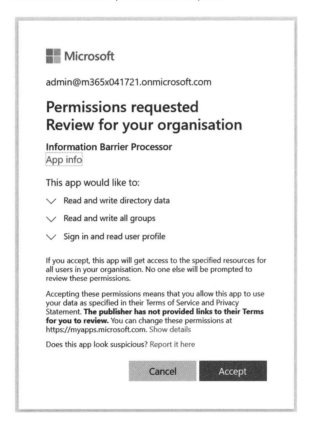

Once the information barrier application can access your Teams tenant, it can help enforce the policies that you configure and can take action against any prohibited interactions that have already taken place. For example, if you create a policy that prevents User A from talking to User B but they already have a conversation going, the chat will be made read-only, and no further interactions will be allowed.

Some scenarios where you would see an impact from applying information barriers between users include:

Searching for a user: Blocked users would be unable to find each other in the directory.

Adding a user to a team: Blocked users would not show up when searching to add a user to the team and if entered manually would be rejected.

Already in a team: The user would be removed from the team.

Starting a new chat: The chat request would not initiate.

In a group chat or existing one-on-one chat: One-on-one chats would be marked read-only, and the user would be removed from group chats (but still be able to see the history to that point).

Joining a meeting: A blocked user would not be able to join meetings.

Starting a Teams call: The call would be blocked.

To read more about the different behaviors shown when information barriers are applied, see docs.microsoft.com/en-us/microsoftteams/information-barriers-in-teams.

Creating Segments

Creating segments is the first step toward creating information barriers; they are what divide your users into groups. Once a segment has been created, you can then either apply a block or allow policy against it to control which other segments it can interact with. A user can belong to up to two segments, but each segment may have only one policy applied to it.

Segments are constructed using filters based on AD attributes, such as Company, Department, or MemberOf (so you can use AD groups to control it).

You can see a full list of supported attributes at docs.microsoft.com/en-us/microsoft-365/compliance/information-barriers-attributes.

To set up the segments you need to connect, use the Security and Compliance PowerShell module, which is part of the Exchange Online modules. Use this code to get it installed and connected:

```
Import-Module ExchangeOnlineManagement

Connect-IPPSSession
```

Once that is connected, you can then construct your segments using the following cmdlets:

```
New-OrganizationSegment -Name "<Name>" -UserGroupFilter "<Attribute> <Match operator> <Value>"
```

So, for example, we will make two segments based on department, one for Consulting and one for Marketing (because we wouldn't want Consulting being bothered by Marketing requests!). The code would look like this:

```
New-OrganizationSegment -Name "Consulting" -UserGroupFilter "Department -eq
'Consulting'"

New-OrganizationSegment -Name "Marketing" -UserGroupFilter "Department -eq
'Marketing'"
```

If successful, you should get some confirmation back (see Figure 4.58). If you receive a timeout error, it may be because you have made a typo in the filter or are using attributes that it doesn't understand.

FIGURE 4.58 Creating a segment

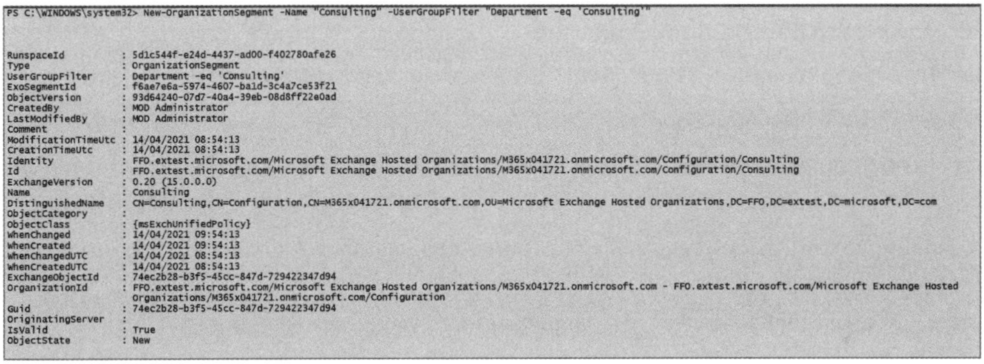

```
PS C:\WINDOWS\system32> New-OrganizationSegment -Name "Consulting" -UserGroupFilter "Department -eq 'Consulting'"


RunspaceId             : 5d1c544f-e24d-4437-ad00-f402780afe26
Type                   : OrganizationSegment
UserGroupFilter        : Department -eq 'Consulting'
ExoSegmentId           : f6ae7e6a-5974-4607-ba1d-3c4a7ce53f21
ObjectVersion          : 93d64240-07d7-40a4-39eb-08d8ff22e0ad
CreatedBy              : MOD Administrator
LastModifiedBy         : MOD Administrator
Comment                :
ModificationTimeUtc    : 14/04/2021 08:54:13
CreationTimeUtc        : 14/04/2021 08:54:13
Identity               : FFO.extest.microsoft.com/Microsoft Exchange Hosted Organizations/M365x041721.onmicrosoft.com/Configuration/Consulting
Id                     : FFO.extest.microsoft.com/Microsoft Exchange Hosted Organizations/M365x041721.onmicrosoft.com/Configuration/Consulting
ExchangeVersion        : 0.20 (15.0.0.0)
Name                   : Consulting
DistinguishedName      : CN=Consulting,CN=Configuration,CN=M365x041721.onmicrosoft.com,OU=Microsoft Exchange Hosted Organizations,DC=FFO,DC=extest,DC=microsoft,DC=com
ObjectCategory         :
ObjectClass            : {msExchUnifiedPolicy}
WhenChanged            : 14/04/2021 09:54:13
WhenCreated            : 14/04/2021 09:54:13
WhenChangedUTC         : 14/04/2021 08:54:13
WhenCreatedUTC         : 14/04/2021 08:54:13
ExchangeObjectId       : 74ec2b28-b3f5-45cc-847d-729422347d94
OrganizationId         : FFO.extest.microsoft.com/Microsoft Exchange Hosted Organizations/M365x041721.onmicrosoft.com - FFO.extest.microsoft.com/Microsoft Exchange Hosted
                         Organizations/M365x041721.onmicrosoft.com/Configuration
Guid                   : 74ec2b28-b3f5-45cc-847d-729422347d94
OriginatingServer      :
IsValid                : True
ObjectState            : New
```

You can then check what segments you have created by running this:

```
Get-OrganizationSegment
```

Applying Information Barriers

Now that the segments are created, you can create a policy that links them together. Remember that the policy can be used either to block or to allow communication between the groups.

Still connected to the PowerShell module from earlier, you would run one of the following cmdlets to either block or allow communications:

```
New-InformationBarrierPolicy -Name "<PolicyName>" -AssignedSegment
"<FirstSegment>" -SegmentsBlocked "<SecondSegment>"

New-InformationBarrierPolicy -Name "<PolicyName>" -AssignedSegment
"<FirstSegment>" -SegmentsAllowed "<SecondSegment>"
```

It is good practice here to name your policies something along the lines of <Segment1> and <Segment2> so that it will be obvious what it was used for if you have to come look at it later. For our example we would therefore run this:

```
New-InformationBarrierPolicy -Name "Consulting-Marketing" -AssignedSegment
"Consulting" -SegmentsBlocked "Marketing"
New-InformationBarrierPolicy -Name "Marketing-Consulting" -AssignedSegment
"Marketing" -SegmentsBlocked "Consulting"
```

Check that the configuration is correct using the following:

```
Get-InformationBarrierPolicy
```

And if you made any mistakes, you can remove them using the following:

```
Remove-InformationBarrierPolicy -Identity <Name>
```

By default, when the policies are created, they are flagged as inactive, so the (nearly) last thing we need to do is set them to be active:

```
Set-InformationBarrierPolicy -Identity <name or ID> -State Active
```

For us, this would be as follows:

```
Set-InformationBarrierPolicy -Identity "Consulting-Marketing" -State Active
Set-InformationBarrierPolicy -Identity "Marketing-Consulting" -State Active
```

Finally, we start the information barrier policy application to make sure that it is checking using the rules we have provided with the following:

```
Start-InformationBarrierPoliciesApplication
```

After the application has started, you should start seeing the effects within 30 minutes or so, but it can take up to 24 hours for the policy to fully apply.

eDiscovery

eDiscovery is the name of a feature that allows you to place content on hold across the different M365 services when they may be subject to legal action, etc. This means you can search through content and provide reports on what is identified, all without fear of the data being deleted or tampered with. eDiscovery itself is a huge topic, so we are really going to skim the surface of what is possible here, but it will be enough to know what you need for the exam.

eDiscovery can be run in three different varieties depending on what you need to achieve:

Content Searches: Used to perform quick searches across content.

Core eDiscovery cases: Places assets on hold and uses a structured case management system to organize the investigation.

Advanced eDiscovery cases: Builds on the core case management system, allowing more complex workflows (such as notifying custodians of the case in progress) and has tools to help organize and structure data that would otherwise require a lot of manual intervention. This type of case requires an E5 or associated add-on license.

 Read more about the types of eDiscovery at docs.microsoft.com/en-us/microsoft-365/compliance/ediscovery.

As you can imagine, for a tool whose primary purpose is to help you respond to legal inquiries about your data, there are a whole set of RBAC roles associated with eDiscovery, as shown in Table 4.4.

TABLE 4.4   eDiscovery RBAC Roles

Role	Compliance Admin	eDiscovery Manager & Admin	Organization Management	Reviewer
Case Management	Y	Y	Y	
Communication		Y		
Compliance Search	Y	Y	Y	
Custodian		Y		
Export		Y		
Hold	Y	Y	Y	
Preview		Y		
Review		Y		Y
RMS decrypt (Rights Management)		Y		
Search & Purge			Y	

docs.microsoft.com/en-us/microsoft-365/compliance/assign-ediscovery-permissions

The role shown in the table as eDiscovery Manager & Admin is actually two roles in practice: eDiscovery Manager and eDiscovery Administrator. The only difference between these roles is that the Manager role can only access their own cases, whereas the Administrator can access all cases in the organization.

Creating an eDiscovery Case

While you can manage eDiscovery cases through PowerShell, we are primarily going to work with them through our new favorite M365 portal, the M365 compliance portal. After logging in, look for eDiscovery in the left menu and choose whether you are going to work with the Core or Advanced tools. For our purposes, click Core (see Figure 4.59).

FIGURE 4.59 Core eDiscovery case list

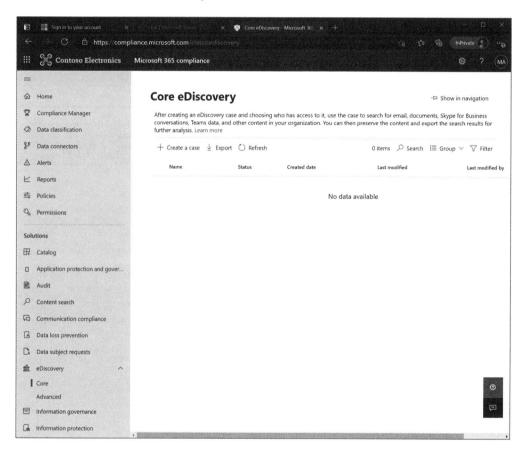

Click Create A Case to open a pop-out on the right side of the screen. Here you can give the case a suitable name and description before clicking Save (see Figure 4.60).

This will make a new blank case. If you click the case, you can then assign users to the case and manage what associated role groups are used. You can also close or delete the case using the buttons at the bottom of the screen.

FIGURE 4.60   Starting a new eDiscovery case

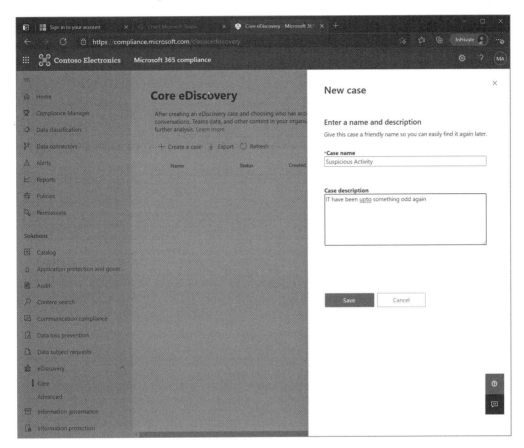

Holding Content in eDiscovery

The next step would usually be to select which content is going to be the subject of the eDiscovery case and place it on hold. This would usually be the team or M365 group relating to the issue you are investigating, or it could be individual users or a combination of the two. In fact, if you are investigating activity inside a team, it may make sense to also include the individual users in the hold as there could be content in private chats that is relevant. In the real world, there is a balance to be had here between overreaching and invading user privacy and the level of scrutiny that is required. Chances are that if you end up having to do this for real, you can take guidance from your company's HR and legal departments about what should be considered in scope.

By placing content on hold, you prevent anyone from deleting or tampering with it until you are finished with the eDiscovery case. You do not have to put content on hold and can still run searches without it, but it is probably a necessary step.

To place a team or users on hold, select the case that was just created and select Open Case from the top menu bar. This will launch a new window with three main sections across the top: Holds, Searches, and Exports. Navigate to the Holds section (see Figure 4.61).

FIGURE 4.61   Including content in a hold

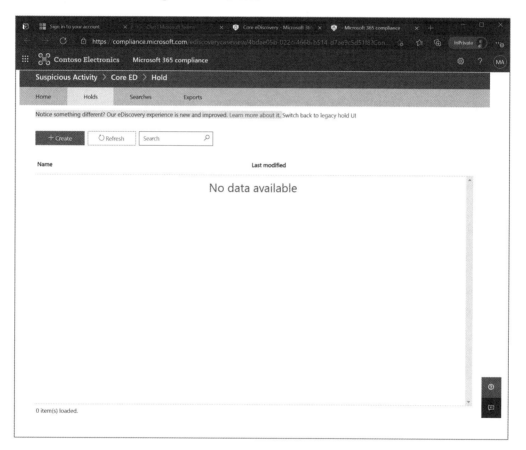

Click Create and give the hold a name (see Figure 4.62).

The locations screen is slightly different from the ones used in the earlier sections as it is split into two categories already, one by user, groups, or teams, and the other by sites. This is because the data that will be subject to the hold generally lives in one of two places, either an Exchange mailbox (top option in Figure 4.63) or a SharePoint site (bottom option in Figure 4.63).

FIGURE 4.62   Naming a hold

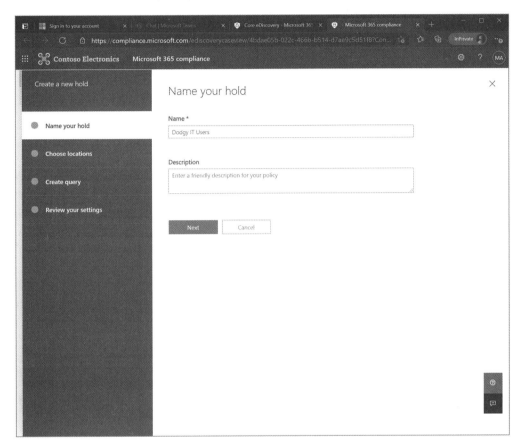

Choose the name of a team and move to the next screen. Here you can specify query conditions; when they are matched, the content will be held. If left blank, all content in the location will be subject to the hold. Complete the wizard, and the hold will now be configured.

 For more information about placing eDiscovery holds on content, see docs.microsoft.com/en-us/microsoft-365/compliance/create-ediscovery-holds.

eDiscovery Searches

Now with the hold sorted, you can generate some searches to go and look for content relevant to the case. In the same case, you can have more than one source for items that are on hold, but you can also have more than one search configured. Also remember that searches

FIGURE 4.63   Scope for a hold

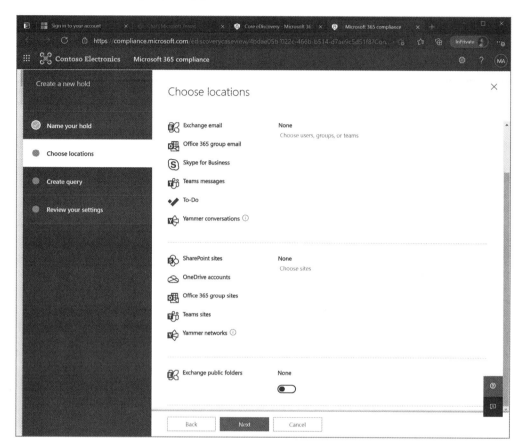

and holds are independent of each other. You can scope a search to look in places beyond what you have on hold.

To build a search, move to the Searches tab and then you can start a manual search by clicking New Search; however, for the first time through, it probably makes sense to start with a Guided Search. Give the search a name and click Next (see Figure 4.64).

On the Locations tab, add the places that you want to include in the search. These can be org-wide (All Locations) or manually specified (like we did on the content hold step), or the search can be scoped to search just the content that this case has already placed on hold (see Figure 4.65).

FIGURE 4.64   Naming an eDiscovery search

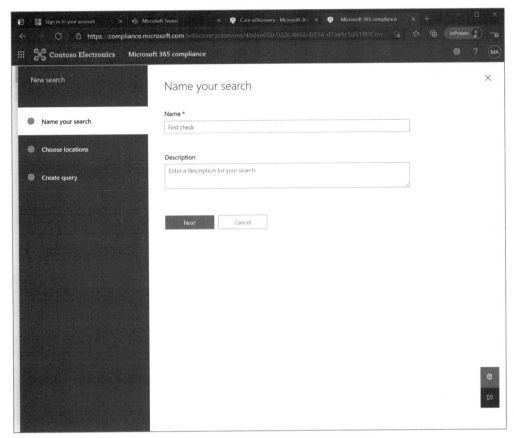

On the next screen you can then create the query that you want to run. By default this will include a box to do a keyword search, but you can add your own conditions or change what is included. The types of criteria you can use include the following:

- Date
- Sender/Author
- Subject
- Type
- Participants

FIGURE 4.65   Scope for an eDiscovery search

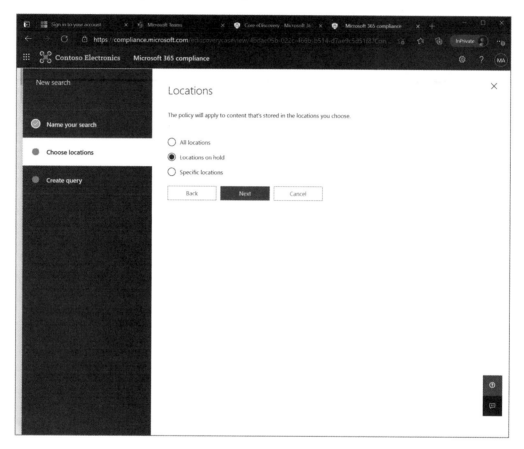

Build up the query that you think will give you the results you are looking for. It would be common to include at least a search date, as you are likely to have a rough idea when the incident you want to check happened (see Figure 4.66).

Click Finish to save the query; this will then take you back to the Searches tab in the interface but with the search open. From here you can modify the conditions as well as check the status of the search. As you can see in Figure 4.67, the query has not come back with any results, so it will need to be refined.

For more information about running eDiscovery searches, see docs. microsoft.com/en-us/microsoft-365/compliance/search-for-content-in-core-ediscovery.

FIGURE 4.66 eDiscovery search query

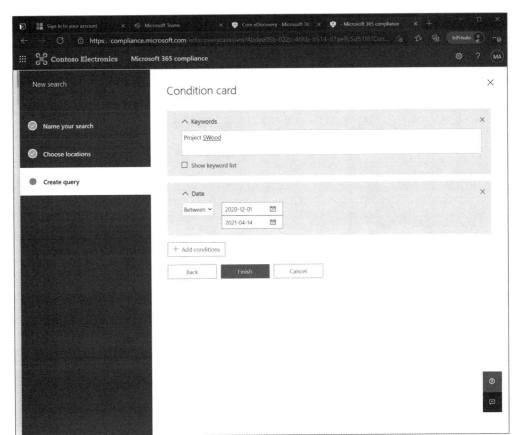

Exporting Results from eDiscovery

Once you have content that you think might be relevant, you can export the results from the search. To do this, select the search, which will show a pop-up on the right side of the screen. Here you can pick Export Results to start the Export Wizard (see Figure 4.68).

Choose what items should be included in the export report. By default the export will only include content that was recognizable, but you might want to also include any content that may have been encrypted, etc., for manual processing. Choose Generate Report to start the export process (see Figure 4.69).

FIGURE 4.67   eDiscovery search query results

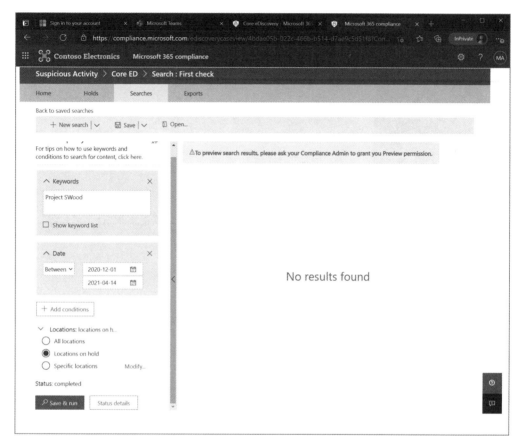

When the report is ready, you can then download it from the Exports tab. To download content generated from an eDiscovery search you need to use a special export tool and provide it with an export key. This key is shown on the report details page, and you can trigger the installation of the export tool from the browser by clicking Download Report (see Figure 4.70).

The export tool will launch, and you need to provide it with the export key (shown in the previous step), along with where on your local computer the files should be downloaded to (see Figure 4.71).

For more information about exporting eDiscovery data, see docs. microsoft.com/en-us/microsoft-365/compliance/export-content-in-core-ediscovery.

FIGURE 4.68   eDiscovery search details

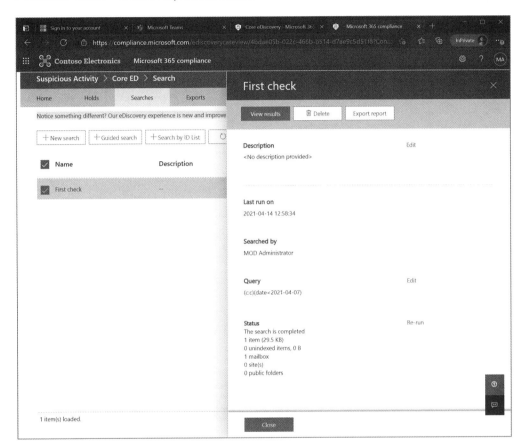

Security and Compliance Alerts

In the last few sections we covered a lot of tools that are at your disposal to help protect and maintain the security of information inside your Teams environment, but that can also mean a lot of things to manually keep track of.

Fortunately, through the use of the built-in auditing capabilities in M365 we can generate alerts when certain activities are carried out. This can range from things like when a new team is created or deleted to when more serious things occur, such as a new eDiscovery hold being created against some content.

FIGURE 4.69 eDiscovery search details

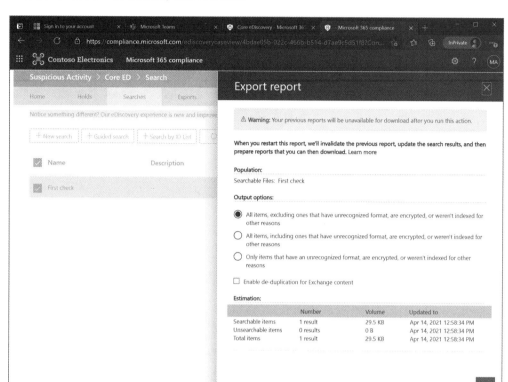

Before getting starting with alerts, we need to make sure that auditing is configured for the tenant, as this is what the alerts monitor. To do this, head back into the M365 compliance portal, under Show All, and then find the Audit section. If you do not have auditing configured for the tenant, you will see a button to activate it (see Figure 4.72).

Configuring Alert Policies

There are several ways to approach creating alert policies, and you can configure them in two locations—either as an O365 Alert or as Cloud App Security (see Figure 4.73).

FIGURE 4.70   eDiscovery export

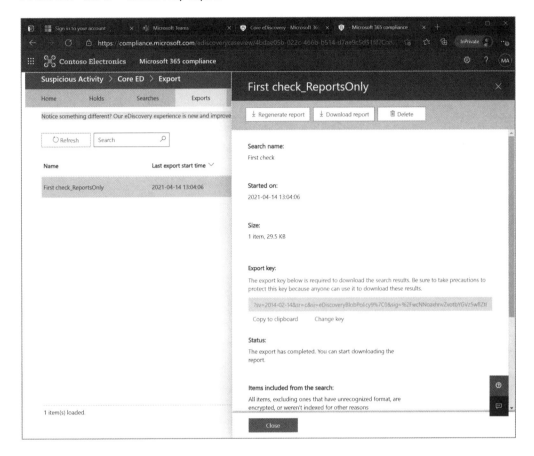

FIGURE 4.71   eDiscovery export tool

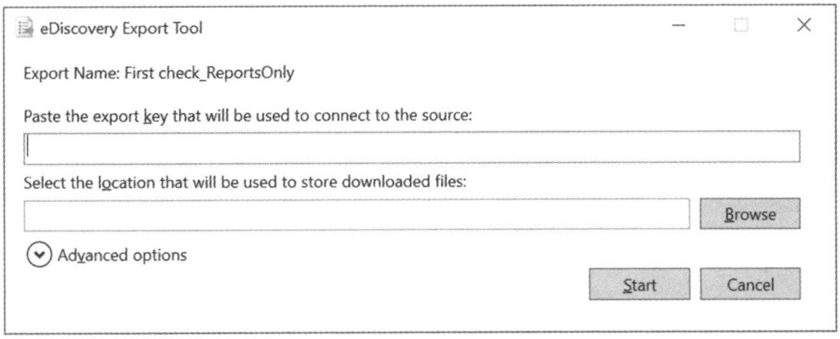

FIGURE 4.72   Configure auditing for the tenant

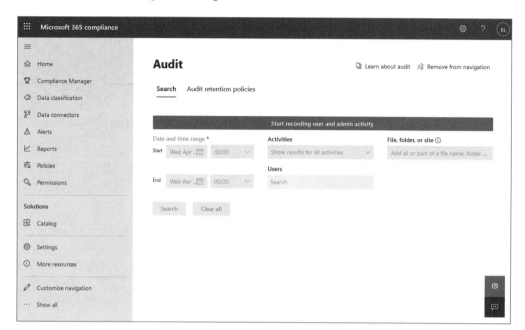

Here we are going to work with Office 365 Alerts, but to learn about the difference between O365 Alerts and Cloud App Security, see docs.microsoft.com/en-us/cloud-app-security/editions-cloud-app-security-o365.

Actually, the quickest way to get some alert policies created is to search through the audit logs for an event that you would like to be alerted to and then use that to generate an alerting policy.

To do that you need to use the deprecated O365 Security and Compliance portal (found at protection.office.com) because, while the new portal will let you search audit logs, it doesn't currently let you then turn that into an alerting policy.

When logged into the portal, open Search ➤ Audit Log Search from the left menu (see Figure 4.73).

Then click in the activities box to search for the type of activity you want to use to generate a report. Options for Teams include the following:

- New Team Created
- Team Settings Updated
- Bot Added To A Team
- Team Deleted

FIGURE 4.73 Starting an audit log search

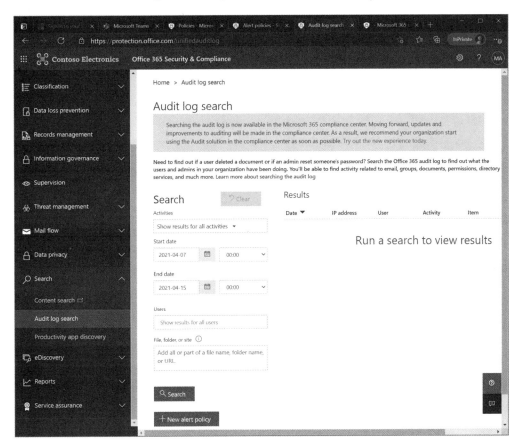

- User Signs Into Teams
- Blocked Teams Device
- Teams Device Configuration Update

Configure a scope to limit the search, and when you're happy, click Search. This will display a list of items that match your criteria (see Figure 4.74).

> **NOTE** Be aware that there can be a delay between the action taken and it showing up in the logs. Depending on the activity, this can be anywhere between 30 minutes and 24 hours.

If you are happy that the search matches the items you want to report on, you can then use the New Alert Policy button at the bottom to turn this search into an alert policy for you. You still need to provide a name as well as specify who receives the alert, but the criteria should already be completed for you. When done, click Save (see Figure 4.75).

FIGURE 4.74   Audit log search results

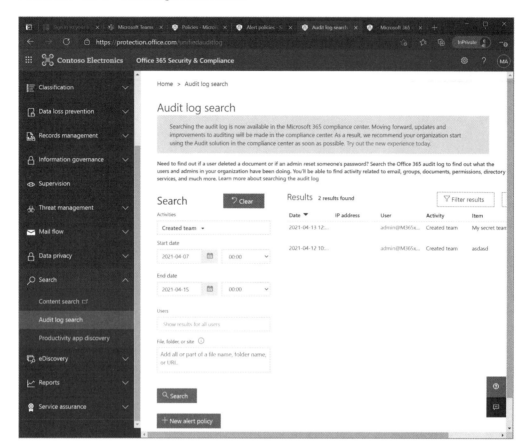

You can then view the created alert (and add more manually) by opening Alerts ➤ Dashboard and selecting Activity Alerts from the Other Alerts section.

Once the alert is triggered, an alert will be shown in the dashboard that can be acknowledged, and if specified during setup, an email alert will be sent.

Teams Apps

As you probably appreciate by now, Teams provides a rich experience for your users, letting them communicate and collaborate in many ways, but if you think about the other tools and systems in place across your organization, it is unlikely that Teams (mighty as it is) can replace them all with native functionality. This is where apps come in: they provide a way

FIGURE 4.75 Turning a search into an alert policy

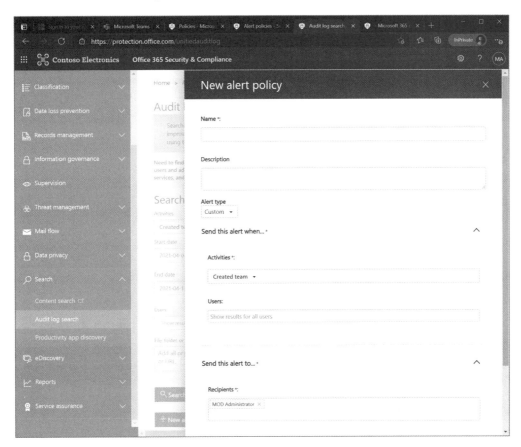

for developers to expand upon the functionality of Teams in a number of different ways so that you can integrate with these other services. Apps can come from Microsoft, other third parties, or even in-house developers. Teams provides the framework, APIs allow integrations, and anyone can write the apps.

Apps can be used in the following ways:

Pinned as a tab or to the app bar: Tabs are the areas found at the top of channels, and with apps you can add custom applications that can be displayed inside a tab. Examples include Yammer Communities or Asana. Apps can also be pinned down the left sidebar for easy access, but we will cover this in the section "App Setup Policies."

Pulling information via a connector: These can be used to post content into channels from external services, such as from Twitter or RSS.

Content messages: Messages can be posted into channels with interactive buttons to perform follow-on actions, for example a workflow requiring an acknowledgment action.

Bots: Chat bots allow interactive conversations to perform workflows or customize information in real time.

 Apps do not need to belong only inside channels. Some apps can be interacted with directly in the Teams client and can appear as another app down the app bar found on the left side of the Teams client.

App Policies

There is the concept of a "store" for Teams, which acts as a curated list of all the apps that your users will have the ability to access or add into their teams. You can control this app store and other behavior related to apps through a dedicated section in the TAC that has the following elements:

Manage Apps: Controls settings at an org-wide level, such as disabling the use of all third-party apps.

Permission Policies: Policies used to control which group of users can access what apps.

Setup Policies: Used to customize what apps are shown in the app bar (the left menu rail in the desktop client).

Customize Store: Used to change the look and feel of the Teams app store. You can add a logo and customize the text colors.

Managing Apps

Access these settings through the TAC under Teams Apps ➤ Manage Apps. The settings that you configure here will apply at a global level, so be careful in blocking apps that you might want to use for a subset of your user base.

The main window lists all applications that are available for use in your tenant (see Figure 4.76). Here you can upload custom apps from a local file or allow or block apps as required at a global level. The uninstall option will show only for custom apps that you have uploaded.

By clicking an application, you can see in more detail if the app has been certified by Microsoft, what permissions it requires, and if it has any settings.

 You can read more about Microsoft's Teams app certification process at docs.microsoft.com/teams-app-certification/all-apps.

To apply some blanket controls for either third-party or custom apps, click the Org-wide App Settings button at the top of the page; this will open a pop-out menu on the side (see Figure 4.77).

FIGURE 4.76   Manage apps in the TAC

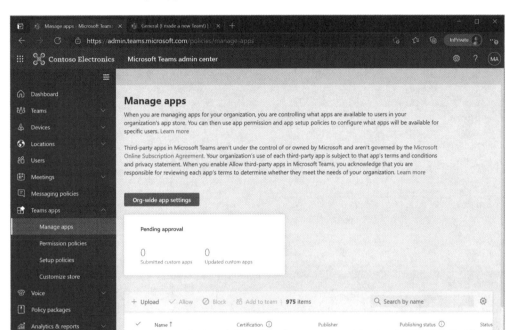

Here you can use the toggles to disable the use of all third-party apps, choose if newly published (by Microsoft) third-party apps show in the store, and choose if you want to disable the use of custom-built applications.

App Permission Policies

App permission policies are used to control which apps are available to users at a more granular level. These policies will behave in the same way as the policies we used for other TAC features in Chapter 3.

To create a policy or modify the global one, go into the TAC and then Teams Apps ➤ Permission Policies. Here you will see a list of the policies created for the organization (see Figure 4.78). Click one to edit it or click Add to start a new policy.

FIGURE 4.77   Org-wide app settings

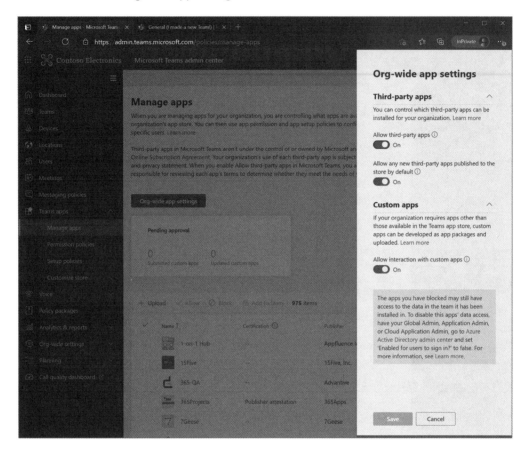

If starting a new policy, give it a name and description at the top of the screen and then choose your options for each of the three categories. The categories of apps you can control are as follows:

Microsoft apps: Apps developed and published by Microsoft

Third-party apps: Apps developed by a third party

Custom apps: Custom apps uploaded directly into the tenant

For each category, there are several further choices to make (see Figure 4.79):

Allow all apps: Like a whitelist, everything in that category is allowed

Allow specific apps and block all others: Useful when you want to only allow a handful of trusted apps

FIGURE 4.78   App Permission Policies page

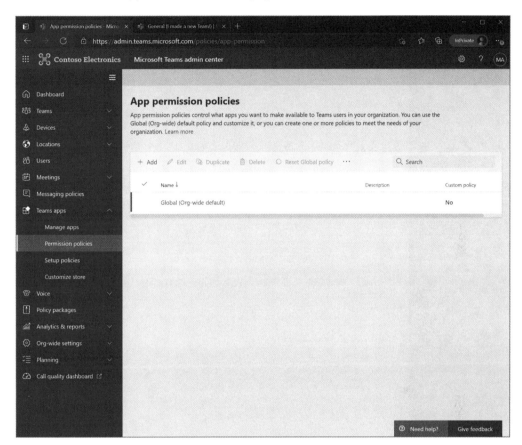

Block specific apps and allow all others: Used when you want to block some specific applications

Block all apps: Blacklist everything

Make your selection from the choices depending on your company's approach to data security and access. You might decide, for example, to allow all Microsoft applications but choose to limit third-party apps to a select few that you know may be beneficial to your users (see Figure 4.80). Click Save to create or update the policy.

FIGURE 4.79 App permission policy options

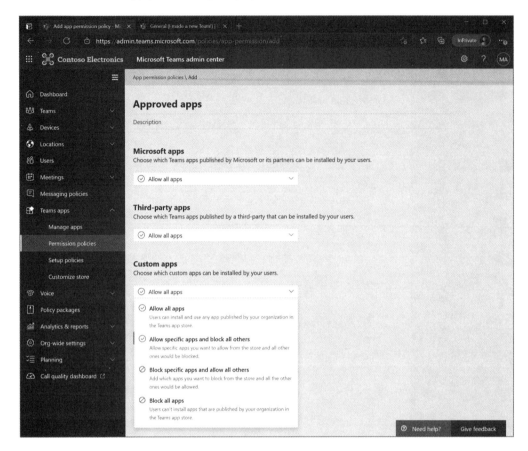

 If you are developing your own applications, this is where you could use a custom policy just for your test users so only they can access your new app until it is ready, at which point you would include it in the global policy (or you can use sideloading, which we will cover next).

Once you have saved or created your policy, you can then go into the user object, and in the long list of policy items, you can specify the new app policy that you have just created.

App permission policies are among the few configuration items for Teams that Microsoft does not recommend you use PowerShell to set, as it can be a complex activity and is important that it is configured correctly. That said, Microsoft does allow the use of the Grant-CSTeamsAppPermissionPolicy cmdlet, which can be used to assign a policy to users.

FIGURE 4.80   Custom app permission policy

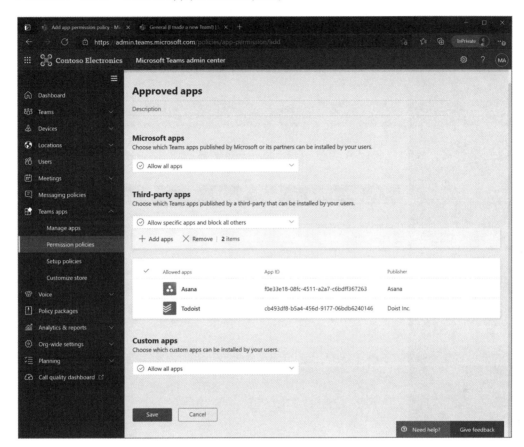

App Setup Policies

App setup polices are used to customize the Teams interface to highlight functionality or apps that are important to your users.

To create a policy or modify the global one, go into the TAC and then Teams Apps ➤ Setup Policies. Here you will see a list of the policies created for the organization (see Figure 4.81); click one to edit it or click Add to start a new policy.

If starting a new policy, give it a name and description at the top of the screen and then choose your options, which are as follows:

Upload custom apps: This allows a user to sideload custom applications into the client; generally this would be off except for developers or users testing an application.

Allow user pinning: This allows users to customize their client by pinning (already installed) apps to the app bar.

FIGURE 4.81   App setup policies

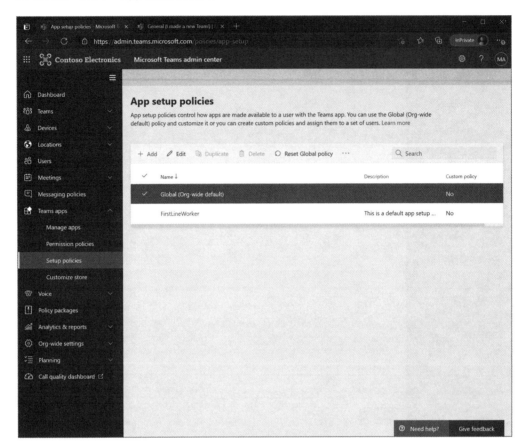

Installed apps: Choose to pre-install certain apps for your users.

Pinned apps: This section lets you arrange the apps pinned to the bar on the left side of the client. You can even remove all the apps from the menu if you choose, but it would probably confuse your users (see Figure 4.82).

Once you have saved or created your policy, apply it to your users as you do for the app permission policies.

Again, do not use PowerShell to configure these policies, but you can assign them to users with the `Grant-CsTeamsAppSetupPolicy` cmdlet.

Once the policy has applied, you can see the changes in the Teams client (see Figure 4.83).

FIGURE 4.82   App setup policy configuration

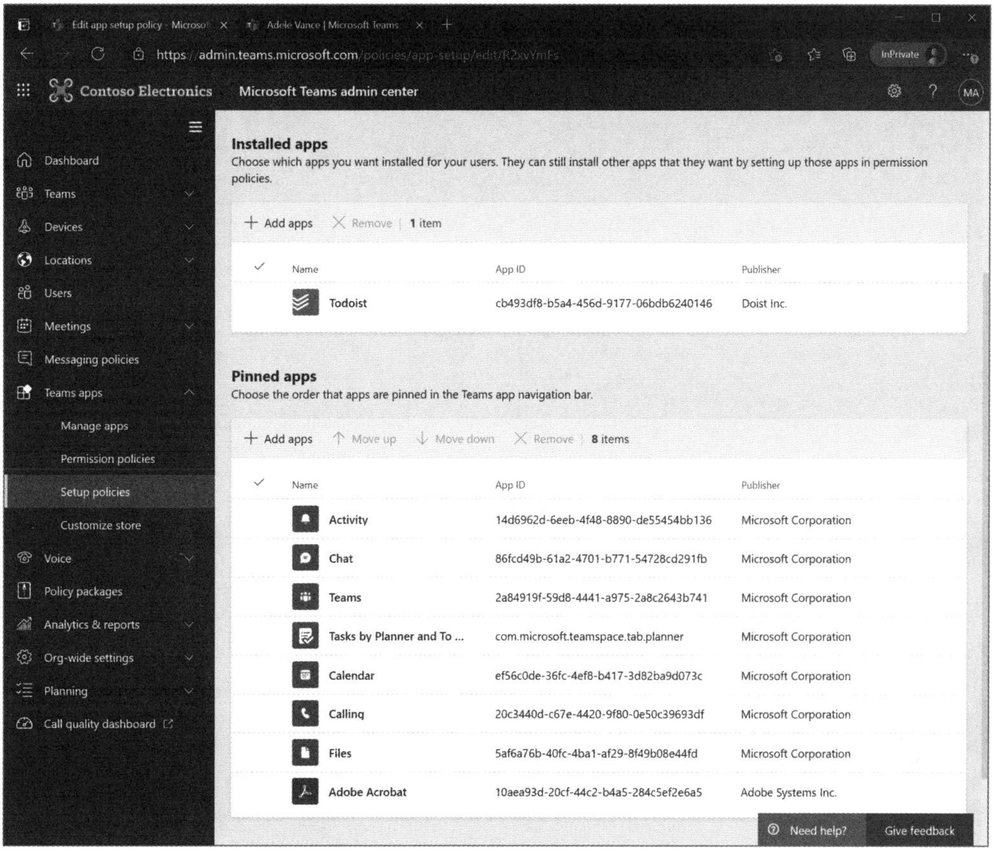

Using Custom Apps

As mentioned earlier, you can write (or have someone else write!) custom applications for use in your company. Perhaps they interact with a particular CRM system that you have deployed, or you want to use a bot to help respond to common service requests to help reduce support tickets.

When creating your custom app (don't worry; you don't have to know how to write them for the exam), you would be using a development environment like the App Studio (which is itself an app for Teams), which will output a ZIP file containing your packaged app.

When working with custom apps, there are four choices for how you can make them available to users:

Loading into the users Teams client: Available only to the single user

Loading into a team: Available to any member of the team

FIGURE 4.83   Custom app bar in the Teams client

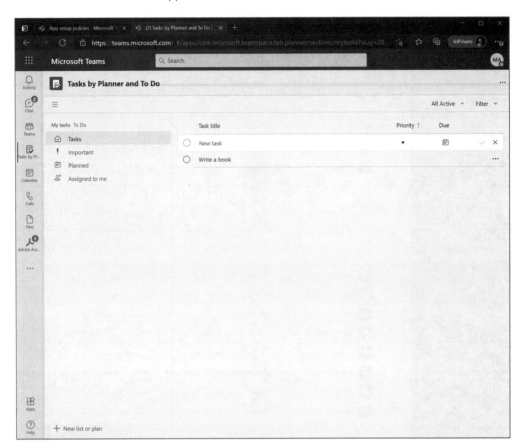

Publishing to the Microsoft Teams app store: The global catalog that all Teams tenants would have access to (usually reserved for proper third-party services)

Publishing to the tenant app catalog: Available to any user in the organization (subject to policy)

The first two options here are referred to as *sideloading*. The ability to control sideloading is found in three places, two of which we covered in the previous section:

Org-wide app settings: Acts as a global on/off setting for custom apps

User app setup policy: Controls if a user can sideload applications

Controlled inside the team itself: Lets a team owner specify if members can upload and use custom apps inside the team

It is important to understand how these different settings overlap and interact with each other; see Table 4.5.

TABLE 4.5 How App Policy Settings Interact

Org-Wide	User App Setup Policy	Team App Setting	Result
Off	On or Off	On or Off	Custom apps cannot be uploaded or used at all.
On	Off	On or Off	User cannot upload custom apps.
On	On	Off	User can upload custom apps to a team if an owner and can use apps in their own client.
On	On	On	User can upload apps to a team as a member and can use them in their own client.

> While writing apps is not in scope, if you are interested in learning how to get started with development, I recommend the following blog/tutorials by Tom Morgan: github.com/tomorgan and thoughtstuff.co.uk. Microsoft also produces a good line of quick-start templates at docs.microsoft.com/en-us/microsoftteams/platform/samples/app-templates. You can even create low-code apps directly inside Teams using the Power Apps app: docs.microsoft.com/en-us/powerapps/teams/use-sample-apps-from-teams-store.

Publishing Custom Apps in the TAC

To upload or upgrade an existing custom app in the TAC, sign in and head to Teams Apps ➤ Manage Apps. Above the list of all applications, select Upload and then select your ZIP file (see Figure 4.84).

Once the application has been uploaded, it will be added to the tenant app catalog and will then appear in the list. You can select it, view its details, or upload a new version.

Publishing Custom Apps in Teams Client

If you are signed into the Teams client with an account that is either a Global or Teams admin user, then from the Teams client in the bottom left of the app bar, open the apps page (see Figure 4.85).

From here select Upload A Customized App, which will give you a choice to upload the app into your own client (or a team) or into the tenant app catalog.

FIGURE 4.84   Uploading a custom app in TAC

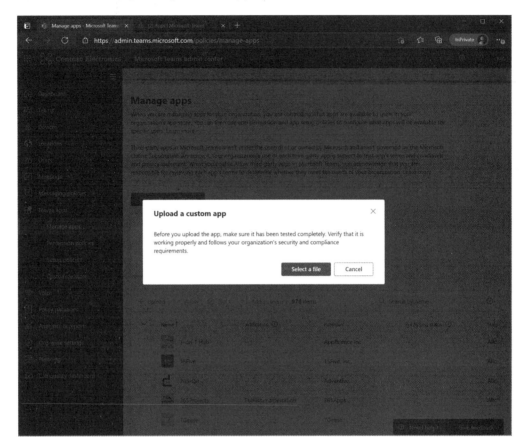

Once it's uploaded to your tenant, you will see a new section appear here called "Built for <Company>." This section shows all apps that you have uploaded to the tenant app catalog, and you can also choose to update any.

FIGURE 4.85   Uploading a custom app in TAC

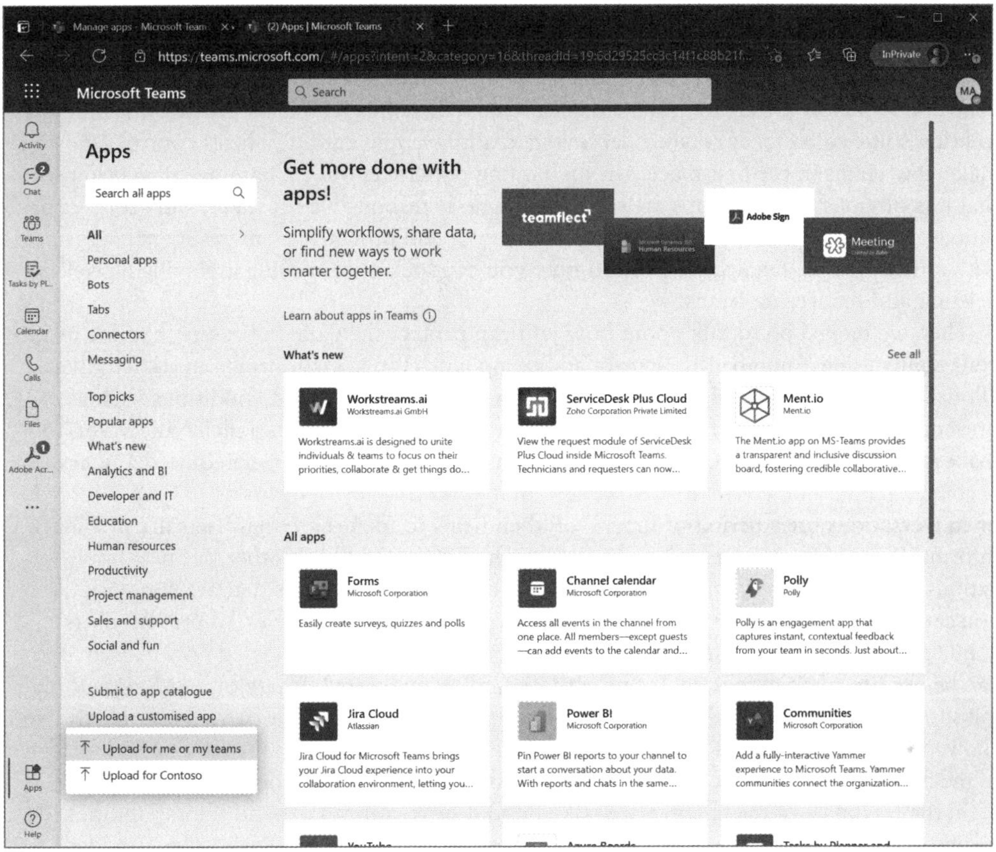

Summary

This chapter has done a lot of hard work with some difficult concepts as we have covered a lot of different ways that you can bring some advanced functionality to your Teams deployment. In the real world, it is likely that your company's requirements are not as clear-cut as those that we have discussed here. As there are a lot of features with similar functionality or overlapping reach, it is really important that before you tackle any of this outside of a lab you sit down and, after gathering requirements from the different parts of your company, map out a deployment plan for how each feature here might achieve one of your goals.

We started by looking at the different RBAC roles that can be used to better manage your Teams environment, meaning that you do not need to give everyone full permissions to modify everything in the deployment. We also looked at how you can be smarter about managing the membership using dynamic membership rules to add or remove people as things change in your company. You can also automate the checking of users' access through the use of access reviews where users have to confirm that they still need access to certain teams.

We learned about how you can manage the lifecycle of a team as well as applying rules to control how teams are created, shaped, and removed. Teams templates provide a simple way to bring some consistency to your deployment, and group creation policies control who can make new teams in the first place. Group naming policies enforce a naming convention so that it is obvious which groups are teams and who is responsible for them, and group expiration provides a way to make sure that you do not end up with an environment clogged up with unused teams. Finally, we showed how you can lock a team using archiving as well as deleting and recovering teams.

Then we moved on to talk about how you can protect the data and assets that live inside your teams using a number of security and compliance tools. First, using sensitivity labels allows you to allocate labels to your teams as well as enforce certain conditions such as preventing sensitive teams from containing external users. Retention policies allow you to make sure that data is removed in a timely fashion when it is no longer required and could become a liability or, conversely, make sure that you meet any obligations to keep a record of conversations for a period of time. DLP then helps to make sure that users are not sharing information with each other inappropriately when it should live in other business applications. If you are a very large organization or dealing with subjects that are contentious, you can use information barriers, built on top of segmentation policies, to prevent users in conflicting groups from communicating with each other. We then showed how eDiscovery can be used to place a hold on Teams activities, allowing users to carry on working but making sure that records are held in time while any investigation work is carried out. Lastly, we showed how you can build alerts to trigger and warn you when certain activities are detected in the tenant, such as users deleting a team, so that you can take appropriate measures.

In the final part of the chapter, we talked about how you can expand the capabilities of Teams beyond those of the native O365 services. We showed how apps can be provided by Microsoft directly or through third parties and how you can deploy your own custom-developed ones. We also showed how you can deploy and pin certain applications to users in your company where they might best add value.

Exam Essentials

Know what the Teams RBAC roles are and how to assign them to users.   Know what the different administration roles are for Teams, where you might use each one, and how to grant permissions to users. Understand that it is best practice to apply the principle of least privilege so that you only give users rights they need to perform their tasks.

Know how to manually control membership of a team. Know that you can control the membership of a team either through the Teams client, via the TAC, or through PowerShell.

Understand how dynamic membership works and know how to configure it. Dynamic membership can be used to create M365 groups that will automatically adjust their membership based on a number of rules and can be created either through the Azure AD portal or in PowerShell.

Know how to use access reviews to regularly reconfirm team memberships. Access reviews allow you to schedule an automatic check of team membership; this can be carried out by the team owner, by the user themselves, or by an administrator. Understand how you would deploy and configure these.

Know that you can use templates to make teams. Templates can be used to create a repeatable structure inside your team; this is helpful if you need to make a lot of teams with the same channel structure and app integrations (for example, for projects).

Understand how you can restrict creation of groups using group creation policies. You may not want to allow users to create teams; instead, you can use group creation policies to limit who in the company can make new M365 groups and therefore teams. Regardless of your group creation policies, some RBAC roles (including Teams Service Administrator, User Administrator, etc.) can still make new groups and teams.

Understand where and how you might use group naming policies to structure your teams. Group naming policies let you add metadata or fixed suffix/prefix information to your teams so that you can control what they look like. You can also use these policies to prevent certain words from being used in your group names when you want to reserve them for other purposes.

Know how group expiration works. After you have had Teams deployed for a long time, you might find that you end up with a lot of abandoned or orphaned teams that are no longer required. By configuring group expiration policies, you can automate a way to stay on top of these and make sure that you only have live teams in the environment.

Understand what the impact of archiving a team would be. Archiving can be used to freeze a team and make it read-only; the team can then be kept available for reference, but no new material can be added.

Know how to delete and recover teams. When you delete a team, it is actually soft-deleted, and you can recover it for up to 30 days; however, after this point it will disappear and cannot be recovered.

Know how to configure and use sensitivity labels. To use sensitivity labels with Teams, you should enable them for containers at the tenant level. They then can be used to control some functionality in the team, for example, if a team is public or private, and to invite external users into it.

Know how to work with retention policies.   Retention policies let you manage old data in your team. They can prevent users from deleting content until it is over a certain age, or automatically enforce the deletion of content past a certain time. This can be helpful when you have legal obligations to maintain or remove data.

Understand how DLP can prevent the sharing of unauthorized data.   DLP rules can be configured using templates to look for certain types of sensitive data, including health-care or credit card information. When DLP detects it, action can be taken to either remove the content or flag it for review. DLP can be essential if you have users who may be handling confidential material to make sure they do not accidentally put the company at risk.

Understand where you might use information barriers.   Depending on the size of your company or your industry, you might have a requirement to prevent users from communicating with each other. This could be based on operational roles or geographical locations, for example. You can create segments in Azure AD for your users and then create information barrier policies that either allow or prevent segments of users from communicating with each other. Remember that for this to work properly in the tenant, you need to authorize the information barrier application.

Be aware of how to use eDiscovery.   eDiscovery is a complex tool that can help you deal with any requests to look for user activity. These could be to support internal HR queries or even ongoing legal actions. Using eDiscovery, you can create cases and manage access to searches and data, as well as being able to place users or teams on hold so that data cannot be removed until the case is closed.

Be able to configure security and compliance alerts.   Security and compliance alerts allow you to generate alerts and actions (such as email notifications) when actions of interest occur in the tenant. This could be creating an alert each time a user deletes a team, or perhaps when a new team is created. These alerts use the auditing engine behind the scenes, so this must be configured at a tenant level.

Understand why you might use apps to expand the native functionality of teams.   Apps can be provided by Microsoft or third parties or custom developed. They provide a way to expand the functionality of teams beyond the native capabilities.

Know how to control the use of apps.   You can allow or block apps at several levels, either globally, per user, or per team. Make sure you are familiar with which of the different policy types control what aspect of app behavior, for example that app setup policies are used to install apps in the Teams client for users.

Know how to add your own applications.   You can install custom apps through a process called sideloading or through an in-tenant app store. You should understand how you might do this and when you would use either option.

EXERCISE 4.1

Viewing Teams Admin Role Permissions

In this exercise, we will look through the TAC and check what rights each role has available.

1. Log into the M365 admin center (admin.microsoft.com) with a Global Administrator account.

2. Expand the left menu using the Show All option.

3. Select Roles and scroll down the list to the Teams options.

4. Set the privacy for the team to be Private.

5. Select the Teams Communications Admin role and click the three vertical dots next to the role name.

6. From this menu, choose Run As, and you will be launched into a version of TAC running with those permissions.

7. Click Show All to expand the full left menu and look at what options are available for the admin role.

8. Expand Users and go look at a user account (ideally one enabled for telephony if you have it) to see what the role can view or update.

9. Repeat steps 5–8 using the other RBAC roles.

EXERCISE 4.2

Configuring a Dynamic Membership Rule for a Team

In this exercise, we will configure a pre-existing team to use dynamic membership. Before we start, make sure you have a test team already created that we can work with (and remember this will work only if your users have Azure P1 licensing applied, but you should be able to perform the steps even without this license available).

1. Log in to the Azure AD portal (aad.portal.azure.com) with Global Administrator rights.

2. Select All Services and then find Groups.

3. Search the list to find your test team's group.

4. Open the group properties and under Properties change the membership type to Dynamic User.

5. Click Add Dynamic Query to enter the query builder.

6. Create a rule with at least two conditions that match some of your users (e.g., job title and location).

7. Use the Validate Rules tab to select some users to check your rule with.

8. Save the group.

EXERCISE 4.3

Configuring an Access Review

For this exercise, we are going to set up an access review to help make sure team membership is being monitored. For this exercise, make sure that you have a test already created that you will use.

1. Log in to the Azure AD portal and open the Azure Active Directory section.

2. Click the section for Identity Governance in the left menu, and then on the screen that opens, open Access Reviews from the left menu.

3. You will now see a list of all the reviews currently configured for your organization. Start a new one by selecting New Access Review from the top menu.

4. Select Teams + Groups as the review type, and then limit the scope to a test team that you have created. Choose to apply the scope to all users in the team and move to the next step.

5. In the drop-down, choose who will receive the access review; for this example, select Group Owners. Use the link that appears to configure your email address as a fallback reviewer.

6. Set the review to occur one time, change the duration to be one day, and set the start date to be <today>. Then move to the next page.

7. Explore the options on this page, but for the exercise leave them at defaults; then move to the last page where you can name the review before creating it.

8. Refresh the Access Review page, and you should now see your review. Click it to view progress and information about the review.

9. The review should then be triggered in the next 24 hours. Keep an eye on the mailbox for your test team owner, and when the email arrives, click Start Review and follow the prompts.

EXERCISE 4.4

Deploying a Team from a Template

In this exercise, we will set up a team template and then use it to create a new team.

1. Start by opening the TAC, and then under Teams open the Team Templates page.

2. Click Add and choose Create A New Template; then select Next.

3. At the top of the page give the template a name and a description (in both fields); then move to the next page.

4. Create some new channels to include in your template and pick at least one app to add as well. Then click Submit to save the template.

5. Next create a template policy by going to the Teams Team Templates section in the TAC. Here you can click Add to make a new template policy.

6. Give the template policy a name and select at least the new template you just created. Then click Save at the bottom of the page.

7. Now assign the template policy to your account. Open Users from the left menu and find your user account in the list. Open the user details page and go to the Policies tab.

8. Select Edit next to Assigned Policies, and from the flyout menu scroll down and find the Template Policy section. In the drop-down list, pick the name of the template you just created.

9. Sign into Teams with the user account you just assigned the policy to and head to Teams from the app bar. At the bottom of the team list, select Join Or Create A Team, and then choose Create A Team. When the Create A Team screen loads, you should see your new template in the list. Select it, and then on the next screen confirm the details of what you want (e.g., the channels and apps that will be configured). Complete the wizard to make your new team.

EXERCISE 4.5

Creating a Group Naming Policy

In this exercise, we will make a group naming policy to automatically tag any new teams that are created in the company.

1. Open the Azure AD portal, click Azure Active Directory from the Favorites list, and then click Groups from the left menu.

2. Look under Settings and click Naming Policy. This will open on the Blocked Words tab by default, but move over to the Group Naming Policy tab to view what you have currently configured.

3. Select Add Prefix and then select the box underneath (by default this will say Attribute). Change this to String and enter some text in the box next to the drop-down.

4. In bold above this section will be a preview of what your team naming structure will look like. When you're happy, click Save at the top.

5. From the Teams client, create a new team to see how the policy has been applied. Remember to use a user without any administrative rights, as an admin can create teams without the naming policy taking effect.

EXERCISE 4.6

Setting Up a Group Expiry

For this exercise we are going to set up a group expiry to help keep on top of teams that have been unused for six months. While we can create the policy, you will not be able to see the full cycle of events (without waiting at least 30 days!) as the expiry will only kick in after the period of inactivity has passed.

1. Open the Azure AD portal, click Azure Active Directory from the Favorites list, and then find Groups from the left menu.

2. Look under Settings and find Expiration.

3. Specify at what time after the last activity the expiry should kick in, for example 180 days. Enter an email address that will be used for groups with no owner.

4. At the bottom of the page you can adjust the scope of the policy to apply to all groups or change the option to Selected to apply the policy to only certain groups.

5. Save the policy. Don't forget to change this back if you are testing in a live deployment so you don't remove any groups by mistake!

EXERCISE 4.7

Configuring Administrative Alerts for Team Activities

In the next activity (Exercise 4.8), we are going to be deleting and restoring a team, so in this exercise we are going to configure administrative alerts to make sure we get notified when this happens. This exercise assumes you have auditing already configured in the tenant.

1. Open the O365 Security and Compliance portal (protection.office.com) and look for Search and then Audit Log Search on the left menu.

2. Click in the activity box and start typing **team**. Select Deleted A Team from the list and then pick New Alert Policy.

3. Give the policy a name and expand the Send This Alert To section. Enter your email address in the recipients list.

4. Complete Exercise 4.8 and then check your email for the notification emails.

EXERCISE 4.8

Archiving, Deleting, and Recovering a Team

In this exercise we are going to archive and then delete and restore a team (which will trigger the alerts configured in Exercise 4.7). Before starting, make sure you have created a team that you can use for the exercise.

1. Open the TAC and under Teams go to the Manage Teams screen. Scroll down the list and select the team (by clicking to the left of the name).

2. In the top menu, click Archive.

3. Load the Teams application and find the team in the Teams list. Confirm that the team is no longer displayed in the full list. You should be able to find it by clicking the cog icon next to Join Or Create A Team, and then it will be shown under the section called Archived.

4. Back in the TAC, select the team again, but this time choose Delete from the top menu. The team will then disappear from the list and from the Teams client.

5. To restore the client, open PowerShell and connect to Azure AD; then run `Get-AzureADMSDeletedGroup`. Copy the ID of the group and then run `Restore-AzureADMSDeletedDirectoryObject –ID <ID from above>`.

6. Back in the TAC, refresh the team list and (after some time) the team should be back in the list and should still be in its Archived state.

7. Select the team and chose Unarchive from the top menu to make the team live again.

8. Confirm in the Teams client that you can access the team.

EXERCISE 4.9

Using Sensitivity Labels to Create an Internal-Only Team Type

Here we are going to use sensitivity labels to create a label that can be used to ensure that some teams cannot have any guest users added to them. This exercise assumes that sensitivity labels for containers have already been enabled in the tenant.

1. Open the M365 compliance portal and select Show All from the left menu; then find Information Protection in the list. Here you will see a list of any labels already created for the tenant.

2. Select Create A Label to make a new classification; give it both kinds of name and at least a user description.

3. On the next screen, change the scope to only include Groups & Sites. Move through the next screen until you get to Define Protection Settings For Groups And Sites. Here you select the box for Privacy And External User Access Settings; then click Next.

4. Do not change the Privacy settings, but make sure the External User access box is not checked. Finish the wizard to save the label. This will then launch the Publish Label Wizard for you.

5. Click Choose The Sensitivity Label to publish, and select the label you just created. Click Next.

6. You can either apply the policy to all users or use the Choose User Or Group option to apply it only to your test account.

7. On the Policy Settings screen you can choose to make the label the new default, or you can mandate that users have to pick a label when creating a team.

8. Complete the wizard to make the label policy.

9. Go into the Teams client as a user who is covered by the policy you just made.

10. From the Teams list, select Join Or Create A Team from the bottom of the list; then select Create A Team. Select From Scratch and on the What Kind of Team Will This Be screen you will see a new drop-down list called Sensitivity, which should have a list containing the label that you just made.

EXERCISE 4.10

Preventing Sharing of Credit Card Information in Chats, and Making Sure That Chat Is Retained for a Period of Time

Here we are going to create two policies to meet a business requirement that all chats by the sales team are maintained for a period of at least one year and that they are not allowed to share credit card data in chat messages. To meet this requirement, we will make one retention policy and one DLP policy. This exercise assumes that you have a preconfigured group for the sales team that we will use to scope the policies.

1. Open the Compliance admin portal and open the section for Information Governance. Then in the top menu go to the Retention section.

2. Click New Retention Policy to start the wizard. Give the policy a name such as **Keep Sales Chats**, and then on the next page update the scope to only include Teams Chat. This will let you change the included users to only be your sales group. Click Next; in the retention settings change the date to Custom and specify one year. Make sure the At The End Of The Retention Period setting is configured to Do Nothing.

3. Complete the wizard to apply the policy.

4. Next set up the DLP rule to detect financial data by moving to the Data Loss Prevention menu in the left menu.

5. Under the Policies section start a new policy by clicking Create Policy. The first screen will show a list of the default templates available. As we want to block sharing of financial information, click the Financial category; then under Templates look down the list and select the one that best applies to your country. Click Next.

6. Give the policy a name, such as **Sales detect financial data**, and on the next screen, change the scope to include only the Teams Chat and Channel Messages. Then change the included scope to only be the sales group that you have for the exercise.

7. Review the policy settings over the next few pages. Change the Info To Protect setting to be Only People Inside My Organization. For Testing set the detection threshold to be 1.

8. On the last page, turn the policy on Right Away.

9. Allow the policies at least an hour to apply; then log into the Teams client as a user covered by the policy, try sending some test financial data to another user, and check that the policy catches it. Note that the policy is pretty good at detecting valid numbers, so you can generate some fake but valid numbers using this website: cardguru.io.

EXERCISE 4.11

Managing Apps

After running a planning session with your company, you have identified the following requirements for app integrations: third-party apps should be blocked for all users, and, as the company is making a push to use the Planner and To Do services, their app should be pinned to the app bar for all users. In this exercise, we are going to meet these requirements.

1. Open the TAC, and under Teams Apps select Manage Apps.

2. From the top right of the screen, select Org-Wide App Settings, and from the right pop-out menu toggle Allow Third-Party Apps to Off. Click Save to apply the settings. This meets the first part of the company requirement.

3. Next head to Teams Apps and then Setup Policies. Click the name of the Global (Org-Wide Default) Policy and under the Pinned Apps section click Add Apps. In the pop-out left menu, click where it says Search By Name and look for Tasks By Planner And To Do. Select it and click Add; then click Add again at the bottom of the pop-out. This will place it at the bottom of the list of pinned apps. Select it and move it up the list if you fancy.

Review Questions

1. You have configured two segments in your organization that you intend to deploy with information barriers. What would you need to do next to prevent the two groups from communicating?

    A. Create one information barrier policy.

    B. Create two information barrier policies.

    C. Create four information barrier policies.

    D. Run `Start-InformationBarrierPoliciesApplication`.

2. You need to display a label inside teams that are being used for temporary projects. How could you achieve this?

    A. Using sensitivity labels

    B. Using retention policies

    C. Creating a DLP policy

    D. Using an M365 group naming policy

3. You want to make sure that your teams are correctly categorized, and you want to prevent users from being able to add guest users into teams containing confidential material. Which feature could help achieve this?

    A. Configuring access reviews

    B. Group creation policy

    C. DLP policies

    D. Enabling sensitivity labels

4. A user has created a custom app for Teams. They have loaded it into their client, but other users are not currently able to access it and need to be able to. What can you do? (Select all that apply.)

    A. Publish the app to the tenant app catalog.

    B. Extract the `manifest.json` file from the Teams client and give it to the other users.

    C. Ask the initial user to share the app ZIP package with the other users and instruct them on how to install it.

    D. Email TeamsPublishing@Microsoft.com with a copy of the app so that Microsoft can add it to the Teams app store.

5. You have a requirement to ensure that private user chats are automatically deleted after a 30-day period. What would you configure?

    A. Create a retention policy scoped to the user's mailbox.

    B. Create a retention policy scoped to Teams channel messages.

    C. Create a retention policy scoped to Teams chats.

    D. Create an archiving policy.

6. Which of the following is a valid type of eDiscovery?

   A. eDiscovery advanced

   B. Content Check

   C. Core eDiscovery case

   D. Detailed eDiscovery case

7. You think that some users in the company may be sharing confidential health records inside team channels instead of using the company line-of-business application. What could you do to check how frequently this is happening without stopping it immediately?

   A. Create a DLP policy configured to generate an administrator alert when medical data is discovered. Configure the scope to include Teams.

   B. Create a DLP policy configured to block the content when medical data is discovered. Configure the scope to include SharePoint sites.

   C. Create a DLP policy configured to block the content when medical data is discovered. Configure the scope to include Teams.

   D. Create a DLP policy configured to generate an alert when medical data is discovered. Configure the scope to include Exchange.

8. You need to be able to restrict the creation of new groups to department heads, and you have a security group containing the department heads already. What can you do?

   A. Make the users Teams Service Administrators in the tenant.

   B. Use the `Set-AzureADDirectorySetting` cmdlet to give the group of department heads permissions to make new groups.

   C. Make the users User Administrators in the tenant.

   D. Use the `Set-AzureADDirectorySetting` cmdlet to give each member permissions to create groups.

9. You need to manually add some users into a team as part of a provisioning PowerShell script. Which cmdlets would you use?

   A. `Get-Team` and `Add-TeamUser`

   B. `Find-Team` and `Add-TeamUser`

   C. `Get-Team` and `New-TeamUser`

   D. `Get-Team` and `Set-TeamUser`

10. You have added a custom app to your tenant app store and want to make sure that it is visible in the main interface of the Teams client for all your users. Which of the following would you use?

   A. App permission policy

   B. App setup policy

   C. Manage apps section of the TAC

   D. Customize store section of the TAC

11. You want to make sure that each team that is created has a suffix of `_Teams` so you can identify which M365 groups are teams-enabled. Which admin portal would you use to configure this?

    A. In the TAC

    B. In the Azure AD Portal

    C. In the M365 admin center

    D. In the M365 compliance portal

12. You want to make teams for your sales department that automatically contain all of the salespeople in your company, split by office location, with the least administrative overhead. Your Active Directory is up to date and can be assumed to contain good metadata. Which of the following would you do?

    A. Create a single dynamic membership rule in Azure AD and apply it to every sales group.

    B. Create new teams for each sales office location and then create a dynamic membership rule for each one with the following query: (`"Department" -eq "Sales"`) `-And` (`"City" -eq "<City>"`).

    C. Create new teams for each sales office location and then create a dynamic membership rule for each one with the following query: (`"Department" = "Sales"`) `-And` (`"City" = "<City>"`).

    D. Create new teams for each sales office location and then create a dynamic membership rule for each one with the following query: (`"Department" -eq "Sales"`) `-And` (`"usageLocation" = "<City>"`).

13. You have recently purchased new devices for each of your meeting rooms but want to delegate the configuration of these devices to one of the support engineers. You have allocated permissions using least-privilege access. Currently the engineer has Teams Communications Support Engineer permissions. What would you need to do to ensure they can configure the new hardware?

    A. Allocate the Teams Service Administrator role.

    B. Allocate the Teams Communications Support Specialist role.

    C. Allocate the Teams Device Administrator role.

    D. Preconfigure the devices in the admin portal and provide the engineer with login details.

14. A team has been automatically deleted following a recent group expiry run. A user comes to you 40 days after the group expiry deadline who needs access to some files that were in the team. What can you do to help?

    A. Run the `Get-AzureADMSDeletedGroup` cmdlet followed by `Restore- AzureAD-MSDeletedDirectoryObject`.

    B. Check in the TAC under the full team list.

    C. Nothing.

    D. Check in the Azure AD portal under Groups.

15. You are looking to add some structure to your Teams deployment and have identified that each time a new project starts for a customer, your users should set it up the same way. Each team contains a specific channel structure and several pinned apps. What could you do to make the process easier for your users?

    A. Give them a PowerShell script that can be run on demand against their new team.

    B. Create a Power Automate workflow that is triggered by a team creation event.

    C. Create an app setup policy to automatically pin the right apps that they need.

    D. Create a team template laying out the channel structure and pinned apps that are needed, and make the template available to your users.

16. Which of the following could you not achieve by configuring access reviews?

    A. Get users to confirm their membership on a team.

    B. Require owners to mark their team as still active.

    C. Receive an email when no owner is configured for a team.

    D. Automatically remove users who do not confirm their membership on a team.

17. Your company has an internal accountability policy that states that users need to reconfirm their membership on teams each quarter. What could you do to help meet this business requirement?

    A. Configure Dynamic membership rules.

    B. Configure access reviews and specify user reviews in the options.

    C. Configure access reviews to be sent to each team owner.

    D. Configure audit alerts for when user group membership changes.

18. You want to find a way to automatically tidy up and remove old teams that are no longer in use but you are concerned that some teams may no longer have owners. What should you do? Your solution should require the least ongoing maintenance.

    A. Configure access reviews for the tenant and enable the justification option so that only teams with an owner can respond.

    B. Enable audit logging in the tenant and use an alert to notify you when new teams are created; use this to track when a team is more than 30 days old.

    C. Set a group expiry for the tenant and make sure that you specify an admin mailbox as a fallback address.

    D. Create a script to check for teams with no owner; schedule the script to run from your computer once a week.

19. Your company has a written policy that requires that after a project is complete any relevant materials are kept for future reference, and no new materials can be added. How could you make sure to meet this policy for any project teams?

    A. Apply a retention policy to the team.

    B. Archive the team when projects have been completed.

    C. Apply a sensitivity label to the team.

    D. Use a segmentation policy to stop users adding more to the team.

20. You configure information barriers in your tenant for the first time but notice that users who should not be able to communicate with each other are not automatically removed from conversations. After confirming that the segmentation is correctly configured, what should you check?

   A. Ensure that the information barrier policy is being applied to their team.

   B. Manually run the information barrier policy from the admin portal.

   C. Wait for AAD connect to synchronize the users.

   D. Make sure that you have authorized the information barrier app to be able to operate in your tenant.

Chapter

5

Adding Telephony

MICROSOFT EXAM OBJECTIVES COVERED IN THIS CHAPTER:

✓ Manage phone numbers

✓ Manage Phone System

In this chapter, we get to play with one of the cooler things that Teams can do: dealing with phone calls over the public switched telephone network (PSTN). Now you might wonder why this is something to get excited about; after all, making calls is easy, right? Any phone can do it, and yes, you would be correct, but let's take a look at what it means to do that alongside all the other things that Teams does.

The official name for making and receiving phone calls in Teams has changed over time, so you might see it referred to as one of the following: Microsoft Teams Phone, Microsoft Teams Calling, or Microsoft Teams Voice Calling. Not to be confused with the specific license type called Phone System that unlocks this functionality inside Teams, or with the general term "phone system," which can be used for any system that deals with phone calls.

Historically a unified communications (UC) platform was one that combined all your different communications mediums together in some way. It would take direct device-to-device calling, online meetings, and text-based messaging (email, IM, or chat) and place them alongside traditional calling as you would have at home with a house phone, or in the office with your traditional phone system from the likes of Cisco, Mitel, or Avaya.

What makes it special in Teams (as well as Skype for Business and those other Microsoft UC products that came before) is that Teams effortlessly combines and integrates real-world phone calling capabilities alongside its other workloads.

When a user places a PSTN call in Teams, the mechanics behind the scenes are very different, dealing with things like SIP trunks and voice gateways. But to the user it looks and behaves just like a regular Teams call or meeting with the same familiar interface and call controls.

You can now deploy this one product, and if correctly configured, it can likely replace your business phone system. This can have a number of side benefits, such as reducing costs by removing the need for expensive and complex voice infrastructure, streamlining management as everything is now in one place, simplifying the end-user experience, as users now just have one tool to learn, and improving productivity, as now anywhere a user goes, if they can run Teams, they can also get their business calls.

This, to me, is what makes Teams a true UC tool (and yes, technically it should be UC&C because we have all that collaboration stuff in there as well) and why it is something to get all enthusiastic about!

Now the telephony workload in Teams is one that people usually have the least experience working with, and it has its own set of special considerations and behaviors that are different from those of the other workloads we have covered. This can make it seem complex or daunting from the outside, but do not worry, in this chapter we are going to take things step by step, and by the end not only will you have enough knowledge for this portion of the MS 700 Exam, but you might even be as enthusiastic about telephony in Teams as I am when you have learned about all the neat things it can do!

Phone System Overview

If you are planning to use Teams to replace your current traditional PBX, it is worth understanding that Teams will likely behave differently from the solutions that you have in place today. It can require rethinking how to best use it, and a common mistake is to try to do a direct feature-to-feature comparison or migration between the old system and Teams. However, as Teams is built to let you work from anywhere, feature comparisons sometimes do not apply or apply differently.

For example, consider this scenario: In the world of fixed-line telephony, a common feature is the call-pickup group. In an office location, if you can hear someone else's phone ringing across the desk cluster but you know that the person is not working in the office today, you could just let the call ring out. But you want to take the call and help whoever it is, so on your desk phone you pick up the receiver, push a special button, and your phone pulls that call over to you.

That sounds great and works well in a static scenario, but now consider that same thing in a Teams world. Just because someone is not in the office doesn't mean that they can't take that call. They might be working from home using their work laptop, or perhaps a home machine using bring your own device (BYOD). They might have Teams running on their mobile device, or they might be using simultaneous ring to also ring their mobile phone over the cellular network. The point is, because Teams lets you work from many locations it may not make sense to apply the same paradigms that work only in the world of fixed line telephony.

Telephony in Teams is all about control. It gives the end user the ability to control how and where they want to answer their calls and to also control what happens if they can't (that is, pass to a colleague, forward somewhere else, or send to voicemail).

Delivery Method

Adding PSTN numbers into Teams can be done in two ways, either through *Calling Plans* or through *Direct Routing*. You can mix and match either of these technologies so that you can have users configured either way in your tenant, depending on what makes the most sense for your scenario.

Calling Plans: This is where Microsoft is your PSTN provider; it gives you the numbers, minutes, and ability to make and receive calls using infrastructure it provides. You do not need anything else (other than licensing, but more on that later).

Direct Routing: This is where you bring your own PSTN connectivity to the Teams service, either through the use of certified gateways or through partner-provided offerings.

Remember from Chapter 2, "Getting Teams Up and Running," that users must be running in Teams Only mode for PSTN calling in Teams to function (via either method)!

Calling Plans

Calling Plans are available only in certain geographies that, at the time of writing, includes the following:

- Austria
- Belgium
- Canada
- Czech Republic
- Denmark
- Finland
- France
- Germany
- Hungary
- Ireland
- Italy
- Netherlands
- New Zealand
- Norway
- Portugal
- Puerto Rico
- Romania
- Singapore
- Slovakia
- Spain
- Sweden
- Switzerland
- United Kingdom
- United States

Microsoft also has agreements with partners in Australia (Telstra) and Japan (Softbank) where tenants created in these regions can use Calling Plans via those providers.

New numbers can be taken from Microsoft for the service in these locations, or numbers can be ported over to them from most major carriers.

The following are some of the considerations for Calling Plans:

- Pros
  - Simple to deploy
  - Fixed monthly fee as part of O365/Microsoft contract
  - No equipment to maintain
- Cons
  - Limited geographical regions available
  - No interop available with current phone systems
  - No option for seamless migrations

Direct Routing is certainly the quickest and simplest way of getting up and running with Phone System in Teams, and quite often companies will use it to test-drive the end-user experience, but this may not be the most cost-effective solution in the long term or provide enough flexibility.

For MS 700 you may be asked to help decide if a company should use Calling Plans or use Direct Routing. Usually this decision will boil down to factors such as coverage (Calling Plans not available in some locations), administrative overhead (Direct Routing can require infrastructure to be maintained), or things like reusing existing PSTN contracts and equipment (not an option in Calling Plans).

Direct Routing

Direct Routing can let you provide coverage in any part of the world, provided you have a suitable Internet connection and some form of PSTN connection via a provider. Direct Routing uses session border controllers (SBCs); think of these as essentially firewalls and routers but for phone calls, to create an encrypted Session Initiation Protocol (SIP) trunk connection to O365. They then also have connections to a local calling provider, which can be via either SIP, Integrated Services Digital Network (ISDN), or Plain Old Telephony Service (POTS) (analog phone lines like you used to get in most parts of the world).

This SBC sits at the center of this deployment, using rules to direct calls between all of the different connectivity methods it has. These can be very complex and let you achieve deep integrations and plan seamless migrations from your old PBX into Teams, or as simple as "any call received by Teams goes to the PSTN and vice versa." It can be easy to get carried away with the possibilities of using gateways for integration, but as a rule of thumb, try to keep things as simple as possible!

It is also possible to host Direct Routing in cloud-based services such as Azure where the SBC runs as a virtual appliance and you have SIP trunks over the Internet. There are also a number of providers that will run a Direct Routing platform for you (often referred to as Direct Routing as a service), but for the purposes of the exam, we will assume that you are deploying it for yourself.

The following are some of the considerations for Direct Routing:

- Pros
  - Can provide coverage anywhere in the world you need it even where there are legal requirements around the use of telephony service. Some countries, such as India, require you to keep PSN calls in country.

- Able to integrate with your current PBX to help smooth migrations or where some workloads have to stay on the PBX.
- Lets you use Teams telephony with any existing carriers, contracts, and numbers that you already have in place.

- Cons
  - Harder than Calling Plans to deploy
  - Requires PSTN provision from a carrier
  - Requires hardware to maintain

Licensing

So far, all the Teams functionality we have talked about (excluding most of what was in Chapter 4, "Teams Lifecycle Management," but those were technically other M365 features that Teams uses) comes included in the base license. Either you have Teams access or you do not. However, for the telephony workload, there are three add-on license types that you need to be aware of that control different aspects of how you can make and receive calls. We will also recap the Audio Conferencing license as it technically enables a type of telephony workload.

Be aware that at the time of writing Microsoft has introduced another license for Teams, the Advanced Communications add-on. This newest license SKU for Teams was meant to cover functionality around meeting customization, enabling compliance recording, and so on, but after some pushback, some of this functionality remained free. Anyway, for the purposes of the exam, this new license type is not yet included, but you can read up more on it at https://docs.microsoft.com/en-us/microsoftteams/teams-add-on-licensing/advanced-communications.

Table 5.1 summarizes what licenses enable which functionality and if they are included in a bundle.

TABLE 5.1   Teams Telephony Licensing

Feature	E1	E3	E5	Phone System (Add-on)	Audio Conferencing (Add-on)	Calling Plan (Add-on)
Chat	Y	Y	Y			
Voice	Y	Y	Y			
Video	Y	Y	Y			
Live Events (Webcasting)		Y	Y			

Feature	E1	E3	E5	Phone System (Add-on)	Audio Conferencing (Add-on)	Calling Plan (Add-on)
Teams Desktop Client	Y	Y	Y			
Teams Mobile Client	Y	Y	Y			
Teams Devices	Y	Y	Y			
PSTN Conferencing			Y		Y	
PSTN Calling capabilities			Y	Y		
Direct Routing			Y	Y		
Microsoft as the carrier (Calling Plans)						Y

Table 5.1 covers the enterprise licensing SKUs only, as that is the scope for the MS 700, and up until recently they were the only Teams SKUs that supported telephony. There is now licensing available for the Small Business plans that unlocks telephony functionality called Microsoft 365 Business Voice.

Audio Conferencing

This is the license that enables users to have dial-in details added to their meetings, as discussed in Chapter 3, "Teams Core Functionality."

By default, dial-in numbers are shared across other O365 tenants and are available in ~180 countries; alternatively, dedicated service numbers can be allocated to a tenant either as standard numbers or toll free. If using toll-free numbers, then you also need to have Communications Credits enabled at the tenant level.

This license is included in the standard E5 SKU but can be purchased as an add-on for other E plans.

You can read more about the Audio Conferencing license in Chapter 3, or you can find information about conferencing rates and features here: https://microsoft.com/en-gb/microsoft-teams/audio-conferencing.

Phone System

The Phone System license is required to unlock the ability to do any PSTN calling in Teams, whether you are using Direct Routing or Calling Plans. This license is included in the standard E5 SKU but can be purchased as an add-on for other E plans.

Calling Plans

Calling Plans are required where you want Microsoft to be your PSTN calling provider. They let you allocate a number hosted by Microsoft (more on this later) to your users and then act as a bundle of minutes that can be allocated to users for spending on calls.

Calling Plans come in two varieties: Domestic, which only includes calls to the same country as the user, and Domestic and International, which also allow calls out to international destinations. They are available in different sizes, should it be required, to help meet the volume of calling your users are likely to make:

- Domestic
  - Small
  - Medium
  - Large
- Domestic and International
  - Same as large with extra international minutes

Calling Plans pool up among users with the same license type and in the same country, so they share the total number of minutes among them. This helps to accommodate situations where usage patterns vary month by month.

For example, 10 users in the United Kingdom all allocated a Domestic/International Calling Plan (1,200 domestic, 600 international minutes) will share a pool of 10 × 1,200 = 12,000 domestic minutes and 10 × 600 = 6,000 international minutes for the month.

Communications Credits can be used to allow pay-as-you-go calling to international destinations where usage does not justify an international calling package.

> **NOTE**   Read more about Calling Plans in O365 at `https://docs.microsoft` `.com/en-us/MicrosoftTeams/calling-plans-for-office-365`.

Communications Credits

Communications Credits are enabled at the tenant level and act as a pot of money that certain telephony features can spend on a pay-as-you-go basis. They can be used in the following scenarios:

- Pay-as-you-go Audio Conferencing
- Paying for people who dial in to a toll-free number associated with your tenant (could be to a conferencing bridge or calling workflow)

- A user dialing out from a Teams meeting to a PSTN number that isn't included in a subscription
- A Calling Plan user making calls to international numbers who doesn't have this covered in their Calling Plan
- A Calling Plan user making any call after any included Calling Plan minutes are exhausted

Users can be assigned Communications Credit licenses individually to control if they are allowed access to pay-as-you-go calling (but this still requires the Phone System license and a Calling Plan license); however, you cannot control their individual level of expenditure.

When the Communications Credits pot is running low, it can be topped up either manually or automatically.

Setting up Communications Credits in your tenant can take a bit of time to arrange, so if you are working with any of the Phone System workloads, it can be handy to set this up with just a small amount of credit so that at least it is there if you need it.

Read more about Communications Credits at https://docs.microsoft .com/en-us/microsoftteams/what-are-communications-credits.

Number Types

When working with phone numbers in Teams, there are two broad categories of numbers:

> **User numbers:** These are numbers allocated to users for making normal calls; they are not expected to have a particularly high volume of incoming calls.

> **Service numbers:** These are used to support Voice Apps and can be allocated to Conference Bridges, Auto Attendants, and Call Queues. They can come in two varieties: either toll or toll-free (requires Communications Credits).

If you are porting numbers into Microsoft (usually when using Calling Plans), you need to identify which category each number, or block of numbers, is to be assigned. You can change numbers from one type to the other, but this needs to be done via a service ticket.

The reason for having different categories of numbers is that Microsoft can plan behind the scenes to handle different volumes of incoming calls. A service number is likely to have a higher call concurrency rate than a standard user number.

We will cover how to add numbers to your tenant in the "Calling Plans" section.

Device Types

This next section discusses something on which you won't be tested specifically on the exam but that is worth having a bit of knowledge about if you ever want to deploy Phone System for real, and that is the different types of devices used to support calling in Teams.

In Chapter 2, we talked about Teams Phones, and in Chapter 3 about Microsoft Teams Rooms, but when you are looking specifically at the Phone System workload, there are a few subcategories for these official Teams phone devices that can be used to help with replacing your current PBX with Teams:

USB handset: This category is essentially a modified headset device that looks like a phone; it cannot operate on its own and relies on the USB connection to a computer for a connection to Teams. All the processing power comes from Teams on your computer, which uses this device as an audio endpoint (microphone/speaker). It can be handy where a user cannot use a headset for some reason.

Core calling: This is a new category of devices that are due to be released in the second half of 2021. They are the no-frills option for where you just need a phone that can make and receive a call via Teams. There is no touch screen, no calendar view, and so on, just a phone that is connected to Teams all by itself (no PC required) that has a handset and dial pad used to make calls. This type of device is what you might put in a hallway or break room where you just need a Teams-native solution to make a call.

Native Teams: This is the default type of Teams-enabled device; it usually has a color touch screen and operates independently of the computer. It runs a forked version of the Teams Android client and is the standard type of device you might issue to a desk-based worker who needs to make calls independently of their computer.

Video phone: This is a fancy version of the native Teams phone that has a webcam and a larger screen, letting you join and participate in Teams video calls. (A native Teams device can also join these calls but doesn't have a camera to share video into the meeting.) These are usually reserved either for very small huddle type meeting rooms or for executives who want shiny toys on their desks.

There are also the two types of interop services Microsoft provides to allow (some) Skype for Business phones and some SIP-based phones (feature due second half of 2021) to connect into Teams.

The other type of device that would be used with Phone System is a headset. This is becoming by far the most popular choice when deploying a Teams-based solution to users, as a headset not only provides a good quality audio experience but is cheaper and more flexible than the type of fixed phone covered earlier. While any headset that can provide audio to the PC (or Mac) would work, you should always consider using certified headsets, as they have the minimum level of quality that they need to meet, and the certification guarantees that buttons such as volume up/down and call answer will operate as expected with Teams.

Just remember that whatever you do, try to make sure that users have a Teams-certified device, because without it, it doesn't matter how good the underlying infrastructure and connections are, if you are putting in bad audio from the microphone you will get bad audio out!

To see a full catalog of the device types and models certified to work with Teams, see `https://microsoft.com/en-gb/microsoft-teams/across-devices/devices`.

Emergency Calling

When adding telephony capabilities to Teams, there is a responsibility to make sure that users can safely make an emergency call if the situation should arise. You may think that dialing the emergency services might be the last thing someone would want to do using the Teams client from their PC, and you might be right, especially with the prevalence of mobile phones. However, you never know what sort of situation a user might find themselves in where this could quite literally be their last resort, so you have to plan and design your telephony deployment appropriately so that should the worst happen, someone can get help.

The phone networks use geographical information to make sure that emergency calls are routed to a public safety answering point (PSAP) located geographically close to the caller, which then means that you are likely to get a quicker response.

This location would have traditionally been the area code portion of the direct inward dial (DID) (the terminology used in the United States) or direct dial in (DDI) (the term used elsewhere) used to place the call, but for Teams this isn't really going to cut it because as we've talked about before, with Teams a user isn't tied to a specific physical location when they make or receive calls. Fortunately, Teams supports both static and dynamic location lookups, so depending on the calling delivery method, you can create different emergency configurations that vary based on the users' locations.

Dynamic services use information gathered from the client such as IP and subnet information or what Wi-Fi access point is being used to perform a lookup to see if any location addresses have been configured that it matches. We will cover the specifics for each deployment method in the following sections.

Regardless of the calling method, if you are using Teams for telephony, it is important that you perform a regular review of your emergency call handling, as it could quite literally be a matter of life and death for someone where Teams could be their lifeline to the outside world in an emergency.

Emergency calling is an important area to make sure you get right when deploying Teams telephony, for obvious reasons. The regulations surrounding it can be complicated and evolve over time and so do the features available in Teams to help meet them. Make sure you are always aware of the current requirements and Teams behavior by reviewing the following link: `https://docs.microsoft.com/en-us/microsoftteams/what-are-emergency-locations-addresses-and-call-routing`.

Location Lookup

The Teams client uses three different types of location lookups to support dynamic emergency calling, which are covered in the following section, but here is a high-level summary of what is used where:

Trusted IP address: This is used to determine if the user is inside the company network.

Location Information Service (LIS): The lookup against LIS will determine the actual physical address that will be sent when an emergency call is placed.

Network settings: This lookup is used to dynamically allocate specific emergency calling policies to the client based on the returned location. Think of this as controlling what happens when an emergency call is made and allowing that behavior to be different based on the location of the user.

 Some of these location settings are used elsewhere by the Teams client too. For example, the trusted IP address is used during *Local Media Optimization* (LMO), and the network settings are used to support *Location-Based Routing* (LBR).

Trusted IP Address

This is arguably the most important of the location lookup tools. It is the first thing that is checked by the Teams client, and if this doesn't match, then further lookups against LIS and Network Settings do not occur.

The Teams client does a lookup of the public IP address that it sees the client using. If this matches a configured range, it determines that the client is inside a company-managed location. This is helpful because you could have a subnet match but be at home or in another location, so the external IP would be different.

To configure trusted IP addresses, head over to the TAC, and from the left menu visit Locations ➤ Network Topology. In this view select the Trusted IP Addresses tab, and you will see a table of the configured IP addresses. Click Add to create a new one, and you will get a pop-up menu on the right (see Figure 5.1). From here you can add the IP address and mask that is used by your site. Remember that if you have both IPv4 and IPv6 public IP addresses, you should configure both here.

You can use PowerShell to configure these with the `-CsTenantTrustedIPAddress` family, so the following, for example, would create a new IPv4 Trusted IP object:

```
New-CsTenantTrustedIPAddress -IPAddress "8.8.8.8" -MaskBits "32"
```

Location Information Service

LIS is used to determine the physical address (Civic Address) where the user is currently located. It does this by using the following information where available:

Network subnet: The broad network subnet in which the client has an IP address (not shared with Network Settings)

Network switches: The chassis ID of the switch through which the client is connected

Switch port: The specific port of the switch that the client is connected to

Wi-Fi access points: The wireless access point through which the client is connected

FIGURE 5.1 Trusted IP address

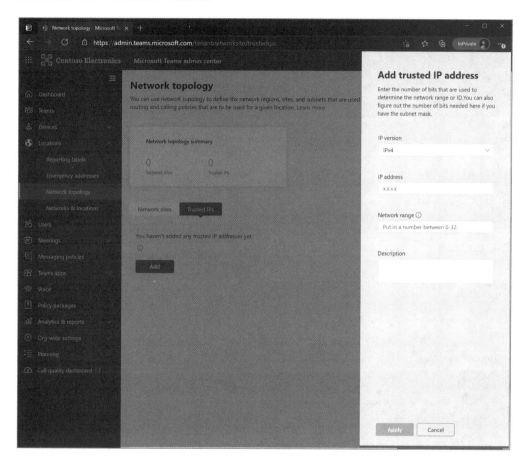

The hierarchy defined using LIS is that a civic address contains one or more locations (e.g., second floor), and a location contains one or more of the items from the previous list such as a subnet or Wi-Fi access point. You should choose as specific a match as is possible; for example, in a large campus network, a subnet might encompass more than one location, so you could perhaps use switch or access point information instead.

When creating a civic address, this should include geographic coordinates so that the physical address can be identified on a map.

To work with the configured addresses in your tenant, open the TAC and head to Locations ➤ Emergency Addresses. Here you will see a list of the locations created for your tenant (see Figure 5.2).

FIGURE 5.2 Emergency Addresses

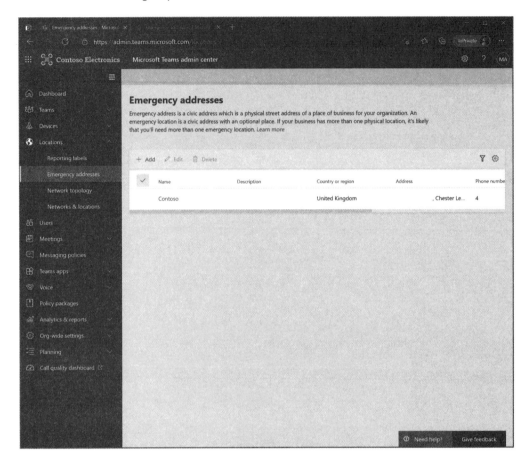

To create a new address, click Add from the menu above the location table. Give the location a name and pick which country it is in. Once you enter a country, additional information will appear on the page, allowing you to either search for the address or enter it manually. If when you start typing the address it is recognized as an address in Azure Maps, then a map will appear, and you can drag the pin to the correct location.

If it cannot find the address you are trying to use, you can use the toggle switch to enter the address manually (see Figure 5.3). This will require you to enter some latitude and longitude coordinates, which you can find through most online mapping websites. If you use Bing or Google Maps, when you right-click the map, it will give you an option to copy the coordinates for that point to the clipboard.

FIGURE 5.3   Entering a new address

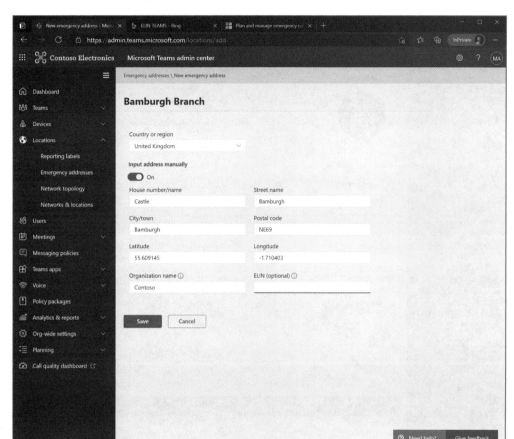

Once the address has been saved, it will show up in your list. Microsoft will automatically attempt to validate the address to check that it can apply emergency services routing to the location. The status of this validation is shown in the first table listing the locations. Once an address has been validated, you are not able to edit it; instead, you should create a new address and remove the old one.

With an address created, you can click its name and use the table at the bottom to define a location (referred to as places in the TAC) inside this address (see Figure 5.4).

Next you can go inside your location to add your network details and define the subnets, switch ports, and so on that will be used to detect this site (see Figure 5.5).

All of these elements can also be created and managed using PowerShell, so if you have a large, complicated networking environment, you could use CSV files and some scripts to automate the creation of these for you.

FIGURE 5.4   Defining a location inside an address

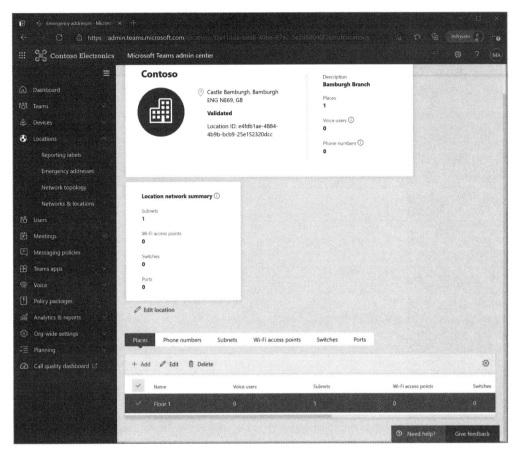

The management cmdlet families are as follows:

- -CsOnlineLisCivicAddress

- -CsOnlineLisLocation

- -CsOnlineLisSubnet

- -CsOnlineLisWirelessAccessPoint

- -CsOnlineLisSwitch

- -CsOnlineLisPort

If you are going to use PowerShell to work with these, it is important to remember the usage hierarchy, so you can't make a new location without associating it to an address (Civic Address), and so on.

FIGURE 5.5   Defining network details inside a location

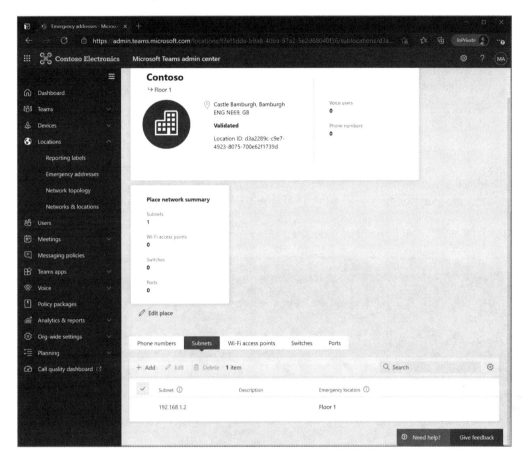

To read up more about emergency addresses and configuring LIS, see https://docs.microsoft.com/en-us/MicrosoftTeams/ add-change-remove-emergency-location-organization.

Network Settings

Lastly we have the lookup against (the generically named) Network Settings. This lookup is used to control what happens when an emergency call is made (should someone be notified, or which SBC should place the call). This *does not* control any information about what address is used when the call is made; that is all on LIS.

A lookup here also uses the client's networking information but at a less granular level. While some of the components of the lookup here may seem to be the same as the one used in LIS, it is a separate system, so you may need to repeat some of your configuration here. Lookups are done using the following:

Network region: A collection of network sites, typically by country; for example, United Kingdom would be a region.

Network site: A collection of IP subnets associated with a physical location. This could be a single office or a campus containing multiple buildings.

Network subnet: A specific network subnet associated to a Network Site, for example: 10.0.10.0/24. (This is independent of the LIS subnet data.)

To configure this in the TAC, head to Locations ➢ Network Topology from the left menu. Here the first tab displayed is called Network Sites and will show you any that you have defined. Click Add to start adding a new one (see Figure 5.6). Give the site a name and add any associated subnets to it. You can also select which emergency calling policies and

FIGURE 5.6   Defining network details inside a location

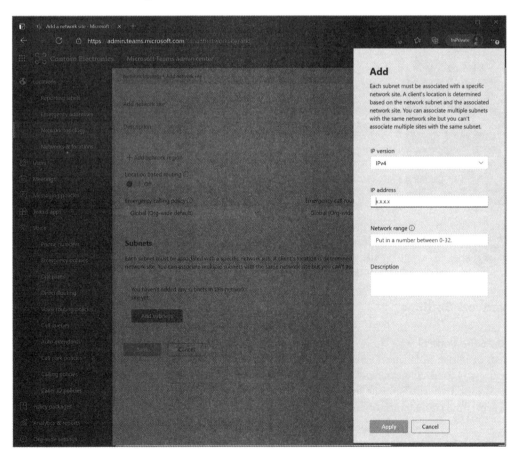

emergency call routing policies will be used when the client is identified as being in this site (more on them later). Click Save, and the site will be added.

Network settings can also be configured in PowerShell using these cmdlets:

- `-CsTenantNetworkRegion`

- `-CsTenantNetworkSite`

- `-CsTenantNetworkSubnet`

 You can read further about configuring network setting locations (and also trusted IP addresses) at https://docs.microsoft.com/en-us/microsoftteams/manage-your-network-topology.

Emergency Policies

There are then two types of policies that help control the behavior when an emergency call is placed:

Emergency calling policy: Used by both Calling Plans and Direct Routing, this policy can be used to configure notifications so that when an emergency call is placed in a building, an appropriate person is notified (for example, building security or management). This can also convert emergency calls into a conference so that the notified party can participate in the emergency call. These policies can be configured at both the site and user levels, and we will look at them in the upcoming Calling Features section.

Emergency call routing policy: Used only by Direct Routing, this policy determines firstly what numbers are classified as emergency numbers and which gateway should deal with the call (the call route). These policies are configured at both a site and a user level.

Emergency Calls with Calling Plans

With Calling Plans, a default emergency location is assigned against the numbers in your tenant. If you are in the United States and Canada, this is configured, as the numbers are allocated to users, but in other countries, such as European countries, it happens when the numbers are provisioned into your tenant.

Which location is used when an emergency call is placed varies from country to country, as they have different regulations and therefore different carrier capabilities.

In the United States, Calling Plans also support Dynamic Emergency Calling, which will cross-reference the client's location using networking information against both the network settings and LIS.

If it finds a match for an updated location, the call will be passed directly to the PSAP for the configured address along with the location information that has been obtained (included in the call setup data).

If the location cannot be determined through a dynamic lookup, the call will be placed toward the PSAP for the default address given when the numbers were assigned. However, before the call reaches the PSAP, it is first answered by a screening service called an Emergency Call Relay Center (ECRC). An operator will answer the call and verify the user's location is correct before placing the call to the PSAP.

This behavior is specific to the United States (which is the most complex), but a summary of the behaviors for the main Calling Plan locations is given here:

- United States
    - If a dynamic location lookup is successful, route to the PSAP for the dynamic address.
    - If not at a dynamic location, calls go to ECRC to determine location before being passed along.
- United Kingdom, Ireland, and Canada
    - Calls go to ECRC to determine location before being passed on to correct handler.
- Australia, Japan
    - As these are partner-provided Calling Plan locations, emergency handling is the responsibility of these partners.
- Other Calling Plan locations (e.g., France, Spain, Germany, Netherlands)
    - Calls are routed to the emergency provider determined by the static location allocated against the numbers when added to the tenant.

If you are in the United States using Calling Plans, you can dial 933 to test your setup. A Microsoft service will answer the call and read back to you what location has been identified and if the call would be screened though an ECRC or not.

Emergency Calling with Direct Routing

Direct Routing has similar behavior to Calling Plans, but there are more configuration steps outside of Teams to make sure that the whole thing joins up correctly.

Emergency call routing policies are used to determine how the call should be processed (through the Network Settings lookup); if both a site and user policy are assigned and valid, then the site-based policy takes priority. If the site does not have one or the site cannot be determined through a lookup, then the user's policy is used. Once the policy is applied to determine where to route the calls, then the lookup against LIS occurs that tells the client what location it to should send should the need occur.

When a call then arrives at the Direct Routing SBC, there are two main things it can do with it, and again this will vary by geography and who the local carrier is. The first is through an *Emergency Routing Service Provider* (ERSP) and the second uses an *Emergency Location Identification Number* (ELIN).

ERSP: Used in the United States (commonly with SIP trunks), this works in a similar way to the Microsoft Calling Plan solution where calls are passed through a screening service to determine the user's location before then connecting the caller to the correct PSAP. This is a service you would need from the upstream carrier connected to your Direct Routing service. It is possible to configure Teams to include the location information when the call is set up. This can further help the ERSP narrow down where the user is located.

ELIN: This is used primarily where you have non–SIP-based connections to the carrier where location information cannot be transmitted alongside the call. It is an application running on your SBC that parses the location information being provided by the Teams client when a call is placed and matches that against its own database. This database is configured according to the SBC vendor's instructions, but when the location data matches, the SBC replaces the caller's number with the ELIN and places the call to a local PSAP. If the emergency services call back to the SBC, it performs a reverse lookup to make sure the call goes back to the correct user.

Emergency calling is a complex subject, so don't worry if you get lost with it; for MS 700 you need to know that emergency calling requires some configuration and that Teams is capable of supporting dynamic location lookups. If you do want to read up further about how it works, see http://docs.microsoft.com/en-us/MicrosoftTeams/configure-dynamic-emergency-calling.

Phone System Delivery

Now we are going to look in more detail at how you can deploy Phone System using either of the connectivity methods that we discussed. In Calling Plans this will mainly focus on number management (provisioning numbers and porting numbers), as Microsoft is acting as the carrier here, whereas in the Direct Routing section it will cover the technical aspects of connecting to the Microsoft service, and the number management isn't as important (because this is done upstream/downstream by your PSTN provider).

Calling Plans

As mentioned, Calling Plans might not be an option for your deployment, depending on what countries you need to have telephony services available in, and they aren't always the most cost-effective solution either. However, they are certainly the simplest way to get up and running because you can do most of it with a few clicks in the Teams Admin Center (TAC). Let's get started by allocating some numbers into a tenant.

Adding Numbers

Remember the two types of numbers that we can use: service numbers or user numbers. For Calling Plans, it is user numbers that you need to have available to allocate to your users. There is a formula that is used to determine how many you can have at any given time. The formula is as follows:

$$\big(\langle \text{Number of Calling Plan licenses} \rangle \times 1.1 \big) + 10$$

So, if you have 100 Calling Plans, you would be able to request the following:

$$100 \times 1.1 = 110 + 10 = \textbf{120}$$

120 user numbers could be allocated to your tenant ready to give out to your users.

Incidentally, to be able to request service numbers, you need to have either Phone System or Audio Conferencing licenses in your tenant. These can then be allocated to either conference bridges (for use in meetings) or to support Voice Apps (more on these later).

> The number of service numbers you can get is worked out by band-ings, based on how many licenses you have. See the full breakdown at http://docs.microsoft.com/en-us/microsoftteams/how-many-phone-numbers-can-you-get.

Numbers via the TAC

To view the numbers assigned to your tenant or to request more, you can open up the TAC and then from the left menu select Voice ➤ Phone Numbers. Here you will see a table with all the current numbers, provided by Microsoft, allocated to you (see Figure 5.7). This will not show any numbers coming from a Direct Routing solution.

To start a new request, click Add in the toolbar, which will start a new request wizard. Each request must be given an order name and description. Then from the drop-down list, pick which country you want to add numbers from. The list of countries shown will be much larger than this. Microsoft can supply Calling Plan numbers, as you could be requesting new numbers for use with Audio Conferencing (see Figure 5.8).

Next you need to choose what type of number you want to request. The list of choices will vary depending on the country you have selected and what is available. For example, in some countries you can only request Toll Free numbers. The drop-down will also show you how many you are able to acquire; as you can see in Figure 5.9, this tenant does not have Communications Credits enabled, so Toll Free numbers are not an option.

Next you must assign a location against the numbers; this is part of the information we covered earlier to help make sure that emergency calls are able to be placed correctly to a handler near the user making the call.

If no locations have been created in the tenant, you can click Add Location to create one, or you can search and select one used previously.

FIGURE 5.7 Numbers shown in the TAC

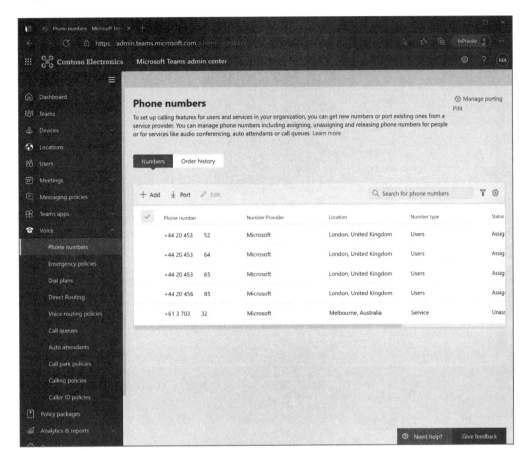

To see the full list of locations that are configured in the tenant, you can find them (still in the TAC) under Locations ➤ Emergency Addresses (see Figure 5.10).

Having selected (or added) a location, you can then pick the area code if more than one is available for the selected country and city and then enter how many numbers you want to select (see Figure 5.11). When requesting numbers this way, it is unlikely that you will get a contiguous block of numbers. This process will go and pull back a selection that Microsoft and its carrier in the region have available and let you select which ones you want.

Companies used to like having large blocks of numbers, as then they knew which range belonged to them and number management was simpler for matching extensions, and so on. However, with Teams there really isn't a requirement to have extensions, and you generally call people (at least internally) by dialing their name, not number. So if you do still need numbers that are all in one chunk, you might be able to request them via a service ticket.

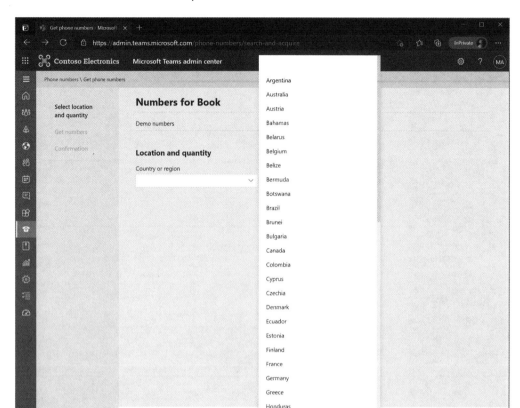

FIGURE 5.8 Number country selection

When you click Next, the system goes and gets a selection of available numbers, which are held for a 10-minute period (see Figure 5.12). If you are happy with the selection, you can place the order, and if not, you can go back and see if you get a different selection.

The final step gives confirmation that the order has been received and that the numbers will become available soon for allocation to users.

Porting Numbers

Another option is to bring numbers that you already have over to the Teams platform. This is done through a process called *porting*, which is a standard industry practice. Microsoft will take over being the service provider from your current supplier and will provide you with the numbers into your tenant and is responsible for their billing, and so on. You can also usually port numbers away from Microsoft if you should need to do so in future.

FIGURE 5.9   Number type selection

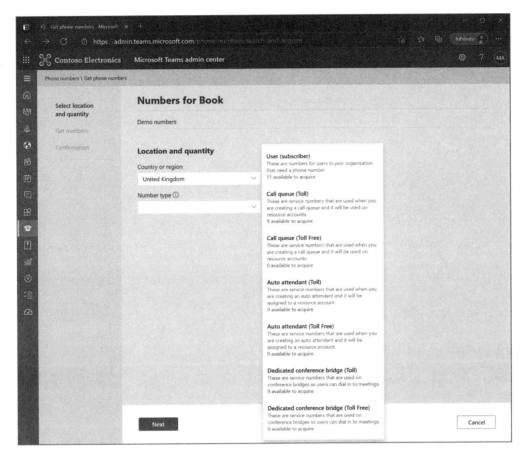

The details will vary from region to region, but the porting process is roughly the same. For example, in the United Kingdom you cannot usually port numbers from the middle of a range. For example, if you have a 50-block number set, you have to port all 50 in one go, and the process can take four to six weeks. However, in the United States, you can port individual numbers, and the process can be fairly rapid.

Be aware of the other implications of number porting. For example, if you port a number that is the primary circuit number for an Integrated Services Digital Network (ISDN) circuit, then it will usually stop the circuit, and your old system will be cut off as the port completes.

FIGURE 5.10 Emergency locations

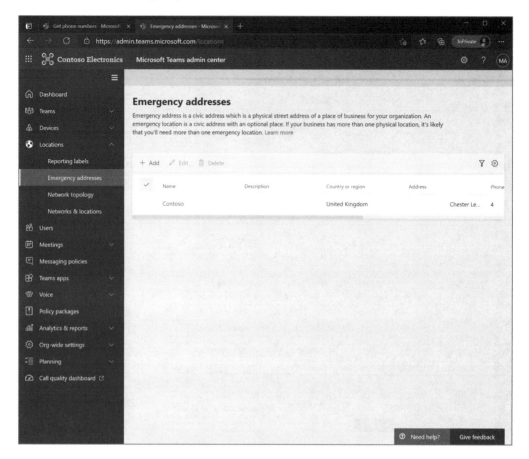

You submit a request to a national clearinghouse that notifies the losing carrier of the port request. They check to see if the details are correct and either accept or reject the port. If any details are incorrect (such as the number range, billing details, or any number of things), the port can be rejected, and you need to update and resubmit the request.

If the port is accepted, then the losing carrier will provide a porting window, which is usually two to four hours in duration (usually you can only get slots during working hours too). In this window, they will update their records to not accept incoming calls anymore, and calls will be passed to the new carrier.

This does mean that the number porting process can be fairly disruptive for an organization, so you should plan for a downtime window during the port where users should expect to not be able to make or receive calls. The reality is that they can probably make outbound call just fine using Teams in the meantime and that the downtime shouldn't be too bad, but it's best to plan for the worst case.

FIGURE 5.11   Number quantity

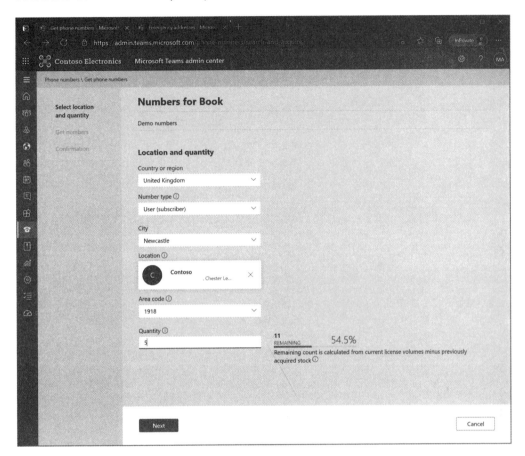

This is a big simplification of what happens, but you do not need to know the specifics of how it works; just have an understanding of the broader process. The number porting process can be one of the most challenging aspects of a phone system deployment as much of the process is out of your direct control. However, Microsoft has done its best to make the process simple, and there is a great team working behind the scenes who specifically support the porting process.

A number port can be started via the TAC from the same number management screen. Go to the left menu, select Voice ➢ Phone Numbers, and above the number list table there is a Port button. This will start the porting wizard. This wizard is intended to capture basic information about the porting process but is not going to cover every eventuality. Sometimes it may be necessary to download and complete a manual form that is then submitted as a support request to the Microsoft porting team.

FIGURE 5.12 Number selection

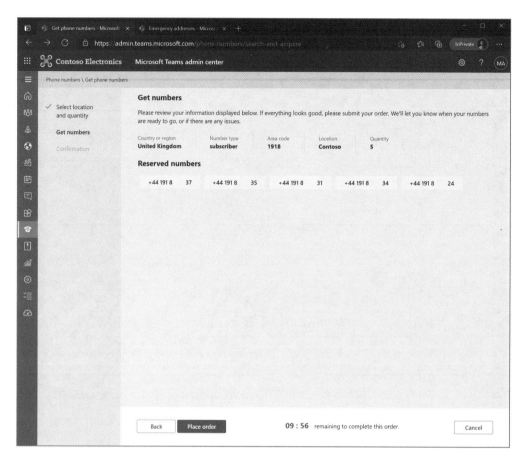

On the first page of the porting wizard are some warning messages and things to note before proceeding (see Figure 5.13):

- Accurate account information is required for the current provider.

- Numbers should still be active. Do not cancel them; the port will usually take care of this.

- Numbers submitted should all be from the same provider.
  - Just submit multiple requests if you need to, but it is unlikely that you will be able to get matching port dates.

- Some number types cannot be ported as they may be handled differently.

- Any transfer dates are provided by the losing provider.
  - If the dates really do not work, you can request to change the dates or cancel and resubmit the request.

FIGURE 5.13   Number porting process

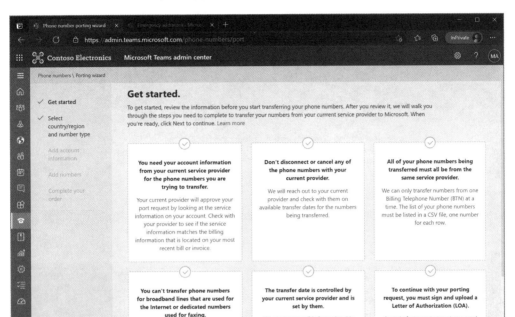

- A letter of authorization (LOA) must be provided, signed by someone with authority to move the numbers.
  - Usually a billing contact or similar who is known to the losing carrier.
- Numbers can be submitted only in E.164 format.

> E.164 is an international standard for writing down phone numbers. Any-time Teams does anything with phone numbers, it is always using E.164. You will recognize this format for numbers as it starts with a + sign and contains no other formatting. Any leading zeros that you might use to dial in-country are also removed.
>
> The first digit represents the country; for example, United States is +1 or United Kingdom is +44. Then the remaining digits are used by the destination country to further identify or route the call (such as which region it is destined for, if it is a mobile number, or if it is a nongeographic number that has special handling conditions).

After acknowledging these constraints, you select the country and number type of either toll free or a geographic number (see Figure 5.14).

FIGURE 5.14 Number porting country selection

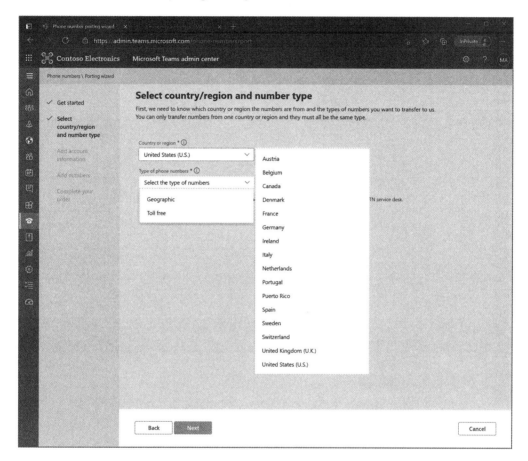

On the next screen you need to have contact information (address) for the authorizing person from your company, the current provider, and the address where the numbers are currently provided (the office location). Some of the information asked for here will vary by country and their specific process, so if you are porting numbers in the United States, you will be asked to choose to port all numbers or just a selection. You can also request a porting date, but this is simply a preference; the date will be set by the losing provider. The Billing Telephone Number (BTN) is the primary number for your service and helps identify the account with the current provider (see Figure 5.15).

FIGURE 5.15 Number porting account information

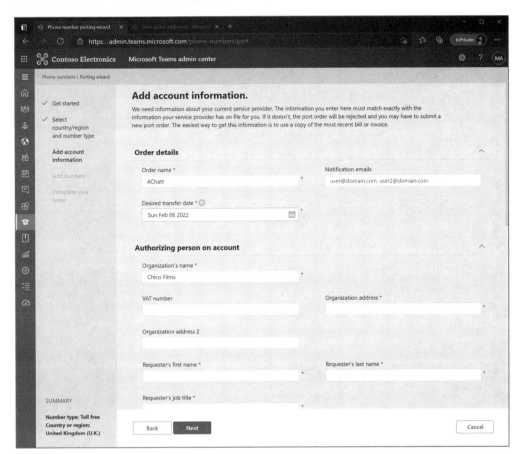

Next you are asked to upload a CSV file containing each number to be ported, one on each line, and in E.164 number format (see Figure 5.16).

NOTE

If you are making the CSV using Excel, be careful, as Excel easily mangles phone numbers by trying to treat them as normal numbers or trying to convert them into scientific format. So, make sure to check using a text editor before you try to upload them.

The form will then validate your inputs and ask for a signed copy of an LOA to be uploaded. If you have not already prepared an LOA, there will be an option to download it or see the reference link to prepare one in advance.

FIGURE 5.16   Number porting number upload

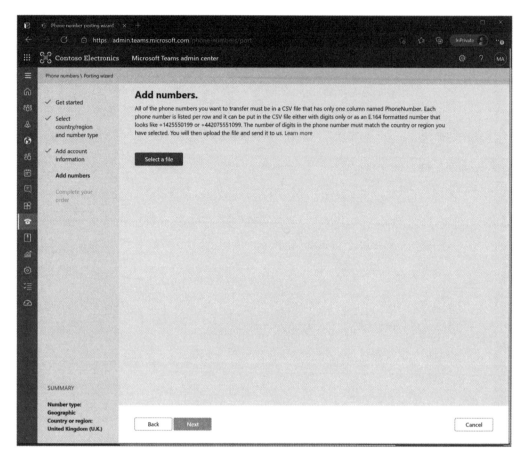

 To see the current porting process details and to find the LOA forms, take a look at the following link (for the US details, but use the left menu to select any of the available countries): `https://docs.microsoft.com/en-us/ microsoftteams/manage-phone-numbers-for-your-organization/ phone-number-management-for-the-u-s`.

After submitting the porting request, you will receive email confirmation and updates as the process progresses.

The first time you do a port, be prepared to have some issues. It is a difficult process and can be common to get ports rejected because the billing information doesn't match what the losing carrier holds, and so on. This isn't a Microsoft process but is standard in the telecoms industry.

If you ever need to port numbers away from Microsoft to a new provider (if, say, swapping from Calling Plans to Direct Routing), then you can specify a porting PIN. For any port requests you make to Microsoft, you will be asked for this PIN to validate the request. You can view and set this PIN from the Manage Porting PIN link at the top right on the Number Management screen in the TAC.

Configuring Users

Once you have the numbers showing in your tenant, allocating them to users is straightforward. Make sure that the users you want to configure have the correct licensing applied, and then from TAC in the left menu select Voice ➤ Phone Numbers.

In the list of numbers, you can see which are currently unallocated, you can select the number, and then you can click Edit. This will open a pop-out menu on the right side of the screen. Click in the search box under the Assigned To section and enter the name of the user you want to assign the number to (see Figure 5.17). In the box underneath, verify that the

FIGURE 5.17   Allocating a number in TAC

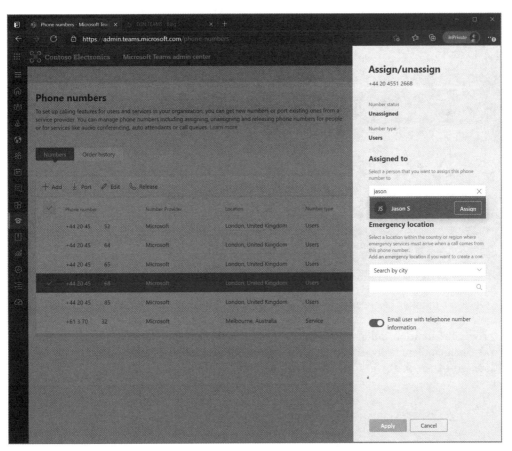

correct emergency location is selected. There is also a toggle switch to control if the user is notified via email about their new number.

Alternatively, you can assign a number by editing the user directly. Head over to Users from the left menu and then search for the user you want to work with. Click the user's name and click Edit next to the General Information section. This will open a pop-out menu on the right side where you can search for and assign a phone number (see Figure 5.18).

FIGURE 5.18   Allocating a number via User Settings

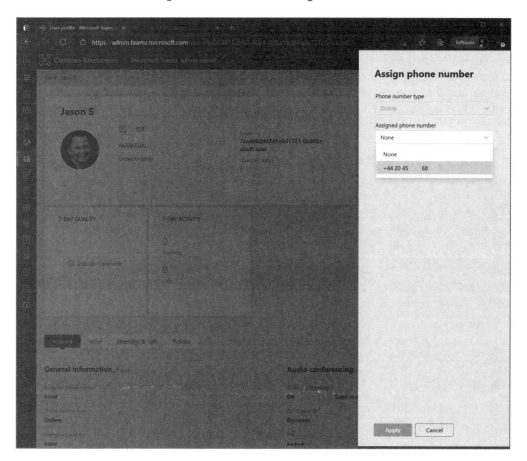

Once the number has been selected, you can also update and select the correct emergency location for the user.

This configuration can also be done via PowerShell using the `-CsOnlineVoiceUser` PowerShell cmdlet family. To manage the emergency addresses, there are also the `-CsOnlineLisLocation` family of cmdlets.

So, to assign a number and location against a user, you could combine the following cmdlets:

```
$Location = Get-CsOnlineLisLocation -Location <LocationName>
Get-CsOnlineVoiceUser -Identity <User> | Set-CsOnlineVoiceUser -TelephoneNumber <PhoneNumber> -LocationID $Location
```

Direct Routing

Direct Routing differs from Calling Plans in that it gives you much more flexibility about how you want to bring telephony into Teams. As you are using SBCs to bring your own connections to the service, you have flexibility:

- Countries that are covered.
- How failover is configured.
- What integrations need to happen with on-premises equipment.
- Control the pace at which you do a migration.
- Maintain current calling contracts and agreements.
- Keep existing number ranges with minimal downtime.

You also have choices about how to deliver Direct Routing. For the rest of this section, we are going to assume that you are deploying it yourself (as does MS 700), but in reality, you could be using Direct Routing through a partner who will run the service for you.

Planning Direct Routing

To get up and running with Direct Routing, there are a number of things you need to consider. We are going to run through them next, but here is a quick checklist:

- Certified SBC
- Internet access to the SBC
- Internet DNS name for the SBC
- Domain activation
- Public certificate for the SBC
- Firewall access allowing traffic to Teams

A fairly significant portion of the Direct Routing configuration is not covered here, and that is how to set up the SBCs themselves. As these gateways are provided by third parties and run their own proprietary software, it is not something that Microsoft can control. You should refer to your SBC manufacturer, who will have guides that should dovetail with the information given here but is focused on the specific configuration tasks for their hardware.

Direct Routing requirements can evolve as the service changes; you can find the current list of requirements at https://docs.microsoft.com/en-us/microsoftteams/direct-routing-plan.

Compatible SBC

First up, you need to have an SBC from a certified vendor. The list of vendors and compatible SBCs is growing but currently includes the following (among others):

- Ribbon
- AudioCodes
- Cisco
- Avaya
- Oracle

To see a full list of certified SBC vendors and gateway versions, look at https://docs.microsoft.com/en-us/microsoftteams/ direct-routing-border-controllers.

Internet Access to the SBC

The SBC must be able to communicate with Teams; to do this, you can either give the SBC a public IP address directly or use NAT to place it inside a DMZ or internal network.

The SBC should also have an internal network connection that can be used by users inside the network when placing calls using something called Media Bypass.

Media Bypass and *Local Media Optimization* (LMO) are features of Direct Routing that allow calls to establish their media connection by the most efficient route instead of having to send them always via the Microsoft Teams Media Processes.

For example, if you have an SBC deployed in a large office, it is fine when users are remote for their calls to go via the Teams service. However, if they are inside the office, this could create a lot of extra Internet traffic and potentially introduce unwanted network quality issues to the call.

With Media Bypass configured, the calls would still be set up using the Teams service, but the audio data (media) would go directly to the SBC over the internal network.

Media Bypass is a large topic in its own right and not something you need to really understand for MS 700, but if you want to read up on it, further check out https://docs.microsoft.com/en-us/ microsoftteams/direct-routing-plan-media-bypass.

DNS Name and Domain

For Teams to be able to address the SBC, it must have a public DNS name configured to point toward the public IP that you have allocated to it. The SBC cannot be registered against the onmicrosoft.com address of the tenant; it must be a non-Microsoft domain. It can be either:

- The normal vanity domain that you use for the tenant
    - SBC1.Contoso.com

- A subdomain of the vanity domain used in the tenant
  - `SBC1.DR.Contoso.com`
- From a totally different namespace (as long as it is unique and not used in any other tenant)
  - `SBC1.DirectRoutingProvider.com`

If a domain namespace is being used that isn't allocated to any users already, then the domain must be added to the tenant, and you will need to jump through the steps to prove ownership (usually by creating specific DNS records against the domain). You must also allocate a temporary user who is configured for Teams with their address configured against the new domain. This process just activates the domain properly behind the scenes against your tenant for use with Teams and therefore with Direct Routing.

Public Certificate

You also need to have a public certificate from a certificate authority that Microsoft recognizes; the list is broad and contains the usual suspects, such as Comodo, GoDaddy, and VeriSign.

The certificate should contain the SBC name either as the subject or in the Subject Alternative Name (SAN) field. It is also possible to use wildcard certificates for the SBC, but these must match the exact subdomain being used by your SBCs in DNS.

It is possible to use wildcard certificates or to include more than one SBC on the same certificate using SANs.

Firewall configuration

Microsoft uses GeoDNS technology to make sure that your SBC establishes a connection to the Direct Routing service points closest to the SBC (Table 5.2 shows the preference for how these resolve). This means that when configuring your SBC, you should always address the following SIP Proxy *fully qualified domain names* (FQDNs) in order. (You can only imagine the discussions behind the scenes that must have happened about if they should have used sip1. in the naming convention).

- `sip.pstnhub.microsoft.com`
- `sip2.pstnhub.microsoft.com`
- `sip3.pstnhub.microsoft.com`

Next you need to make sure that you are allowing access through your firewall between the SBC and the Teams service. There are several ranges of ports that you need to open depending on how you want to configure your Direct Routing service.

MEDIA BYPASS

By default, all media traffic will route through what are called Teams *Media Processors* (MP). These are the components of Teams that handle media during a call, but they are limited (relatively speaking) in their geographical distribution, so you might not be close to one, which could have an impact on call quality.

TABLE 5.2 SIP Signaling Failover

Primary (sip.pstnhub. . .)	Secondary (sip2.pstnhub. . .)	Tertiary (sip3.pstnhub. . .)
EU	NOAM	ASIA
NOAM	EU	ASIA
ASIA	NOAM	EU

https://docs.microsoft.com/en-us/MicrosoftTeams/direct-routing-plan#media-traffic-port-ranges

Media processor locations:

- US West and US East
- Amsterdam and Dublin
- Singapore and Hong Kong
- Japan East and Japan West (MP only, not signaling)
- Australia East and Australia Southeast (MP only, not signaling)

One solution to this is called Media Bypass, which allows clients to communicate either directly with the public IP address off the SBC or through something called a *Transport Relay*. If you want to open up the firewall and allow incoming Internet connections, the media path from the client would be: client → SBC public IP → PSTN Carrier.

Transport relays are used to help keep media going via the shortest path possible and to help maximize the chances of a call succeeding. They live at the edge of Microsoft's network, so you should not ever be too far away from one.

For Direct Routing, if you have Media Bypass configured and do not want to allow incoming Internet connections directly to your SBC from any Internet IP address, you can restrict it to just accept connections from the transport relays (and media processors). When a client then places a call (from outside your WAN), the media would be established from client → transport relay → SBC public IP → PSTN carrier.

SIGNALING PORTS

Table 5.3 shows the firewall ports required for the SBC to establish a connection to Teams (these are always required).

TABLE 5.3 Direct Routing SIP Signaling Ports

Traffic Type	From	To	Source	Destination
SIP/TLS	Teams SIP Proxy	SBC Public IP	1024-65525	Defined on the SBC
SIP/TLS	SBC Public IP	Teams SIP Proxy	Defined on the SBC	5061

https://docs.microsoft.com/en-us/MicrosoftTeams/direct-routing-plan#media-traffic-port-ranges

MEDIA PORTS (WITHOUT MEDIA BYPASS)

Table 5.4 shows the firewall ports required to allow media to be established to the Teams media processors (these are always required).

TABLE 5.4   Direct Routing Ports to Media Processors

Traffic Type	From	To	Source	Destination
UDP/SRTP	Media Processor	SBC Public IP	3478-3481 49152-53247	Defined on the SBC
UDP/SRTP	SBC Public IP	Media Processor	Defined on the SBC	3478-3481 49152-53247

```
https://docs.microsoft.com/en-us/MicrosoftTeams/direct-routing-
plan#media-traffic-port-ranges
```

MEDIA PORTS (WITH MEDIA BYPASS)

If you are configuring Media Bypass, you should also add the ports shown in Table 5.5 to allow communications from Transport relays, or if you want to allow communications from any Internet IP, use the values from Table 5.4, but do not restrict the source or destinations to the Media Processor IP addresses.

TABLE 5.5   Direct Routing Ports for Media Bypass

Traffic type	From	To	Source	Destination
UDP / SRTP	Transport Relays (52.112.0.0/14)	SBC Public IP	50000-59999	Defined on the SBC
UDP / SRTP	SBC Public IP	Transport Relays (52.112.0.0/14)	Defined on the SBC	50000-59999 3478 3479

```
https://docs.microsoft.com/en-us/MicrosoftTeams/direct-routing-
plan#media-traffic-port-ranges
```

Deploying Direct Routing

As previously discussed, you should consult with your SBC vendor to get their instructions for how to perform the actual SBC configuration itself. Here we are going to look at what you have to set up in the tenant, assuming that you have met all of the infrastructure requirements laid out earlier.

Adding SBCs to the Tenant

SBCs can now be added either through the TAC or using PowerShell. To start with setting one up in TAC, head to Voice ≻ Direct Routing from the left menu. Here you will see a list of the configured SBCs along with an overview of their status.

To configure a new SBC, click Add from the menu above the list; then at the top enter the FQDN for the gateway and then complete the rest of the form with the required options (see Figure 5.19). The following is a list of the main options you can configure:

SIP Signaling Port: The port used on the SBC for the incoming connection from Teams.

Send SIP Options: Used to determine whether the SBC is online (rather than just that a connection is established).

Forward Call History: If call forwarding information is provided along with calls placed to the SBC.

PAI Header: If identifying information should be sent to the SBC when a call is placed.

Capacity: A figure used only in monitoring to help identify when an SBC may be reaching capacity. This is not used to prevent new calls being sent to the SBC.

Response Codes: Lets you customize what codes the SBC can send back to indicate it is unable to route calls.

Failover Time: How long to wait before trying a call to another SBC.

Country For Media: Useful if the geolocation is routing media via a region not local to the SBC.

PIDF/LO For Emergency Calls: If presence and location data is supported by the SBC for emergency calling (as discussed earlier in the chapter).

At the bottom of the page you can configure settings specific to LMO and Media Bypass.

You can read up on the full list of options available at `https://docs` `.microsoft.com/en-us/microsoftteams/direct-routing-connect-` `the-sbc`.

To configure an SBC using PowerShell, you can use the `–CSOnlinePSTNGateway` set of cmdlets.

To create a new SBC, you would run the following:

```
New-CsOnlinePSTNGateway -FQDN <Public name of SBC> -SIPSignalingPort <port>
```

And to view all the SBCs in your tenant, use `Get-CSOnlinePSTNGateway`.

Full documentation for these cmdlets can be found at `https://` `docs.microsoft.com/en-us/powershell/module/skype/` `new-csonlinepstngateway`.

FIGURE 5.19   Adding a new SBC via the TAC

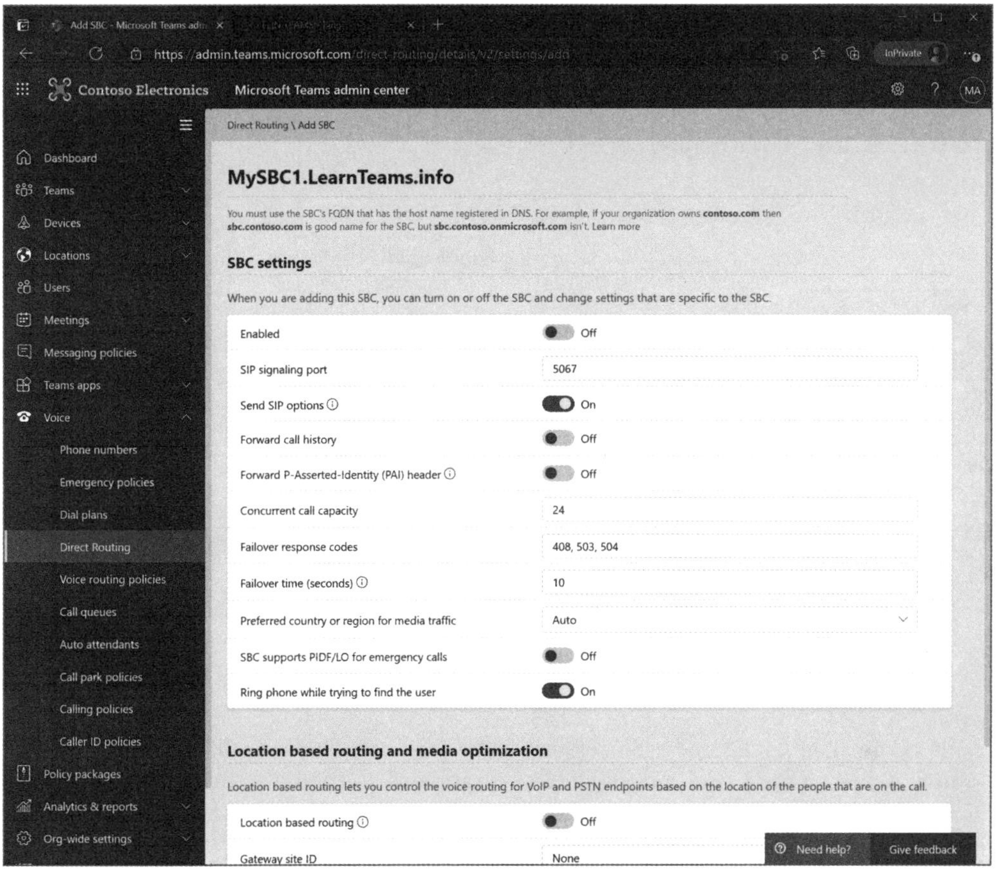

Configuring Voice Routing

To control what types of numbers users can call, and how these calls are routed between gateways configured in the tenant, Teams uses a voice routing system made up the following components:

Voice routing policy: These are the policies that are assigned against users. They contain one or more PSTN usages.

PSTN usages: A PSTN usage contains voice routes; they can be included in one or more voice routing policy.

Voice routes: Voice routes contain number patterns that must be matched by the dialed number; these can be very specific or totally open. They also contain a record of which SBC should handle the calls that match the defined rule.

Online PSTN gateways: These are objects that we created earlier for the actual SBCs.

Using these components you can build up resiliency to match whatever scenario you want to support for call failover, for example Active/Active, where all outbound calls are split between two SBCs, or Active/Passive, where calls only click the second SBC when the first fails. Or perhaps you want to route only certain types of numbers to one SBC and the others somewhere else. Figure 5.20 shows how these can be combined as required.

FIGURE 5.20   Voice routing options

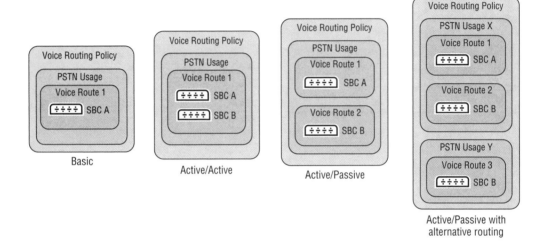

These can all be configured again, either via the TAC or in PowerShell.

To find them in the TAC, head to the same location we created the SBCs in (Voice ➢ Direct Routing), but this time change to the Voice Routes tab. Here you can see a list of the Voice Routes tab used in the tenant, and you can add new ones or edit the existing ones (see Figure 5.21).

To create a voice routing policy, once you have set up your routes, go over to Voice ➢ Voice Routing Policies. Here you can see the list of the ones already created in the tenant and can add new ones. Click Add and then select the PSTN usages you created earlier—nice and simple (see Figure 5.22).

Managing these elements in PowerShell uses the following cmdlet families:

-CsOnlinePSTNUsage

-CsOnlineVoiceRoute

-CsOnlineVoiceRoutingPolicy

FIGURE 5.21   Voice routes

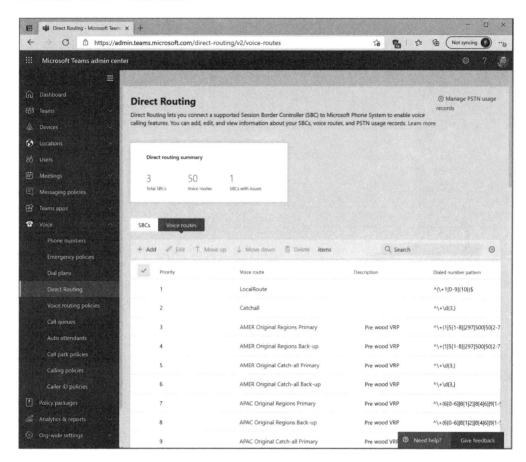

The code to create a basic configuration would look like this:

```
Set-CsOnlinePstnUsage -Identity Global -Usage @{Add="All PSTN Calls PSTNU"}
New-CsOnlineVoiceRoute -Identity "All Call Route" -NumberPattern "p^\*" -OnlinePstnGatewayList <SBC1>, <SBC2> -Priority 1 -OnlinePstnUsages "All PSTN Calls PSTNU"
New-CsOnlineVoiceRoutingPolicy "All Calls VRP" -OnlinePstnUsages "All PSTN Calls PSTNU"
```

This makes a voice route to send all calls to SBC1 and SBC2 and then adds that route to a PSTN usage, and that PSTN usage is then assigned to a voice routing policy.

FIGURE 5.22 Voice routing policies

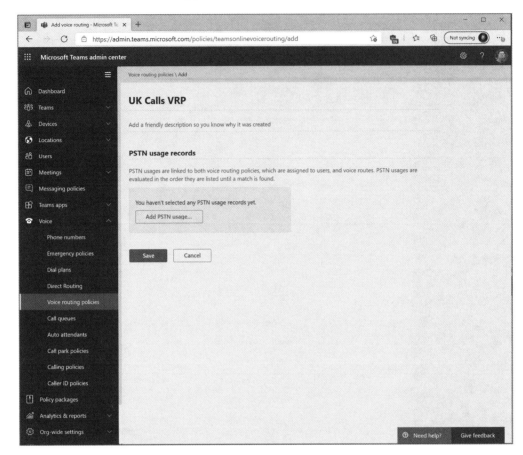

Configure Emergency Routing

As discussed in the "Emergency Calling" section earlier, there are specific policies used by Teams when you are using Direct Routing that let you control how to identify and route emergency calls.

To set up or view the current configuration, head to the TAC and from the left menu select Voice ➤ Emergency Policies. This will open by default on the emergency calling policies (we are going to cover them in the next section), but you can move over to the screen for call routing policies using the option at the top of the page (see Figure 5.23). This will show a list of the policies currently configured, and you can edit them or add more.

FIGURE 5.23   Emergency call routing policies

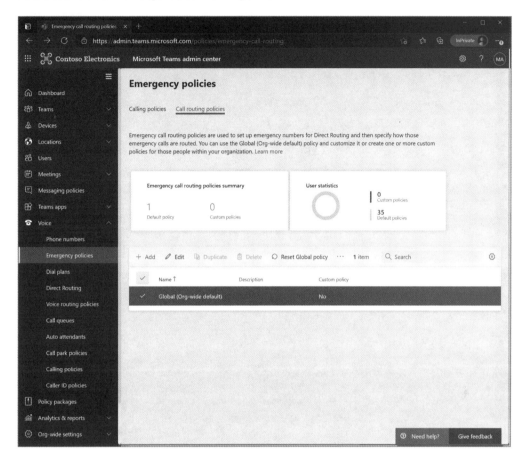

Click Add to make a new policy and give it a suitable name. Here you can configure the following options (see Figure 5.24):

Dynamic Emergency Calling: Specifies if dynamic location information can be included in the call setup.

Emergency Numbers: Used to specify three bits of information to identify and handle an emergency string.

   Emergency Dial String: A regular expression string used to match the dialed number; for example, ^\+911$ would match both +911 and 911.

   Emergency Dial Mask: An optional item that specifies alternative numbers that match to the same rule; for example, you could include 999 so that a UK user dialing an emergency number in the United States still matches this rule for 911.

FIGURE 5.24   Dial string and dial mask settings

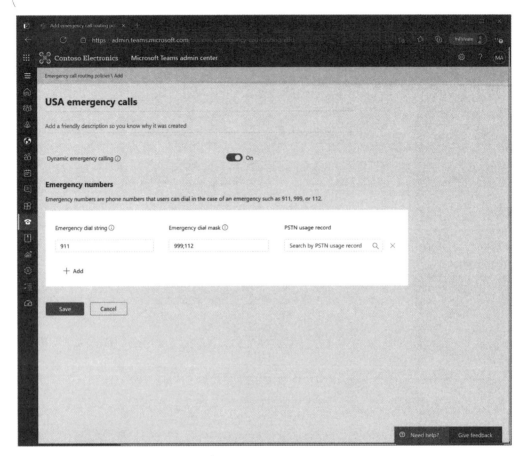

PSTN Usage Record: Select which PSTN usage record should handle the call to determine how to route it. These could be the same PSTN usages you created for users, or a dedicated set just used for emergency calls (perhaps with more resilient SBCs included).

Be aware that dial strings and masks should be unique inside each policy, but you can have more than one string and mask set should you require it.

To configure these in PowerShell, you could use the `-CsTeamsEmergencyCallRouting Policy` family of cmdlets.

We covered how to dynamically assign these policies based on location back in the Network Settings section.

Read more about emergency call routing policies at `https://docs.microsoft.com/en-us/MicrosoftTeams/manage-emergency-call-routing-policies`.

Configuring Users

The last step is to then enable users for calling with Direct Routing. This is done via Power-Shell, as currently the Teams tenant doesn't know anything about the number ranges or allocation that you might have coming in through the SBC.

To configure a user, connect a Skype for Business Online PowerShell session and then use the `Set-CSUser` cmdlet to configure some attributes:

EnterpriseVoiceEnabled: This is a True or False value to specify if the user is enabled for telephony.

HostedVoiceMail: This is a True or False value indicating if Azure Voicemail will be enabled for the account.

OnPremLineURI: This specifies the phone number to be used by the user, which must be in E.164 format and be formatted as a TEL URI (starts with TEL:<number>).

So, to enable an account, the command would look like this:

```
Set-CSUser -Identity <User> -OnPremLineURL <TelURI> -EnterpriseVoiceEnabled
$True -HostedVoiceMail $True
```

Here's an example:

```
Set-CSUser -Identity `Ben@LearnTeams.info`-OnPremLineURL Tel:+44191111111 -
EnterpriseVoiceEnabled $True -HostedVoiceMail $True
```

Once a user has been configured, you assign a voice routing policy that you created in the previous step. This can either be done in PowerShell using `Grant-CsOnlineVoiceRoutingPolicy`:

```
Grant-CsOnlineVoiceRoutingPolicy -Identity `ben@LearnTeams.info`-PolicyName
`All Calls VRP`
```

Or they can be configured in the TAC either by selecting the voice routing policy from the table where they were created and allocating to a user or by editing the user policies directly from the User screen (as with all the other types of Teams policies).

 Remember that once you have enabled a user for Teams telephony, there can be a delay before their client picks up the changes due to the various configuration items that have to happen behind the scenes.

Direct Routing Health Dashboard

Once you have your SBCs set up in your tenant and configured, Teams provides a health dashboard that you can use to monitor the SBCS. This can help you identify issues before they turn into problems and can help troubleshooting when you do get any issues. In Chapter 6 "Review Usage and Maintain Quality," we are going to cover some other tools that can help identify calling-related trends and issues, but as this dashboard specifically relates to Direct Routing, we are going to cover it here.

FIGURE 5.25   Direct Routing health dashboard

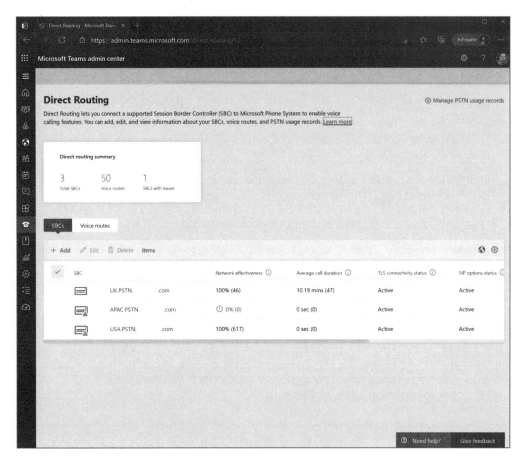

You can find the dashboard in the TAC under Voice ➤ Direct Routing (see Figure 5.25). Here you will see a summary of the information for your SBC estate along with any warning flags. The table then offers a breakdown by SBC of some key metrics:

Network Effectiveness Ratio (NER): This is a calculated value based on the number of calls that have succeeded versus those that have failed. The formula used to work it out can skew the number if you have had fewer than 100 calls going through the gateway recently!

Average Call Duration: This shows the average length of calls through the SBC.

TLS Status: This shows the status of the connection to the SBC as well as warning if the SBC SSL certificate is due to expire within 30 days.

SIP Option Status: When configuring the SBC, there will have been a choice to configure options. These are a special kind of SIP message that helps both sides know that the connection is available. This will show if there is any problem with receiving these messages.

Detailed SIP Options: This shows extra information if anything is wrong.

Concurrent Call Capacity: If you recall, when adding the SBC to the tenant, a capacity value was set. This shows if the SBC is under or over that value.

Enabled: This is a toggle showing if the SBC is in use or not.

If you click the name of an SBC, you will then access a detailed screen with more information (and you can view and modify its settings if you require). This screen (see Figure 5.26) shows a number of graphs giving information about the historical performance of the SBC. Here you can see the following:

NER Value: Same as above, but this time with the total number of calls

Average Call Duration: Again this time shown with the number of calls placed

Concurrency: Shown as a percentage of the peak against the configured value

Network Information: Details about the key networking metrics (Latency, Jitter, and Packet Loss)

FIGURE 5.26   Direct Routing health dashboard SBC details

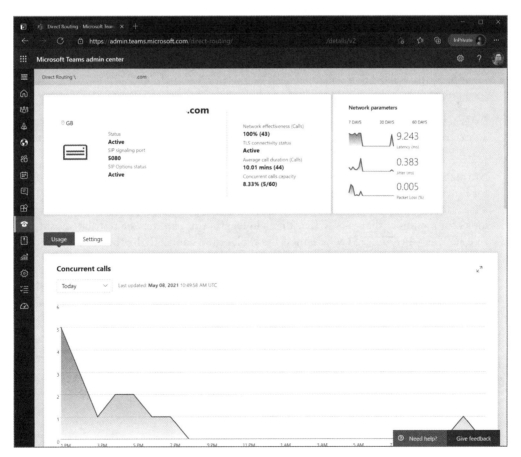

Controlling Phone System Features

Now that we have looked at how to bring telephony into your Teams deployment, we are going to explore some of the features that are available and how you can use Teams to build calling workflows to handle some fairly advanced calling scenarios.

Calling Features

Teams uses several policies to control the availability and behavior of a number of telephony-related features; here we are going to look at each policy in turn. All of these can be configured and controlled through either the TAC (found under the left Voice menu option) or PowerShell and are created and applied in the same way as the other policy types that we have covered in this book so far.

Dial Plans

As we have talked about before, Teams does all PSTN calling using the E.164 numbering format, but users do not necessarily know how to dial numbers in this format. A dial plan is a set of number rules that converts what the user enters into the dial pad into E.164 format (or something else if you need to handle something specific through a Direct Routing SBC).

The good news is that Microsoft provides a set of default dial plans that are automatically applied based on the region that a user is configured with. You should need to create your own dial plans only if there are some specific scenarios that you need to accommodate, such as supporting a short dial code that calls the service desk helpline.

When configuring a dial plan, there are the following options (see Figure 5.27):

External Access Prefix: This specifies if a dialed specific prefix needs to be used to access an external line; this concept comes from legacy PBXs where it was common to need to dial a 9 before your number.

Normalization Rules: Normalization rules are rules based on regular expressions (rules for how to handle strings of characters). These rules will match the number entered by a user and control how the output should be formatted. For example, a rule of ^(\d(4))$ looks for a number that is only four digits in length; this can then be translated using a rule such as +44777777$1 where the $1 is replaced dynamically by the digits entered by the user.

Dial plans in PowerShell are referred to as tenant dial plans, and they can be managed in PowerShell using the -CsTenantDialPlan cmdlet set. This set has a companion set of cmdlets called the -CsEffectiveTenantDialPlan, which lets you test what dial plan would apply for a specified number against a specified user.

 To read more about how dial plans operate and about the default ones see https://docs.microsoft.com/en-us/microsoftteams/ create-and-manage-dial-plans.

FIGURE 5.27 Dial plan options

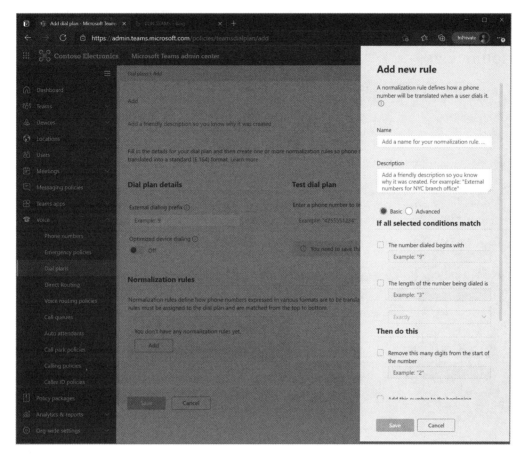

Call Park Policies

Call parking allows you to place a call on hold against a temporary parking number inside the Teams service. Any other telephony user who is also covered by the call parking policy in your tenant can then dial the number of the parked call and bring it over to their device. You could use this scenario to move a call between devices (although this is functionality being added directly into the Teams client without having to use call parking), or if you need to transfer the call to someone through a Teams channel conversation where you have requested assistance but are not sure who can help.

Call parking uses an arbitrary number range such as 10–99 that should not be used for any other purposes.

The following items are included in a policy (see Figure 5.28):

Allow: A master toggle to enable/disable the feature

Call Pickup Start Of Range: The lowest number in the range allocated

Call Pickup End Of Range: The highest number in the range allocated

Park Timeout: How long a call can be parked before it is returned to the original recipient

FIGURE 5.28 Call park policy options

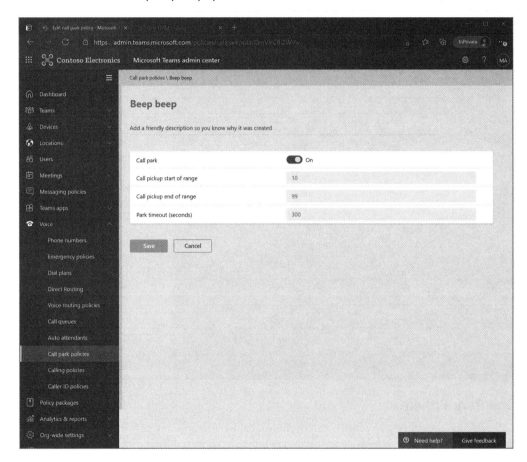

Call parking can be managed in PowerShell using the -CsTeamsCallParkPolicy cmdlet set.

> Learn more about call parking at https://docs.microsoft.com/en-us/microsoftteams/call-park-and-retrieve.

Calling Policies

Calling policies are used to control what calling and forwarding features are available to users in their client, such as being able to forward calls, use call groups, and delegate.

The following settings are available inside a calling policy (see Figure 5.29):

User Can Make Private Calls: Can make 1:1 calls; disabling this disables calling.

Call Forwarding And Simultaneous Ring To Other People In The Organization: Allow incoming calls to be forwarded, or to ring at the same time, against other users in your company.

Call Forwarding And Simultaneous Ring To Other People In The Organization: Allow incoming calls to be forwarded, or to ring at the same time, but this time to any telephone number.

Voicemail Availability: Can be forced on, off, or user controlled.

Inbound Calls To Call Groups: Call groups are a user-controlled group of users who can receive the original users' phone calls.

Delegation For Inbound And Outbound Calls: Allows calls to be managed through delegates.

Prevent Toll Bypass: Used to force calls to go via the external PSTN network instead of routing them as Teams calls. This can be required to meet some geographical calling restrictions alongside Location Based Routing.

Busy On Busy: Controls what happens to subsequent PSTN calls if the user is already in a call. This can let the second call ring through to the client or force it to voicemail.

Web PSTN Calling: Support making PSTN calls through a supported web browser.

Calling policies can be managed in PowerShell using the `-CSTeamsCallingPolicy` cmdlet set.

More information on calling policy behavior is available at `https://docs.microsoft.com/en-us/MicrosoftTeams/teams-calling-policy`.

Caller ID Policy

By default, the incoming caller ID is displayed for incoming calls, and a user's DID/DDI is shown when they make outbound calls. There may be some scenarios where you want to override this, for example, having all users calls show as coming from the main office DID/DDI. This behavior can be configured and controlled through the caller ID policies.

FIGURE 5.29   Calling policy options

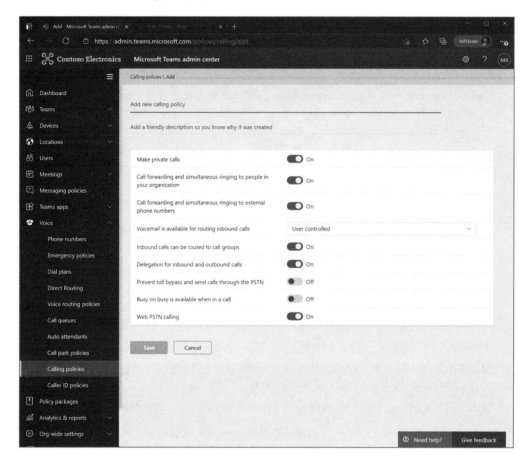

The following options are available (see Figure 5.30):

Block Incoming Caller ID: Hides the inbound number for incoming calls.

Override Caller ID Policy: Lets the user override the caller ID policy and choose to hide their number or not.

Replace Caller ID: Specifies what should be used instead of the user's number when making an outbound call. This can be either set to anonymous or masked by a service number.

Caller ID policies can be managed in PowerShell using the -CsCallingLineIdentity cmdlet set.

Read more about caller ID policies at https://docs.microsoft.com/ en-us/microsoftteams/caller-id-policies.

FIGURE 5.30 Caller ID options

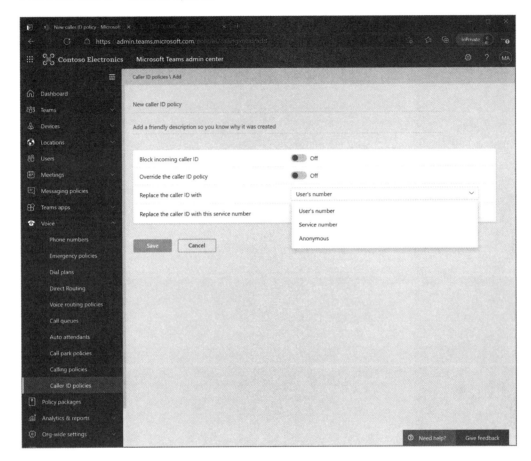

User Calling Configuration

Some per-user telephony settings can be configured administratively if necessary. This can be helpful to view a user's configuration when helping troubleshoot an issue with them, or if you need to change their configuration for them (such as if they are out sick).

You can view or update a user's configuration by opening the TAC, heading to the User view, and then searching for the user and clicking their name to open their configuration page. Head to the tab for Voice tab, and you can then view or edit their calling configuration (see Figure 5.31).

In here you can configure the following settings:

FIGURE 5.31 User calling configuration

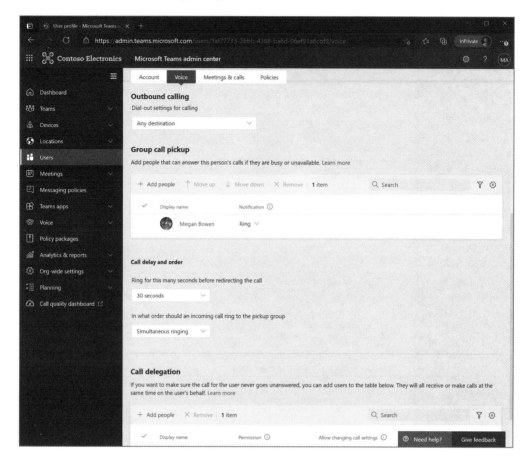

Group Call Pickup: Group call pickup is a personal call management feature where a user can define a list of other users (who also need to be configured for telephony) who can receive their incoming calls. This can be helpful, for example, if you are working on a particular project but are out of the office for a day. You could configure the group call pickup to contain other people on the project team who for that period of time could receive your incoming calls and deal with any project-related work. Here you can also configure how the notification appears: like a normal incoming call or just as a banner notification. A maximum of 25 users can be added to a user's group call pickup list.

Call Delay And Ring Order: Apply to the previous group call pickup configuration and dictate how long a call will try the original user before also calling to the group call pickup group.

Call Delegates: Teams allows the delegation of calling tasks to other users; this is separate from other delegation such as for calendar information in Exchange. A delegate has three types of permissions: the ability to make a call on behalf of the user, the ability to receive incoming calls for the user, and lastly the ability to update their calling settings.

Emergency Calling Policies

In the earlier sections, we talked about how you can identify and handle routing for emergency calls. Using emergency calling policies, you can also control if you need to notify anyone else in the organization when a user places an emergency call. Perhaps this could be building security or an HR function.

To set up or view the current configuration, head to the TAC and from the left menu select Voice ➢ Emergency Policies. Here you will see a list of the policies currently configured (see Figure 5.32).

FIGURE 5.32   Emergency calling policies

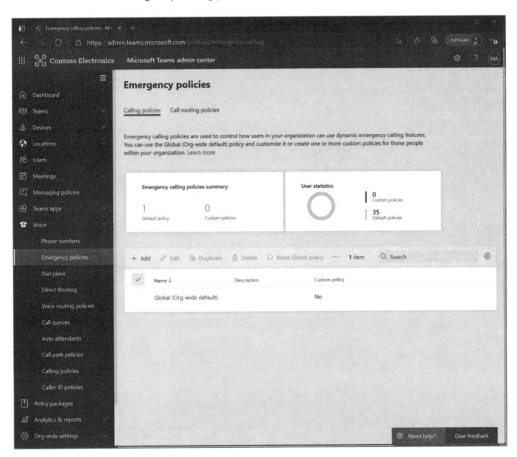

To add a new policy, click Add and configure the following options (see Figure 5.33):

Policy Name: Name the policy.

Notification Mode: How to notify someone that an emergency call has been placed; there are three options available.

> **Send Notification Only:** A Teams chat message only is sent to the user or group specified.

> **Conference In Muted:** Ring the number specified (can be user or a group) and add them to the call via a conference, but they are unable to unmute to interact with the user or PSAP agent.

> **Conference In Unmuted:** Ring the number specified (can be a user or a group) and add them to the call via a conference, and they are able to communicate with both the user and the PSAP agent.

FIGURE 5.33 Creating a new emergency calling policy

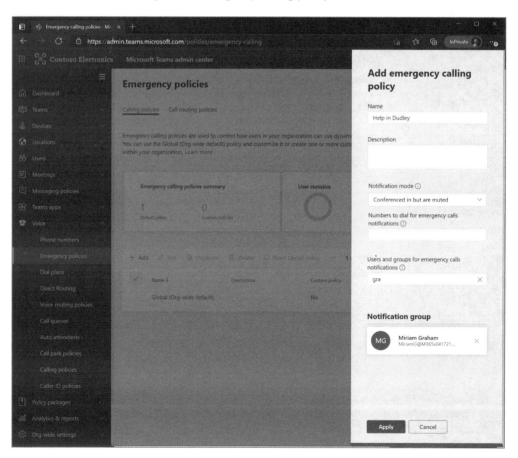

Numbers To Dial: Specify the E.164 number of the user or group to call if either conference option is selected.

Notification Group: The names of users or groups to notify via chat when a call is placed.

To work with these using PowerShell, you would use the -CsTeamsEmergencyCalling-Policy set of cmdlets.

Read more about emergency calling policies at https://docs.microsoft .com/en-us/MicrosoftTeams/manage-emergency-calling-policies.

Calling Workflows/Voice Apps

A common requirement when dealing with PSTN calling is the ability to handle calls that are not directed to specific users, for example calls into a main office number or to a help desk function.

Teams supports creating voice workflows to handle such scenarios using functionality called *call queues* and *auto attendants*. You may see these collectively referred to as Voice Apps. You can use these two elements to build up fairly complex call flow scenarios, which isn't bad considering that on some legacy PBXs you might need extra hardware or licenses to have similar functionality (that doesn't mean they are a perfect fit for all scenarios; sometimes you will still need third-party contact centers). You can also combine them and link them in any way that you require (see Figure 5.34 in the next section). Before we dig into each one, here is a quick summary of the differences between the two:

Auto Attendants: An auto attendant can provide callers with a menu of choices for how they want to direct the call. This menu can be driven either by voice input or by key presses. An auto attendant will also allow different behaviors to be configured during working hours and nonworking hours (for example overnight or on public holidays).

Call Queues: A call queue is used to distribute incoming calls against a number of different users. You can configure how the call is routed: does it call all users in one go or try them one by one? It also has options for how many calls can be waiting in the queue, for how long, and what happens if they breach these values.

Resource Accounts

To help direct incoming calls to the correct queue or attendant, Teams uses resource accounts. A resource account is a disabled user object created in Azure AD. If the queue or attendant needs to have a phone number associated with it, then the resource account needs a license allocated to it. This can be either a special, free, virtual user license (Microsoft 365 Phone System—Virtual User) or a paid for phone system license. Resource accounts do not need to have Calling Plan licenses assigned to them if you are using them with service numbers.

Using resource accounts in this way lets you allocate either a service number (direct from Microsoft) or a Direct Routing number (from your PSTN provider) against the account so that the Teams service can determine which queue or attendant should process the call when it arrives. You do not need to give each resource account a phone number, but each queue and attendant does require a resource account. If you need to associate more than one phone number with a queue, you can simply add more resource accounts with the desired numbers into the same queue or attendant.

Figure 5.34 shows an example of how a workflow can be built out of these components. In this example, the main office number is answered by an auto attendant and then passed

FIGURE 5.34 Auto attendants and call queues in an example workflow

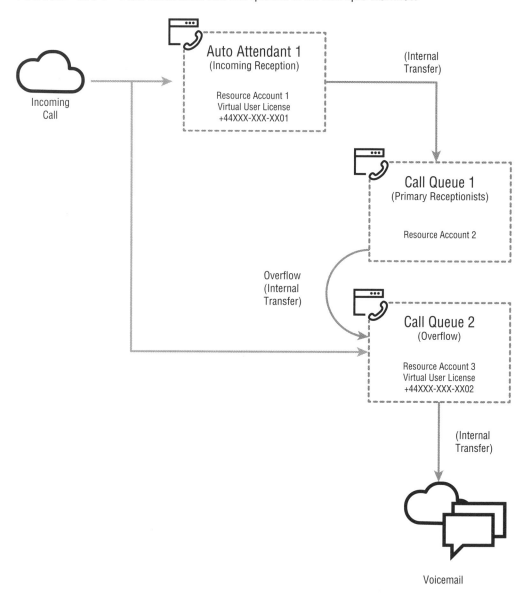

through to a call queue containing the main reception users. If this call is not answered, it overflows to a second queue containing more users. This overflow queue also has its own PSTN number, so anyone who has the correct number could dial straight into this queue. If the call isn't answered, there is an overflow configured to send the calls to voicemail. To support this scenario, you would have three resource accounts, but only two would have a virtual user license allocated to them.

If you have not used resource accounts before, even though they are free, they must still be purchased before they are available to allocate to accounts. You can purchase them via the main M365 admin center under Billing ➢ Purchase Services ➢ Add-Ons and then searching for Phone System—Virtual User. The license will be listed as zero cost, but you still need to complete the transaction.

Any organization with at least one phone system license automatically can request 25 virtual user licenses; this number then increases by one for every 10 phone system licenses that are purchased.

Read more about the Microsoft 365 Phone System—Virtual User license at https://docs.microsoft.com/en-us/microsoftteams/ teams-add-on-licensing/virtual-user.

Once you have a license available, you can create the resource accounts using the TAC. Head to Org-Wide Settings ➢ Resource Accounts. This will give you a list of the accounts already created in the tenant (see Figure 5.35).

Click Add to open a pop-out on the right side of the screen. Give the account a display name and username and choose if it is going to be allocated against an auto attendant or a call queue (see Figure 5.36).

Once the account is created, you need to assign it a virtual user license from the M365 admin center if you want to allocate it a phone number. This is done the same way as with a normal user and any other M365 license.

You can also create the accounts when using the wizard in the TAC that can build your auto attendant or call queue, and if you create a resource account this way, it will be automatically allocated a virtual user license if one is available.

If you want an auto attendant or call queue to have more than one number associated with it, then you can create a resource account for each number that you want to use and then associate more than one resource account against the voice app.

To create them via PowerShell, you can use the -CsOnlineApplicationInstance cmdlet, but you do need to provide an application ID that tells Teams if the account is to be used for an attendant or queue. The application IDs are as follows:

Auto attendant: ce933385-9390-45d1-9512-c8d228074e07

Call queue: 11cd3e2e-fccb-42ad-ad00-878b93575e07

FIGURE 5.35   Resource accounts

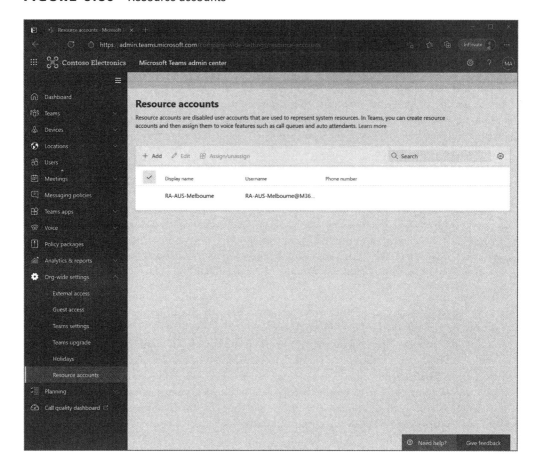

So, the code to create a new call queue would be as follows:

```
New-CsOnlineApplicationInstance -UserPrincipalName
"ReceptionQueue@learnteams.info" -ApplicationID 11cd3e2e-fccb-42ad-ad00-
878b93575e07 -DisplayName "Reception"
```

To read more about resource accounts, see https://docs.microsoft
.com/en-us/microsoftteams/manage-resource-accounts.

FIGURE 5.36   Creating a new resource account

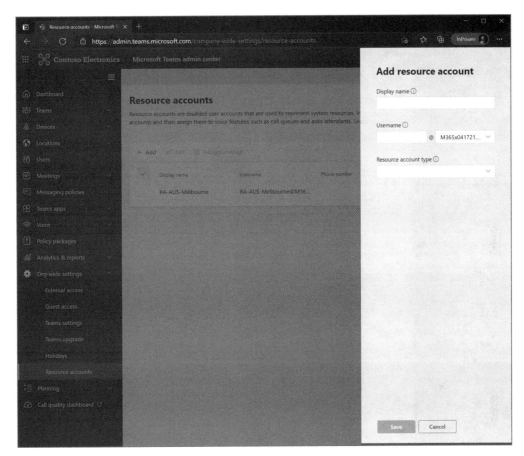

Auto Attendants

To make an auto attendant, open the TAC and under Voice ➤ Auto Attendants, you will see a list of those deployed in your organization. This table will show you some key information about the attendants (see Figure 5.37).

To make a new attendant, click Add and then give it a name and complete the following information (see Figure 5.38):

Operator: This is an optional configuration item that can then be used as a named item in the configuration. It is usually someone who can assist a caller if they are stuck. You have four choices to select from, and these are going to be common in other places when we set up these queues and attendants.

FIGURE 5.37   Auto attendant list

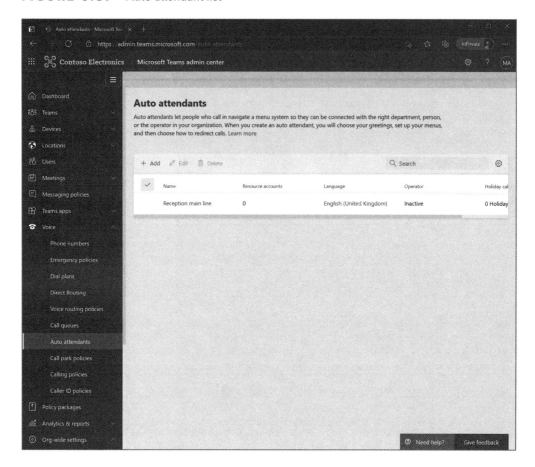

No Operator: Disabled.

Person In The Organization: A named user.

Voice App: Another queue or attendant.

External Phone Number: An E.164 phone number that will be dialed.

Time Zone: What time zone the time-based operations (such as in/out of hours) will be based on.

Language: Auto attendants can use text to speech read-out messages to callers; this selects which voice should be used.

FIGURE 5.38   Auto attendant initial configuration

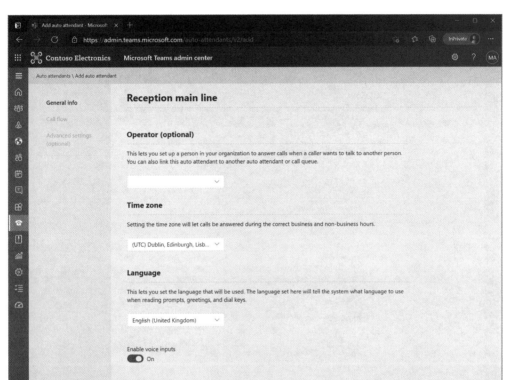

Moving to the next page, you then build up what happens to the call as it is answered (see Figure 5.39). The choices are as follows:

Greeting Message: No greeting, upload your own file, or read the entered greeting message out in the voice selected on the previous screen.

Then Route: You can choose to disconnect the call, redirect it to the same options we had earlier (person, voice app, external number, and also this time direct to voicemail), or play a menu.

FIGURE 5.39 Auto attendant call routing

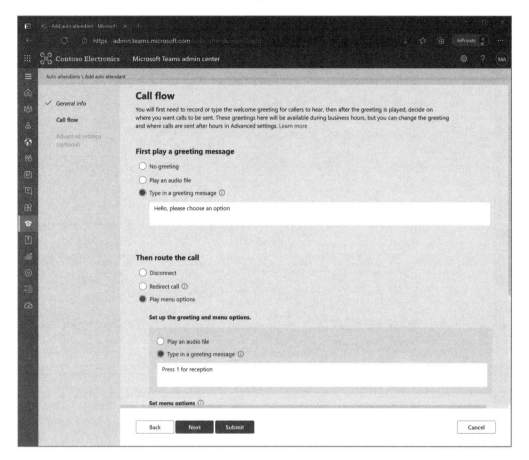

If you choose to use a menu, you can build up several options to then direct the call as you like (see Figure 5.40):

Set up a greeting: Either upload an audio file or enter text to be read to the caller; make sure this contains all the options that you are going to give in the menu!

Build your menu: Use the table to add options against a dial key. Each option can also contain a voice command if you allow it, where the system will match what the caller says using voice recognition. Each menu item then has a set of destination options:

Operator: Defined in the previous step.

Person In The Organization: A named user.

Voice App: Another queue or attendant.

FIGURE 5.40   Auto attendant initial configuration

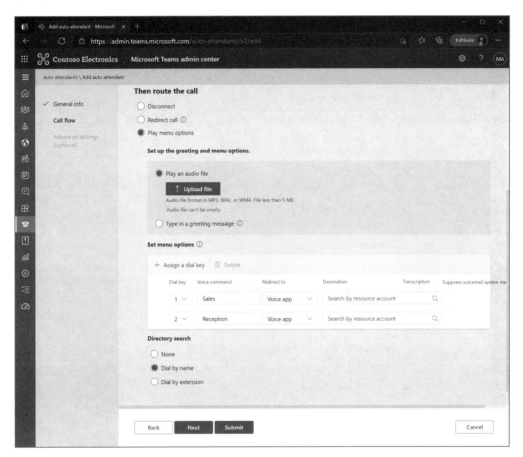

VoiceMail: A user or group voicemail box.

External Phone Number: An E.164 phone number that will be dialed.

Announcement: Either play an uploaded audio clip or read an announcement.

The last option on this screen is for directory search. This is a feature of auto attendants where users can search for a user by name using either their voice or the dial pad. For most call routing attendants, you would probably have this option disabled. Be careful when creating an attendant that allows external callers to search and dial users in the directory, although you can limit the scope of the directory to exclude certain users or groups of users.

After configuring your menu and choices, click Next to move to the next screen where you can configure different behaviors to happen during business and out of hours. Use the table displayed to define what the working hours are for the attendant (see Figure 5.41),

FIGURE 5.41   Auto attendant working hours configuration

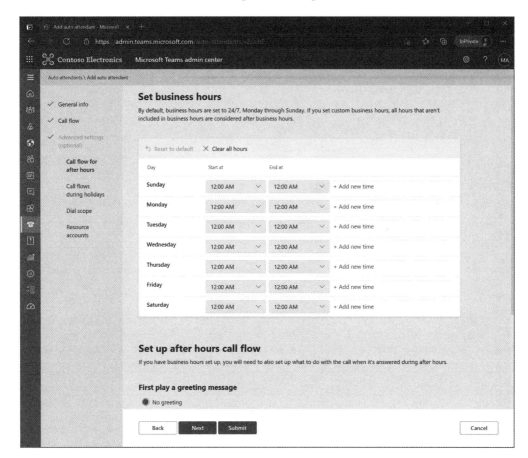

and then in the table underneath configure either another menu of choices or what different behavior you want to happen when outside of those hours. The choices and options are the same as you had on the previous screen.

The next screen (see Figure 5.42) lets you define holidays for the attendant, which again can have a different configuration from the working or nonworking hours setup. Use the Add button in the table to create your holidays and desired behavior.

Moving to the next screen, you can choose the scope for the directory lookup. Here you can either include or exclude specific AD groups from the lookup feature; for example, you might want to not include your executives in the lookup (see Figure 5.43)!

Lastly, you choose what resource account you want to use (or create a new one) with this attendant (see the previous section). Click Submit, and your attendant will be configured.

FIGURE 5.42   Auto attendant working holiday settings

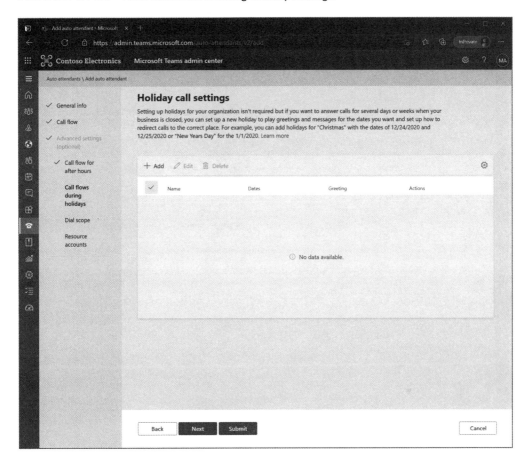

You can configure auto attendants using PowerShell, but given the nested nature of how they work and that so many choices and options are available, it is not something I would recommend unless you fancy a challenge or need to create a vast number of them! Just so you are aware, the cmdlet groupings are as follows:

- –CsAutoAttendant
- –CsAutoAttendantMenu
- –CsOnlineAudioFile
- –CsAutoAttendantCallFlow
- –CsAutoAttendantHolidays
- –CsOnlineTimeRange
- –CsOnlineDateTimeRange

FIGURE 5.43 Auto attendant dial scope

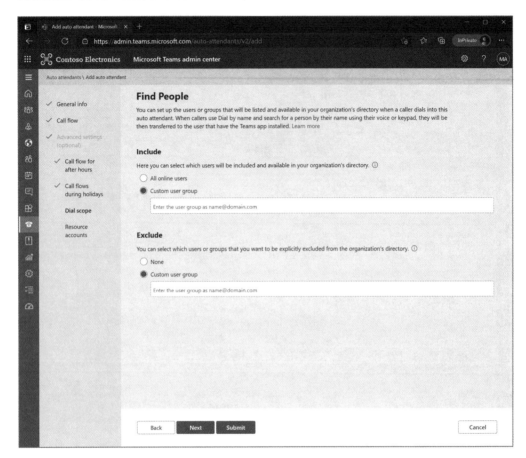

- `-CsOnlineSchedule`
- `-CsAutoAttendantSupportedTimeZone`
- `-CsAutoAttendantCallHandlingAssociation`
- `-CsAutoAttendantSupportedLanguage`
- `-CsAutoAttendantCallableEntity`

 Auto attendants provide a huge amount of flexibility for how to handle incoming calls; you can read up further on them at `https://docs .microsoft.com/en-us/microsoftteams/create-a-phone- system-auto-attendant`.

Call Queues

Call queues are created and managed in the same way as auto attendants, but they have their own section in the TAC. To view what you currently have go to the TAC and then select Voice ➤ Call Queues (see Figure 5.44).

FIGURE 5.44   Call queue list

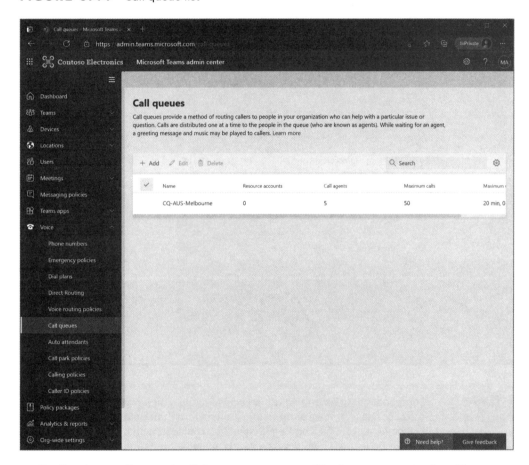

Configuring a call queue is all done on one page, unlike for an auto attendant. To start, click Add and then enter the name of the queue you want to create. Straightaway this time you are asked to select (or create) a resource account. Either select one you have previously created or, if you enter something in the box and nothing is returned, you will have an option to make a new resource account (see Figure 5.45).

Next select the language that the queue will use for any system-generated prompts (the selection here is the same as for auto attendants). You can also specify a greeting, which is played to users when they first click the queue (probably not required if you are passing calls from an auto attendant) as well as any hold music that should be played while the queue is hunting for a user to answer the call.

FIGURE 5.45   Call queue resource account selection

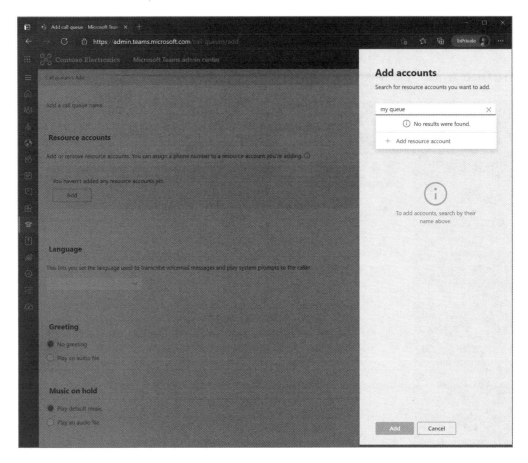

 I personally find having hold music on a queue a bit jarring, especially if the caller has come straight to the queue. From their point of view, they will have heard a ringing tone that is then replaced with hold music. What I like to do is upload hold music that is actually the ringback tone used in the local country so that to the caller it still just sounds like the call is ringing as normal.

Next is the core of the call queue, whom to route the call to. Until recently this had to be users, but functionality has been added so that you can use a team to manage access to the call queues (see Figure 5.46).

FIGURE 5.46   A call queue integrated with a channel

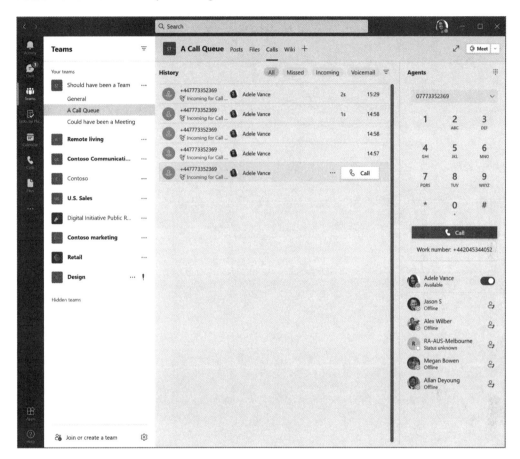

When a team has been integrated with a queue, it is placed into an existing channel with a special dashboard tab added where you can view information about calls currently in progress as well as historical calling information. To integrate with a team, select Add A Channel and then search for your team and pick the channel you want to use (see Figure 5.47).

If you are going for a more traditional approach, you can instead select up to 20 named users or a group. If you use a group, then the queue can call up to 200 users (see Figure 5.48).

Once you have added users, you can adjust the order in which they appear in the list. This will be important because of the call routing selection we are about to make, but first you can select if you want to force the incoming call to run as a conference. Using a conference for the queue should make hunting for and joining different agents into the call faster, but it does require a current Teams client (this wasn't available at launch), and the users in the queue need to be assigned an Audio Conferencing License.

FIGURE 5.47   Call queue, selecting a channel

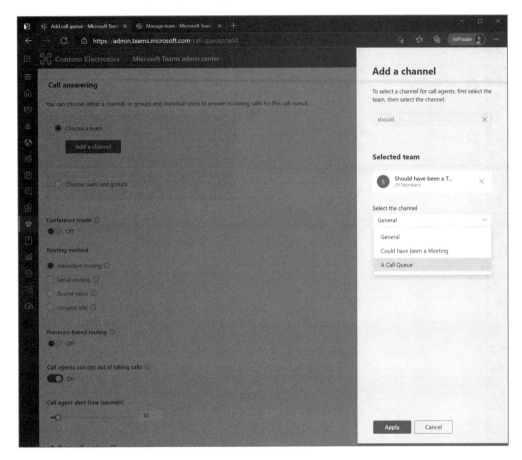

Next under Routing Methods, you can choose how calls are split between the agents that are participating in the queue (see Figure 5.48 from the previous step). The choices are as follows:

Attendant Routing: Calls out to all users in the queue at the same time.

Serial Routing: Calls the users in the order displayed in the User list.

Round Robin: Splits the incoming calls between the users so that they are called evenly.

Longest Idle: Sends the call to an agent who hasn't received a call for the longest time (if an agent is showing as Away for more than 10 minutes, they are considered to not be present and won't receive calls).

FIGURE 5.48 Call queue, choosing users

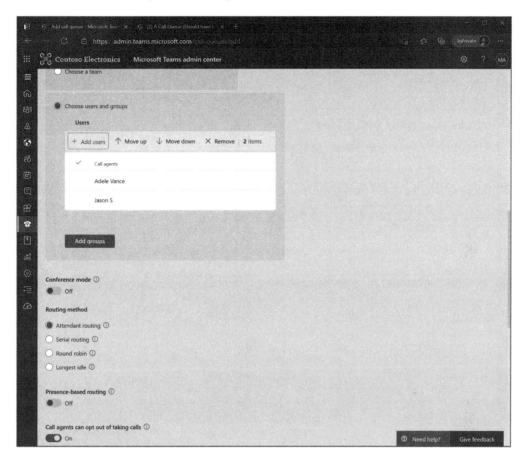

There is a toggle box for presence-based routing. This makes Teams take into consideration the presence state of users when determining who to send a call to. If a user is available, they are viewed as able to take calls and will be included in the routing decision. If the status is anything else, they are not considered.

The next toggle lets users control themselves if they are able to receive calls from the queue. For example, you might want to let users toggle themselves out of the queue when they go for lunch or are working on another project for a period of time.

The last slider in this section controls how long the system should attempt to route a call to a user before moving on to the next choice (not valid if using attendant mode, as all agents are called in parallel). For example, you might want a call to only try one person for 20 seconds before moving on so the caller doesn't have to wait for a long time.

In the last section of the queue (see Figure 5.49), we get to configure what happens when calls exceed the boundaries we configure. This could be if too many calls are waiting to be

FIGURE 5.49 Call queue overflow options

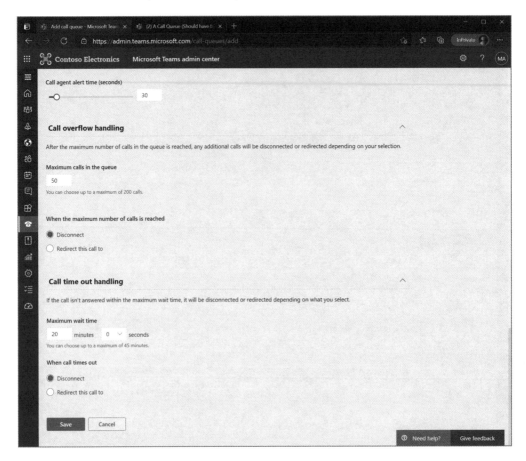

answered or if the call has been waiting for too long. The options available are the same for either scenario and are similar to what we had in the auto attendant:

Disconnect The Call: Does what it says.

Person In The Organization: A named user.

Voice App: Another queue or attendant.

External Phone Number: An E.164 phone number that will be dialed.

VoiceMail: An M365 group voicemail box.

After setting up your queue, click Save, and then you can integrate it with your auto attendants, and so on.

When mapping out your organization's calling workflow requirements, you might find that you would be better off creating your queues first before creating your auto attendants.

Again, as with auto attendants, you can manage them through PowerShell, and while they are simpler as there are fewer choices to manage, it might not be something you want to do for fun (or perhaps it is). Should it take your fancy, the cmdlet grouping you'd need is -CsCallQueue.

> Call queues let you do some really neat routing with calls around your environment. To explore them further, visit https://docs.microsoft .com/en-us/microsoftteams/create-a-phone-system-call-queue.

Summary

I hope after reading this chapter you can see why Teams makes quite a compelling case to become your phone system and replace your current PBX. Being able to combine all those telephony features alongside the flexibility and control that Teams inherently allows makes for a slick end-user experience.

While it may seem that we went through Teams's telephony features in a lot of detail, there are still many areas that we haven't covered as they aren't directly in scope for MS-700. If you have gotten the taste for this calling stuff you will want to go do some further reading. Here are some interesting areas that we didn't cover:

Azure voicemail: How the voicemail system associated with Teams works, and how it can have its own layer of calling controls.

Local Media Optimization and Media Bypass: While we talked a little about these, there is some smart technology at play that tries to make sure your calling media always takes the shortest path possible. You can even use LMO to connect downstream SBCs to the Teams platform without having to have Internet access and certificates in use (a parent SBC can take care of this for you).

Location-Based Routing: The ability to choose to route calls differently based on the location of the client's device.

Analog Device Support: How you can bring some analog devices to the Teams platform through a suitable SBC.

Standard SIP Device Support: At the time of writing, Microsoft has announced that you can soon connect non-Teams SIP-based devices to the Teams service; this will be helpful to allow companies to reuse existing devices.

Carrier Connect: An announced feature that will allow Direct Routing Service Providers to integrate with the TAC so you can manage the provision of new numbers and services from a partner's Direct Routing platform.

Branch Survivability: The ability to run some Teams server code on an SBC to allow clients to still make outbound calls through that SBC if the Teams service is unavailable.

So back to the things we did cover in this chapter. At the start, we talked about the two key delivery methods for PSTN connectivity and how they differ. We also recapped the types of licensing used by Teams for calling, as telephony functionality is not included in the base Teams license. We covered the different types of numbers that you can have in the tenant and where you would use either one, as well as some of the telephony-specific devices that you might come across when deploying phones for your users.

In the first section, we also covered how Teams can support emergency calling in different scenarios. This is a complex topic as there are a lot of technologies involved and, depending on the country, strict legal requirements that must be met. In this section, we first looked at how the Teams client can identify its location using three different types of network-based lookups that, when combined with emergency policies, let Teams meet these obligations. We then showed how these different tools combine to let you safely offer emergency services capabilities to users.

In the next section, we dug into the specifics of how you can deploy Calling Plans and Direct Routing. With Calling Plans, this is primarily how you can add numbers into your tenant, either by using the TAC or by porting them to Microsoft. Once you have numbers available, you can then assign them to users or resource accounts.

For Direct Routing, we covered the technical prerequisites that need to be in place for a successful deployment, such as Public DNS names and certificates. In the firewall configuration, we talked about how media bypass can help to keep traffic using the most effective route possible, and then in the section about deploying Direct Routing we went through the steps and choices for settings up an SBC in your tenant. Remember that you will need to refer to the vendor's own instructions for how to configure its SBC hardware to work with Teams, as none of this will work without that setup too! Lastly, we showed how you can monitor the health of your SBCs and keep on top of any connectivity and calling issues.

Finally, we ran through some of the features available when using Phone System, starting with the different policies that are available to help control the features and behaviors of calling in your environment. These policies are (mostly) configured and applied in the same way as the other policies that we have covered in this book where you can either specify the global default or create a specific policy to apply against a user. Lastly, we covered call queues and auto attendants that allow you to build some pretty complex workflows to handle incoming calls, such as those to a support helpline or a main incoming office number.

Exam Essentials

Know that there are two types of calling delivery for Teams. Know about the key differences between Calling Plans and Direct Routing and understand how you would choose which you would deploy.

Understand the different types of licensing used for telephony.   Know that telephony functionality requires a Phone System license and that Calling Plans come in two main types for either domestic or international calling capabilities. You should also remember how Calling Plan package minutes are shared between users of the same region and license type.

Know that there are two categories of numbers that can be added to a tenant.   Know that you can have both user and service numbers and know where each one is used.

Understand how Teams can define static addresses for emergency calls.   Understand how you can define locations (addresses) in the tenant that are referenced by Teams when a user dials an emergency number.

Know that Teams can also use dynamic address assignment to meet stricter regulations around emergency calling.   You should also understand how Teams uses networking information to identify if a client is connecting from a company location and that it can then modify the address used (and other behaviors such as notification preferences) based on this information.

Know how to request or port numbers for your tenant.   Know that you can request numbers in any Calling Plan region for your users, and know that you can also port numbers that you currently have from another provider and bring them for use inside Teams.

Know how to assign numbers to your users.   Having added numbers to your tenant (for Calling Plans), you should be able to allocate them to users so that they can make and receive calls. If you are using Direct Routing, know how to use PowerShell to configure a user and assign them a number manually.

Know about the prerequisites for setting up Direct Routing.   Understand how you could connect an SBC to the Teams service (you do not need to know the SBC-specific side of the configuration) and what is required to make it work.

Know how to set up an SBC in your tenant.   Know how you would configure an SBC in your tenant so that it shows in the SBC health dashboard and you can view its status. Know how you can configure voice routing policies to address SBCs and allow users to make and receive calls using your SBCs.

Know why you would use a dial plan.   Dial plans are used to modify the numbers that a user enters into a standard E.164 format. Know how you would configure and apply one if needed.

Know what call parking is and how to set up a policy.   Call parking can help store and retrieve calls if you need to pass them to other users. Know how to configure one via the TAC.

Know that you can control telephony functionality through calling policies.   Calling policies let you control functionality, such as the ability to forward calls, or how incoming calls are handled if you are already in a call (busy on busy). If you need to block or change the default behavior for your users, you can do so by creating these policies.

Know when to use a caller ID policy.   You can control how a user's number is displayed when they place a call to the PSTN using a caller ID policy. These either can hide the user's number or can be masked using a service number.

Know that you can control certain aspects of a user's calling behaviors via the TAC.   From the TAC you can modify a user's group call pickup configuring or their delegate settings. This can be handy if a user is not available for a prolonged period and you need to make sure someone can answer their calls.

Know that call queues and auto attendants use resource accounts.   Call queues and auto attendants are built on top of resource accounts. These accounts can be configured with the phone numbers used by the queue or attendants, but each account also needs some form of phone system license (paid, or a virtual free license).

Know the key functionality for an auto attendant.   Auto attendants can let you route calls to different destinations based on a caller's input (voice or via dial pad), the time of day, or if it is during holidays. These destinations can be other voice apps in Teams, specific users, or external phone numbers, depending on what is required. An attendant will also let you do a voice search against the directory.

Know the key functionality for a call queue.   A queue controls how an incoming call is distributed among users in your organization. This can be either in parallel (attendant mode) or some form of weighting (either round robin, longest idle, or serial). You can then also configure what happens when a call breaches the metrics for a queue by either waiting too long or having too many waiting in front of it.

Exercises

EXERCISE 5.1

Ordering New User Numbers

In this exercise, we will order some user numbers ready to allocate to users. You may not be able to complete this entire exercise, depending on the location of your tenant and the licenses available. Please refer to the section adding numbers, under Phone System Delivery for pictures of the steps being taken.

1. Log into the TAC with a Teams administrator account.

2. Expand Voice ➤ Phone Numbers.

3. Click Add and enter an order name and description.

4. Select your region from the drop-down list, making sure it is a Calling Plan region.

5. Under number type, select User (subscriber).

6. Select a city.

7. Next to Location, click Add A Location.

8.   Select your country and then enter an address to see if the automatic map selection will find it.

9.   If the address is not identified for you, use the toggle box and enter it manually.

10.   Name the organization for the address.

11.   Save the address and return to the previous screen.

12.   Select the area code for the order (based on the city selected; the list may have options).

13.   Enter **1** as the quantity.

14.   Click Next and wait for the system to allocate a number.

15.   If you are able, click Place Order to confirm these numbers for your tenant.

Configuring an Address

In this exercise, we will configure an emergency address with a place and some networking information configured.

1.   Log into the TAC with a Teams administrator account.

2.   Expand Locations ➤ Emergency Addresses.

3.   If you were able to complete Exercise 5.1, you should have a location here; if not, click Add and complete the questions.

4.   Click the name of the location to see its details.

5.   Under Places, click Add and enter a name such as **Floor 1**.

6.   Click the name of the place you just added to view the place information.

7.   Select subnets and then click Add; select if this is an IPv4 or IPv6 subnet and enter a subnet before clicking Apply.

8.   Move through the other tabs for Wi-Fi, Switches, and Ports; click Add to see what information is asked for.

9.   Next go to the Locations ➤ Networks & Locations section in the TAC. Here you should see the subnets or other networking information you just created. You can set these up here if it is easier.

EXERCISE 5.3

Configuring a Trusted IP

In this exercise, we will configure a trusted IP used to identify whether a client is on a company network.

1. Log into the TAC with a Teams administrator account.

2. Expand Locations ➤ Network Topology.

3. Click the Trusted IPs tab.

4. Click Add and enter an IP address and how many bits are in the mask for the network range (32 for a single IP).

5. Click Apply to save it.

EXERCISE 5.4

Creating an Emergency Calling Policy

In this exercise, we will configure an emergency calling policy used to notify a test account if a user dials an emergency number. Be careful when testing these steps to not disrupt any real emergency calling configuration that you have in place!

1. Log into the TAC with a Teams administrator account.

2. Expand Voice ➤ Emergency Policies.

3. Above the list of calling policies, click Add.

4. Give the policy a name and description.

5. Configure the notification mode to either of the Conference options.

6. Search for and add a test user in the Users And Groups section.

7. Click Apply to save the policy.

EXERCISE 5.5

Creating an Emergency Call Routing Policy

In this exercise, we will configure an emergency call routing policy that would be used with Direct Routing. Be careful when testing these steps to not disrupt any real emergency calling configuration that you have in place!

1. Log into the TAC with a Teams administrator account.

2. Expand Voice ➤ Emergency Policies.

3. Navigate to the Call Routing Policies section at the top of the page.

EXERCISE 5.5

4. Click Add to start creating a new policy.

5. Give the policy a name and description.

6. Enable the toggle for Dynamic Emergency Calling.

7. Click Add in the Emergency Numbers section.

8. Enter an emergency dialing string for your country (911 in the United States).

9. In Emergency Dial mask, enter another country's dialing string (999 in the United Kingdom).

10. Click Save to save the policy.

EXERCISE 5.6

Configuring a Location-Based Emergency Policy Assignment

In this exercise, we will configure a subnet to then allow location-based emergency policy assignment. Be careful when testing these steps to not disrupt any real emergency calling configuration that you have in place!

1. Expand Locations ➤ Network Topology.

2. Under Network Sites, click Add.

3. Enter a site name and description.

4. Select the two policies that you created in Exercise 5.4 and Exercise 5.5 in the drop-down boxes.

5. Under Subnets, click Add.

6. Enter the details for an internal subnet using the IP address and subnet range (mask).

7. Click Apply to save the subnet, and then click Save to save the network site.

EXERCISE 5.7

Assigning a Number to a User

In this exercise, we will now assign a user number to a user account. You will need to have both Phone System and Calling Plan licenses assigned to the test account before starting.

1. Expand Voice ➤ Phone Numbers.

2. in the numbers table, sort by Status to find the number we requested in Exercise 5.1.

3. Select the number and click Edit.

4. In the right pop-out, search for the test user account and select it.

continues

5.   Under Emergency Location, search for the location created in Exercise 5.2.

6.   Normally you would now click Apply and save the configuration, which would then allocate the number to the user; however, you can also assign numbers directly from the user account itself, so click Cancel.

7.   Head over to Users on the left menu in the TAC.

8.   Search for the test user account and click its name.

9.   In the main General Information screen, click Edit.

10. In the pop-out menu on the right, click the Assigned Phone Number and select the number you have reserved.

11. Under Emergency Locations, search for the address created earlier and then click Apply.

Creating a Basic Call Queue

In this exercise, we will create a call queue. You will need either some test accounts or a test group (user accounts will need Phone System configuring) to act as the destination for the queue.

1.   Expand Voice ➤ Call Queues.

2.   Click Add and give the queue a name.

3.   Under Resource Accounts, click Add.

4.   Start entering the name for the resource account that you want to use.

5.   When the search returns no items, click Add Resource Account.

6.   Enter the details for the account we are going to create for the example, selecting Call Queue as the type. Make sure to have no spaces in the username field.

7.   Save the account and then click Add to place it against the queue.

8.   Configure the language to your preference.

9.   If you have an audio file available in the right format (less than 5MB, MP3, WAV, or WMA) upload it as a greeting for music on hold; if not, leave the defaults.

10. Select Choose Users and Groups and add the users or group you have available for this test.

11. Leave Conference mode off unless you have the right licenses (Audio Conference) available for your test accounts.

12. Read the information bubbles next to the Routing Methods selection and pick one that suits your fancy.

EXERCISE 5.8 (continued)

13. Change the agent alerting down to something like 10 seconds so you can see the call behavior.

14. Configure numbers in the queue to be low (like 2) and then choose Redirect This Call and browse the available options.

15. If you have enough test accounts, configure one of them as the destination for the overflow; if not, set it back to Disconnect.

16. Save the queue.

17. You can test the queue behavior by calling the resource account that you created using its UPN. After testing how the queue works, come back and edit the queue to try different options for routing and overflow handling.

EXERCISE 5.9

Creating a Basic Auto Attendant

In this exercise, we will create a basic auto attendant linked to the queue you created in Exercise 5.8. If you are unable to allocate numbers, you should still be able to call it using a Teams ➢ Teams call. Note that auto attendants have a lot of options; this exercise is just going to cover building a simple flow. After creating one, please go back and edit it to experiment with the options yourself.

1. Expand Voice ➢ Auto Attendants.

2. Click Add and give the auto attendant a name.

3. Under Operator set it to be a person in the organization and pick one of your test accounts (if you don't have any leave it as No Operator).

4. Select your time zone from the list and your language if it is available; then click Next.

5. On the Call Flow page, select a greeting message and either type something or upload a file if you have a suitable audio file available.

6. Choose to then route the call to Play menu options.

7. Enter a Greeting message for the menu.

8. Click Assign a Dial Key and then select 1 for the key and Voice App2 for the Redirect To option. In the Destination box, enter the name of the queue you created in Exercise 5.7.

9. Disable Directory Search and then click Next.

10. Modify the working hours for a day and click Add new Time to see how you can customize the working hours for the attendant.

11. Click Next. Here you would add any holidays to also trigger an out-of-hours behavior.

continues

12. Click Next twice to get to the Resource Account screen. Click Add and search for the resource account you want to use with the attendant. If you do not have one created, copy steps 3–6 from Exercise 5.8 (but change the type to Auto Attendant).

13. Click Submit to save your attendant.

EXERCISE 5.10

Creating a Call Policy to Modify Some User Calling Policies

Here we are going to create a calling policy that controls some telephony-related features for our users. We want to send calls to voicemail when a user is already on a call, and we do not want to allow forwarding to external numbers.

1. Expand Voice ➢ Calling Policies.

2. In the list, click Add and give the policy a name.

3. Give the policy a name in the top box.

4. Turn off the toggle next to Call Forwarding and simultaneous ringing to external phone numbers.

5. Turn on the toggle next to Busy On Busy.

6. Save the policy.

7. To assign it to a user, go to Users from the left menu.

8. Search for your test user account and click the name.

9. Go to the Policies tab and then click Edit next to the Assigned Policies section.

10. Scroll down and find the Calling Policy; select the new policy in the drop-down box.

EXERCISE 5.11

Configuring a Caller ID Policy to Hide a User's Phone Number

We are going to create a caller ID policy that will mask an outbound user's calls. If you have a service number associated with your tenant, you can replace the number with this; if not, we will set it to Withheld.

1. Expand Voice ➢ Caller ID Policies.

2. Click Add and give the policy a name.

3. Toggle the Override The Caller ID Policy setting.

4. In the Replace The Caller ID With drop-down box, select Anonymous.

5. Save the policy and assign it to a user, repeating steps 7–10 from Exercise 5.10.

Review Questions

1. You have users in France who need to make PSTN calls, and you currently have E3 licenses and want to use Microsoft to provide the numbers. What are the minimum additional licenses that you should purchase? (Select all that apply.)

    A. E5

    B. Calling Plan domestic

    C. Audio Conferencing

    D. Phone System

2. You want to use dynamic emergency calling against your Direct Routing configuration. You have configured both the LIS and emergency voice routing policies correctly, but when tested, it does not work, and the call routes to the user's default SBC. What other configuration is required?

    A. A calling policy enabling emergency dialing.

    B. An emergency address associated with the user's number.

    C. Update the SBC configuration.

    D. Configure Trusted IP Address.

3. You have deployed Direct Routing and need to make sure that emergency calls are all routed to a specific SBC configured with ELIN support. What would you use to achieve this?

    A. An Emergency Call Routing Policy

    B. An Emergency Calling Policy

    C. An Online Voice Routing Policy

    D. A Caller ID Policy

4. You need to configure an auto attendant to handle incoming sales calls from external callers. You want there to be no call charges to the caller when placing an order. What would you do?

    A. Assign a toll-free service number to the auto attendant.

    B. Create a resource account and assign it a toll-free service number.

    C. Create a user account and assign it a toll-free user number.

    D. Buy more Communications Credits.

5. You want to migrate to Teams telephony for your users. When choosing between Calling Plans and Direct Routing, which of the following should you consider? (Select all that apply.)

    A. Teams telephony features required

    B. Countries where service is required

    C. Location of your tenant

    D. How many voice apps you need to deploy

6. You need to build a voice workflow to meet the following requirements: during business hours send the calls to a group of three users; if they do not answer the call after one minute, send it to another group of 10 users. When the office is closed, accept a voicemail. What would you need to configure?

   A. Three call queues

   B. An auto attendant and two call queues

   C. Two auto attendants and a call queue

   D. Three auto attendants

7. You need to plan a smooth migration from your old PBX to Teams telephony and must maintain your numbers. You cannot port your numbers due to remaining in-contract time with the current provider, and all your offices are in the United States. What should you do?

   A. Get a signed LOA document.

   B. Purchase Direct Routing–compatible SBCs.

   C. Add Communications Credits to your tenant.

   D. Set your tenant into Teams Only mode.

8. You have users who are going to participate in a call queue. The queue will be configured to use conferencing mode. What licenses are required by the users to answer calls from the queue? (Select all that apply.)

   A. Phone System license

   B. Communications Credits

   C. Audio Conferencing

   D. Azure AD P1

9. You want to enable 10 users for Calling Plans. Half of these users also need to be able to make international calls but only on an infrequent basis. What can you do to minimize the spend on calling?

   A. Buy 10 Domestic and International Calling Plans.

   B. Buy 5 Domestic and 5 Domestic and International Calling Plans.

   C. Buy 10 Domestic Calling Plans.

   D. Buy 10 Domestic Calling Plans and assign Communications Credits to 5 users.

10. You have deployed Direct Routing and need to monitor the health of your SBCs. Where would you find this information?

   A. Teams usage reports

   B. Call Quality Dashboard

   C. Direct Routing Health Dashboard

   D. SBC Status updates portal

11. While migrating from your PBX to Teams, you want to maintain support for users to dial the IT service desk using a short code of 1234. What would you configure to support this?

   A. A dial plan

   B. A normalization rule on the SBC

   C. A caller ID policy

   D. A group-based auto attendant

12. You need to add a new SBC to your tenant for Direct Routing using PowerShell. The SBC is called MYSBC2.Learnteams.info, and it is on port 5068. What cmdlet would you run?

   A. `New-CsOnlinePSTNGateway -FQDN MYSBC2.Learnteams.info -SIPSignalingPort 5068.`

   B. `New-CsOnlinePSTNGateway -FQDN MYSBC2.Learnteams.info -Port 5068.`

   C. `New-TeamsPSTNGateway -domain MYSBC2.Learnteams.info -SIPSignalingPort 5068.`

   D. `New-DirectRoutingPSTNGateway -FQDN MYSBC2.Learnteams.info -Port 5068.`

13. You are trying to build a new auto attendant that must have an external number associated with it. You created the resource account in the TAC and placed an order for a new service number. When you attempt to associate the number with the resource account, no numbers are available. What has not been configured?

   A. The service number has not properly applied to the tenant.

   B. The resource account needs to be placed into TeamsOnly mode.

   C. The resource account region does not match the service number region.

   D. The resource account needs to be allocated a Virtual User License.

14. A user goes on long-term leave and you are contacted by their line manager who wants to make sure that someone can deal with the user's incoming calls instead of them all going to voicemail. What can you do that involves the least administrative effort and maintains appropriate security measures?

   A. Reset the user's password, and give it to the line manager so they can adjust calling settings.

   B. Reset the user's password, and log in through a private browser to update their calling settings.

   C. Assign the line manager as a delegate for the user by modifying the user's calling settings in the TAC.

   D. Remove the user's number and assign it a call queue.

15. You are configuring an SBC to use with Direct Routing and have elected to place the SBC on a domain that currently isn't associated with your tenant. After validating the domain using a DNS record lookup, what else must you do before you can use the SBC?

   A. Configure a user with an Online Voice Routing Policy.

   B. Configure a temporary licensed account using the new domain.

   C. Create an account with the Teams Service Administrator role permission against the new domain.

   D. Authorize the SBC in the Direct Routing Health dashboard.

16. You have been asked to configure a call queue that will call all agents at the same time. Which routing method would you use?

    A. Serial

    B. Round robin

    C. Longest idle

    D. Attendant mode

17. You have configured Direct Routing for your tenant and need to assign numbers to your users. What is the quickest way to assign the phone number?

    A. Using TAC

    B. Via PowerShell

    C. In the Teams client

    D. Using Active Directory

18. Some of your users need to be able to place outbound calls without showing their phone numbers. How could you achieve this?

    A. Using a Calling Policy

    B. With a Call Parking Policy

    C. Using a Dial Plan

    D. By creating a Caller ID Policy

19. You want to use Calling Plans for Teams telephony. You have purchased and assigned Calling Plan and Phone System licenses to your users (who are already configured with E3). You have assigned a user number via the TAC for the correct region, but when testing, your users are not able to make PSTN calls. Where would you check the configuration next?

    A. Caller ID Policy.

    B. Calling Policy.

    C. Activate the SBC domain.

    D. Assign and emergency call routing policy.

20. You are configuring some users in the United States with Calling Plan numbers. The numbers have been allocated to the portal, and you are using the TAC to manually assign the numbers one by one. What else will you need to set up at the same time?

    A. An Online Voice Routing Policy

    B. A Call Queue

    C. An Emergency Address

    D. Network Settings

Chapter

6

Review Usage
and Maintain Quality

**MICROSOFT EXAM OBJECTIVES COVERED
IN THIS CHAPTER:**

✓ Monitor and analyze service usage

Over the last few chapters, we have looked at getting everything prepped, working out how to configure and apply policies, and understanding security and compliance requirements that may apply to your organization. Now in this, our last chapter together, we are going to look at how you can track and measure usage of Teams. It's all very well if you have spent all this time and effort trying to get things working, but it won't matter at all if no one then uses it or if they have issues using it.

Teams gathers a lot of great data about what people are doing on the platform (not in a compliance tracking kind of a way; that's what eDiscovery and the like were for back in Chapter 4, "Advanced Teams Functionality and Management") so you can help identify where people are not getting the most out it. For example, if you knew that you had deployed webcams to all of your staff but then find that no one is using video during meetings, you could investigate why this might be: people may not know how to start video, or perhaps they don't understand how it can help improve engagement during a call. It could even be that the network performance is poor, so if they used video, the call quality would suffer. Being able to get this type of insight into how your environment is being used is a great way to make sure things are running smoothly, and if not, you can start nudging things back in the right direction. By using these reports, you can be a proactive administrator and identify problems before they become large-scale issues.

Adoption and Deployment Approach

User adoption is a phrase you will see quite a lot in the Microsoft training materials. It is a term for making sure that you approach how to get engagement from users when you deploy a new solution or product. You usually can't just get away with a "build it and they will come" type approach to implementing something like Teams. You should try to get people on board with why you are deploying it and what the benefits are. If you can get people excited (it *is* possible) about what you are deploying and why, they are much more likely to get on board, and you will see better uptake of the solution.

When covering benefits, you should focus on benefits to the users themselves, rather than focusing on the larger corporate benefits. While overall company benefits are great, the average user might not get as excited about saving money on an IT deployment as the board would.

Some examples of focusing on end-user benefits might be highlighting that using Teams document-sharing capabilities keeps users from having to manually deal with versions of documents sent in email or that using presence and chat can cut down on the volume of time-wasting emails in their inboxes. These are things that offer small improvements to someone's working day, and so are things they can really get behind.

Deployment Planning

When starting to deploy Teams, you should consider creating a high-level deployment plan that you can follow, looking at both what features you want to enable at each point and which groups of users you are targeting.

This book has been structured roughly according to how you might look at approaching the deployment for your company:

- Getting started and preparation

- Deploying simple workloads

- Enabling more advanced features

- Monitoring and reviewing results and quality

One of the places that you can access some tailored guides and information about how you could deploy Teams is by using Teams Advisor. This used to be a separate service but is now integrated into the TAC, which can help you plan the steps of an adoption by analyzing what you have configured and deployed in your tenant.

Teams Advisor

The idea behind Teams Advisor is it can perform some automated readiness assessments against your tenant to check things such as licensing availability for certain workloads or whether guest access is configured. Then, depending on which workload you select, Teams Advisor will create a team for you with an associated planner board and task lists allocated to the users that you specify during setup. This gives you a step-by-step action plan to follow for deploying that capability. To get the most out of Teams Advisor, you will need, as well as a Teams license, one for Planner and Forms.

To access Teams Advisor, open the TAC and then from the left menu expand Planning ➤ Teams Advisor. This will open the main screen of Teams Advisor, where several possible deployment workload options are laid out depending on what you are looking to achieve:

- Collaboration focused

  - Chat, teams, channels, and apps

- Meeting focused

  - Meetings and conferencing

- Skype for Business upgrade focused

If you click View next to the item, you will see a list of the tasks in each stage (see Figure 6.1).

FIGURE 6.1   Teams Advisor task list

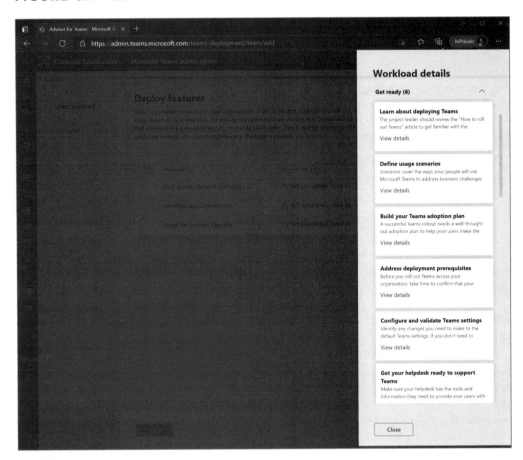

To set up the team and planner, pick an option and click Next; it will ask you to select which users are going to be part of the team that will be created. These should be people you will work closely with on the deployment (see Figure 6.2). You can always expand the membership after the team has been created.

Once the team has been created, you will see a dashboard of the overall progress and what tasks have been selected (see Figure 6.3).

While the pre-created task lists and prescribed steps might not be 100 percent accurate for your needs, they do provide a good idea of where to start and a framework that you can use to adapt things to your company.

To read more about what Teams Advisor can do for you, see `https://docs.microsoft.com/en-us/microsoftteams/use-advisor-teams-roll-out`.

FIGURE 6.2   Teams Advisor team members

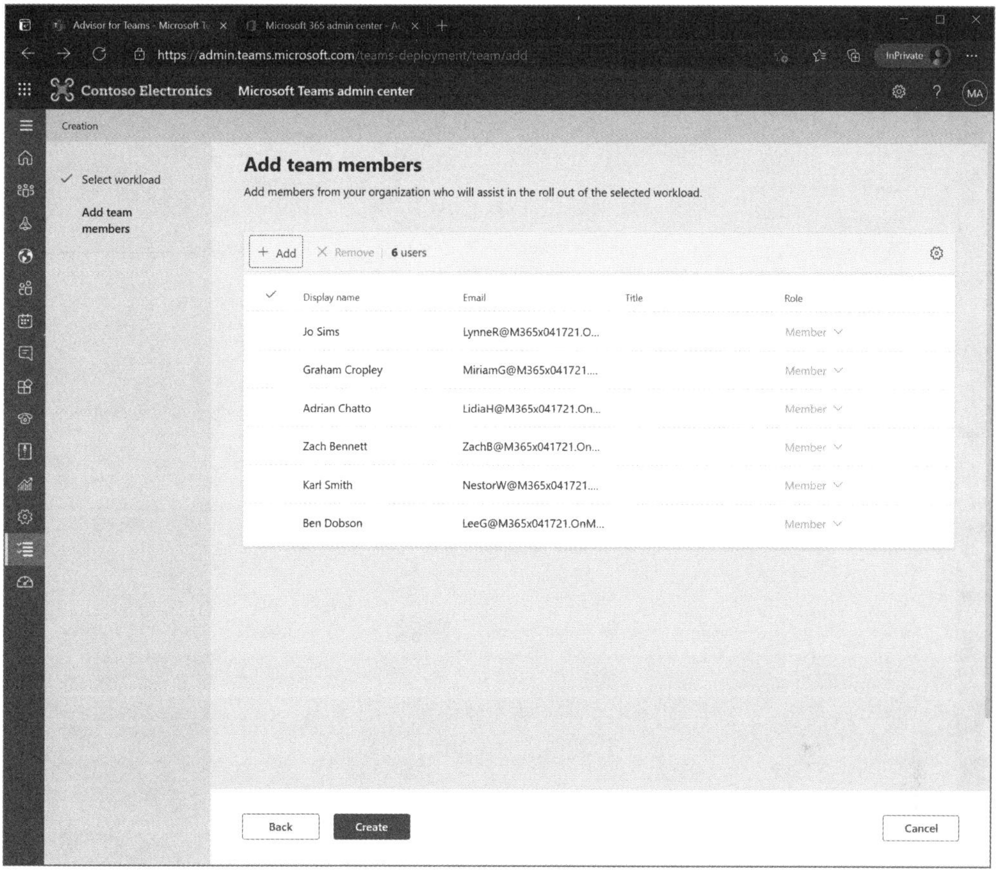

User Adoption

User adoption is a complex topic in its own right, so here are just a few nods in its direction so that you know some of terms that might be mentioned on the MS 700 exam. Take a look at some of the links in the references for this section and you will find a wealth of training material and information on the subject that might be of particular interest.

In the prebuilt plans that Teams Advisor will create for you, there will be references to different roles that are commonly used during a Teams deployment project. These are as follows:

Executive sponsors: These are people high up in the company structure with the weight to help clear blockers and be trendsetters. If they are seen to be big proponents of the technology, then it makes the process easier as others are more likely to follow.

FIGURE 6.3   Teams Advisor deployment dashboard

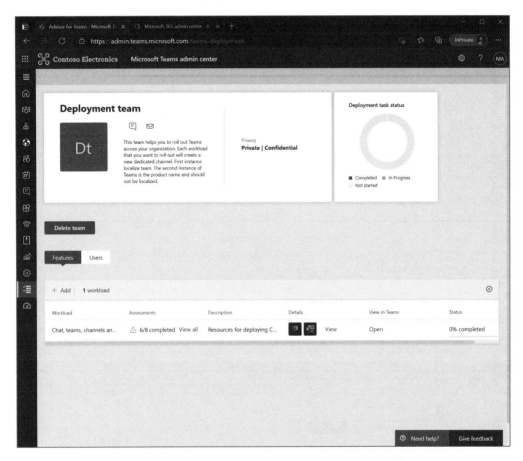

Service operators: They are responsible for running the solution after it has been deployed. This isn't necessarily the same group that deployed it, as often the service will transition over from the business's IT support.

User champions: Champions are enthusiastic ordinary users whom you can use to help drive uptake in the user base. They are people who during testing or pilot project phases will provide you with invaluable feedback on the deployment, and when you deploy for real, they can help influence others to use the technology.

By identifying these roles early in the project, especially your executive sponsors, you can smooth your path because they can influence others in the company when you hit roadblocks or issues that may require a change in company processes.

Some companies invest a lot of time and energy in their champions programs, and these users are given special treatment and sometimes perks like more expensive headsets. Do not underestimate the importance of generating enthusiasm and support from users across the company, as you will greatly benefit from their support when the deployment goes live.

During your deployment, or pilot, of the project, you should be looking at the usage statistics and data to check that people are using the products in the way you anticipated. We will look at how Teams can provide you with invaluable reporting in the next section.

Depending on your deployment project, you may conduct a pilot phase where you move some users onto the platform to test the behavior and features/functionality before planning a larger rollout. Be careful using IT users for this pilot. By all means, include IT in a pilot, but they should not be the only users!

This is because IT users are not normal users. They have different expectations of technology than ordinary users, as well as sometimes having non-standard hardware and software and access permissions. This means the feedback you will receive from IT users will not necessarily align with that of other users from different parts of the business. A successful pilot should be inclusive and cover a good cross section of your user base.

Microsoft provides some good deep guides about how to deploy Teams and the different workloads here: https://docs.microsoft.com/en-gb/ MicrosoftTeams/planning-workshop-practical-guide.

You will also find the Customer Success Kit, which contains a number of templates for things like emails and internal communications to help with the deployment.

You can find a dedicated site for user adoption methodology and overall approach here: https://adoption.microsoft.com.

Monitoring Collaboration

When deploying a complex product like Teams, it can be helpful to think of the process as operating in a cycle where you can tackle workloads one by one. Perhaps you start with a project to deploy the basic Teams collaboration features, then come around to add in the meeting workloads, and lastly add telephony. Business priorities may dictate a different order, say, for example, if everyone in the company suddenly had to work from home for the best part of a year. Then deploying meetings and telephony quickly may make sense!

However, even when you may think that you have finished your deployment with no more workloads left to enable, it isn't really the end of the deployment process. It is good practice to make sure you are monitoring the usage and uptake (as we have talked about before) to ensure that people are getting the most out of the system. Here we are going to look at some of the reports available for both Teams and Microsoft 365. There are some specific reporting tools and methodologies that cover monitoring and troubleshooting the voice workload to a greater level of detail; these are covered in the next section.

Teams Usage Reports

Inside the TAC you can pick to run one of the predefined reports for a specific time span (7 days, 30 days, or 90 days) and can even choose to export the data yourself and download it as a CSV file for your own processing.

To be able to access the reports, you must have one of the administrator RBAC roles, such as Global Administrator, Teams Administrator, or Teams Communications Administrator. The reports will return data only when it exists for your tenant; for example, the PSTN calling reports will not return data if you do not have any appropriate licenses in your environment.

To see the list of reports available, open TAC ➤ Analytics & Reports ➤ Usage Reports. Here you can pick from the following report types:

Apps usage: Shows information about the Teams integrated apps that have been used in your teams. This lets you track which apps are popular and keep an eye on what third-party apps are being used (see Figure 6.4).

FIGURE 6.4 Teams apps usage report

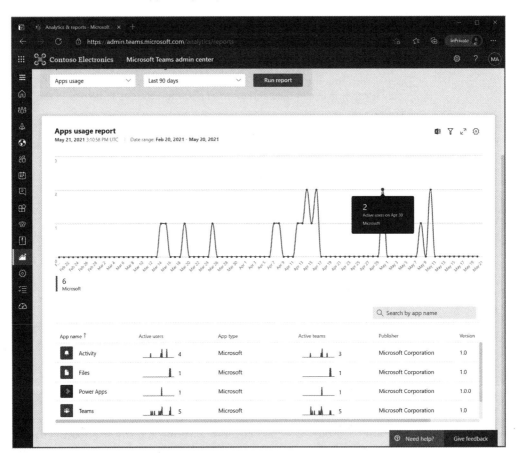

PSTN blocked numbers: Shows information about internal users who were blocked from making a call. This report does not have a customizable date range (see Figure 6.5).

FIGURE 6.5 Teams PSTN blocked users report

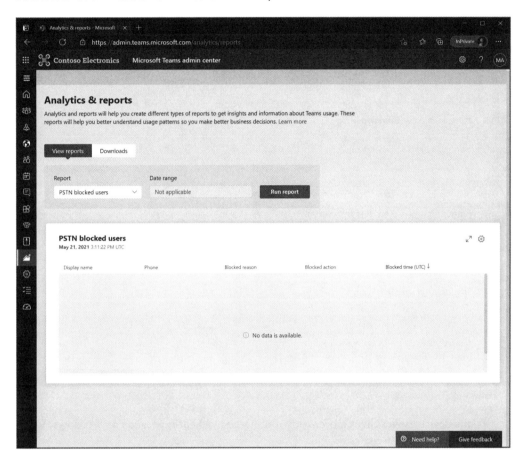

PSTN minutes pools: Shows the usage of minutes in calling plan bundles; remember that users in the same region with the same calling plan license share their minutes (see Figure 6.6).

PSTN usage (Calling Plans/Direct Routing): Shows a breakdown of the calls in and out in the time range specified. This report will have a tab at the top to toggle between calling-plan calls and direct-routing calls (see Figure 6.7, which shows the calling plan report).

FIGURE 6.6   Teams PSTN minute pools report

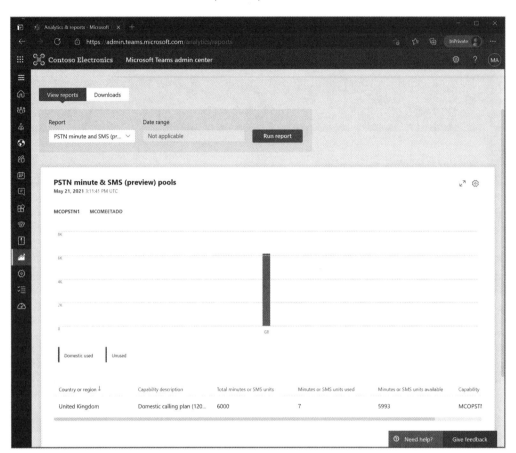

Teams device usage: Gives a breakdown of usage by client type, such as Windows, Web, or iOS (see Figure 6.8).

Teams live event usage: Shows a list of live events that have run during the specified time. You can optionally search just for events by a specified user (see Figure 6.9).

Teams usage: Gives a report of activity inside a team showing information such as active users, number of guests, and number of messages (see Figure 6.10).

Teams user activity: Gives a breakdown of activity type by user. Activities shown include things like the number of messages and how many meetings were organized versus scheduled (see Figure 6.11).

FIGURE 6.7 Teams PSTN usage report

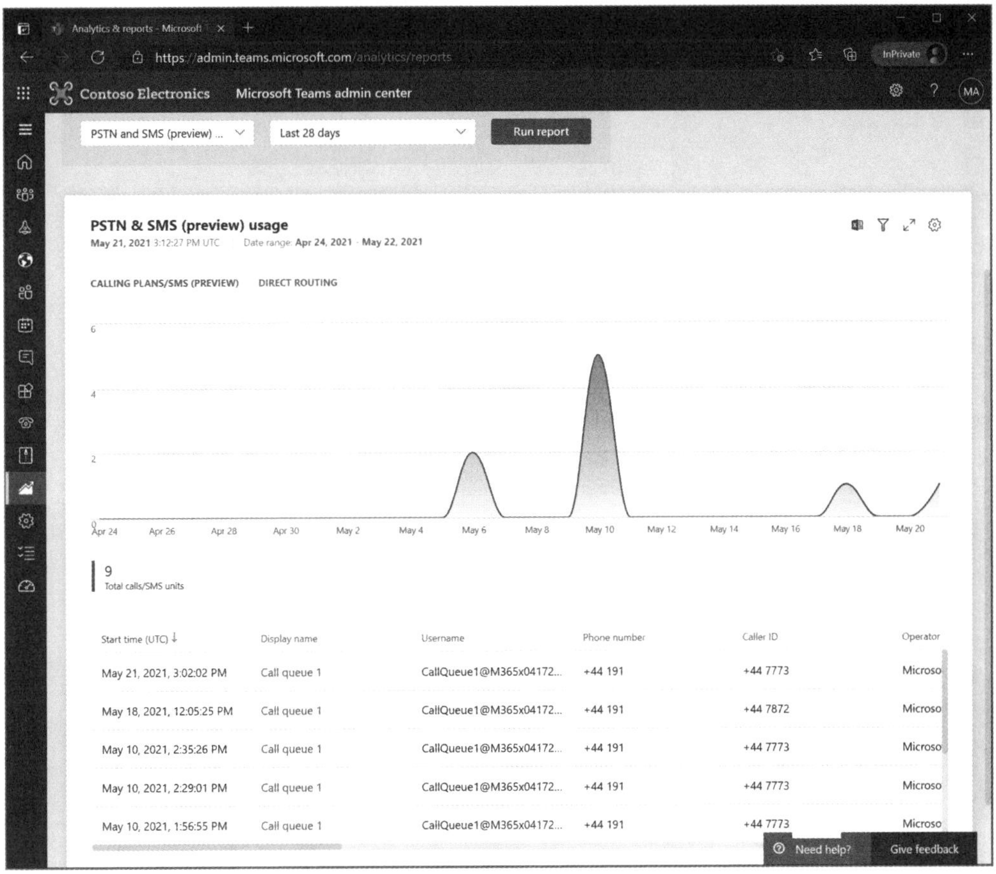

In the reports that contain usage information, the following definitions are used:

Active users: Number of unique users who have performed an action inside the team during the date range used

Active channels: Number of channels where some level of user activity has been performed during the date range of the report

I hope you can see that by monitoring these reports you can get an idea whether the structure that you have put in place is being used as intended or if it may need some tweaking. They will tell you, for example, if you had lots of teams but only a few were active, or if you had a team with lots of channels but only a few were used.

FIGURE 6.8 Teams device usage report

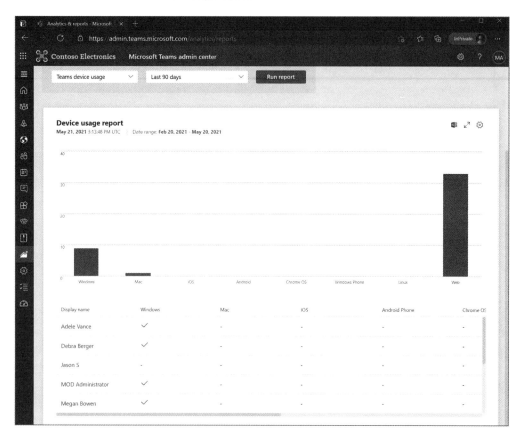

To export the data for further processing, you can click the little Excel icon that appears when you hover on any of the charts. This starts generating the report in the background, and you can then download the output CSV file from the analytics and reports page in the TAC by selecting the Downloads tab (see Figure 6.12).

Click Download to save the CSV to your local machine where you can then generate your own reports by perhaps cross-referencing other information. For example, you could add office or country information so that you can then report usage by specific location.

NOTE   You can read more about the report specifics here: https://docs.micro-soft.com/en-us/microsoftteams/teams-analytics-and-reports/teams-reporting-reference.

FIGURE 6.9   Teams live event usage report

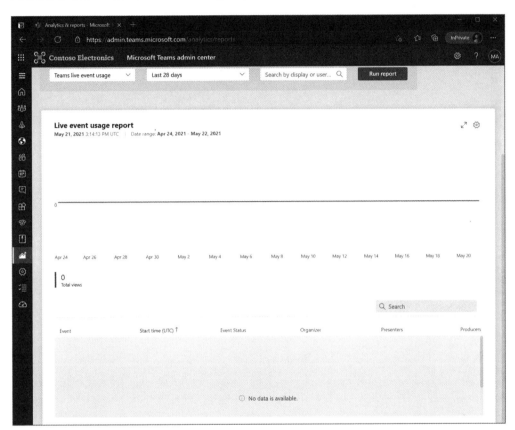

Microsoft 365 Usage Reports

The reports found in the TAC are focused on Teams-specific workloads and tasks, but sometimes it can be helpful to see the usage in Teams in the context of the other Microsoft 365 workloads (such as Exchange or SharePoint). To see this type of information, there are some high-level reports available in the main Microsoft 365 admin center.

To view the reports, go to Show All from the left menu and then open Reports ➤ Usage. Here you can select a timespan and then see some high-level information about the usage across your tenant (see Figure 6.13).

As you can see in Figure 6.14, the report gives you a breakdown of active users by service. Here you can see that there was a lot of email activity in Exchange, but it was comparable to the number of active users in Teams. This type of data could help you track against your Teams deployment project goals, for example if one of the goals was to reduce email volume for internal communications. You would use these reports to help track that sort of information.

FIGURE 6.10 Teams usage report

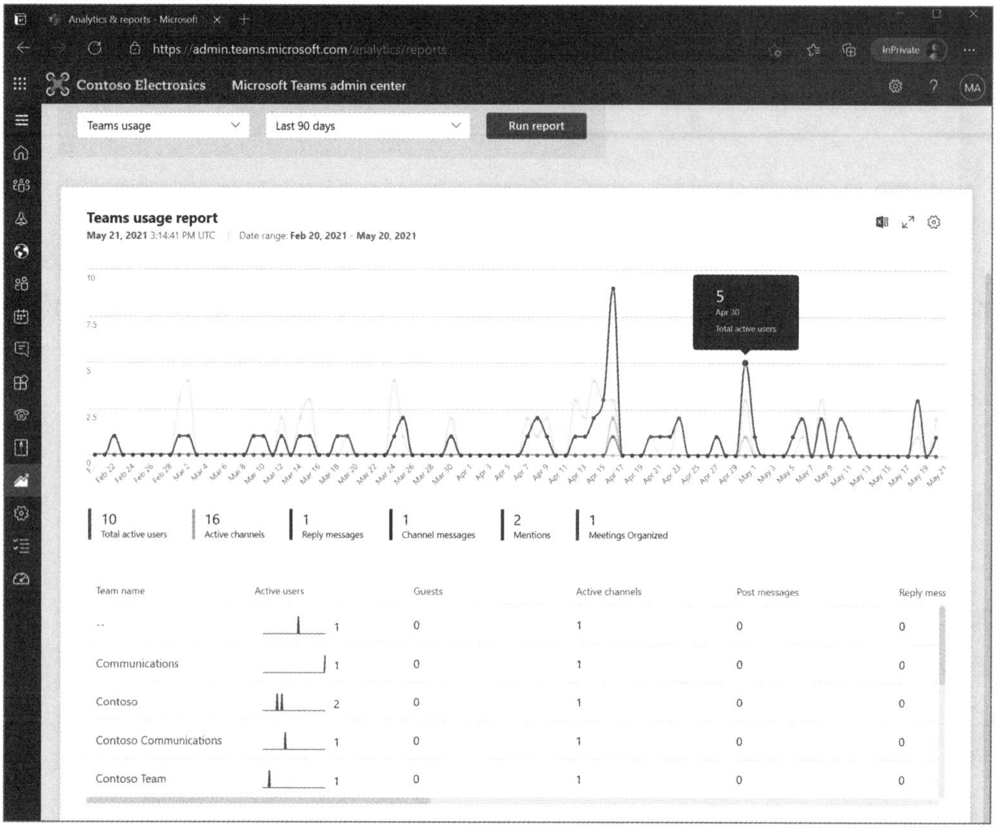

You can click the View More button to drill into any of the reports, and the Teams activity report is split into two categories for either user activity or device usage. When comparing the Teams workload to that of other services, it is probably the user activity that is of most interest.

Monitoring Telephony

While the reports we just covered in the TAC and the Microsoft 365 admin center are good, they do not provide enough detailed information to reveal trends and troubleshoot the communications workload in Teams. Fortunately, there are some alternative tools that we can use to help us here.

FIGURE 6.11   Teams user activity report

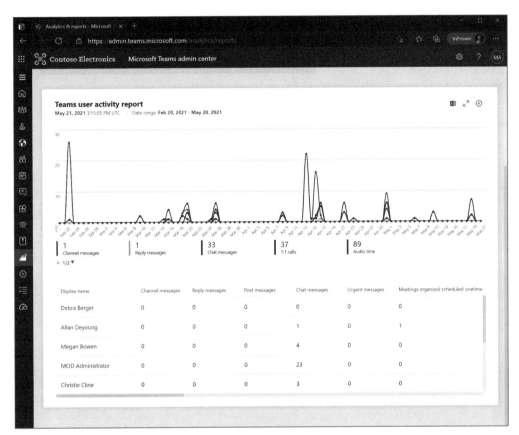

Each time, in Teams, when the client does something major during a call, some metrics are collected and passed back to the Teams service for processing. This means that even if the client is disconnected from a call because their client crashes or the network disconnects, the server has a good amount of information available to help work out what might have gone wrong.

The following are the key points during a call when data is captured:

- Call setup when the call is being established

- During a call at periodic intervals, or if a warning is raised (these show as little notifications displayed in the client)

- Call clear down, when the call has ended and been wrapped up

FIGURE 6.12   Analytics & reports downloads

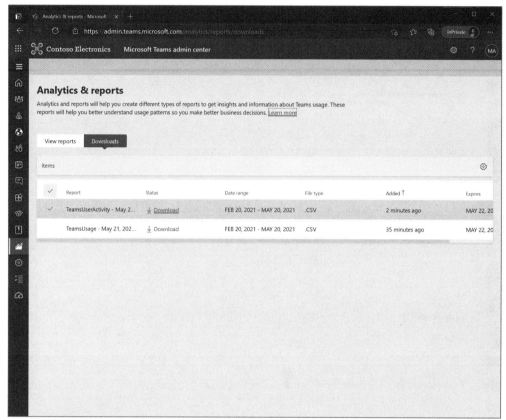

This data is then accessed in two different ways depending on your requirements:

Call analytics: This information shows per-user call information and is usually used for targeted troubleshooting, for example, when a user raises a ticket for a specific issue in which they had a poor call experience. Here you could go find the user, find the call, and then see what happened.

Call Quality Dashboard (CQD): CQD is used to detect trends in data at an organization-wide level. It allows the uploading of building data to let you identify if specific locations are having issues with calling quality, and it can show trends in deployments during migration.

FIGURE 6.13 Microsoft 365 usage report

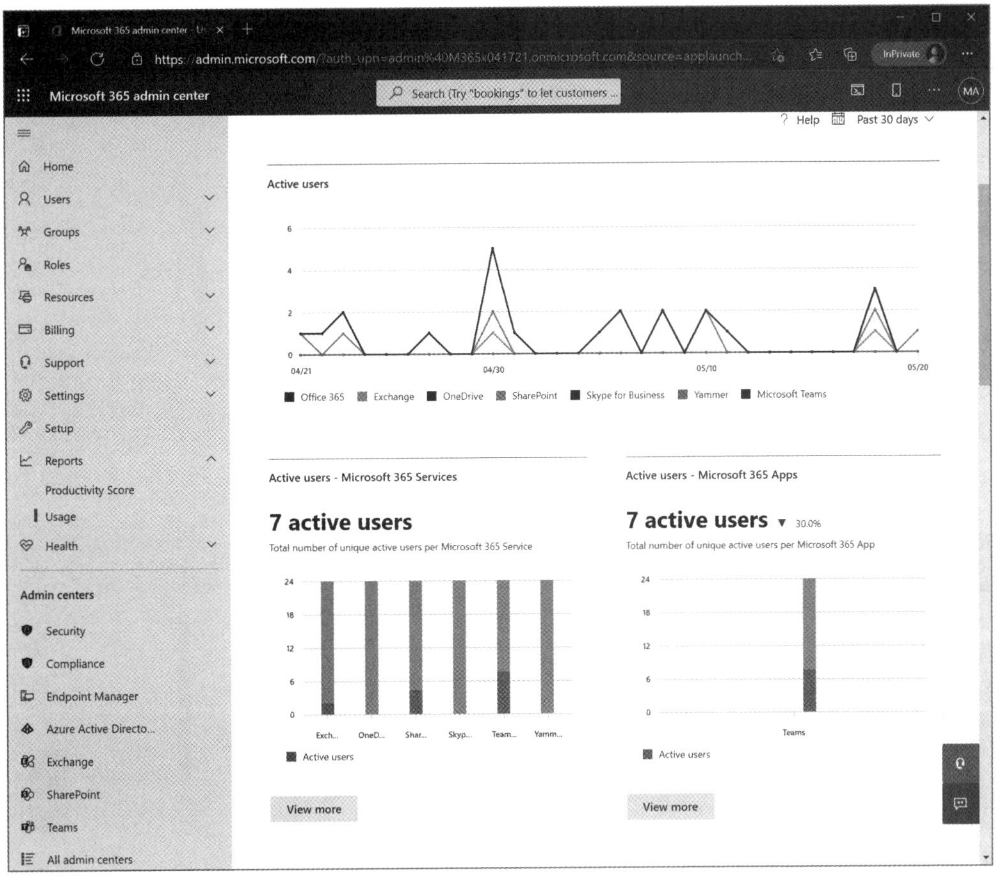

Call Analytics

Call analytics are accessed from the user page in the TAC, and if you cast your mind back to Chapter 4 where we discussed the Teams administrator roles, this was one of the tools where the level of access permission affects what data you have access to.

Teams administrators, Teams communications administrators, and Teams communications support engineers have full access to the data held in call analytics, including showing all participant information for everyone in a call. Teams communications support specialists will still have access to the same data, but other participant information will be obfuscated.

FIGURE 6.14   Microsoft 365 usage report workload detail

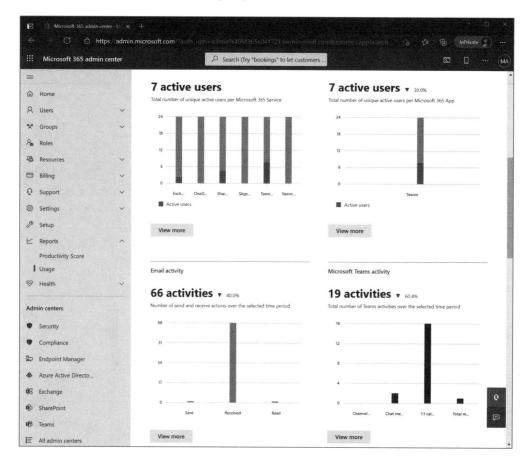

The data shown in call analytics is for Teams-to-Teams calls, Teams meetings, or Teams phone calls. To access it, log into the TAC, and then from the left menu select Users. Search through the list for the user whose call you want to troubleshoot and then click their name. Move to the Meetings & Calls tab shown partway down the page under the summary of their information and activity (see Figure 6.15).

You will then see a large list of all the meetings and calls that the user has participated in. Be aware that while this information is displayed in as close to real time as possible, you may not see calls show up for 30 minutes or so depending on how busy things are behind the scenes.

To see detailed information about a specific call, click the ID number, and you will be taken to a screen containing more information (see Figure 6.16). On the overview page, the data is split into four parts and then divided by each side of the call, so information such as

FIGURE 6.15   Call analytics information

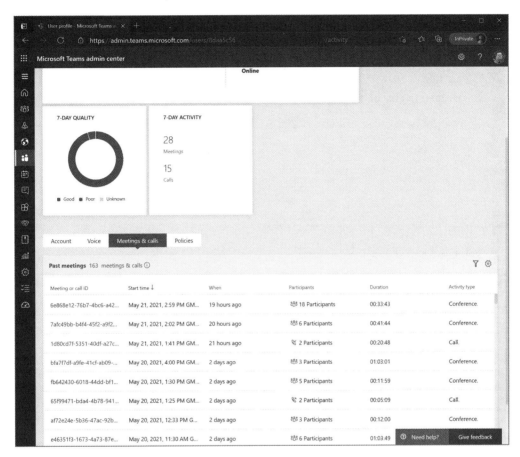

device, system, and connectivity are shown for the selected user and the remote participant where available. If the call is with an external user, there may be gaps in the information gathered by your tenant about their half of the call.

If the call contained more than just audio, then data is gathered and represented against streams. A stream is one type of data sent or received in the call; for example, if you used screen share and video, then you would have three streams, one for each modality. If the call was a meeting (or conference as the call analytics information refers to it), then you can also view a neat overview of who joined at which point and what modalities they were using (see Figure 6.17).

You can use the data from the call analytics to try to help identify what might have caused the problem. Teams will highlight data on the summary pages if things like the recommended network metrics (see Chapter 2, "Getting Teams Up and Running") were breached.

FIGURE 6.16 Detailed call information

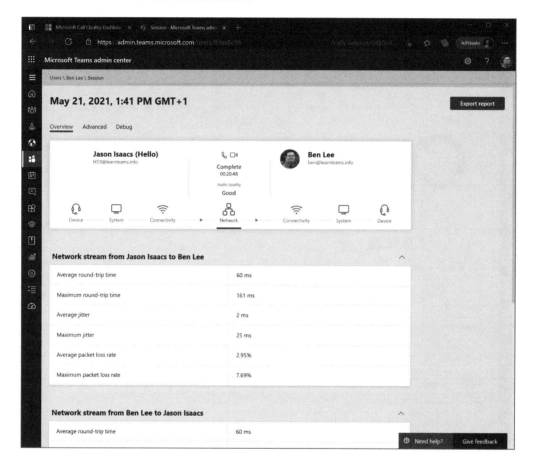

Some areas that can commonly cause problems for calls include the following:

Devices: Not using certified devices or using built-in microphones and speakers in a call. Built-in devices may seem great to the person who is using them, but for everyone else on the call, they may be causing a large amount of feedback or distortion. Check what devices everyone was using for the call.

Overall network conditions: The network may not be able to support those key metrics for round-trip time, jitter, packet loss, and packet reorder ratio that we discussed in Chapter 2.

FIGURE 6.17   Conference timeline

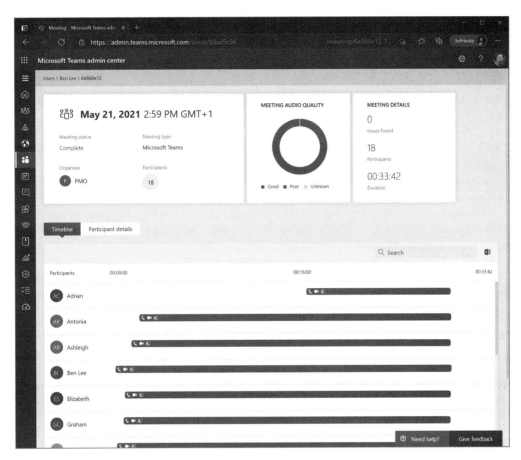

Wi-Fi or VPN: Another clue can be to check if the caller was on a Wi-Fi network or using a VPN, as these can impact the overall networking conditions, and Wi-Fi especially can be subject to external influences (such as someone using a microwave in a nearby kitchen!).

To learn more about troubleshooting call quality with call analytics, see https://docs.microsoft.com/en-us/microsoftteams/use-call-analytics-to-troubleshoot-poor-call-quality.

Call Quality Dashboard

Call Quality Dashboard (QCD) is also designed to help troubleshoot calling issues, but instead of looking at specific calls and users, it aggregates information from across all calls in the tenant and lets you review this data for trends.

For example, if a user has an issue with a call that is identified as being caused by a networking issue, call analytics would help identify that, but it wouldn't tell you that the problem could be office-wide. In CQD you would be able to view a dip in overall call quality by location so that you could proactively find and fix the problem.

To get the most out of CQD, it helps to tell it what network ranges are used inside your organization—called *building data*. This way when you look at reports, you can compare performance for managed locations where it should always be good (for example in your office building using the company WAN) versus on an unmanaged connection where you do not have as much influence or control over it (for example using Wi-Fi from a local coffee shop). Ideally, you will have this information available, as you already used it in the previous chapter for the Location Information Services and Network Settings configuration. This is the last time we need it, I promise (subject to Microsoft changing it all).

To access CQD, either you can find a link to it at the bottom of the TAC menu or you can go directly to https://cqd.teams.microsoft.com.

You may find that when accessing CQD, it will give you an error saying you need to sign in even if you have already been signed into the TAC or another admin portal. Just click Sign In in the top-right corner, and it should then log you in correctly.

Access to CQD is not just based on the Teams admin roles; some of the other M365 admin roles can also access and view reports. CQD also contains some amount of end-user identifiable information (EUII), which may or may not be accessible depending on your permissions. Table 6.1 summarizes the different permissions.

TABLE 6.1 CQD Admin Roles

M365 RBAC Role	View/ Create Reports	View User Information (EUII)	Upload Building Data
Global Administrator	Y	Y	Y
Teams Administrator	Y	Y	Y
Teams Communications Administration	Y	Y	Y
Teams Communications Engineer	Y	Y	N
Teams Communications Support Specialist	Y	N	N
Global Reader	Y	Y	N
Reports Reader	Y	N	N

https://docs.microsoft.com/en-us/microsoftteams/turning-on-and-using-call-quality-dashboard

The EUII data is automatically removed after 28 days, so any report you are looking at that contains data past this time frame will be free from user information. The following is what Microsoft classifies as EUII data:

- Full IP address
- Media Access Control (MAC) address
- User principal name and object ID
- Computer name
- User feedback

After logging in, you will see a page of summary reports that are available to all users in the tenant (see Figure 6.18). They show high-level trend information of the split between good, unclassified, and poor calls, which then calculates a percentage of poor calls. Calls can sometimes be unclassified if they did not last long enough to successfully establish or something happened that meant some of the data was not available for processing.

FIGURE 6.18   CQD summary reports

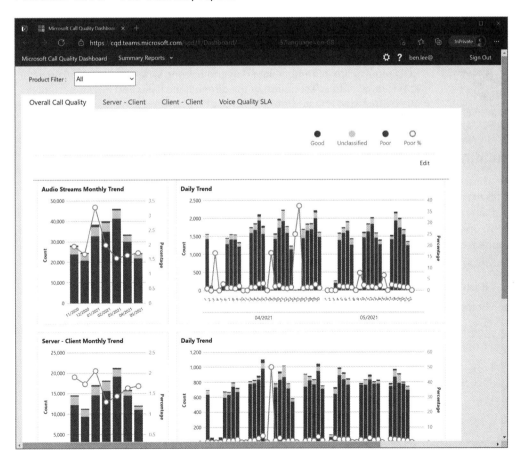

You may think that the percentage of poor calls should be as close to zero as possible, but, in reality, somewhere less than 4 percent is pretty good going. This is partly because you will never have absolute control over all the factors influencing a call, and having people connecting from home or over unmanaged Wi-Fi networks will contribute to poor or failed calls.

The data that is collected inside CQD is housed in a gigantic data warehouse, and when you view or create reports, CQD uses what are called *dimensions* to filter the data. You will see many of these labeled twice, one as first and the other as second. This reflects the different ends of each stream and, slightly confusingly, does not always correlate with which direction the call was made, that is, from caller to callee. The following is used to determine which is labeled as first or second:

- If a server endpoint was involved in the call, the server is always marked as first.

- The client in a server/client call is therefore always second.

- If endpoints are the same type (client/client or server/server), then an order of precedence is applied.

To help when using this data in reports, there is a True/False field called First Is Caller that can help identify the direction of a call.

CQD reports are incredibly data rich and beyond what you need to know at this level. A full description of the dimensions used and how they apply can be found at https://docs.microsoft.com/en-us/microsoftteams/ dimensions-and-measures-available-in-call-quality-dashboard.

Building Data

As mentioned earlier, to get the most out of CQD, it is best to build a network map that allocates network subnets to specific buildings and locations so that when you are playing with and filtering reports, you know which locations you are dealing with.

To upload building data into the tenant, create either a comma-separated value (CSV) or a tab-separated value (TSV) file that is formatted as follows:

- It should not include a header row in the file.

- It can contain only strings or numbers; true/false (Boolean) is indicated by a 0 or 1.

- Empty columns must be included if the field has no data.

- A total of 15 columns are needed.

- 1,000,000 rows is the limit (that's a lot of locations!).

Table 6.2 shows the fields included in the building data.

TABLE 6.2   Building Data Fields

Column	Data Expected	Example	Include
NetworkIP	String	10.10.10.0	Yes
NetworkName	String	UK/NE/DUR1	Yes
NetworkRange	Number	24	Yes
BuildingName	String	Durham-D1	Yes
OwnershipType	String	LearnTeams	Optional
BuildingType	String	Lease	Optional
BuildingOfficeType	String	Office	Optional
City	String	Durham	Recommended
ZipCode	String	DHXX	Recommended
Country	String	UK	Recommended
State	String	County Durham	Recommended
Region	String	North East	Recommended
InsideCorp	Boolean	1	Yes
ExpressRoute	Boolean	0	Yes
VPN	Boolean	0	Optional

https://docs.microsoft.com/en-us/microsoftteams/cqd-upload-tenant-building-data

There are three items in the building data list that are worth explaining further. They are the Booleans at the end that are used to identify characteristics of the network:

InsideCorp: True when the network specified is part of the managed company WAN. For example, if you had a rented office space with a shared Internet-only network connection, you would still want to add that location into CQD but mark it as not part of the company network so you know not to expect calls to go peer-peer when this location is involved.

ExpressRoute: True if the network has a dedicated network connection to Microsoft (Express Route).

VPN: Used when you have dedicated network ranges or sites that connect over VPN. VPNs can be among the factors contributing to poor call quality, so being able to identify VPN locations in reports is useful.

It can be easy to get stuck with how to name your buildings and locations. In reality, all that matters is that something is entered that is understandable to other people in the organization (and you) so that when reports are generated, they can identify which location was having an issue.

Once you have prepared your file, the next step is uploading it to the tenant. To do this, click the cog in the top-right corner of the CQD window and select Tenant Data Upload. This will take you to a screen where you can select the file from your local computer and specify the start date (and optional end date) for the file. This date information is used because you might be undergoing a network restructure where subnets will be moved or adjusted across physical locations. By being able to specify a start/end date for the upload, you can make sure that the network ranges you are specifying display the right information at the right time (see Figure 6.19).

FIGURE 6.19 Tenant data upload

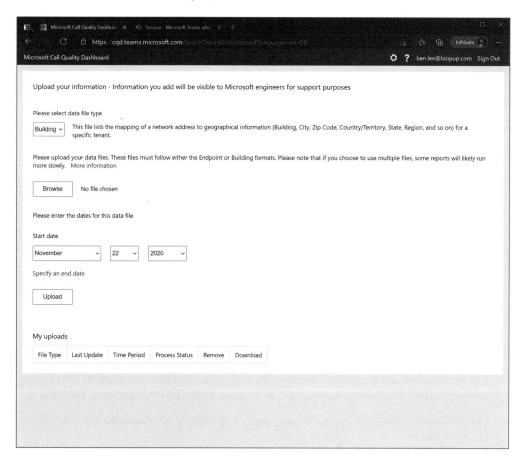

Recently Microsoft also added a section into the TAC where you can upload this data. It seems likely that over time uploading it directly into CQD will be deprecated, and ideally more of the location information used across Teams will start to be centralized inside the TAC. To upload your building data file (still the same format as you just created), go to the TAC, select Locations ➤ Reporting Labels, and then choose Upload. Here you can upload your file or download a template. When uploading via the TAC, you cannot specify a life span or any dates for the file.

Once the building data has been uploaded and processed, you should start being able to see the location information inside your reports. You will also notice that reports that use filters, such as Inside / Outside and Managed / Unmanaged, will reflect the locations of the clients. For example, a client in a known subnet flagged as InsideCorp (see Table 6.2) would be classed as Inside and Managed.

Detailed Reports

While the summary reports included in CQD can be helpful, some of the power comes from being able to create your own customized sets of reports showing the information that you care about in a way best suited to your organization. To start creating detailed reports from the top of the CQD menu bar, click the small drop-down arrow. Here you will see a full list of the built-in reports:

- Summary Reports

- Location-Enhanced Reports (may show only once building data is uploaded)

- Reliability Reports

- Quality of Experience Reports

- Quality of Drill-Down Reports

- Failure Drill-Down Reports

- Rate My Call Reports

- Help Desk Reports

- Client Version Reports

- Endpoint Reports

The names of most of these built-in reports are self-explanatory, but it is worth noting that on the Rate My Call report you can access the feedback submitted by your users when, at the end of the call, Teams asks the user about how their experience was.

To start adding your own reports, select the Details Reports option from the drop-down list, and you will then see a pre-created detailed report looking at all your audio streams. Note that when the titles of reports are in blue, you can usually click them to drill into the data and go to another more detailed breakdown report.

To start creating your own reports, use the buttons on the left menu to either edit the current report, start a new one, or import a report set from a template. Any reports that are created here are visible only to your user account, so if you are working with a team of people who access CQD, it can be good practice to keep a template file somewhere centrally so that everyone has the same set of reports to use.

A good starting point for creating customized CQD reports is to download a set provided by Microsoft and import them. To do this, first download the ZIP file from `https://aka.ms/QERtemplates` and unzip the contents. Then inside CQD and from the detailed reports page click Import on the left menu and upload the CQDX files. You should then have some reports that look like those shown in Figure 6.20. You will need to scroll the window to the right to see the new imported reports.

FIGURE 6.20   CQD detailed reports

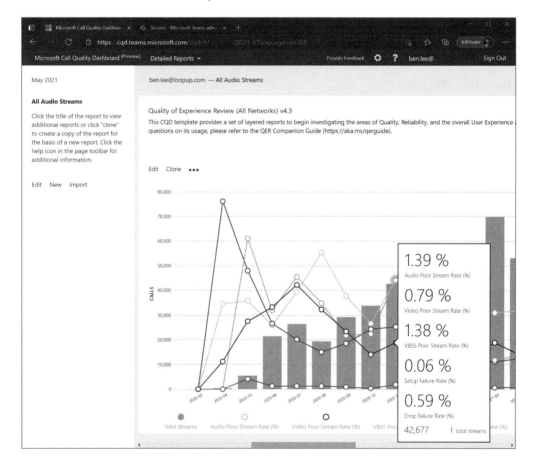

If you drill into these reports, you can get some great information about how your environment is performing. Reports like TCP versus UDP can show if you might have a firewall issue where not all the correct ports are open to Teams. (UDP should always be used in preference to TCP.) Or the HTTP Proxy report can tell you if lots of user calls are routing through a proxy server (remember from Chapter 2 how this can affect call performance). There are even reports that help you identify where there are subnets with lots of calls originating in them but no building data assigned.

While being able to customize all of these reports to make some great-looking dashboards, sometimes you want to be able to combine CQD with other data or display it in ways that the CQD web interface just isn't capable of. Fortunately, to help, Microsoft has made it possible to directly access the data behind CQD using its Power BI engine.

 To learn a bit more about the details reports and how CQD works, visit https://docs.microsoft.com/en-us/microsoftteams/cqd-data-and-reports.

CQD Power BI Connector

Power BI is Microsoft's large-scale data visualization and presentation tool. It lets you work with large sets of data and then process, filter, and report on them in many ways so that you can then build up visual dashboards and reports to best display your data. Power BI comes in several different flavors, including for Teams (an app to integrate with a channel), but here we are going to just look at how to access the CQD data from the desktop client (currently Windows only).

First you should download and install the Power BI Desktop client, either from the Windows Store or from https://powerbi.microsoft.com/en-us/desktop.

Once you download and install it, you will need the latest version of the CQD Power BI connector, which you can find linked from here: https://docs.microsoft.com/en-us/microsoftteams/cqd-power-bi-connector.

Save the connector ZIP file and extract the contents to somewhere safe on your computer. Inside the contents should be several PBIT files, which are templated reports, and a PQX file, which is the connection file that Power BI needs. Copy this file into your Documents\Power BI Desktop\Custom Connectors\ folder (if it does not exist in My Documents, then create it).

Next launch Power BI, and from the splash screen choose Get Data. This will open a screen showing all the possible sources you can hook Power BI into. Search the list for *Microsoft Call Quality* (see Figure 6.21) and click Connect.

When prompted, sign in with your tenant administrator credentials. You will then see a window with a lot of CQD column names; click Load and then select DirectQuery when asked how Power BI should access the data. Given that CQD is so vast, you are not able to access it by importing or downloading the data; you have to connect using a direct query only! Click Connect and then wait for a minute or two while the connection is established.

When you see a blank report, you can now start building the report you want to see, but given that this can be quite a daunting task, luckily Microsoft also included some report templates in the CQD connector pack. Find the files you extracted earlier; look at the PBIT files and choose one to open. Figure 6.22 shows the Teams usage report template file open and connected to CQD.

The following are the default reports included in the template pack:

- Helpdesk Report
- Location Enhanced Report
- Mobile Device Report

- PSTN Report
- Summary Report
- Teams Usage Report
- User Feedback Report

FIGURE 6.21   Power BI CQD data source

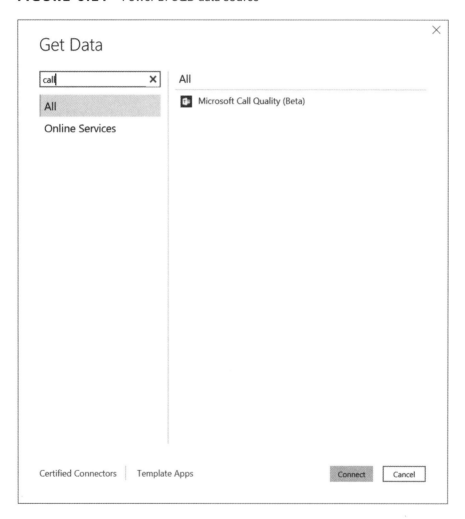

Once you have customized your reports, you can save them for use later or publish them to locations such as a SharePoint site or team for others to view. Earlier in the chapter we talked about how a deployment project could run and that monitoring uptake was an important part of that. Having a templated report that is reviewed at each project meeting can be a simple way of making sure that happens.

FIGURE 6.22   Power BI Teams usage report template

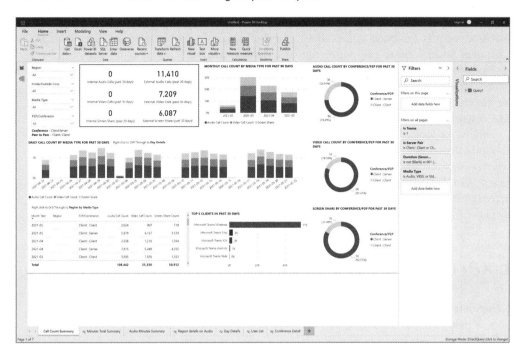

Power BI, while it has a free edition that can be used for stand-alone reporting like this, does have subscription licensing tiers that cover some of the features and capabilities. For example, if you want to publish a dashboard in a location for other people to view or edit, this usually requires a license, and so on. Power BI licensing is out of scope for MS 700, but you can learn more about it at `https://powerbi.microsoft.com`.

Linking CQD is incredibly powerful as you can build some great reports that give a huge insight into what is happening with your Teams deployment. Learn more about it at `https://docs.microsoft.com/en-us/microsoftteams/cqd-power-bi-query-templates`.

Summary

In this chapter, we looked at how you can start to approach your deployment of Teams and covered some of the built-in tools that Microsoft provides to help make this process simpler.

Teams Advisor can be a great way to start your deployment planning, and even if you do not follow all the steps to the letter, it can make a good starting point for a framework that you can modify to suit your company and your business requirements. By using Teams Advisor, you also get quick access to a lot of the Microsoft materials in one place such as the Customer Success Kit to help with your own deployment.

We then talked about how you can look at the use of Teams and its different workloads across all of your users. This is displayed in two locations, either inside the TAC as part of the more detailed Teams usage reports or at a higher level compared to the other M365 workloads shown in the Microsoft 365 admin center.

Finally, we looked at some of the tools available to help with spotting trends and troubleshooting the communications workload. These are split between call analytics information, which is designed more for focused troubleshooting of a specific user or issue that has been raised, and CQD, which helps analyze and show trend data at a high level so you can proactively monitor and deal with issues as you spot them. We talked about how you could display CQD data using Power BI to produce your own customized dashboards and reports.

Exam Essentials

Know that you can use Teams Advisor to help plan your project. Teams Advisor is available to help with the deployment of several workloads in Teams; it provides a set of predefined project outlines that can be used to help you plan and manage your deployment. To use Teams Advisor, you should have a Teams, Planner, and Forms license assigned.

Understand how user adoption is an important part of a deployment. Deploying a project is not as simple as just enabling the right licenses and features. You should always consider the impact on users and how this is managed. Champions provide a good way of building support from your user base to help the project succeed.

Be able to interpret Teams usage reports. Know how to access and run the Teams usage reports as well as how to export data for further processing. You should also be aware of which RBAC roles can access the reports.

Know how to access the M365 usage reports. Know how to access the M365 usage reports and how they differ from the Teams usage reports (they are more high level and less Teams workload specific).

Understand which tool you would use to troubleshoot calling quality issues. Know the difference between call analytics and CQD. Be able to choose between them when investigating issues. You should also understand which RBAC roles have access to what data inside a report (access to personal data is limited for the support specialist's role).

Know how to access call analytics. Know that call analytics, which can be accessed via the user account information inside the TAC, provide detailed information about specific calls.

Know how to access CQD.   Know that CQD is used to provide higher-level analytics for trending and an overall insight into calling quality across your environment.

Understand why adding building data helps improve CQD reports.   Know that you should upload your networking data into CQD, either from CQD itself or in the TAC under Locations ➤ Reporting Labels, to help map which locations are on the company network and to help identify where problems are occurring for further analysis with your networking teams.

Know that you can work with CQD data inside Power BI.   While CQD provides a lot of detailed information, you can also use it inside Power BI for advanced processing and integration with other reporting data that you might have in the company.

Exercises

EXERCISE 6.1

Using Teams Advisor to Create a Deployment Plan

In this exercise, we will set up a deployment plan for the Meetings and Conferencing work-load, but feel free to repeat this exercise for another workload.

1. Log into the TAC and navigate to Planning ➤ Teams Advisor.

2. Select the workload to deploy, in this case Meetings and Conferencing. Click the Assessments column to read the information about what tasks are recommended before starting.

3. With the workload selected, click Create.

4. Add any team members who may help you with the deployment on the next screen and then click Create.

5. Back in the TAC, still in the Teams Advisor screen, click Open in the View In Teams column. This will take you to the team that was just created.

6. Inside the team open the Planner tab pinned to the top bar of the channel and review the recommended tasks.

EXERCISE 6.2

Reviewing Teams Usage Reports

In this exercise, we will look at the current Teams usage in our tenant from inside the TAC and then in the next exercise we will compare it with the wider M365 activity.

continues

EXERCISE 6.2 *(continued)*

1. Log into the TAC and under Analytics & Reports select Usage Reports.

2. Select the Teams Usage Report from the drop-down list and set the date range to 30 days. Click Run Report.

3. Browse through the report to see which teams are busy.

4. Next change to the Teams User Activity Report and run it.

5. This will show you the activity broken down by user.

EXERCISE 6.3

Reviewing M365 Usage Reports

Now we will run the M365 usage reports and see how the Teams activity compares to that in the rest of the tenant.

1. Log into the M365 admin center (`https://admin.microsoft.com`).

2. Expand the list on the left by clicking Show All.

3. Under Reports click Usage.

4. Scroll down the report and notice the breakdown of activity by workload.

5. Find the activity for Teams and compare it to the breakdown for email.

6. Click View More under the Teams Activity Report and notice the different kind of data displayed here versus that shown in Exercise 6.2. (This is more service oriented rather than giving a deeper look at the work in Teams.)

EXERCISE 6.4

Reviewing the Call Data for a User

Here you need to have a user account or a test account that has placed some calls in Teams recently. We are going to look at the data for some real calls and see if they were good or bad.

1. Log into the TAC and from the left menu select Users.

2. Find or search the list to find your selected user account.

3. Click the user's name and then move to the Meetings & Calls section of their profile information.

4. Look down the list, and if you have the data in your tenant, notice that some are calls and others are conferences.

5. Select a call and click through the different parts to see the available data (Device, System, Connectivity, and Network).

continues

6. Look for the key things you would check if you were troubleshooting the call:

    - Did they use a certified headset or device?
    - Were they on Wi-Fi?
    - Were they connected to a VPN?
    - Did the network meet the minimum standards for supporting Teams calls?

7. Switch to the Advanced and Debug tabs in the page to see the level of information that was captured during the call (it was a lot; you do not need to follow everything that you see here!).

8. If the user also participated in a meeting, go back a page and select a meeting.

9. Repeat the process of looking through the data for the call.

EXERCISE 6.5

Opening CQD and Viewing the Online Reports

In this exercise, we are going to look at the default reports inside CQD and then download and set up custom detailed reports.

1. Log into CQD from `https://cqd.teams.microsoft.com`.

2. On the main page, browse through the default reports for overall call quality and the different types of calls (server-client and client-client).

3. From the drop-down at the top, select Detailed Reports.

4. Download the current custom report file from `https://aka.ms/QERtemplates` and extract it to your computer.

5. In the left menu, select Import and select the files that you just extracted to upload (`.cqdx` files).

6. Import both of them, but note that the location reports will work only if you have configured building data in your tenant (see the "Call Quality Dashboard" section for information about how to do this).

7. When the import has succeeded, find the new reports to the right of the default All Audio Streams report and click the title.

8. Browse through the reports exploring the available data.

Review Questions

1. What tool would you use to create a customized dashboard that can display call quality statistics for senior management to access on demand?

   A. Teams Advisor

   B. CQD with Power BI

   C. CQD

   D. Teams usage reports

2. Which of the following RBAC roles cannot access Teams usage reports?

   A. Teams Administrator

   B. Teams Communications Administrator

   C. Global Administrator

   D. Teams Device Administrator

3. Which tool would you use to help troubleshoot a user who reported a bad experience in a call?

   A. Call analytics

   B. CQD

   C. Teams usage reports

   D. M365 usage reports

4. How long is personal data (EUII) available in CQD reports?

   A. 10 days

   B. 21 days

   C. 28 days

   D. 90 days

5. You need to track the number of live meetings being configured in the tenant and who is creating them. Which report would you use?

   A. Teams Live Event usage report

   B. CQD with a filter to only show Live Events

   C. Teams usage report

   D. Call analytics by user

6. Why is it important to add building data to CQD?

   A. It makes the reports more engaging as it relates to real locations.

   B. It helps CQD identify which are managed networks and lets you identify which locations need work.

   C. You cannot create custom reports without adding it.

   D. Building data automatically imports from the rest of the TAC.

7. You want to use CQD with Power BI and have downloaded the custom connector from Microsoft and installed the Power BI client. Where should you place the CQD connection files?

    A. `Documents\Power BI\Custom Connectors`

    B. `Desktop\Power BI Desktop\Connectors`

    C. `Documents\Power BI\Connectors`

    D. `Documents\Power BI Desktop\Custom Connectors`

8. Which of the following user interactions would you find in a CQD report? (Select all that apply.)

    A. Teams to Teams call

    B. Teams meeting

    C. Teams channel conversation

    D. Teams multiparty messaging

9. Which of the following workloads can Teams Advisor help plan? (Select all that apply.)

    A. Calling and Meetings

    B. Live Meetings

    C. Skype for Business Upgrades

    D. Chat, teams, channels, and apps

10. What groups of users is it recommended that you include in your deployment project?

    A. User champions

    B. Service operators

    C. Consultants

    D. Executive sponsors

Appendix

Answers to Review Questions

Chapter 1: Introducing Teams

1. B. The Calling tab shows recently made calls and frequently contacted users.

2. D. Away, Do Not Disturb, and Available are all standard presence states. Idle is not an option, but when a user is automatically set to Away, a last seen time is displayed.

3. B. When in a one-to-one chat (not a team), shared files are stored in the user's OneDrive for Business in a special folder called Microsoft Teams Chat Files.

4. A. Of the available options, E1 is the cheapest plan and also grants access to use Teams. The E4 plan is no longer offered for sale as it contained on-premises usage rights for Skype for Business.

5. B. User licensing is configured in the Microsoft 365 Admin Center.

6. D. Call Quality Dashboard (CQD) will show you summaries about all the calling quality in your environment; you can use this data to identify issues.

7. A. You can view a user's Teams configuration in the Teams Admin Center.

8. B. Domains are set up and managed out of the Microsoft 365 Admin Center.

9. C. The Microsoft Teams PowerShell module includes the components required to manage both Teams and the relevant Skype for Business Online components.

10. D. Most PowerShell commands that modify settings have a `-Confirm` option and a `-WhatIf` option. `-Whatif` provides output that shows what would have been updated, whereas `-Confirm` makes you confirm with a y/n the command as it is executed.

11. C. Only one policy can apply to a user at a time. If the user has a specific policy applied directly to them, this will always take priority.

Chapter 2: Getting Teams Up and Running

1. C. The escalation is supported only in the Click-to-Run version of Skype for Business starting in the July 2019 builds. Option A does not apply as the user is able to chat in Skype for Business, so they must be in a coexistence mode that allows the use of Skype for Business. Option B is not relevant as escalation is not being initiated by the Teams client for this interaction. For option D, UDP port 4568 is not used for application sharing.

2. D. If the meeting invite was copied by the user, while it may still be joinable, it could be missing some hidden metadata that the Meeting Migration Service uses to detect and therefore update meetings. The Meeting Migration Service will update valid Skype for Business meetings regardless of which application created the invite (i.e., Outlook Desktop or Outlook for the Web). For option B, the Audio Conferencing license has no impact on running the Meeting Migration Service. With option C, the location again does not impact running the Meeting Migration Service.

3. D. Option A is incorrect because the Meeting Migration Service can take up to 24 hours to try to update the meetings and might not have completed; use PowerShell to check the status of the report. Option B is incorrect because meetings with no future occurrence are ignored by the Meeting Migration Service. Option C is incorrect because if Outlook is offline, its client will be displaying old information.

4. A. To allow escalation in Teams, the user must be able to create ad hoc meetings. For option B, while this is a valid setting, it has no bearing on escalation. In option C, the presence status does not matter for the initiating user. For option D, the Tenant coexistence mode is not relevant if the users are already signed in and communicating.

5. B. Setting the preferred app to the Skype Meetings app will set the meeting join preference to the browser plugin option where available. Option A would use the full client, option C would not automatically remove Skype for Business, and in option D, the Outlook plugin is not relevant to joining meetings.

6. D. Use the organization-wide policy to quickly have the user's computers install Teams in the background. While options A and B would work, it is not efficient. Option C would not prompt to install Teams.

7. B. Teams media will use either the UDP ports (3478–3481) or TCP 443; however, UDP should be used for the best quality. For option A, QoS policies can help in some situations, but with TCP 443 being used as the primary protocol for media, this is not likely to be the largest issue. For option C, the Network Assessment Companion can help identify blocked ports but can't fix the problem. Option D would not have any impact on real users; it is for planning only.

8. A. `Grant-CsTeamsUpgradePolily –PolicyName SfBWithTeamsCollabAndMeetings –Identity <user>` will let the user use Teams for meetings but still keep PSTN calling in Skype for Business. Option B would not let the user create Teams meetings. Options C and D are not valid cmdlets.

9. B. When the organization-wide policy is updated, the Meeting Migration Service will not run, so if you need to update user meetings, you must run it manually. Regarding option A, this should not be required for each user. Regarding option C, the Communications Credit license does not impact meeting scheduling. For option D, disabling and reenabling user accounts will not trigger the Meeting Migration Service.

10. C. This cmdlet will allow Exchange to automatically process incoming meeting requests and accept where they do not conflict with existing meetings. In option A, the Teams Admin Center does not let you adjust calendar processing. In option B, you cannot process calendar appointments using mailbox rules, and the cmdlet in option D is not valid.

11. A and C. For option A, WiFi connections can be susceptible to packet loss or other interference. By getting them to try calls on a wired connection, you can remove this as the cause. Option C could also be contributing to the problem; if they are working from home, they might have some sort of VPN running, and Teams traffic (especially for media) should bypass the VPN connection. Option B would be unlikely to help on a home user's network connection, and with option D, a home ISP would be unlikely to assist here.

12. C. For a shared area phone, the Common Area Phone license should be sufficient (you will still need either to supply a Calling Plan license or to configure Direct Routing, but more on this in Chapter 5, "Adding Telephony"). In option A, it would be impractical to expect users to log in and out of the phone to use a common area phone. Option B would work; however, it is a waste of an expensive license type. For option D, this license would again work, but we do not require any Exchange or calendar functionality.

13. A. The clue here is the small meeting room with video functionality. This is where Microsoft Teams Rooms on Android devices would be best suited. For option B, desk phones do not support video, and in option C a full Microsoft Teams Rooms would be overkill for a small space. While option D could work, it could be complicated and requires a lot of customization to work reliably.

14. A, B, C, D. Option A will make Windows machines correctly tag traffic as they put it on the network. Option B makes sure any other client traffic (i.e., from non-Windows devices) will be tagged. Option C will catch and tag traffic returning from O365, and option D makes sure that clients use the port ranges you have configured.

15. C. As we are testing from the network edge, jitter is above the threshold we would like; it should be under 15ms. If we were testing from a client across another WAN link, this figure would be acceptable. For option A, packet loss is within the acceptable bounds; however, any packet loss is not a good sign. For option B, round-trip time is just okay at under 60ms. For option D, the packet reorder ratio is acceptable.

16. A. You can force devices to update immediately (they will wait until not in use) from the Teams Admin Center using multiselect. For option B, Microsoft does not provide a Power-Shell interface for updating devices at this time. In option C, the Teams client cannot manage any other endpoints beyond those directly connected to the device. In option D, the O365 admin portal does not show Teams devices.

17. B. If you had QoS deployed via GPO for Skype for Business, this will be referencing `lync .exe` and needs to be updated to include `teams.exe`. For option A, you should check the client port ranges you have configured in the tenant, but unless you have updated your configuration from the defaults this is not likely to be the problem as Skype for Business Online uses the same ranges as Teams. For option C, `msteams.exe` is not the valid executable used by Teams, and in option D, there is no QoS user-specific configuration policy.

18. A, D. Teams is installed independently of the Office version, so either the x86 or the x64 edition can be deployed (usually via a `.exe` for Windows, the MSI is used for automated deployment methods). Option B, the `.pkg` package, is for macOS, and option C, the `.deb` package, is for Linux.

19. B. The user's `%userprofile%\AppData\Local\Microsoft\Teams` folder is the default user profile location where Teams will install itself unless you specify a per-machine installation (used only for VDI environments). For options A and C, Teams does not install to the Program Files folders by default. The location in option D does contain Teams data but is a cached folder, not the actual installation path.

20. D. To use Teams for PSTN calls, a user must be in Teams Only mode. The global configuration will apply only where users have not had something manually specified. Options A and B, while part of the cleanup process if you are removing on-premises to Skype for Business, do not impact Teams and PSTN calling. For option C, the client will not need to be reinstalled to pick up new settings.

Chapter 3: Teams Core Functionality

1. B. When you allow a domain, this automatically blocks all other domains that are not included. As no other domains are included in the external access list, they have all been blocked. Options A and D do not apply for external access, and option C would apply only if users are communicating with Skype consumer users.

2. A. Guests have their own global configuration items. These are controlled under the org-wide settings. For option B there are no specific controls against the Azure AD guest object. In option C you can control some settings for meetings but not guest access, and in option D external access is a non-authenticated user (guests are authenticated).

3. B and C. By default an E3 does not include the Audio Conferencing license, but the E5 does. You can either apply a separate add-on to the user or change them to an E5 if you have them available. In option A, dial-in availability is not controlled by the default number or through meeting policy (option D).

4. D. Org-wide teams can only be created for up to 10,000 users. Option A is something you would configure afterward in your team. For option B, Teams administrator has enough permissions to be able to create org-wide teams. In option C, while there is a limit on the number of org-wide teams that can be created (five), we do not have that information at hand, but we do know the user count is too high.

5. A. Creating a new meeting policy and assigning it using the existing group means that as long as the group is kept up to date, then the right users will have the policy. In option B the group does not need to be an M365 group. Technically option C would work but is not efficient and does not guarantee that all users are covered. Changing the ports in option D will not affect the ability to attempt to use video.

6. C. You should create two custom messaging policies and assign them to the Sales and Marketing groups, ideally using policy assignment and AD groups. Org-wide Teams settings do not control the ability to edit and send urgent messages (option A), and you need more than one policy as you should not affect other users (option B). Teams permission policies are used to control app integrations.

7. B. As User 2 is not a guest in any teams, they are an anonymous user as far as Teams is concerned. You must make sure that the meeting setting (applied org-wide) to allow anonymous users to join meetings is enabled. In option A this would control only whether User 2 would have to wait in a lobby. Licensing is not usually a consideration for normal meeting access or permissions, and option D would apply only to live events, not regular Teams meetings.

8. A. As guests are able to join the teams, then we know that guest access is at least partially working (so not option B or C). If they are unable to access the team notebook, this is stored in the SharePoint site, so it is likely that the SharePoint sharing permissions are too restrictive to allow the guests access to the file. You can check and change this in the SharePoint Online Center (or the OneDrive for Business Admin Center). You cannot control this type of access directly inside the team itself, so option D is incorrect.

9. D. A meeting of that scale should be a Teams live event, and live events can be configured to work with third-party eCDN solutions to cache and distribute media to local clients, thus reducing the internet bandwidth required. Options A and B aren't really in the spirit of driving Teams usage and an SBC in option C is used for telephony media, not meetings.

10. A. Currently you can only restore deleted channels through the Teams client, so options B and C are not valid. As for option D, when a channel is deleted, it can be recovered for 30 days. As the user reported, the channel was there last week, so we should be able to simply restore it.

11. C. To reduce the duplication of groups and ongoing management tasks, you can convert the distribution list into an M365 group and then make this the basis for the new team. Options A and D would leave the existing distribution list in place. Option B creates an unnecessary SharePoint site first.

12. B. Moderation settings are applied at the individual channel level, so options B and D are incorrect. The "fun stuff" settings do not cover moderation but are for things like Giphy support.

13. A. The description of the problem matches how priority notifications work. While you could talk to Finance and ask them to not use the urgent tags all of the time, you can also disable this feature for them by creating a custom messaging policy. For option B, there is no ability to disable receiving urgent notifications. In options C and D, it is not tagging or mentions as this generates a standard notification, not one that lasts for 20 minutes.

14. C. When you remove email integration from a team and set it back up, the email address will change. It is automatically generated by Microsoft and is unique. You will need to update the friendly contact object that you created with the new email address. You cannot change the generated email (option A), and while replication can usually be blamed for most delays in Teams, it is unlikely to be the cause (option B). Team settings do not cover email integration (option D).

15. A, D. You need to create a new private team and then set `ShowInTeamsSearchandSuggestions` to `$false`. Option C is incorrect as a public team would allow users to automatically join. In option B, `-TeamDiscovery` is not a valid option for the `Set-Team` cmdlet.

16. B. Creating a new private channel is the simplest solution, and they can support up to 250 members. While option A would technically solve the problem, you are creating another team that needs to be managed. In option C, you cannot hide channels (unless they are private channels). In option D, while this template name will be associated with the Share-Point site that a private channel would create, it is done automatically for you.

17. A. Allowed SMTP domains are configured in TAC under the Teams Settings page. The settings in option B would control the ability to interact with users in Teams (chat, etc.), and in option C these settings do not control email domains. The PowerShell in option D is not a valid cmdlet.

18. D. Once you start and then stop a Teams live event, you cannot reuse it. For any test runs, a separate scheduled Teams live event should be created. As they have already opened and then closed the real call, another one needs to be created and any join information updated with the new details. Options A, B, and C will not make a difference as the event has already been "used."

19. A and D. Owners should always be able to create new private channels, so option A could solve the problem, but if the user is just a member, you can control their ability to make private channels inside the team settings. The 250 limit is only for membership of a private channel and doesn't affect the ability to create them (option B) and it does not matter if a team has guest members or not (option C).

20. B. When removing accounts from an org-wide group, you must do this in Teams or they will be automatically be added back in when the group is updated. So options A, C, and D might temporarily remove access, but they will be placed back in over time.

Chapter 4: Advanced Teams Functionality and Management

1. B. Information barrier policies need to be created in both directions, so A-B and B-A; therefore. you would need two policies. Option D should be run when the policies are created, not before.

2. A. When sensitivity labels are applied to the M365 group at a container level, the tag is shown inside the team in the top-right corner. Options B and C would control the content inside the team, and option D would control the naming of any new teams created.

3. D. Sensitivity labels could be used to create a Confidential classification for teams. This can also then restrict the ability to allow guest users to be members. For option A, access reviews would only allow auditability for membership, not enforce a rule. Group creation policies in option B would restrict making new groups, not behavior, once created. DLP would help prevent content being shared but doesn't stop users from being part of the group.

4. A, C. The app can be sideloaded into the other user's clients (C), or you can add the app to the tenant catalog. Option B is not how to sideload apps, and option D is not how to submit an application to Microsoft for consideration.

5. C. A retention policy configured to delete content over 30 days old would be needed; this should be scoped to Teams chats, which cover one-to-one and one-to-many messages. Option A would cover just emails, option B would cover messages in a team, and for option D Teams does not have archiving policies.

6. C. The valid types of eDiscovery workloads are Content Search, Core eDiscovery, and Advanced eDiscovery.

7. A. This would detect the medical content and generate an admin alert so you could monitor how frequently it is occurring. In options B and D, the scope does not cover Teams channels, and option C would block the content.

8. B. You can restrict the creation of new groups to the AD group containing department heads. Options A and C will also allow those users to create groups but gives them access to configure other items in your tenant. In option D you should specify the existing group, not use named individuals.

9. A. `Get-Team` returns a team, and `Add-TeamUser` adds a user to a team. The other cmdlets are not valid.

10. B. App setup policies are used to install apps to the Teams client as well as pin them to the sidebar of the teams client. Option A controls what kind of apps are allowed, option C lets you load and update deployed apps, and option D is where you can customize the store's look and feel.

11. B. This requires an M365 group naming policy to be configured, which is done from the Azure AD portal.

12. B. You will need a team for each group that you want to use, and the correct query would be the one shown in option B using the `-eq` operator and the Sales and City attributes. In option C, the = sign is not a valid operator, and in option D `usageLocation` defines the country where a user's data should be held in the tenant (if enabled for multinational corporation support).

13. C. A user with Teams Device Administrator permissions will be able to set up and configure any Teams hardware device. Option A would also allow this permission but also grant access to all other configuration items, which we would not want. Option B has fewer permissions than the engineer already has, and option D doesn't prevent us from having to perform the configuration!

14. C. While obviously the right thing to do is to try to find the group using the cmdlets in A, as the group expired more than 40 days ago, chances are you will not be able to find it. Options B and D will not show the deleted groups.

15. D. Using team templates will let them create a new team based on the standard layout each time without any other administrative overhead or tools being required. Technically options A and B could work but have their own sets of complications. Option C would only control apps in the client.

16. B. Group expiry can be used to confirm if teams are still required; all the other features are found in access reviews.

17. B. By configuring access reviews with "users review their own access," the emails will be sent to each group member for them to confirm that they still require access. Option A does not help track group membership, and option C requires the owner to confirm membership. Option D would have a significant administrator overhead and does not automate the confirmation process.

18. C. Using group expiry can automate the process of removing unused teams, and by specifying a fallback address, you will receive the notification for groups with no owner. The one thing this doesn't do is find you groups that are still in use with no owner, as they will be automatically refreshed. Option A would let groups expire without making you aware, in option B audit logging would require you to manually track the teams over time, and option D would rely on your local machine being on and does not identify unused teams (but would tell you all teams with no owner).

19. B. By archiving the team, you can ensure that the content is preserved as it stands and is still available for reference. In option A, a retention policy could help ensure content cannot be deleted, but it would still allow new material to be added. Options C and D would not help preserve the content.

20. D. To be able to manipulate user interactions (such as removing users from conversations), the information barrier app needs to have access into your tenant. It is likely that something either did not work or was incorrectly configured at this stage. In option A, policies are not applied at a team level, and you do not need to run the policy manually (option B). For option C this could impact how a policy applies if a user's attributes have recently been updated, but the question hints that the segmentation data is correct.

Chapter 5: Adding Telephony

1. D, B. You would need Phone System to allow calling and a calling plan to let you have numbers from Microsoft. While option A (E5) would include Phone System, the questions asked for the minimum licenses, and this includes a lot of other components that are not relevant. We do not have enough information in the question to know if Audio Conferencing is needed.

2. D. The external IP of the client is checked first to see if it matches the IP of a company location; if not, then no other checks are used, and the default user or global Emergency Voice Routing Policy is used. In option A, calling policies do not control emergency dialing. Emergency addresses (option B) are not used for Direct Routing numbers, and the SBC configuration in option C would not apply, as the issue is in selecting the SBC to route a call to.

3. A. An Emergency Call Routing Policy allows you to specify what are classed as emergency numbers and how to route them differently to other calls. An Emergency Calling Policy in option B controls who would be notified when an emergency call is placed. An Online Voice Routing Policy (option C) controls routing normal calls, and a Caller ID Policy (option D) doesn't play a part in routing calls.

4.   B. To assign a number to an auto attendant, you use resource accounts. A resource account can have a normal or toll-free service number allocated to it. In option A, you cannot directly assign the number to a voice app. In option C, user accounts cannot have service numbers and cannot be assigned to a voice app. In option D, while Communications Credits are needed to use toll-free numbers, buying more will not achieve the goal of the question.

5.   B, C. Calling Plans are available only in some countries, and where they are provided through partners (Japan and Australia), they apply only for tenants hosted in that region. For option A, Teams telephony functionality is the same regardless of the delivery method, and in option D, the number of voice apps is not constrained by the calling delivery method.

6.   B. With different behavior required during office hours versus out of hours, you would configure an auto attendant first. This then sends the call to a call queue to ring the first group of users. Another queue is then needed for the group of 10 users. The ability to send to voicemail is configured as part of the auto attendant (and would probably require a group mailbox or user account too). Options A, C, and D do not.

7.   B. To deliver Teams telephony with your existing numbers without porting, you must deploy SBCs and use Direct Routing to bring them to Teams. In option A, an LOA is used to port numbers to the service, which you do not want to do. Communications Credits (option C) may be required but do not impact the delivery method for telephony. It is similar for option D. Teams Only mode would be required for your users but not as the next step.

8.   A, C. Users must be configured for Teams telephony, which requires a Phone System license; as the queue is set for conference mode, then they must also have an Audio Conferencing license. Communications Credits (option B) is not required for answering a call queue, and neither are any of the Azure AD licenses (option D).

9.   D. The key here is the infrequent use of international dialing. It is likely that spending on an International Calling Plan will cost more than your users need, so by using Communications Credits, the international calls become "pay as you go." Options A and B would be costly for an infrequent use of international calls, while option C would not allow the international calling at all.

10.   C. After configuring SBCs in your tenant, they will show in the Direct Routing Health Dashboard in TAC, where you can see their current status and previous performance. Teams usage reports (option A) show you overall feature usage, and CQD (option B) shows you call trends but not specifically related to an SBC. The portal in option D does not exist, although you can view specific SBCs data from inside the Direct Routing Health Dashboard.

11.   A. Dial plans let you create normalization rules to modify what the user enters into the dial pad. This way you can convert 1234 into the real number of the service desk voice app. In option B, a rule on the SBC could also achieve this, but we do not know if Direct Routing is being used, and the call would have left the Teams environment by that point. In option C, a caller ID policy controls the outbound number presentation, and option D would affect the membership of the auto attendant, not how it is called.

12.   A. The correct cmdlet is `New-CsOnlinePSTNGateway`, and the right options are `FQDN` and `SIPSignalingPort`. The other combinations shown in options B, C, and D are not valid options.

13. D. When creating a resource account, if it needs to have a phone number, it must have either a full Teams + Phone System license or a Virtual User license allocated. With option A, while it is possible that something has gone wrong, it is more likely that a license hasn't been applied to the account. When a resource account is created, it is configured for Teams Only mode, so option B shouldn't apply, and with option C, the region of the service account is not taken into consideration.

14. C. You can modify the users Team Group Calling settings and delegates using TAC; if you assign the line manager as a delegate, they can then receive incoming calls from the user. The other answers will let you modify the user's settings to turn on forwarding, but options A and B aren't great from a security point of view, and option D certainly doesn't keep things simple!

15. B. When using a new domain for the SBC, it must be activated using a licensed user. This kicks off some provisioning processes behind the scenes to make sure the tenant is going to accept SIP requests on this domain. An Online Voice Routing Policy is not required to activate the domain (option A), and option C does not activate a domain either, as an administrative account doesn't need to have a license assigned. The Direct Routing Health Dashboard does not play a part in activating the domain (option D).

16. D. Attendant mode rings out to all agents at the same time, so it meets the requirement. The other methods ring an agent one at a time using different patterns.

17. B. You can configure numbers for Direct Routing using PowerShell, which is not available from TAC (option A) or the Teams client (option C). For option D, you can technically synchronize this information depending on your configuration, but it would require everything to perform a sync cycle first.

18. D. A Caller ID policy allows you to specify masking a user's calls to be either anonymous or with a specified service number. A Calling policy controls general telephony functionality (option A), a Call Parking policy (option B) controls the ability to park calls to a holding number, and dial plans (option C) control how numbers are manipulated when required.

19. B. In the Calling policy, you can disable the ability to make private calls. This disables all Teams telephony functionality; while it may be unlikely that this has been disabled, everything else is correctly assigned so you would check here next. For option A, this would only affect number presentation; options C and D would apply for Direct Routing only.

20. C. When allocating numbers in the United States from Calling Plans, you need to specify an Emergency Address that is the default. Option A is used for Direct Routing calls, and Option B doesn't relate to emergency calling capabilities. The network settings in option D can help with dynamic emergency calling but can be configured after assigning the numbers.

Chapter 6: Review Usage and Maintain Quality

1. B. While CQD has the data to be able to publish it elsewhere, you would need to use Power BI. Teams Advisor (option A) just helps with deployment planning, CQD (option C) could work but you would need to assign RBAC roles to all managers and make them log into CQD and import the custom reports, and option D doesn't allow for customization.

2. D. The Teams Device Administrator can only configure and manage devices. The other roles (options A, B, C) are all able to view usage reports.

3. A. You would visit the user's page in TAC and look at their call history using call analytics. This would let you then review the specific call to identify what happened. CQD (option B) will show overall call trends, Teams usage reports (option C) will show team and channel activity, and M365 usage (option D) will show general Teams activities but not specific user interactions.

4. C. CQD removes EUII data from the database after 28 days.

5. A. There is a specific usage report for Teams Live Events that shows how many and who has been creating them. CQD (option B) would not help track Teams Live Events, the Teams usage report (option C) shows team and channel activity, and while call analytics (option D) would show who has been using live meetings, it would be onerous to check each user one by one.

6. B. The building data helps CQD identify networks so that calling data can be split out from locations that belong on the corporate network (where call quality should be higher) and those from other unmanaged locations. Also, by naming the networks, you know where to start troubleshooting. Option A may be slightly accurate, but it isn't the primary reason. You can make custom reports even if building data does not exist (option C), and as much as I wish it were true, option D is wrong because the building data is a separate location configuration from the rest of Teams!

7. D. The correct location is under the user's My Documents location, then in a subfolder called Power BI Desktop, and then another subfolder for Custom Connectors. The other folder paths will not be checked by Power BI Desktop.

8. A, B. CQD shows information about the voice workload, so channel conversations (option C) and multiparty chat or IMs (option D) will not be surfaced inside Power BI.

9. A, C, D. Teams Advisor has built-in project outlines for all the workloads except for Live Meetings (option B).

10. A, B, D. You should help create engagement in your user base through champions (option A). Service operators (option B) need to be involved to understand how the deployment will change their day-to-day activities, and executive sponsors (option D) will help drive change through the business and unblock issues. And as for option C, while consultants are quite often involved in deployment projects to help bring expertise and knowledge, they are not always an essential part of the deployment.

Index